Vi IMproved— Vim

New Riders

New Riders Professional Library

Vi IMproved— Vim

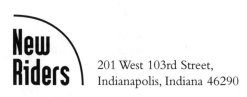

New Riders
201 West 103rd Street,
Indianapolis, Indiana 46290

Steve Oualline

Vi IMproved—Vim

International Standard Book Number: 0-7357-1001-5

Library of Congress Catalog Card Number: 00-101489

05 04 03 02 01   7 6 5 4 3 2 1

Interpretation of the printing code: The rightmost double-digit number is the year of the book's printing; the right-most single-digit number is the number of the book's printing. For example, the printing code 01-1 shows that the first printing of the book occurred in 2001.

Composed in QuarkXpress and MCPdigital by New Riders Publishing

Printed in the United States of America

Trademarks

All terms mentioned in this book that are known to be trademarks or service marks have been appropriately capitalized. New Riders Publishing cannot attest to the accuracy of this information. Use of a term in this book should not be regarded as affecting the validity of any trademark or service mark.

Warning and Disclaimer

This book is designed to provide information about *Vim*. Every effort has been made to make this book as complete and as accurate as possible, but no warranty or fitness is implied.

The information is provided on an as-is basis. The authors and New Riders Publishing shall have neither liability nor responsibility to any person or entity with respect to any loss or damages arising from the information contained in this book or from the use of the discs or programs that may accompany it.

Publisher
David Dwyer

Associate Publisher
Al Valvano

Executive Editor
Stephanie Wall

Managing Editor
Gina Brown

Product Marketing Manager
Stephanie Layton

Publicity Manager
Susan Nixon

Acquisitions Editor
Ann Quinn

Development Editor
Nancy E. Sixsmith

Project Editor
Elise Walter

Copy Editor
Keith Cline

Indexer
Steve Oualline

Book Designer
Louisa Klucznik

Cover Designer
Aren Howell

Proofreader
Debbie Williams

Composition
Octal Publishing, Inc.

Contents At a Glance

Contents

About the Author

Steve Oualline is a software engineer specializing in C++ programming and LINUX. He lives in southern California and spends his spare time as a real engineer on the Poway Midland Railroad. Other hobbies include blimp-making and collecting old Jack Benny radio shows.

About the Reviewer

This reviewer contributed his considerable hands-on expertise to the entire development process for *Vi IMproved—Vim*. As the book was being written, this dedicated professional reviewed all the material for technical content, organization, and flow. His feedback was critical to ensuring that *Vi IMproved—Vim* fits our reader's need for the highest quality technical information.

Ron Aaron co-owns a custom software development firm in Bellevue, Washington, where he lives with his wife and daughters, their toys and his tools. He has been using *Vim* on a daily basis for several years, and finds it indispensable for his work. He may be reached at ron@mossbayeng.com.

To my wife Chi Mui Oualline
Steve Oualline

Acknowledgements

A special thanks goes to Bram Moolenaar. Not only did he create a high quality *Vim* clone, but he documented it as well. (Good software and good documenation are rarely found together.) After he produced *Vim*, he was nice enough to release it as Charityware, thus enriching the Kibaale Children's Centre instead of himself.

Finally, I wish to thank the fine staff at New Riders, including Elise Walter, Ann Quinn, Nancy Sixsmith, Stephanie Wall, and Keith Cline for all the work they've done to make sure that this book is a first class production.

Tell Us What You Think

As the reader of this book, you are our most important critic and commentator. We value your opinion and want to know what we're doing right, what we could do better, what areas you'd like to see us publish in, and any other words of wisdom you're willing to pass our way.

As Executive Editor for New Riders, I welcome your comments. You can fax, email, or write me directly to let me know what you did or didn't like about this book—as well as what we can do to make our books stronger.

Please note that I cannot help you with technical problems related to the topic of this book, and that due to the high volume of mail I receive, I might not be able to reply to every message. When you write, please be sure to include this book's title and author, as well as your name and phone or fax number. I will carefully review your comments and share them with the author and editors who worked on the book.

Fax: 317-581-4663
Email: stephanie.wall@newriders.com
Mail: Stephanie Wall
        Executive Editor
        New Riders Publishing
        201 West 103rd Street
        Indianapolis, IN 46290 USA

Foreword

In 1988 I got myself a new computer, an Amiga 2000 (a fancy computer in those days). Being used to the *Vi* editor on Unix, I looked around for a *Vi*-like editor for the Amiga; I did find a program that looked a bit like *Vi*, but not close enough for an experienced *Vi* user. Fortunately the source code was available, so I started improving it: at first to make it more *Vi* compatible, then adding a few simple features that I needed for my work… then some more features… it seems I never stopped doing this. That's how the editor became Vim.

During the time you spend behind a computer, how much consists of reading and typing text? If I look at myself, I can say it's more than half the time. If you use a good editor, it will help you to do your work effectively, and you can save a lot of time—*Vim* is such an editor. It has many powerful features that you can use to do your work quickly, but you will have to learn them. There is an investment you need to make before you can reap the gain in effective editing. That is where this book will help you.

I am glad there is finally a book completely dedicated to *Vim*. Now you can learn how to get the most out of this powerful editor without learning the obsolete *Vi* commands first; this is especially useful for beginners. The basic commands are explained with pictures and lots of examples; I don't know any other text that gets you started using *Vim* in such a nice way. Steve has done a great job of explaining *Vim* commands in a style that is easy to read and understand.

People who have been using *Vim* for some time will find many hints for less-often-used commands in the second half of this book. Not every detail is covered; you can find those in the online help. If this book explained every little detail you wouldn't be able to hold it in one hand!

Seeing the commands that are explained in this book helps me understand how a user works with Vim. In Chapter 4, Steve mentions the use of the **:last** and **:rewind** commands; he would have expected **:first** to pair up with **:last**. That makes sense. I'll add it in the next version! If you come up with a remark like this, feel free to mention it to me—but first check the latest version, as your wish might already have been implemented!

In case you still have questions that you don't find answered in this book, check out the *Vim* Web site at `http://www.vim.org`. It contains a lot of useful information and links, such as the link to the download area. You can also find pointers to the *Vim* mailing lists, where *Vim* users and developers talk about problems and solutions.

Besides working on *Vim* I try to help needy people. I have done voluntary work in Uganda for a year, helping the numerous AIDS victims in this African country. After leaving this project I wanted to continue supporting the work there. I managed to connect these two activities by making *Vim* charityware. It's freeware with a twist. You might wonder why I decided to do this and what it means for you, so here's an explanation:

Vim is open source, free software. It doesn't cost you anything. But when you use *Vim* for your editing, you will hopefully feel that it is worth something. Some users suggested that I could ask for money for Vim, but I didn't like the idea of turning *Vim* into a commercial program. And I didn't really need the money myself. However, the project in Uganda could really use help. The charityware concept was a logical combination of these thoughts.

The purpose of *Vim* coming with a charityware license is that I ask you, as a *Vim* user, to donate some money to the project in Uganda. This project helps orphans that suffer from the AIDS epidemic, which kills many parents in this poor area. It provides them with food and medical help to survive now, and education to help them learn to take care of themselves in the future. I have visited the project several times, and have seen that the help that is provided really makes a difference. One boy that I got to know during my first visit, called Boaz, arrived at the project as one of the many orphans, without parents or food and dressed in rags. Now Boaz is finishing his training as a medical assistant, and has started working in the clinic at the project. Not only did we manage to help him survive, but now he is able to help others.

When you are using Vim, please consider making a donation to help these orphans. Appendix G tells a bit more about the project. You can find recent information here: `http://iccf-holland.org`. Or use this command in Vim: `:help uganda`.

I would like to thank Steve for writing this book and spending so much time on explaining *Vim* properly. The people at New Riders also deserve my appreciation; I have given them a hard time with all my remarks and suggested corrections. Furthermore, *Vim* would not be what it is now without the hundreds of people who helped me build and improve *Vim*—not only by sending me patches and bug reports, but also by encouraging me to continue working on *Vim*.

I hope you will find this book useful and enjoy using *Vim* effectively.

Happy Vimming!

Bram Moolenaar
(Creator of Vim)

Introduction

The *Vim* editor is designed to edit text. It does this job very well and is considered one of the best text editors in existence.

Like it or not, the basic text file is not going away. You want to write a program, it's a text file; change a configuration file, it's a text file; create a script—again, it's a text file. The *Vim* editor does all these jobs superbly.

A Short History of *Vim*

When the UNIX operating system first gained popularity, it came with an editor called *Vi*. This program quickly became a hit with programmers, system administrators, and other people who spent a lot of time writing text. Part of this popularity was due to the fact that it was so efficient.

For example, the commands to move the cursor left, down, up, and right are the keys "h", "j", "k", and "l." At first this mapping may seem silly, but if you look at a keyboard you'll see that these keys make up the "home" row for the right hand. So the designers of *Vi* put the most popular commands (cursor movement) on the keys that were easiest to type (home row, right hand).

An interesting thing happened to *Vi*: it stagnated. This can happen to commercial software that the marketing department doesn't consider "sexy." But about 20 years ago, people stopped adding new features to *Vi*. This in spite of the fact that people wanted such things as multiple windows and integration with the make utility.

To get around these limitations, people started writing Open Source clones of *Vi*. The best and most popular one is *Vim*.

It all started when Bram Moolenaar wanted an editor for his Amiga 2000. He got the source for a *Vi* clone and started fixing and modifying it. He published the source and was joined by a number of people who help enhance and maintain the editor. One of these, Sven Guckes, joined the effort and became the webmaster for www.vim.org.

The leadership of Bram Moolenaar is the reason that *Vim* has risen to the top of the *Vi* clones. He has two simple rules when it comes to adding features to *Vim*:

1. The feature must be useful.

2. It must be documented.

The *Vim* editor has been released under a unique license. It's charityware. If you like the editor, the authors ask that you donate to the Kibaale Children's Center in Uganda. (See Appendix G, "*Vim* License Agreement," for complete information.)

How to Read This Book

The *Vim* editor has hundreds of commands. You probably won't use all of them for your daily editing. In Part I of *Vi IMproved—Vim*, we start with the most useful subset of the commands. These are the commands you'll use for most editing. These chapters are organized around common editing tasks and features such as editing text files, using *Vim* windows, program editing, and so on.

Don't try to read the entire book at once. The *Vim* editor has a ton of features designed for almost every conceivable editing task. About the only person who could possibly use all these features would have to be a Jewish Arab living in Hong Kong working for a Japanese software company. (That's the only way I can see someone using the Farsi, Hebrew, Japanese, Chinese, and programming features.)

The best way is to read the chapters that concern you and skip the ones that don't. You will probably want to read the book in stages. For example, if you are new to *Vim*, you'll want to read Chapter 1, "Basic Editing." When you are comfortable with these commands and start to chafe at their limitations, you can then go on to other chapters.

Also remember that you don't have to learn all the commands. The *Vim* editor has many commands that perform similar functions. I'm what I consider a power user of *Vim*, yet I estimate that I use only about 25% of its commands. You don't need to learn about *Vim*'s three sets of commands to scroll the screen. One will do just fine.

Notation

The `Courier` font is used for screen output. **Bold** is used for text that you type. For example:

```
$ vim file.txt
```

Parameters to commands, where you need to enter the approbate values, are set in italics. For example:

```
:set makeprg=program
```

In this case you should replace program with the name of a program.

Optional parameters are enclosed in square brackets ([]):

```
:quit [!]
```

Optional parameters for which you select a value are enclosed in square brackets ([]) and set in italics:

```
:[count]tag
```

This indicates that you can optionally specify a count. For example, the commands:

```
:tag
:5tag
```

are both valid.

Control characters are indicated by the prefix CTRL. For example, CTRL-A, is "Control-A", or the key you get when you hold down the "Ctrl" key and press "A."

Both *Vim* and this book use the ^ notation to display control characters. For example, we can say, "If you enter CTRL-A in the text it appears as ^A."

Finally, special keys are displayed using the <> notation. For example `<F1>`, `<Enter>`, `<Esc>`, etc. For a complete list of the special keys see Appendix B.

Commands

Sometimes there are multiple ways to enter a command. For example, to expand the current window so it's the only window on the screen, you can enter the command `CTRL-Wo`, `CTRL-W CTRL-O`, `:on`, or `:only`. In such cases we select the single clearest version of the command to use in the text. All versions are listed in the Appendixes.

The *Vim* editor has a huge number of commands. For example, there are six commands just to scroll the text in the window (and that does not include options). In order to keep thing manageable we've selected what we consider the best working subset for our tutorial chapters.

How this Book is Organized

Chapter 1: Basic Editing

This chapter describes the minimum number of commands you'll need to do editing.

Chapter 2: Editing a Little Faster

After you master Chapter 1, this chapter will help you edit faster and more efficiently.

Chapter 3: Searching

The Vim editor contains a sophisticated search capability. This chapter describes how to use the basic capabilities of this searching.

Chapter 4: Text Blocks and Multiple Files

This chapter covers how to use the *Vim* commands to cut, paste, and move blocks of text. Editing more than one file at once is also covered.

Chapter 5: Windows

The *Vim* editor can display more than one editing window at a time. In this chapter the basic use of this feature is covered.

Chapter 6: Basic Visual Mode

The *Vim* visual mode allows you to highlight a block of text and then perform a cut, paste, or other editing command on it. Thus, with visual mode, you can see exactly what text you are going to affect by your editing command.

Chapter 7: Commands for Programmers

The *Vim* editor contains a number of features just for programmers. These include syntax highlighting, the ability to compile the programs from *Vim* (and browse through the error list afterwards), automatic C style indentation, and many more.

Chapter 8: Basic Abbreviations, Keyboard Mapping, and Initialization Files

The abbreviation feature of *Vim* allows you to define an abbreviation that, when entered in your text, will automatically be expanded to the full word.

A keyboard mapping lets you redefine how the keyboard is used. For example, you can define a mapping so that when you type `<F10>` the `:quit<CR>` command is executed.

If you define more than one or two abbreviation or keyboard mappings, you might want to create an initialization file so that they are loaded automatically when you start your program.

Chapter 9: Basic Command (:) Mode Commands

Command mode lets you enter very sophisticated (and complex) editing commands. For example, global search and replace can only be done from command mode.

Chapter 10: Basic GUI Usage

This chapter describes the basic features of the GUI version of *Vim*.

Chapter 11: Dealing with Text Files

If you are editing text documentation or any plain text file, the commands in this chapter will concern you. It covers things such as formatting and automatic line wrapping.

Chapter 12: Automatic Completion

The autocompletion feature of *Vim* lets you type in half a word and tell *Vim* to finish it. The editor will search through the words in your file (and other places) and try to complete your word. This chapter describes the commands used to control this feature.

Chapter 13: Autocommands

Basically an "autocmd" is a command that gets executed when an "event" happens. In practice, these commands are very powerful initialization commands for your editor. Among other things, they can be used to turn on or off features based on file type.

Chapter 14: File Recovery and Command Line Arguments

The *Vim* editor has the ability to recover from a crashed editing session. The command line argument to do this, as well as other useful command line arguments, are discussed in this chapter.

Chapter 15: Miscellaneous Commands

This chapter covers exotic commands that don't fit in any other chapters.

Chapter 16: Cookbook

The cookbook contains step-by-step instructions for performing many common and useful editing tasks.

Chapter 17: Topics Not Covered

Unfortunately this book can't cover everything. Some things had to be left out, such as foreign languages that the author doesn't know or interfaces to tools that the author does not have. This chapter gives a brief description of these topics as well as references for more information.

Chapter 18: Complete Basic Editing

All the basic editing commands, all their options, and all their details. (We spend 3 pages on "move forward word," for example.)

Chapter 19: Advanced Searching Using Regular Expressions

If you're doing a lot of searching and replacing, you'll want to go beyond the basic regular expressions and use the full power of the syntax. All the regular expression elements are describe here.

Chapter 20: Advanced Text blocks and Multiple Files

Everything you can do with a text block and all the commands that deal with multiple files can be found here.

Chapter 21: All about Windows and Sessions

This chapter covers all the window-related commands as well as session files which allow you to save you window layout (and other things) for later use.

Chapter 22: Advanced Visual Mode

The complete list of visual mode commands is discussed here.

Chapter 23: Advanced Commands for Programmers

This describes all the options you can use to customize the interface to the `make` program as well as many more commands useful to programmers.

Chapter 24: All about Abbreviations and Keyboard Mapping

How to define abbreviations that are valid only in certain modes as well as mode dependent keyboard mappings.

Chapter 25: Complete Command (:) Mode Commands

This chapter covers advanced line specification and all the command mode commands. Many of the operations these commands do can be more easily done using the normal editing mode commands, but the commands here might be of interest to script writers.

Chapter 26: Advanced GUI Commands

More on commands only available in the GUI version of the editor.

Chapter 27: Expressions and Functions

The *Vim* editor contains an extensive macro language which is described here.

Chapter 28: Customizing the Appearance and Behavior of the Editor

This chapter describes how to customize the appearance of the GUI as well as how to define your own menu items.

Chapter 29: Language-Dependent Syntax Options

How to customize the syntax coloring for specific languages.

Chapter 30: How to Write a Syntax File

How to write a syntax file for a new language. This file tells *Vim* how to do the syntax coloring for your new language.

Appendix A: Installing Vim

This appendix goes through the steps needed to install the Vim editor.

Appendix B: The <> Key Name

A list of the key names understood by Vim, such as <F1>, <Left>, and <Space>.

Appendix C: Normal Mode Commands

A list of normal mode commands with a short explanation of each one.

Appendix D: Visual Mode Commands

A list of normal visual mode commands with a short explanation of each one.

Appendix E: Insert Mode Commands

A list of insert mode commands with a short explanation of each one.

Appendix F: Option List

A list of all the options including the option name, the abbreviated name, the default value, and a short explanation of each.

Appendix G: Vim License Agreement

Vim is charityware. The author asks that if you want to pay for the software, you should send a donation to the Kibaale Children's fund. For details, read this appendix.

Appendix H: Quick Reference

A list of the most useful Vim commands in an easy-to-read format.

Support for *Vim*

The *Vim* editor is Open Source software. It comes with no official support. Hey, it is both high quality and free, what more do you want?

However, there is considerable unofficial support. The group Vim.org maintains a web site where you can get the latest *Vim* news and information. Here you can also find documentation, tips, tools, mailing list information, and other stuff. This organization is located on the Web at http://www.vim.org.

There are a number of mailing lists managed by Vim.org group which you can subscribe to for support, help, and information. You can even email the top *Vim* guy at bram@Vim.org.

Web Support

Additional resources and support can be found at www.newriders.com.

I

The Tutorial

Basic Editing

T HE *VIM* EDITOR IS ONE OF THE MOST powerful text editors around. It is also extremely efficient, enabling the user to edit files with a minimum of keystrokes. This power and functionality comes at a cost, however: When getting started, users face a steep learning curve.

This chapter teaches you the basic set of 10 *Vim* commands you need to get started editing. In this chapter, you learn the following:

- The four basic movement commands
- How to insert and delete text
- How to get help (very important)
- Exiting the editor

After you get these commands down pat, you can learn the more advanced editing commands.

Before You Start

If you have not installed *Vim*, you need to read Appendix A, "Installing *Vim*," and install the editor.

If you are running on UNIX, execute the following command:

```
$ touch ~/.vimrc
```

By creating a ~/.vimrc, you tell *Vim* that you want to use it in *Vim* mode. If this file is not present, *Vim* runs in *Vi*-compatibility mode and you lose access to many of the advanced *Vim* features. However, you can enable the advanced features from within *Vim* at any time with this command: `:set nocompatible<Enter>`.

If you are running on Microsoft Windows, the installation process creates the Microsoft Windows version of this file, _vimrc, for you.

Running *Vim* for the First Time

To start *Vim*, enter this command:

```
$ gvim file.txt
```

Note that the $ is the default UNIX command prompt. Your prompt might differ.

If you are running Microsoft Windows, open an MS-DOS prompt window and enter this command:

```
C:> gvim file.txt
```

(Again, your prompt may differ.)

In either case, *Vim* starts editing a file called `file.txt`. Because this is a new file, you get a blank window. Figure 1.1 shows what your screen will look like.

The tilde (~) lines indicate lines not in the file. In other words, when *Vim* runs out of file to display, it displays tilde lines. At the bottom of a screen, a message line indicates the file is named `file.txt` and shows that you are creating a new file. The message information is temporary and other information overwrites it when you type the first character.

Figure 1.1   Initial *Vim* window.

The *vim* Command

The **gvim** command causes the editor to create a new window for editing. If you use the command **vim**, the editing occurs inside your command window. In other words, if you are running inside an *xterm,* the editor uses your *xterm* window. If you are using an MS-DOS command prompt window under Microsoft Windows, the editing occurs inside the window. Figure 1.2 shows a typical MS-DOS command prompt window.

```
A very intelligent turtle
Found programming UNIX a hurdle
    The system, you see,
    Ran as slow as did he,
And that's not saying much for the turtle.
~
~
~
~
~
~
~
~
~
~
~
~
~
~
"turtle.txt" 5L, 158C                        1,1            All
```

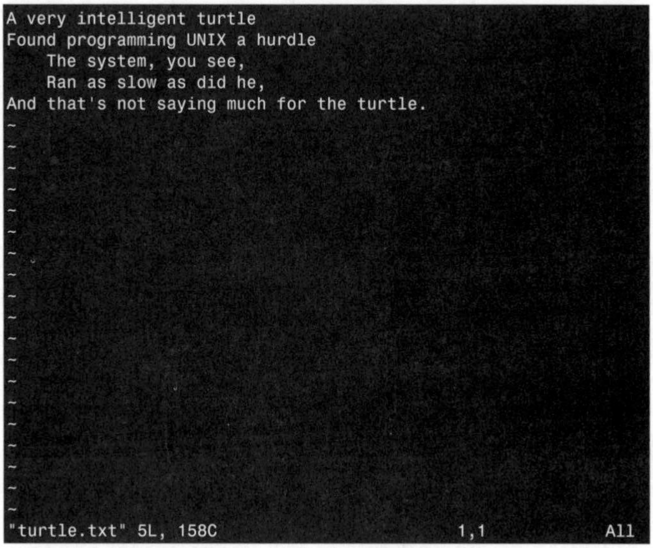

Figure 1.2   Editing with the **vim** command in an MS-DOS window.

Modes

The *Vim* editor is a modal editor. That means that the editor behaves differently, depending on which mode you are in. If the bottom of the screen displays the file-name or is blank, you are in normal mode. If you are in insert mode, the indicator displays - - INSERT - -; and if you are in visual mode, the indicator shows - - VISUAL - -.

Editing for the First Time

The next few sections show you how to edit your first file. During this process, you learn the basic commands that you have to know to use *Vim.* At the end of this lesson, you will know how to edit—not fast, not efficiently, but enough to get the job done.

Inserting Text

To enter text, you need to be in insert mode. Type **i**, and notice that the lower left of the screen changes to - - INSERT - - (meaning that you are in insert mode).

Now type some text. It will be inserted into the file. Do not worry if you make mistakes; you can correct them later. Enter the following programmer's limerick:

```
A very intelligent turtle
        Found programming UNIX a hurdle
        The system, you see,
        Ran as slow as did he,
And that's not saying much for the turtle.
```

After you have finished inserting, press the **<Esc>** key. The --INSERT-- indicator goes away and you return to command mode.

Your screen should now look something like Figure 1.3.

```
A very intelligent turtle
Found programming UNIX a hurdle
    The system, you see,
    Ran as slow as did he,
And that's not saying much for the turtle█
~
~
~
~
```

Figure 1.3   Screen after the text has been inserted.

Getting Out of Trouble

One of the problems for *Vim* novices is mode confusion, which is caused by forgetting which mode you are in or by accidentally typing a command that switches modes. To get back to normal mode, no matter what mode you are in, press the **<Esc>** key.

Moving Around

After you return to command mode, you can move around by using these keys: **h** (left), **j** (down), **k** (up), and **l** (right). At first, it may appear that these commands were chosen at random. After all, who ever heard of using **l** for right? But actually, there is a very good reason for these choices: Moving the cursor is the most common thing you do in an editor, and these keys are on the home row of your right hand. In other words, these commands are placed where you can type them the fastest.

> **Note**
>
> You can also move the cursor by using the arrow keys. If you do, however, you greatly slow down your editing—because to press the arrow keys, you must move your hand from the text keys to the arrow keys. Considering that you might be doing it hundreds of times an hour, this can take a significant amount of time. If you want to edit efficiently, use h, j, k, and 1.
>
> Also, there are keyboards which do not have arrow keys, or which locate them in unusual places; therefore, knowing the use of these keys helps in those situations.

One way to remember these commands is that **h** is on the left, **l** is on the right, **j** is a hook down, and **k** points up. Another good way to remember the commands is to copy this information on a Post-It Note and put it on the edge of your monitor until you get used to these commands.

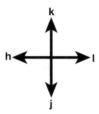

Deleting Characters

To delete a character, move the cursor over it and type **x**. (This is a throwback to the old days of the typewriter, when you deleted things by typing xxxx over them.)

Move the cursor to the beginning of the first line, for example, and type **xxxxxxx** (eight **x**'s) to delete the first eight characters on the line. Figure 1.4 shows the result. To enter a correction, type **iA young <Esc>**. This begins an insert (the **i**), inserts the words *A young*, and then exits insert mode (the final **<Esc>**). Figure 1.5 shows the results.

```
ntelligent turtle
Found programming UNIX a hurdle
    The system, you see,
    Ran as slow as did he,
And that's not saying much for the turtle.
~
~
~
~
```

Figure 1.4   Screen after delete (xxxxxxxx).

```
A young intelligent turtle
Found programming UNIX a hurdle
    The system, you see,
    Ran as slow as did he,
And that's not saying much for the turtle.
~
~
~
~
```

Figure 1.5   Result of the insert.

> **Note**
>
> *Vim* is a text editor. By default, it does not wrap text. You must end each line by pressing the <Enter> key. If you don't and just keep typing when you reach the right margin, all you will do is insert a very long line into the editor. You will not automatically go to the next line. To do so, you need to press the <Enter> key. (This is the default mode of operation. You can configure the *Vim* editor to word wrap, however, as discussed in Chapter 11, "Dealing with Text Files.")

Undo and Redo

Suppose you delete too much. Well, you could type it in again, but an easier way exists. The **u** command undoes the last edit.

Take a look at this in action. Move the cursor to the *A* in the first line. Now type **xxxxxxx** to delete *A young*. The result is as follows:

```
intelligent turtle
```

Type **u** to undo the last delete. That delete removed the *g*, so the undo restores the character.

```
g intelligent turtle
```

The next **u** command restores the next-to-last character deleted:

```
ng intelligent turtle
```

The next **u** command gives you the *u*, and so on:

```
ung intelligent turtle
oung intelligent turtle
young intelligent turtle
young intelligent turtle
A young intelligent turtle
```

If you undo too many times, you can press **CTRL-R** (redo) to reverse the preceding command. In other words, it undoes the undo.

To see this in action, press **CTRL-R** twice. The character *A* and the space after it disappear.

```
young intelligent turtle
```

There's a special version of the undo command, the **U** (undo line) command. The undo line command undoes all the changes made on the last line that was edited. Typing this command twice cancels the preceding **U**.

> **Note**
> If you are an old *Vi* user, note that the multilevel undo of *Vim* differs significantly from the single level available to a *Vi* user.

> **Note**
> Throughout this book we assume that you have turned off *Vi* compatibility. (*Vi* compatiblity disables many advanced features of *Vim* in order to be compatible with *Vi*.) This feature is automatically turned off for Unix users when they create the *$HOME/.vimrc* file. For Microsoft Windows, it is turned off during installation. (If compatibility is turned on the v command provides one level of undo.)

```
A very intelligent turtle
         xxxx                          Delete very
A intelligent turtle
                  xxxxxx               Delete turtle
A intelligent
                                       Restore line with U
A very intelligent turtle
A intelligent                          Second U undoes the preceding U
```

Getting Out

To exit, use the **ZZ** command. This command writes the file and exits.

Unlike many other editors, *Vim* does not automatically make a backup file. If you type **ZZ**, your changes are committed and there's no turning back. (You can configure the *Vim* editor to produce backup files, as discussed in Chapter 14, "File Recovery and Command-Line Arguments.")

Discarding Changes

Sometimes you will make a set of changes and suddenly realize you were better off before you started. Don't worry; *Vim* has a "quit-and-throw-things-away" command. It is **:q!**.

For those of you interested in the details, the three parts of this command are the colon (:), which enters command mode; the **q** command, which tells the editor to quit; and the override command modifier (!). The override command modifier is needed because *Vim* is reluctant to throw away changes. Because this is a command mode command, you need to type **<Enter>** to finish it. (All command mode commands have **<Enter>** at the end. This is not shown in the text.)

If you were to just type **:q**, *Vim* would display an error message and refuse to exit:

```
No write since last change (use ! to override)
```

By specifying the override, you are in effect telling *Vim*, "I know that what I'm doing looks stupid, but I'm a big boy and really want to do this."

Other Editing Commands

Now that you have gone through a few simple commands, it is time to move on to some slightly more complex operations.

Inserting Characters at the End of a Line

The **i** command inserts a character *before* the character under the cursor. That works fine; but what happens if you want to add stuff to the end of the line? For that you need to insert text after the cursor. This is done with the **a** (append) command.

For example, to change the line

```
and that's not saying much for the turtle.
```

to

```
and that's not saying much for the turtle!!!
```

move the cursor over to the dot at the end of the line. Then type **x** to delete the period. The cursor is now positioned at the end of the line on the *e* in turtle:

```
and that's not saying much for the turtle
```

Now type **a!!!<Esc>** to append three exclamation points after the *e* in turtle:

```
and that's not saying much for the turtle!!!
```

Deleting a Line

To delete a line, use the **dd** command, which deletes the line on which the cursor is positioned. To delete the middle line of this example, for instance, position the cursor anywhere on the line *The system, you see*, as shown in Figure 1.6.

Now type **dd**. Figure 1.7 shows the results.

Opening Up New Lines

To add a new line, use the **o** command to open up a new line *below* the cursor. The editor is then placed in insert mode.

```
A very intelligent turtle
Found programming UNIX a hurdle
    The System, you see,
    Ran as slow as did he,
And that's not saying much for the turtle!!!
~
~
"turtle.txt" 5L, 155c written
```

Figure 1.6   Screen before **dd** command.

```
A very intelligent turtle
Found programming UNIX a hurdle
    Ran as slow as did he,
And that's not saying much for the turtle!!!
~
~
~
```

Figure 1.7   Screen after **dd** command.

Suppose, for example, that you want to add a line to the sample text just below the third line. Start by leaving the cursor on the *Ran as slow. . .* line, as seen in Figure 1.7.

Now type **o** to open up a new line. Enter the text for the line and then press **<Esc>** to end insert mode. Figure 1.8 shows the results.

If you want to open a line above the cursor, use the **O** (uppercase) command.

```
A very intelligent turtle
Found programming UNIX a hurdle
    Ran as slow as did he,
and that was very slow
And that's not saying much for the turtle.
~
~
~
~
```

Figure 1.8   Screen after using the **o** command.

Help

Finally, there's one more important command, the help command. To get help, enter the following:

```
:help
```

(Remember the implied **<Enter>** for command-mode commands.) This displays a general help window, as seen in Figure 1.9.

```
*help.txt*     For Vim version 5.7.  Last change: 2000 Jan 01

                     VIM - main help file
                                                               k
          Move around: Use the cursor keys, or "h" to go left,      h   l
                       "j" to go down, "k" to go up, "l" to go right.    j
Close this window: Use ":q<Enter>".
    Get out of Vim: Use ":qa!<Enter>" (careful, all changes are lost!).
Jump to a subject: Position the cursor on a tag between |bars| and hit CTRL-].
    With the mouse: ":set mouse=a" to enable the mouse (in xterm or GUI).
                    Double-click the left mouse button on a tag between |bars|.
         jump back: Type CTRL-T or CTRL-O.
Get specific help: It is possible to go directly to whatever you want help
                   on, by giving an argument to the ":help" command |:help|.
                   It is possible to further specify the context:
                        WHAT              PREPEND     EXAMPLE
                   Normal mode commands   (nothing)   :help x
                   Visual mode commands   v_          :help v_u
                   Insert mode commands   i_          :help i_<Esc>
                   Command-line commands  :           :help :quit
help.txt [help][RO]

[No File]
"help.txt" [readonly] 1297L, 61009C
```

Figure 1.9   Help screen.

If you don't supply a subject, `:help` displays the general help window. The creators of *Vim* did something very clever (or very lazy) with the help system. They made the help window a normal editing window. You can use all the normal *Vim* commands to move through the help information. Therefore **h**, **k**, **j**, and **l** move left, up, down, right, and so on.

To get out of the help system, use the same command you use to get out of the editor: **ZZ**.

As you read the help text, you will notice some text enclosed in vertical bars (for example, `|:help|`). This indicates a hyperlink. If you position the cursor anywhere between the bars and press **CTRL+]** (jump to tag), the help system takes you to the indicated subject. (For reasons not discussed here, the *Vim* terminology for a hyperlink is tag. So **CTRL+]** jumps to the location of the tag given by the word under the cursor.)

After a few jumps, you might want to go back. **CTRL+T** (pop tag) takes you back to the preceding screen. Or in *Vim* terms, it "pops a tag off the tag stack."

At the top of this screen, there is the notation `*help.txt*`. This is used by the help system to define a tag (hyperlink destination). Chapter 7, "Commands for Programmers," explains tags in detail.

To get help on a given subject, use the following command:

`:help subject`

To get help on the **x** command, for example, enter the following:

`:help x`

To find out how to delete text, use this command:

`:help deleting`

To get a complete index of what is available, use the following command:

`:help index`

When you need to get help for a control character command (for example, **CTRL-A**, you need to spell it with the prefix CTRL-.

`:help CTRL-A`

The *Vim* editor has many different modes. By default, the help system displays the normal-mode commands. For example, the following command displays help for the normal-mode **CTRL-H** command:

`:help CTRL-H`

To identify other modes, use a mode prefix.

If you want the help for the insert-mode version of this command, prefix the key with `i_`. This gives you the following command:

`:help i_CTRL-H`

Table 1.1 lists several other mode prefixes.

When you start the *Vim* editor, you can use several command-line options. These all begin with a dash (-). To find what the -t command-line option does, for example, use the command

```
:help -t
```

The *Vim* editor has a number of options that enable you to configure and customize the editor. If you want help for an option, you need to enclose it in single quotation marks. To find out what the number option does, for example, use the following command:

```
:help 'number'
```

The following table summarizes the special prefixes.

Table 1.1   **Help Prefixes**

What	Prefix	Example
Normal-mode commands	(nothing)	:help x
Control character	CTRL-	:help CTRL-u
Visual-mode commands	v	:help v_u
Insert-mode commands	i	:help i_<Esc>
ex-mode commands	:	:help :quit
Command-line editing	c	:help c_<Del>
Vim command arguments	-	:help -r
Options	' (both ends)	:help 'textwidth'

Special keys are enclosed in angle brackets. To find help on the up-arrow key, for instance, use this command:

```
:help <Up>
```

Appendix B, "The <> Key Names," provides a complete list of the key names.

Other Ways to Get Help

You can get to the help screen by pressing the <F1> key. This displays the general help screen, and you can navigate from there. If your keyboard has a <Help> key, you can use it as well.

Using a Count to Edit Faster

Suppose you want to move up nine lines. You can type **kkkkkkkkk** or you can enter the command **9k**.

In fact, you can precede all the movement commands with a number. Earlier in this chapter, for instance, you added three exclamation points to the end of a line by typing **a!!!<Esc>**. Another way to do this is to use the command **3a!<Esc>**. The count of **3** tells the **a** command to insert what follows (!) three times.

Similarly, to delete three characters, use the command **3x**.

The *Vim* Tutorial

The UNIX version of the *Vim* editor comes with an interactive tutorial. Lesson 1 covers many of the commands described in this chapter.

To invoke the tutorial on UNIX, use the following command:

```
$ vimtutor
```

The tutorial starts by explaining the movement commands so that you can move through the tutorial. After that it gradually introduces more complex commands.

If you are on a non-Unix system, execute the command

```
:help tutor
```

for information on how to get the *Vim* tutorial working on your system (it isn't difficult).

Summary

You now know enough to edit with *Vim*. Not well or fast, but you can edit. Take some time to practice with these commands before moving on to the next chapter. After you absorb these commands, you can move on to the more advanced commands that enable you to edit faster and easier.

Editing a Little Faster

THE BASIC COMMANDS COVERED IN CHAPTER 1, "Basic Editing," enable you to edit text. This chapter covers some additional commands that enable you to edit more efficiently. These commands include the following:

- Additional movement commands
- Quick searches along a single line
- Additional delete and change commands
- The repeat command
- Keyboard macros (how to record and play back commands)
- Digraphs

One of the things I noticed as I wrote this chapter is the amazing number of different ways you can move through a file. Although I have been using *Vi* and now *Vim* as my main editor for the past 15 years, I have never bothered to learn all of them. I get by with the 10% I like.

There are lots of different ways of doing things in *Vim*. This chapter discusses one useful selection of all the possible commands.

Word Movement

Let's start with movement. To move the cursor forward one word, use the **w** command. The **b** command moves backward one word. Like most *Vim* commands, you can use a numeric prefix to move past multiple words. For example, **4b** moves back four words. Figure 2.1 shows how these commands work.

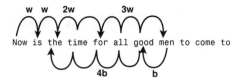

Figure 2.1   Word movement.

Moving to the Start or End of a Line

The **$** command moves the cursor to the end of a line. Actually, a bunch of keys map to the "end-of-line" command. The *Vim* names for these keys are **$**, **<End>**, and **<kEnd>**. (The **<kEnd>** key is *Vim's* name for the keypad End key.)

The **$** command takes a numeric argument as well. If present, it causes the editor to move to the end of the next line. For example, **1$** moves you to the end of the first line (the one you're on), **2$** to the end of the next line, and so on. Figure 2.2 illustrates how this command works.

The **^** command moves to the first nonblank character of the line. The **<Home>** or **<kHome>** key moves to the first character of the line, as seen in Figure 2.3. (The **0** [zero] command does the same thing.)

Like every other command previously discussed, these three commands can take a numeric argument. They do not do anything with it, but you can specify it if you want to.

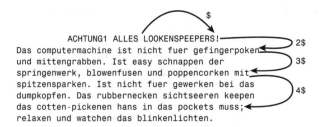

Figure 2.2   The **$** command.

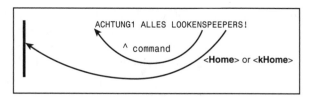

Figure 2.3   The ^ and `<Home>` commands.

Searching Along a Single Line

Moving is the most common editing activity you do. One of the most useful move-ment commands is the single-character search command. The command **fx** (forward search) searches the line for the single character *x*.

Suppose, for example, that you are at the beginning of the following line:

```
To err is human. To really foul up you need a computer.
```

Suppose you want to go to the *h* of *human*. Just execute the command **fh** and the cur-sor will be positioned over the h:

```
To err is human. To really foul up you need a computer.
```

To go to the end of the word *really*, use the command **fy**. You can specify a count; therefore, you can space forward five words by using the command **5f<Space>**:. Note: this only moves five *space characters*, not five words. If there are multiple spaces between words, this will *not* move five words!

```
To err is human. To really foul up you need a computer.
```

The **F** command searches to the left. Figure 2.4 shows the effect of the **f** and **F** commands.

The **tx** (search 'til) command works like the **fx** command, except it stops one char-acter before the indicated character. The backward version of this command is **Tx**. Figure 2.5 shows how these commands work.

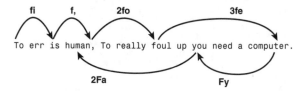

Figure 2.4   Operations of the **f** and **F** commands.

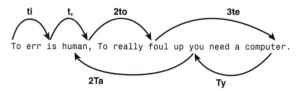

Figure 2.5   The t and T commands.

Sometimes you will start a search, only to realize that you have typed the wrong command. You type **f** to search backward, for example, only to realize that you really meant **F**. To abort a search, press **<Esc>** as the search key. So **f<Esc>** is an aborted forward search. (Note: **<Esc>** cancels most operations, not just searches.)

Moving to a Specific Line

If you are a C or C++ programmer, you are familiar with error messages such as the following:

```
prog.c:3: 'j' undeclared (first use in this function)
```

This tells you that you might want to fix something on line 3. So how do you find line 3?

One way is to do a **9999k** to go to the top of the file and a **2j** to go down two lines. It is not a good way, but it works.

A much better way of doing things is to use the **G** command. With an argument, this command positions you at the given line number. For example, **3G** puts you on line 3. (Likewise, use the **1G** command to go to the top of the file rather than **9999k**.)

With no argument, it positions you at the end of the file.

(For a better way of going through a compiler's error list, see Chapter 7, "Commands for Programmers," for information on the **:make** and **:clist** related commands.)

Telling Where You Are in a File

How do you really know where you are in a file? You can do so in several ways. The first is to turn on line numbering with the following command (see Figure 2.6):

```
:set number
```

```
1176        Ode to a maintenance programmer
1177        ================================
1178
1179  Once more I travel that lone dark road
1180  into someone else's impossible code
1181  Through "if" and "switch" and "do" and "while"
1182  that twist and turn for mile and mile
1183  Clever code full of traps and tricks
1184  and you must discover how it ticks
1185  And then I emerge to ask anew,
1186  "What the heck does this program do?"
1187
1188                    ****
1189
:set number
```

Figure 2.6   Window with numbering turned on.

The *Vim* editor is highly configurable and has a huge number of options. You can use the **:set** command in many different ways, which are described in Chapter 28, "Customizing the Appearance and Behavior of the Editor."

The number option is a Boolean option, meaning that it can be on or off. To turn it on, use this command:

```
:set number
```

To turn it off, use this command:

```
:set nonumber
```

```
Ode to a maintenance programmer
=================================
Once more I travel that lone dark road
into someone else's impossible code
Through "if" and "switch" and "do" and "while"
that twist and turn for mile and mile
Clever code full of traps and tricks
and you must discover how it ticks
And then I emerge to ask anew,
"What the heck does this program do?"

                ****

:set nonumber
```

Figure 2.7   Results of **:set nonumber**.

Figure 2.7 shows the results of this command.

Where Am I?

The **CTRL-G** command displays a status line that indicates where you are in the file. For example:

```
"c02.txt" [Modified] line 81 of 153 —52%— col 1
```

This indicates that you are editing a file called c02.txt, and that it has been modified since the editing started. The cursor is positioned on line 81 out of a total of 153, or about 52% of the way through the file. The cursor is currently sitting in column 1.

Note

These line numbers are for your information only; they are not written into the file when you exit.

```
to open up the packing crate and find the manual. (What
did they think
we were reading anyway?)

<H1>Dumb programmer stories

    Ode to a maintenance programmer
Once more I travel that lone dark road
into someone else's impossible code
Through "if" and "switch" and "do" and "while"
that twist and turn for mile and mile
"sun-o.txt" [Modified] line 186 of 1119 --16%-- col 2-9
```

Figure 2.8   The **CTRL-G** command.

Sometimes you will see a split column number (for example, col 2-9). This indicates that the cursor is positioned on character 2. But because character one is a tab,
the screen column is 9. Figure 2.8 shows the results of a typical **CTRL-G** command.

Scrolling Up and Down

The **CTRL-U** command scrolls up half a screen of text. (Up in this case is backward in
the file; the text moves down on the screen. Don't worry if you have a little trouble
remembering which end is up. Most programmers have the same problem.)

The **CTRL-D** command scrolls you down half a screen.

Figure 2.9 shows how these two commands work.

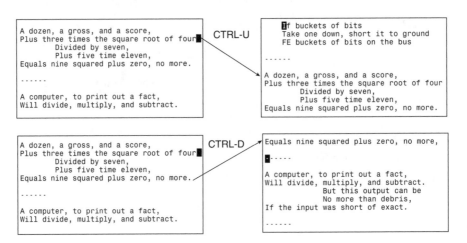

Figure 2.9   Results of the **CTRL-U** and **CTRL-D** commands.

Deleting Text

As you learned in Chapter 1, the **dd** command deletes a line. The **dw** command deletes
a word. You may recognize the **w** command as the move word command. In fact, the **d**
command may be followed by any motion command, and it deletes from the current

location to the place where the cursor winds up. (Therefore, we say the syntax of the **d** command is **d***motion*.)

The **3w** command, for example, moves the cursor over three words. The **d3w** command deletes three words, as seen in Figure 2.10. (You can write it as **d3w** or **3dw**; both versions work the same.)

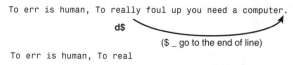

```
To err is human, To really foul up you need a computer.
d3w
                        (three words)
To err is human, To realyou need a computer.
```

Figure 2.10   The **d3w** command.

The **$** command moves to the end of a line. The **d$** command deletes from the cursor to the end of the line, as seen in Figure 2.11. A shortcut for this is the **D** command.

```
To err is human, To really foul up you need a computer.
d$
                        ($ _ go to the end of line)
To err is human, To real
```

Figure 2.11   The **d$** command.

Where to Put the Count (*3dw* or *d3w*)

The commands **3dw** and **d3w** delete three words. If you want to get really picky about things, the first command, **3dw**, deletes one word three times; the command **d3w** deletes three words once. This is a difference without a distinction.

You can actually put in two counts, however (for example, **3d2w**). This command deletes two words, repeated three times, for a total of six words.

Changing Text

The **c** command changes text. It acts just like the **d** command, except it leaves you in insert mode. For example, **cw** changes a word. Or more specifically, it deletes a word and then puts you in insert mode. Figure 2.12 illustrates how this command works.

There is a saying that for every problem there is an answer that's simple, clear, and wrong. That is the case with the example used here for the **cw** command. The **c***motion* command works just like the **d***motion* command, with one exception: the **cw** and **dw** commands. Whereas **cw** deletes the text up to the space following the word (and then enters insert mode), the **dw** command deletes the word and the space following it.

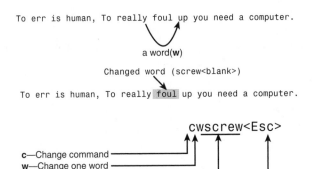

Figure 2.12   How **cw** works.

The **cc** command works on the entire line. That is, it deletes the line and then goes into insert mode. In other words, **cc** works on the current line just like **dd**. Likewise, **c$** or **C** change from the cursor to the end of the line.

The . Command

The . command is one of the most simple yet powerful commands in *Vim*. It repeats the last delete or change command. For instance, suppose you are editing an HTML file and want to delete all the <B> tags. You position the cursor on the first < and delete the <B> with the command **df>**. You then go to the < of the next </B> and kill it using the . command. The . command executes the last change command (in this case, **df>**). To delete another tag, position the cursor on the < and press the . command. Figure 2.13 illustrates how this can work.

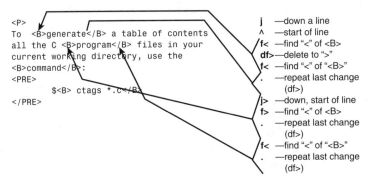

Figure 2.13   Using the . command.

Joining Lines

The **J** command joins the current line with the next one. A space is added to the end of the first line to separate the two pieces that are joined, as illustrated by Figure 2.14. If a count is specified, the count lines are joined (minimum of two).

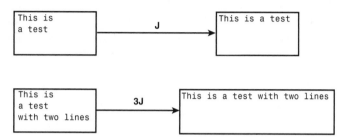

Figure 2.14   The **J** command.

Replacing Characters

The **r**x command replaces the character under the cursor with *x*. Figure 2.15 shows how you can use the **r** command to replace a *z* with an *s*.

The **r** command can be preceded with a count, indicating the number of characters to be replaced. In Figure 2.16, we go to the beginning of line (the ^ command) and execute **5ra** to replace the first five characters with a.

Figure 2.15   The replace (r) command.

Figure 2.16   Replace (r) command with count.

> **Note**
>
> The **r** command treats **<Enter>** in a special way. No matter how big the count is, only one **<Enter>** is inserted. Therefore, **5ra** inserts five *a* characters, whereas **5r<Enter>** replaces five characters with one **<Enter>**.

Be careful where you place the count. The **5rx** command replaces five characters with the character *x*, whereas **r5x** replaces the character under the cursor with *5* (**r5**) and then deletes a character (**x**).

Changing Case

The ~ command changes a character's case. It changes uppercase to lowercase and vice versa. If a count is specified, the count characters are changed. Figure 2.17 contains examples.

Figure 2.17   Use of the ~ command.

Keyboard Macros

The . command repeats the preceding change. But what if you want to do something more complex than a single change? That's where the keyboard macros come in. The **q***character* command records keystrokes into the register named *character*. (The character must be between *a* and *z*.)

To finish recording, just type a **q** command. You can now execute the macro by typing the **@***character* command. (This can be preceded by a count, which will cause the macro to be executed that number of times.)

Take a look at how to use these commands in practice. You have a list of filenames that look like this:

```
stdio.h
fcntl.h
unistd.h
stdlib.h
```

And what you want is the following:

```
#include "stdio.h"
#include "fcntl.h"
#include "unistd.h"
#include "stdlib.h"
```

You start by moving to the first character of the first line. Next you execute the following commands:

qa	Start recording a macro in register a.
^	Move to the beginning of the line.
i#include "<Esc>	Insert the string **#include** " at the beginning of the line.
$	Move to the end of the line.

a"<Esc>	Append the character double quotation mark (") to the end of the line.
j	Go to the next line.
q	Stop recording the macro.

Now that you have done the work once, you can repeat the change by typing the command **@a**. Alternatively, because you have three lines to go, you can change them using the command **3@a**.

Figure 2.18 shows how to define and then execute a macro.

```
stdio.h
fcntl.h
unistd.h
stdlib.h
```
Start

```
#include "stdio.h"
fcntl.h
unistd.h
stdlib.h
```
qa-Record into register a
^-Go to the geginning of a line
i#include '<Esc>-Insert text
a"<Esc>-Insert more text
j-Go to the next line
q-Stop macro

```
#include "stdio.h"
#include "fcntl.h"
unistd.h
stdlib.h
```
@a-Execute macro "a"

```
#include "stdio.h"
#include "fcntl.h"
#include "unistd.h"
#include "stdlib.h"
```
2@a-Execute macro "a" twice

2.18 Defining and using a macro.

Digraphs

Some characters are not on the keyboard—for example, the copyright character (©). To type these letters in *Vim*, you use digraphs, where two characters represent one. To enter a ©, for example, you type **CTRL-Kc0**.

To find out what digraphs are available, use the following command:

```
:digraphs
```

The *Vim* editor will display the digraph-mapping table, as seen in Figure 2.19.

This shows, for example, that the digraph you get by typing **CTRL-K~!** is the character (¡). This is character number 161.

> **Warning**
>
> The digraphs are set up assuming that you have a standard ISO-646 character set. Although this is an international standard, your particular display or printing system might not use it.

```
~
:digraphs
~! ¡ 161      c| ¢ 162      $$ £ 163      ox ¤ 164      e= ¤ 164      Y- ¥ 165
|| ¦ 166      pa § 167      "" ¨ 168      cO © 169      a- ª 170      << « 171
-, ¬ 172      -- 173      rO ® 174      -= ¯ 175      ~o ° 176      +- ± 177
22 ² 178      33 ³ 179      ´´ ´ 180      ju µ 181      pp ¶ 182      ~. · 183
,, ¸ 184      11 ¹ 185      o- º 186      >> » 187      14 ¼ 188      12 ½ 189
34 ¾ 190      ~? ¿ 191      A` À 192      A´ Á 193      A^ Â 194      A- Ã 195
A" Ä 196      A@ Å 197      AA Å 197      AE Æ 198      C, Ç 199      E` È 200
E´ É 201      E^ Ê 202      E" Ë 203      I` Ì 204      I´ Í 205      I^ Î 206
I" Ï 207      D- Ð 208      N~ Ñ 209      O` Ò 210      O´ Ó 211      O^ Ô 212
O~ Õ 213      O" Ö 214      /\ × 215      OE × 215      O/ Ø 216      U` Ù 217
U´ Ú 218      U^ Û 219      U" Ü 220      Y´ Ý 221      Ip p 222      ss ß 223
a` à 224      a´ á 225      a^ â 226      a- ã 227      a" ä 228      a@ å 229
aa å 229      ae æ 230      c, ç 231      e` è 232      e´ é 233      e^ ê 234
e" ë 235      i` ì 236      i´ í 237      i^ î 238      i" ï 239      d- ð 240
n~ ñ 241      o` ò 242      o´ ó 243      o^ ô 244      o- õ 245      o" ö 246
:- ÷ 247      oe ÷ 247      o/ ø 248      u` ù 249      u´ ú 250      u^ û 251
u" ü 252      y´ ý 253      ip p 254      y" ÿ 255
Press RETURN or enter command to continue█
```

Figure 2.19   Digraph-mapping table.

3

Searching

THIS CHAPTER INTRODUCES YOU TO THE VARIOUS *Vim* search commands. The basic search commands in *Vim* are rather simple, which means that you can get started with searching fairly easily.

In this chapter, you learn about the following:

- Simple forward searches
- Search options
- Incremental searches
- Changing directions
- Basic regular expressions

Simple Searches

To search for a string, use the */string* command. To find the word *include,* for example, use the command **/include**. An **<Enter>** is implied at the end of this command. (Any time the cursor jumps to the bottom of the screen and you type something, you must end it with **<Enter>**.)

Note: The characters .*[]^%/\?~$ have special meaning. If you want to use them in a search you must put a \ in front of them. Example: to find . use the search string\ . .

The cursor now moves to the *i* of include, as seen in Figure 3.1.

```
/*********************************************************
 * cd-speed                                              *
 *      Report the speed of a cd-rom                     *
 *                  (Also works on hard drives and other *
 *                  devices)                             *
 *                                                       *
 * Usage:                                                *
 *      cd-speed <device>                                *
 *                                                       *
 *********************************************************/
#█nclude <iostream.h>
#include <iomanip.h>
/include
```

Figure 3.1   Searching for include.

To find the next include, use the command /**<Enter>**. The cursor now moves to the
next occurrence of the string, as shown by Figure 3.2.

```
/*********************************************************
 * cd-speed                                              *
 *      Report the speed of a cd-rom                     *
 *                  (Also works on hard drives and other *
 *                  devices)                             *
 *                                                       *
 * Usage:                                                *
 *      cd-speed <device>                                *
 *                                                       *
 *********************************************************/
#include <iostream.h>
#█nclude <iomanip.h>
/include
```

Figure 3.2   Search again, forward (/**<Enter>**).

Another way to find the next match is with the **n** command. This command does the
same thing as /**<Enter>**, but does it with one less keystroke. Figure 3.3 shows the result
of this search.

```
 * cd-speed                                              *
 *      Report the speed of a cd-rom                     *
 *                  (Also works on hard drives and other *
 *                  devices)                             *
 *                                                       *
 * Usage:                                                *
 *      cd-speed <device>                                *
 *                                                       *
 *********************************************************/
#include <iostream.h>
#include <iomanip.h>
#█nclude <unistd.h>
```

Figure 3.3   Search again (**n**).

Both the /**<Enter>** and **n** commands can have a count specified. If there is a count, the
command searches for the count number of matches from the current location.

Search History

The search command has a history feature. Suppose, for example, that you do three
searches:
    /one
    /two
    /three

Now let's start searching by typing a simple / without pressing **<Enter>**. If you press **<Up>**, Vim puts **/three** on the prompt line. Pressing **<Enter>** at this point searches for *three*. If you do not press **<Enter>**, but press **<Up>** instead, *Vim* changes the prompt to **/two**. Another **<Up>** command moves you to **/one**.

In other words, after you do a number of searches, you can use the **<Up>** and **<Down>** keys to select one of your recent searches.

Searching Options

Many different options control the way you perform a search. This section discusses a few of them.

Highlighting

The following command causes *Vim* to highlight any strings found matching the search pattern:

```
:set hlsearch
```

If you turn on this option and then search for *include*, for example, the results in all the *include* strings are highlighted, as seen in Figure 3.4.

To turn off search highlighting, use this command:

```
:set nohlsearch
```

To clear the current highlighting, use the following command:

```
:nohlsearch
```

Search highlighting is now turned off; matched text will not be highlighted. However, the highlighting will return when you use a search command.

Incremental Searches

By default, *Vim* uses the traditional search method: You specify the string, and then *Vim* performs the search. When you use the following command, the editor performs incremental searches:

```
:set incsearch
```

```
*                    devices)                              *
*                                                          *
*  Usage:                                                  *
*      cd-speed <device>                                   *
*                                                          *
***********************************************************/
#include <iostream.h>
#include <iomanip.h>
#include <unistd.h>
#include <stdlib.h>
#include <stdio.h>
#include <sys/ioctl.h>
```

Figure 3.4 The **'hlsearch'** option.

The editor starts searching as soon as you type the first character of the string. Each additional character further refines the search.

Suppose, for example, that you want to search for ioctl.h, but this time you want to use an incremental search. First, you turn on incremental searching.

Next, you start the search by typing the /i command. Figure 3.5 shows how the editor searches for the first *i* and positions the cursor on it.

```
* Usage:                                                  *
*    cd-speed <dev█ce>                                     *
*                                                          *
***********************************************************/
#include <iostream.h>
#include <iomanip.h>
#include <unistd.h>
#include <stdlib.h>
#include <stdio.h>
#include <sys/ioctl.h>
#include <sys/types.h>
#include <sys/mtio.h>
/i█
```

Figure 3.5   Results after /i.

You continue the search by typing an **o**. Your search now is **/io**, so the editor finds the first io, as seen in Figure 3.6.

This is still not the place you want, so you add a **c** to the search, resulting in the **/ioc** command. The *Vim* editor advances, as illustrated in Figure 3.7, to the first match of *ioc*.

This is what you want to find, so you press **<Enter>**, and you're there.

To turn off incremental searches, use the following command:

:set noincsearch

```
* Usage:                                                  *
*    cd-speed <device>                                     *
*                                                          *
***********************************************************/
#include <█iostream.h>
#include <iomanip.h>
#include <unistd.h>
#include <stdlib.h>
#include <stdio.h>
#include <sys/ioctl.h>
#include <sys/types.h>
#include <sys/mtio.h>
/io█
```

Figure 3.6   Incremental search after /io.

```
* Usage:                                                  *
*    cd-speed <device>                                     *
*                                                          *
***********************************************************/
#include <iostream.h>
#include <iomanip.h>
#include <unistd.h>
#include <stdlib.h>
#include <stdio.h>
#include <sys/ioc█tl.h>
#include <sys/types.h>
#include <sys/mtio.h>
/ioc█
```

Figure 3.7   Incremental search after /ioc.

Searching Backward

The reverse search command (**?**) searches backward. The **n** command repeats the last search. If a reverse search was the last one used, the **n** command searches in the reverse direction. If the last search was a forward search, the **n** command searches forward.

Figure 3.8 shows how the **?** and **n** commands can work together.

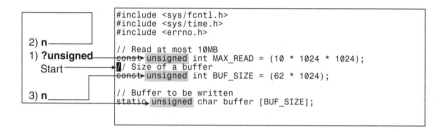

Figure 3.8   **?** and **n** commands.

Changing Direction

Suppose you start a forward search for unsigned using the **/unsigned** command. You can turn around and search in the reverse direction by using the **?** command. The **n** command repeats the search in the same direction. The **N** command reverses the direction on the search and repeats it.

To make things a little clearer, line numbering has been turned on using the following command:

`:set number`

In this example, we use the following search commands:

Command	Meaning	Result
/unsigned	Forward search for unsigned	Line 24
n	Repeat search in the same (forward) direction	Line 26
n	Search again	Line 29
?	Reverse search for the preceding string (unsigned)	Line 26
N	Reverse direction and repeat the search	Line 29

Figure 3.9 shows the /**unsigned** command used to perform a search. The **n** command was used twice to go the next occurrences of the string. Then we reversed course with a **?** command (which always goes backward.) Finally, we reverse course again with the **N** command. Figure 3.9 shows this tortured path.

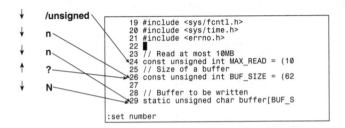

Figure 3.9 Different kinds of search commands.

Basic Regular Expressions

The *Vim* editor uses regular expressions to specify what to search for. *Regular expressions* are an extremely powerful and compact way to specify a search pattern. Unfortunately, this power comes at a price because regular expressions are a bit tricky to specify.

Let's start with the simple stuff. In a regular expression, the normal letters match themselves. So the regular expression *Steve* will match *Steve*.

The Beginning (^) and End ($) of a Line

The ^ character matches the beginning of a line. (It is no coincidence that this is also the command to move to the beginning of the line.) The expression **include** matches the word *include* anywhere on the line. But the expression ^**include** matches the word *include* only if it is at the beginning of a line.

The **$** character matches the end of a line. Therefore, **was$** finds the word *was* only if it is at the end of a line. Figure 3.10, for example, shows a search for the pattern *the* with highlighting enabled.

```
<H1> Dumb user tricks

At one university the computer center was experience
trouble with a new type of computer terminal. Seems
that the professors loved to put papers on top of
the equipment, covering the ventilation holes. Many
terminals broke down because they became so hot that
the solder holding one of the chips melted and the
chip fell out.

The student technicians were used to this problem. One
day a technician took the back off a terminal
/the
```

Figure 3.10 Searching for *the*.

Next you see what happens when searching for the regular expression ^**the**. The results, as seen in Figure 3.11, show that only two occurrences, both of which begin lines, are highlighted.

Finally a search for **the$**. As you can see from Figure 3.12, only one *the* ends a line.

If you want to search for a line consisting of just the word *the*, use the regular expression ^**the$**. To search for empty lines, use the regular expression ^**$**.

```
<H1>Dumb user tricks

At one university the computer center was experience
trouble with a new type of computer terminal. Seems
that the professors loved to put papers on top of
the equipment, covering the ventilation holes. Many
terminals broke down because they became so hot that
the solder holding one of the chips melted and the
chip fell out.

The student technicians were used to this problem. One
day a technician took the back off a terminal
/^the
```

Figure 3.11   Searching for ^**the**.

```
<H1>Dumb user tricks

At one university the computer center was experience
trouble with a new type of computer terminal. Seems
that the professors loved to put papers on top of
the equipment, covering the ventilation holes. Many
terminals broke down because they became so hot that
the solder holding one of the chips melted and the
chip fell out.

The student technicians were used to this problem. One
day a technician took the back off a terminal
/the$
```

Figure 3.12   Searching for **the$**.

Match Any Single Character (.)

The character **.** matches any single character. For example, the expression **c.m** matches a string whose first character is a *c*, whose second character is anything, and whose the third character is *m*. Figure 3.13 shows that the pattern matched the *com* of *computer* and the *cam* of *became*.

```
At one university the computer center was experience
trouble with a new type of computer terminal. Seems
that the professors loved to put papers on top of
the equipment, covering the ventilation holes. Many
terminals broke down because they became so hot that
the solder holding one of the chips melted and the
chip fell out.

The student technicians were used to this problem. One
day a technician took the back off a terminal
expecting to find a loose chip and instead found a
/c.m
```

Figure 3.13   Special character ..

Matching Special Characters

Most symbols have a special meaning inside a regular expression. To match these special symbols, you need to precede them with a backslash (\). To find *the.* (period), for example, use the string **the\.**.

Regular Expression Summary

The following list assumes that the **'magic'** option is on (the default).

x	The literal character x
^	Start of line
$	End of line
.	A single character
\character	Turns off the special meaning of many characters, gives special meaning to a few others

4

Text Blocks and
Multiple Files

THIS CHAPTER SHOWS YOU HOW TO DEAL with larger text blocks. This includes the commands that enable you to define a large text block as well as perform cut, paste, and copy operations.

With most editors, you can just cut and paste. However, the *Vim* editor has the concept of a register. This enables you to hold data for multiple cut, copy, or paste operations. Most other editors are limited to a single cut/paste clipboard. With the *Vim* registers you get more than 26 clipboards.

One of the strengths of UNIX is the number of text manipulation commands it provides. This chapter shows you how to use the filter command to take advantage of this power to use UNIX filters to edit text from within *Vim*.

Up until now, you have worked with single files in this book. You will now start using multiple files. This will enable you to perform the same edits on a series of files, and to cut and paste between files.

This chapter discusses the following topics:

- Simple cut-and-paste operations (in *Vim* terms, delete and put)
- Marking locations within the text
- Copying text into a register using the yank commands
- Filtering text
- Editing multiple files

Cut, Paste, and Copy

When you delete something with the **d**, **x**, or another command, the text is saved. You can paste it back by using the **p** command. (The technical name for this is a *put*).

Take a look at how this works. First you will delete an entire line with the **dd** command, by putting the cursor on the line you want to delete and pressing **dd**. Now you move the cursor to where you want to place the line and use the **p** (put) command. The line is inserted on the line following the cursor. Figure 4.1 shows the operation of these commands.

Because you deleted an entire line, the **p** command placed the text on the line after the cursor.

If you delete part of a line (a word with the **dw** command, for instance), the **p** command puts it just after the character under the cursor (see Figure 4.2).

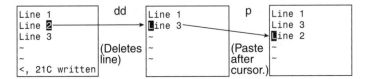

Figure 4.1   Deleting (cutting) and putting (pasting).

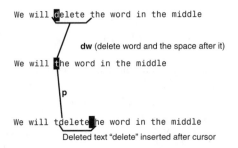

Figure 4.2   Deleting a word and putting back again.

Character Twiddling

Frequently when you are typing, your fingers get ahead of your brain. The result is a typo such as *teh* for *the*. The *Vim* editor makes it easy to correct such problems. Just put the cursor on the *e* of *teh* and execute the command **xp**. Figure 4.3 illustrates this command. This works as follows:

x   Deletes the character 'e' and places it in a register.

p   Puts the text after the cursor, which is on the 'h'.

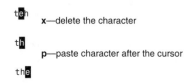

Figure 4.3   Character twiddling with xp.

More on "Putting"

You can execute the **p** command multiple times. Each time, it inserts another copy of the text into the file.

The **p** command places the text after the cursor. The **P** command places the text *before* the cursor. A count can be used with both commands and, if specified, the text will be inserted *count* times.

Marks

The *Vim* editor enables you to place marks in your text. The command **ma** marks the place under the cursor as mark *a*. You can place 26 marks (*a* through *z*) in your text. (You can use a number of other marks as well.)

To go to a mark, use the command `` `mark ``, where *mark* is the mark letter (and `` ` `` is the backtick or open single-quote character).

The command `'mark` (single quotation mark, or apostrophe) moves you to the beginning of the line containing the mark. This differs from the `` `mark `` command, which moves you to the marked line and column.

The `'mark` command can be very useful when deleting a long series of lines. To delete a long series of lines, follow these steps:

1. Move the cursor to the beginning of the text you want to delete.

2. Mark it using the command **ma**. (This marks it with mark *a*.)

3. Go to the end of the text to be removed. Delete to mark *a* using the command **d'a**.

   Note: There is nothing special about using the *a* mark. Any mark from *a* to *z* may be used.

There is nothing special about doing the beginning first followed by the end. You could just as easily have marked the end, moved the cursor to the beginning, and deleted to the mark.

One nice thing about marks is that they stay with the text even if the text moves (because you inserted or deleted text above the mark. Of course, if you delete the text containing the mark, the mark disappears.

Where Are the Marks?

To list all the marks, use the following command:

```
:marks
```

Figure 4.4 shows the typical results of such a command.

The display shows the location of the marks *d* through *d* as well as the special marks: ', ", [, and].

Marks *a* through *d* are located at lines 1, 8, 14, and 25 in the file.

The special marks are as follows:

'	The last place the cursor was at line 67 of the current file
"	Line 1 (we were at the top of the file when last closed it)
[	The start of the last insert (line 128)
]	The end of the insert (line 129)

To view specific marks, use this command:

```
:marks args
```

Replace *args* with the characters representing the marks you want to view.

```
*            the data from an input
* (.c) file.
*/
struct in_file_struct {
:marks
mark line col  file/text
 '     67    0  *^I^I^I   into the "bad" list^I^I*
 a      1    0  #undef USE_CC^I/* Use Sun's CC com
 b      8    1  * Usage:^I^I^I^I^I*
 c     14    1  *^I^I^I   (default = proto_db)^I^I
 d     25    1  *^I--quote^I^I^I^I^I*
 "      1    0  #undef USE_CC^I/* Use Sun's CC com
 [    128   42  * in_file_struct -- structure that
 ]    129   12  *            the data from an input
Press RETURN or enter command to continue█
```

Figure 4.4   `:marks`.

Yanking

For years, I used a simple method for copying a block of text from one place to another. I deleted it using the **d** command, restored the deleted text with the **p** command, and then went to where I wanted the copy and used the **p** to put it into the text.

There is a better way. The **y** command "yanks" text into a register (without removing it from the file). The general form of the **y** command is **y***motion*. It works just like the delete (**d**) command except the text is not deleted. And the shorthand **yy** yanks the current line into the buffer.

(Note: Most other editors call this a "copy" operation.)

Take a look at how you can use this command to duplicate a block of text. First go to the top of the text to be copied and mark it with **ma**. Then go to the bottom and do a **y'a** (yank to mark *a*).

Now go to where the copied text is to be inserted and put it there using the **p** command.

Figure 4.5 shows these commands in action.

Yanking Lines

The **Y** command yanks a single line. If preceded by a count, it yanks that number of lines into the register. You might have expected **Y** to yank until the end of the line, like **D** and **C**, but it really yanks the whole line.

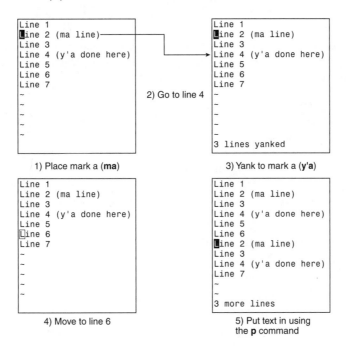

Figure 4.5 Yank (copy) and put (paste).

Filtering

The **!***motion command* takes a block of text and filters it through another program. In other words, it runs the system command represented by *command*, giving it the block of text represented by *motion* as input. The output of this command then replaces the selected block.

Because this summarizes badly if you are unfamiliar with UNIX filters, take a look at an example. The **sort** command sorts a file. If you execute the following command, the unsorted file `input.txt` will be sorted and written to `output.txt`. (This works on both UNIX and Microsoft Windows.)

```
$ sort <input.txt >output.txt
```

Now do the same thing in *Vim*. You want to sort lines 1 through 10 of a file. You start by putting the cursor on line 1. Next you execute the following command:

```
!10G
```

The **!** tells *Vim* that you are performing a filter operation. The *Vim* editor expects a motion command to follow indicating which part of the file to filter. The **10G** command tells *Vim* to go to line 10, so it now knows that it is to filter lines 1 (the current line) through 10 (**10G**).

In anticipation of the filtering, the cursor drops to the bottom of the screen and a **!** prompt displays. You can now type in the name of the filter program, in this case **sort**.

Therefore, your full command is as follows:

```
!10Gsort<Enter>
```

The result is that the **sort** program is run on the first 10 lines. The output of the program replaces these lines.

The **!!** command runs the current line through a filter. (I have found this a good way to get the output of system commands into a file.)

I'm editing a `readme.txt` file, for example, and want to include in it a list of the files in the current directory. I position the cursor on a blank line and type the following:

```
!!ls
```

This puts the output of the **ls** command into my file. (Microsoft Windows users would use **dir**.)

Another trick is to time stamp a change. To get the current date time (on UNIX), I use the following command:

```
!!date
```

This proves extremely useful for change histories and such.

> **Note**
>
> Using *!!* like this is technically not filtering because commands like *ls* and *date* don't read standard input.

Editing Another File

Suppose that you have finished editing one file and want to edit another file. The simple way to switch to the other file is to exit *Vim* and start it up again on the other file.

Another way to do so is to execute the following command:

```
:vi file
```

This command automatically closes the current file and opens the new one. If the current file has unsaved changes, however, *Vim* displays a warning message and aborts the command:

```
No write since last change (use ! to override)
```

At this point, you have a number of options. You can write the file using this command:

```
:write
```

Or you can force *Vim* to discard your changes and edit the new file using the force (**!**) option, as follows:

```
:vi! file.txt
```

> **Note**
>
> The **:e** command can be used in place of **:vi**. The fact that these commands are equivalent has led to a flame war between Steve Oualline, who prefers **:vi** and Bram Moolenaar, who prefers **:e**. (Okay, it was limited to three slightly discordant emails, but it's hard to introduce real drama in a book like this.)

The `:view` Command

The following command works just like the **:vi** command, except the new file is opened in read-only mode:

```
:view file
```

If you attempt to change a read-only file, you receive a warning. You can still make the changes; you just can't save them. When you attempt to save a changed read-only file, *Vim* issues an error message and refuses to save the file. (You can force the write with the **:write!** command, as described later in this chapter.)

Dealing with Multiple Files

So far the examples in this book have dealt with commands that edit a single file. This section introduces you to some commands that can edit multiple files.

Consider the initial **Vim** command, for example. You can specify multiple files on the command line, as follows:

```
$ gvim one.c two.c three.c
```

This command starts *Vim* and tells it that you will be editing three files. By default, *Vim* displays just the first file (see Figure 4.6).

To edit the next file, you need to change files using the **:next** command. Figure 4.7 shows the results. Note that if you have unsaved changes in the current file and you try to do a **:next**, you will get a warning message and the **:next** will not work.

You can solve this problem in many different ways. The first is to save the file using the following command:

```
:write
```

In other words, you can perform a **:write** followed by a **:next**.

The *Vim* editor has a shorthand command for this. The following command performs both operations:

```
:wnext
```

```
/* File one.c */
~
~
~
~
```

Figure 4.6   Editing the first of multiple files.

```
/* File two.c */
~
~
~
"two.c" 1L, 17C
```

Figure 4.7   **:next**.

Or, you can force *Vim* to go the next file using the force (**!**) option. If you use the following command and your current file has changes, you will lose those changes:

```
:next!
```

Finally, there is the **'autowrite'** option. If this option is set, *Vim* will not issue any No write... messages. Instead, it just writes the file for you and goes on. To turn this option on, use the following command:

```
:set autowrite
```

To turn it off, use this command:

```
:set noautowrite
```

You can continue to go through the file list using the following command until you reach the last file:

```
:next
```

Also, the **:next** command can take a repeat count. For example, if you execute the command

```
:2 next
```

(or **:2next**), *Vim* acts like you issued a **:next** twice.

Which File Am I On?

Suppose you are editing a number of files and want to see which one you are on. The following command displays the list of the files currently being edited:

```
:args
```

The one that you are working on now is enclosed in square brackets. Figure 4.8 shows the output of the command.

```
/* File two.c */
~
~
~
~
one.c [two.c] three.c
```

Figure 4.8   Output of **:args**.

This figure shows three files being edited: one.c, two.c, and three.c. The file currently being editing is two.c.

Going Back a File

To go back a file, you can execute either of the following commands:

```
:previous
```

or

```
:Next
```

These commands act just like the **:next** command, except that they go backward rather than forward.

If you want to write the current file and go to the previous one, use either of the following commands:

```
:wprevious
:wNext
```

Editing the First or Last File

You might think that `:first` would put you at the first file and `:last` would edit the last file. This makes too much sense for use with computers. To start editing from the first file, no matter which file you are on, execute the following command:

```
:rewind
```

To edit the last file, use this command:

```
:last
```

Note: Bram has promised to add a `:first` command in the next release of *Vim*.

Editing Two Files

Suppose that you edit two files by starting *Vim* with the following:

```
$ gvim one.c two.c
```

You edit a little on the first file, and then go to the next file with the following:

```
:wnext
```

At this point, the previous file, `one.c`, is considered the *alternate file*. This has special significance in *Vim*. For example, a special text register (#) contains the name of this file.

By pressing **CTRL-^**, you can switch editing from the current file to the alternate file. Therefore, if you are editing `two.c` and press **CTRL-^**, you will switch to `one.c` (`two.c` becoming the alternate file). Pressing **CTRL-^** one more time switches you back.

Suppose that you are editing a bunch of files, as follows:

```
$ gvim one.c two.c three.c
```

The command *count***CTRL-^** goes to the count file on the command line. The following list shows the results of several **CTRL-^** commands:

1 CTRL-^   one.c

2 CTRL-^   two.c

3 CTRL-^   three.c

CTRL-^   two.c   (previous file)

> **Note**
>
> When you first start editing (file `one.c`) and press CTRL-^, you will get an error message: No
> `alternate file`. Remember the alternate file is the last file you just edited before this one (in this
> editing session). Because `one.c` is the only file edited, there is no previous file and therefore the error
> message.

5

Windows

S O FAR YOU HAVE BEEN USING A SINGLE window. In this chapter, you split the screen into multiple windows and edit more than one file simultaneously. This chapter also discusses the use of editing buffers. A *buffer* is a copy of a file that you edit along with the setting and marks that go with it.

The topics discussed in this chapter include the following:

- How to open a new window
- Window selection
- Editing two files at once
- Controlling the size of a window
- Basic buffer usage

Opening a New Window

The easiest way to open a new window is to use the following command:

```
:split
```

This command splits the screen into two windows (and leaves the cursor in the top one), as seen in Figure 5.1.

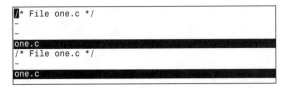

Figure 5.1   Splitting a window.

Both are editing the same file, so you can view two different parts of a file simultaneously.

If you are at the bottom window, the **CTRL-Ww** command moves the cursor to the top window (alternate command: **CTRL-W CTRL-W**). If you are at the top window, the editor jumps to the bottom one on the screen.

To change windows, use **CTRL-Wj** to go down a window and **CTRL-Wk** to go up a window (see Figure 5.2). Or if you are using *Vim* with a mouse, you can just click in the window you want.

To close a window, use **ZZ** or the following command:

    `:q`

CTRL-Wc does the same thing.

Usually you would expect **CTRL-W CTRL-C** also to close a window. It would if all the **CTRL-W** commands were consistent. Because **CTRL-C** cancels any pending operation, however, **CTRL-W CTRL-C** does nothing.

Opening Another Window with Another File

The following command opens a second window and starts editing the given file:

    `:split file`

Figure 5.3 shows what happens when you start editing `one.c` and then execute the following command

    `:split two.c`

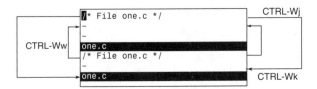

Figure 5.2   Window navigation.

```
/* File two.c */
~
~
~
two.c
/* File one.c */
~
one.c
"two.c" 1L, 17C
```

Figure 5.3   Results of `:split two.c`.

The `:split` command can also execute an initial command using the *+command* convention.

Figure 5.4 shows what happens when you are editing one.c and execute the following command:

```
:split +/printf three.c
```

```
    {
        printf("%2d squared is %3d\n", i, i*i);
    }
three.c
/* File one.c */
~
one.c
"three.c" 11L, 160C
```

Figure 5.4   Result of `:split` with a + command

Controlling Window Size

The `:split` command can take a number argument. If specified, this will be the number of lines in the new window. For example, the following opens a new window three lines high and starts editing the file alpha.c:

```
:3 split alpha.c
```

A space appears here for clarity. You could have just as easily write the following:

```
:3split alpha.c
```

Figure 5.5 shows the results.

```
/* This is alpha.c */
~
~
~
alpha.c
/* File one.c */
~
~
~
~
~
~
~
one.c
"alpha.c" 1L, 22C
```

Figure 5.5   `:3split`.

Split Summary

The general form of the **:split** command is as follows:

```
:count split +command file
```

count   The size of the new window in lines. (Default is to split the current
             window into two equal sizes.)

+command   An initial command.

file   The name of the file to edit. (Default is the current file.)

The *:new* Command

The **:new** command works just like the **:split** command except that the **:split**
command splits the current window and displays the current file in both windows.

   The following command splits the current window and starts a new file in the
other window:

```
:new
```

Split and View

The **:sview** command acts like a combination of **:split** and **:view**. This command
proves useful if you want to look at, but not edit, a file in another window.

Changing Window Size

Changing window size when you are using **gvim** is easy. To change the size of a window, use the mouse to drag the separator up or down (see Figure 5.6).

   If you are using the terminal version of *Vim*, you need to type in some commands.

   The command *count***CTRL-W+** increases the window size by *count* (default = 1).
Similarly *count***CTRL-W-** decreases the window's size by *count* (default = 1).

   The command **CTRL-W=** makes all the windows the same size (or as close as possible).

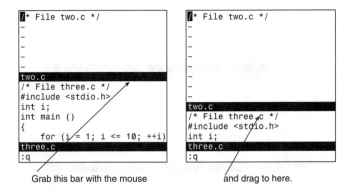

Grab this bar with the mouse   and drag to here.

Figure 5.6   Adjusting the window size.

The command *count***CTRL-W_** makes the current window *count* lines high. If no count is specified, the window is increased to its maximum size.

Buffers

The *Vim* editor uses the term *buffer* to describe a file being edited. Actually, a buffer is a copy of the file that you edit. When you finish changing the buffer and exit, the contents of the buffer are written to the file. Buffers not only contain file contents, but also all the marks, settings, and other stuff that go with it.

Normally it is pretty easy to tell what buffers you have: If it has a window on the screen, it is a buffer; if it is not on the screen, it is not a buffer.

Now for a new concept thrown into the mix, that of the hidden buffer. Suppose you are editing a file named one.c and you need to do some work on two.c. You split the screen and create two windows, one for each file. But you do not like split-screen mode; you want to see one file at a time.

One solution is to make the window for two.c as big as possible. This works, but there still is an annoying little bit of one.c showing. Another solution is to close the one.c window, but then you lose all the changes for that file.

The *Vim* editor has another solution for you: the **:hide** command. This causes the current buffer to become "hidden." This causes it to disappear from the screen. But *Vim* still knows that you are editing this buffer, so it keeps all the settings, marks, and other stuff around.

Actually, a buffer can have three states:

Active   Appears onscreen.

Hidden   A file is being edited, but does not appear onscreen.

Inactive   The file is not being edited, but keep the information about it anyway.

The inactive state takes a little explaining. When you edit another file, the content of the current file is no longer needed, so *Vim* discards it. But information about marks in the file and some other things are still useful and are remembered along with the name of the file. Also, a file that was included in the command with which you started *Vim*, but was not edited, will also be an inactive buffer.

To find a list of buffers, use the following command:

```
:buffers
```

Figure 5.7 shows the results of this command.

The first column is the buffer number. The second is a series of flags indicating the state of the buffer. The third is the name of the file associated with the buffer.

The state flags are as follows:

–   Inactive buffer.

h   Buffer is hidden.

%   Current buffer.

Alternate buffer.

+   File has been modified.

```
~
~
~
~
~
~
two.c
:buffers
  1 #h   "one.c"                        line 1
  2 %    "two.c"                        line 1
  3  -   "three.c"                      line 1
  4  -   "four.c"                       line 0
  5  -   "help.txt"                     line 1
  6  -   "editing.txt"                  line 234
Press RETURN or enter command to continue
```

Figure 5.7 **`:buffers`**.

In this case, you see six buffers:

1. The next to last file you were working on, also known as the alternate file (# flag). This buffer has been hidden (h flag). You were editing file one.c and left the cursor on line 1.
2. The active buffer (% flag). This is the file you are editing.
3. An inactive buffer. You want to edit `three.c`, but you have made no changes to it.
4. Another file on the argument list that has not been edited.
5. When you executed a **`:help`** command, the Vim editor opened two files. The first one of these is called `help.txt`.
6. This is another help file called `editing.txt`.

Selecting a Buffer

You can select which buffer to use by executing the following command:

`:buffer` *`number`*

number is the buffer number. If you do not know the number of the buffer, but you do know the filename, you can use this command:

`:buffer` *`file`*

Figure 5.8 shows the results of a typical **`:buffer`** command.

```
/* File three.c */
#include <stdio.h>
int i;
int main()
{
    for (i = 1; i <= 10; ++i)
    {
        printf("%2d squared is %3d\n", i, i*i);
    }
    return (0);
}
~
~
three.c
```

Figure 5.8   `:3buffer` or `:buffer three.c`.

```
/* File one.c */
~
~
~
~
~
one.c
/* File three.c */
#include <stdio.h>
int i;
int main()
{
    for (i = 1; i <= 10; ++i)
three.c
"one.c" line 1 of 1 --100%-- col 1 ((2) of 3)
```

Figure 5.9   Result of `:sbuffer`.

The following command splits the window and starts editing the buffer:

`:sbuffer` *number*

If a number is specified, the new window will contain that buffer number. If no number is present, the current buffer is used. This also takes a filename as an argument. If you are editing the file three.c and execute the following command, for example, you get the results seen in Figure 5.9:

`:sbuffer one.c`

Other buffer-related commands include the following:

`:bnext`	Go to the next buffer.
`:count` `bnext`	Go to the next buffer count times.
`:count` `sbnext`	Shorthand for `:split` followed by `:count` `bnext`.
`:count` `bprevious`	Go to previous buffer. If a count is specified, go to the *count* previous buffer.
`:count` `sbprevious`	Shorthand for `:split` and `:count` `bprevious`.
`:count` `bNext`	Alias for `:bprevious`.

`:count sbNext`	Alias for `:sbprevious`.
`:blast`	Go to the last buffer in the list.
`:sblast`	Shorthand for `:split` and `:blast`.
`:brewind`	Go to the first buffer in the list.
`:sbrewind`	Shorthand for `:split` and `:rewind`.
`:bmodified count`	Go to count modified buffer on the list.
`:sbmodified count`	Shorthand for `:split` and `:bmodified`.

Buffer Options

Usually when the last window of a file is closed, the buffer associated with the file becomes inactive. If the option **hidden** is set, files that leave the screen do not become inactive; instead they automatically become hidden. Therefore if you want to keep the contents of all your old buffers around while editing, use the following command

```
:set hidden
```

Note

The `:hide` command always hides the current file no matter what the "hidden" option is set to.

Normally, the split/buffer related commands split the current window. If the **"switch-buf"** is set to "useopen" and there is a window displaying the buffer you want to display already on the screen, the *Vim* will just make that window the current one instead of performing the split (see Figure 5.10).

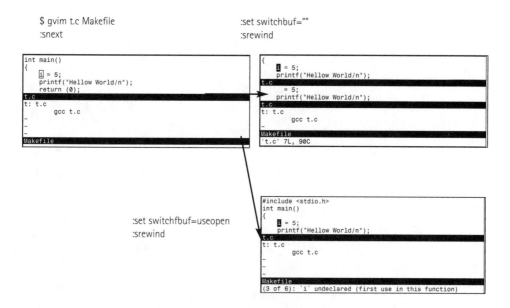

Figure 5.10   The "switchbuf" option.

Note the "switchbuf" option can have the values: "(nothing), 'split,' 'useopen' and 'split,useopen'." For a description of the "split" argument see Chapter 23, "Advanced Commands for Programmers."

6

Basic Visual Mode

ONE FEATURE THAT SETS *VIM* APART from its predecessor is something called visual mode. This mode gives you the ability to highlight a block of text and then execute a command on it. You can highlight a block of text, for example, and then delete it with a **d** command.

The nice thing about visual mode is that, unlike other *Vim* commands where you operate blindly, with visual mode you can see what text is going to be affected before you make a change.

In this chapter, you learn about the following:

- How to start visual mode
- Visual yanking
- Using visual mode to change text
- Visual commands for programmers
- Visual block mode

Entering Visual Mode

To enter visual mode, type the **v** command. Now when you move the cursor, the text from the start position to the current cursor location is highlighted (see Figure 6.1).

After the text has been highlighted, you can do something with it. For example, the **d** command deletes it. Figure 6.2 shows the results.

The Three Visual Modes

There are actually three different visual modes. The **v** command starts a character-by-character visual mode. All the characters from the start to the cursor are highlighted. Figure 6.3 shows this mode in action.

The **V** command starts linewise visual mode. You can highlight only full lines in this mode (see Figure 6.4).

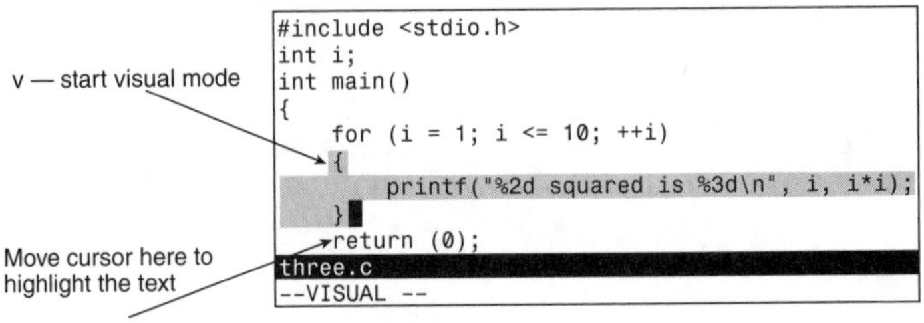

Figure 6.1   Visual mode.

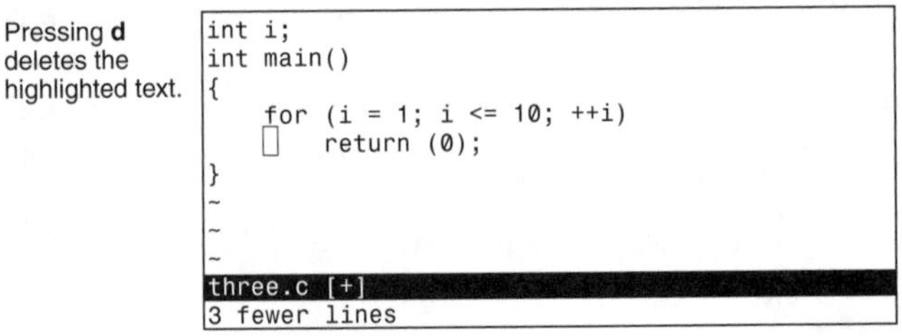

Figure 6.2   Visual delete.

> **Note**
>
> To get help on the commands that operate in visual mode, use the prefix **v_**. Therefore
>
> `:help v_d`
>
> describes what the **d** command does in visual mode.

Visual start
(Cursor is here
when **v** is pressed.)

Visual end
(Cursor is moved
to here.)

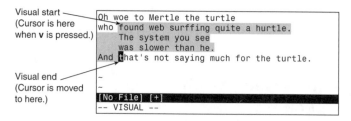

Figure 6.3   v (visual mode).

Visual start
(Cursor is here
when **V** is pressed.)

Visual end
(Cursor is moved
to here.)

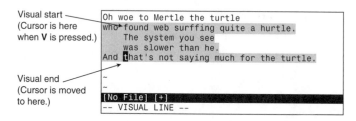

Figure 6.4   v (line visual mode).

To highlight a rectangle on the screen, use **CTRL-V**. This mode is extremely useful if you want to work with tables as shown in Figure 6.5. You can highlight a column and delete it using the **d** command.

Visual start
(Cursor is here
when **CTRL-V**
is pressed.)

Visual end
(Cursor is moved
to here.)

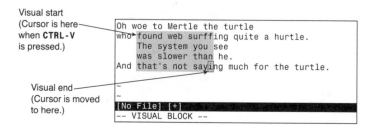

Figure 6.5   CTRL-V (block visual mode).

Leaving Visual Mode

Normally, you leave visual mode by typing a visual-mode command, such as **d** to delete the highlighted text. But you can also cancel visual mode by pressing the **<Esc>** key.

Remember, you can always type **<Esc>** to get back to normal mode so you know where you are. Some people find **<Esc>** a little annoying because it beeps if you type it twice. The first **<Esc>** goes from visual mode to normal mode. The second **<Esc>** in normal mode is an error and generates the beep. (The command **CTRL-C** will do the same thing as well.)

If you want to make sure that you are in normal mode and do not want to generate a beep, use the **CTRL-\CTRL-N** command. This acts just like **<Esc>** but without the noise.

Editing with Visual Mode

Editing with visual mode is simple. Select the text using the visual commands just discussed, and then type an editing command. This section shows you how to perform simple edits using a visual selection.

Deleting Text in Visual Mode

The **d** command deletes the highlighted text, as shown in Figure 6.6.

The **D** command deletes the highlighted lines, even if only part of a line is highlighted (see Figure 6.7).

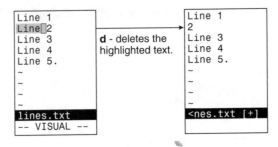

Figure 6.6   Deleting text in visual mode.

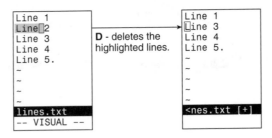

Figure 6.7   The visual **D** command.

Yanking Text

The **y** command places the highlighted text into a register. The linewise version of this command, **Y**, places each line of the highlighted text into a register.

Switching Modes

Suppose you are in character mode (started by **v**) and you realize you want to be in block mode. You can switch to block mode by just pressing **CTRL-V**.

In fact, you can switch visual modes at any time by just selecting the new mode. To cancel visual mode, press the **<Esc>** key; or you can switch to the mode you are already in. (In other words, if you use **v** to start visual mode, you can use another **v** to exit it.)

Changing Text

The **c** command deletes the highlighted text and starts insert mode. The **C** command does the same thing, but it works only on whole lines.

Joining Lines

The **J** command joins all the highlighted lines into one long line. Spaces are used to separate the lines.

If you want to join the lines without adding spaces, use the **gJ** command.

Figure 6.8 shows how the **J** and the **gJ** commands work.

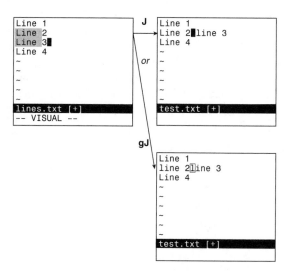

Figure 6.8   The visual **J** and **gJ** command.

Note
r and **s** do the same thing as **c** in visual mode. The same thing goes for **R** and **S**.

Commands for Programmers

The > command indents the selected lines by one "shift width." (The amount of white space can be set with the `'shiftwidth'` option.) The < does the process in reverse. (Note that these commands have a different meaning when using visual block mode.)

The = command indents the text. The `CTRL-]` command will jump to definition of the function highlighted.

Keyword Lookup

The `K` command is designed to look up the selected text using the "man" command. It works just like the normal-mode `K` command except that it uses the highlighted text as the keyword.

Visual Block Mode

Some commands work a little differently in visual block mode. Visual block mode is started by pressing `CTRL-V` and is used to define a rectangle on the screen.

Inserting Text

The command `Istring<Esc>` inserts the text on each line starting at the left side of the visual block, as seen in Figure 6.9.

You start by pressing `CTRL-V` to enter visual block mode. Now you define your block. Next you type `I` to enter insert mode followed by the text to insert. As you type, the text appears on the first line. After you press `<Esc>` to end the insert, the text will magically be inserted in the rest of the lines contained in the visual selection. Figure 6.9 shows how this process works.

If the block spans short lines that do not extend into the block, the text is not inserted in that line. Figure 6.10 illustrates what happens to short lines.

If the string contains a newline, the `I` acts just like a normal-mode insert (`i`) command and affects only the first line of the block.

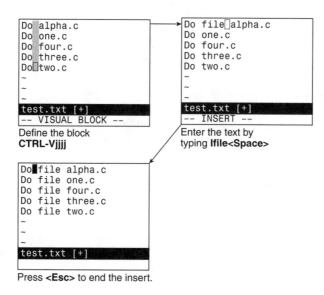

Define the block
CTRL-Vjjjj

Enter the text by
typing **Ifile<Space>**

Press **<Esc>** to end the insert.

Figure 6.9   Inserting text in visual block mode.

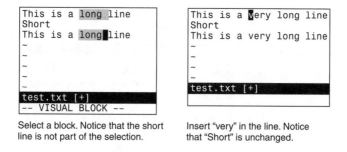

Select a block. Notice that the short
line is not part of the selection.

Insert "very" in the line. Notice
that "Short" is unchanged.

Figure 6.10   Inserting with short lines.

Changing Text

The visual block **c** command deletes the block and then throws you into insert mode to enable you to type in a string. The string will be inserted on each line in the block (see Figure 6.11).

The **c** command works only if you enter less than one line of new text. If you enter something that contains a newline, only the first line is changed. (In other words, visual block **c** acts just normal-mode **c** if the text contains more than one line.)

Note

The string will not be inserted on lines that do not extend into the block. Therefore if the block includes some short lines, the string will not be inserted in the short lines.

The **C** command deletes text from the left edge of the block to the end of line. It then puts you in insert mode so that you can type in a string, which is added to the end of each line (see Figure 6.12). Again, short lines that do not reach into the block are excluded.

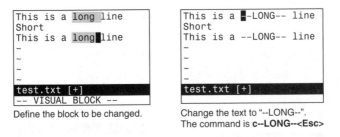

Define the block to be changed.   Change the text to "--LONG--".
                                   The command is **c--LONG--<Esc>**

Figure 6.11   Block visual **c** command.

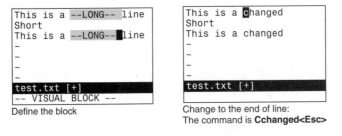

Define the block   Change to the end of line:
                    The command is **Cchanged<Esc>**

Figure 6.12   Block visual **c** with short lines.

The visual block **A** throws *Vim* into insert mode to enable you to input a string. The string is appended to the block (see Figure 6.13). If there are short lines in the block, spaces are added to pad the line and then string is appended.

You may notice that the **A** command affects short lines, whereas the other editing commands do not. The developers of *Vim* have noticed this and will fix this bug in a future version of the editor.

You can define a right edge of a visual block in two ways. If you use just motion keys, the right edge is the edge of the highlighted area. If you use the **$** key to extend the visual block to the end of line, the **A** key will add the text to the end of each line (see Figure 6.14).

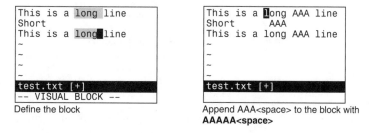

Define the block   Append AAA<space> to the block with
                                      AAAAA<space>

Figure 6.13 Block visual A command.

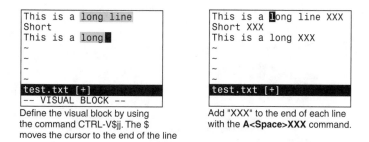

Define the visual block by using   Add "XXX" to the end of each line
the command CTRL-V$jj. The $ with the **A<Space>XXX** command.
moves the cursor to the end of the line

Figure 6.14 Block visual $ and A commands.

Replacing

The r*char* command applies all the selected characters with a single character (see Figure 6.15). Short lines that do not extend into the block are not affected.

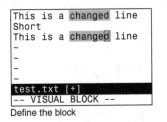

Define the block

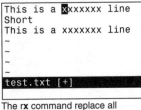

The **rx** command replace all characters in the block with "x"

Figure 6.15 Block visual-mode r command.

Shifting

The command **>** shifts the text to the right one shift width, opening whitespace. The starting point for this shift is the left side of the visual block (see Figure 6.16).

The **<** command removes one shift width of whitespace at the left side of the block (see Figure 6.17). This command is limited by the amount of text that is there; so if there is less than a shift width of whitespace available, it removes what it can.

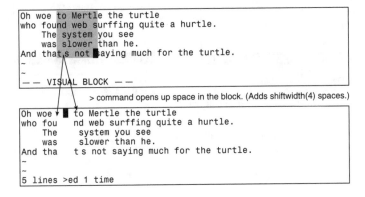

Figure 6.16 Block visual-mode > command.

```
aaa BBBBBBBBBB
aaa  BBBBBBBBBB
aaa   BBBBBBBBBB
aaa    BBBBBBBBBB
aaa     BBBBBBBBBB
aaa      BBBBBBBBBB
-- VISUAL BLOCK --
```

< command removes shiftwidth (4) spaces from the text

```
aaaBBBBBBBBBB
aaaBBBBBBBBBB
aaaBBBBBBBBBB
aaaBBBBBBBBBB
aaaBBBBBBBBBB
aaa BBBBBBBBBB
aaa  BBBBBBBBBB
7 lines <ed 1 time
```

Figure 6.17   Block visual < command.

Visual Block Help

Getting help for the commands that use visual block mode differs a little from other commands. You need to prefix the command with **v_b_**. To get help on the visual block **r** command, for example, type the following:

```
:help v_b_r
```

Commands for Programmers

THE VIM EDITOR CONTAINS A LARGE NUMBER of commands to make life easier for programming. For example, *Vim* contains a number of commands to help you obtain correct indentation, match parentheses, and jump around in source files.

One of the best features of *Vim* as far as a programmer is concerned are the commands that enable you to build a program from within *Vim* and then go through the error list and edit the files that caused trouble.

In this chapter, you learn about the following:

- Syntax coloring
- Automatic indentation
- Indentation commands
- Commands to navigate through the source code
- Getting information through the **man** command.
- The use of tags to go up and down a call stack
- Making programs with the **:make** command
- File searching with **:grep**

Syntax Coloring

The following command turns on syntax coloring.

```
:syntax on
```

That means that things such as keywords, strings, comments, and other syntax elements will have different colors. (If you have a black-and-white terminal, they will have different attributes such as bold, underline, blink, and so on.)

You can customize the colors used for syntax highlighting as well as the highlighting method itself.

Syntax Coloring Problems

Most of the time syntax coloring works just fine. But sometimes it can be a little tricky to set up. The following sections take a look at some common problems and solutions.

Colors Look Bad When I Use *Vim* (UNIX only)

Ever try and read light yellow text on a white background? It is very hard to do. If you see this on your screen, you have a problem. The *Vim* editor has two sets of syntax colors. One is used when the background is light, and the other when the background is dark.

When *Vim* starts, it tries to guess whether your terminal has a light or dark background and sets the option **'background'** to **light** or **dark**. It then decides which set of colors to use based on this option. Be aware, however, that the editor can guess wrong.

To find out the value of the **'background'** option, use the following command:

```
:set background?
```

If *Vim*'s guess is not correct, you can change it using a command such as this:

```
:set background=light
```

You must use this command before executing the command:

```
:syntax on
```

I Turned on Syntax Colors, but All I Get Is Black and White (UNIX)

A common problem affects the *xterm* program used on many UNIX systems. The problem is that although the *xterm* program understands colors, the terminal description for *xterm* frequently omits colors. This cripples syntax coloring. To correct this problem, you need to set your terminal type to the color version. On Linux this is **xterm-color**, and on Solaris this is **xtermc**.

To fix this problem, put the following in your $HOME/.cshrc file:

```
if ($term == xterm) set term = xterm-color
```

This works on Linux with the *csh* shell. Other systems and other shells require different changes.

I'm Editing a C File with a Non-Standard Extension. How Do I Tell *Vim* About It?

The *Vim* editor uses a file's extension to determine the file type. For example, files that end in .c or .h are considered C files. But what if you are editing a C header file named `settings.inc`? Because this is a non-standard extension, *Vim* will not know what to do with it. So how do you tell *Vim* that this is a C file?

The answer is to use the option `'filetype'`. This tells *Vim* which type of syntax highlighting to use. With a C file, you use the following command:

```
:set filetype=c
```

Now *Vim* knows that this file is a C file and will highlight the text appropriately.

If you want to make this setting automatically, look in the help files with this command:

```
:help new-filetype
```

Running the Color Test

If you are still having trouble with colors, run the *Vim* color test. This is a short *Vim* program that displays all the colors on the screen so that you can verify the correctness of the *Vim* colors.

The color test can be started with these two commands:

```
:edit $VIMRUNTIME/syntax/colortest.vim
:source %
```

Shift Commands

The *Vim* editor has lots of commands that help the programmer indent his program correctly. The first ones discussed here merely shift the text to the left (`<<`) or the right (`>>`).

The left shift command (`<<`) shifts the current line one shift width to the left. The right shift command (`>>`) does the same in the other direction. But what is a shift width? By default, it is 8. However, studies have shown that an indentation of 4 spaces for each level of logic is the most readable. So a shift width of 4 would be much nicer. To change the size of the shift width, use the following command:

```
:set shiftwidth=4
```

Figure 7.1 shows how the shift width option affects the `>>` command.

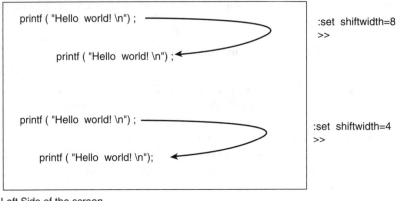

Left Side of the screen

Figure 7.1   shiftwidth and >>.

The << command shifts a single line. As usual you can prefix this command with a count; for example, **5<<** shifts 5 lines. The command <*motion* shifts each line from the current cursor location to where *motion* carries you.

Automatic Indentation

The *Vim* editor has a variety of automatic indentation options. The major indentation modes are the following:

cindent	This works for C-style programs (C, C++, Java, and so on). When this style of indentation is enabled, the *Vim* editor automatically indents your program according to a "standard" C style.
smartindent	In this mode, *Vim* indents each line the same amount as the preceding one, adding an extra level of indentation if the line contains a left curly brace ({) and removing a indentation level if the line contains a right curly brace (}). An extra indent is also added for any of the keywords specified by the **'cinwords'** option.
autoindent	New lines are indented the same as the previous line.

The next few sections explore these indentation modes in detail.

C Indentation

The *Vim* editor knows something about how C, C++, Java, and other structured language programs should be indented and can do a pretty good job of indenting things properly for you. To enable C-style indentation, just execute the following command:

```
:set cindent
```

With this option enabled, when you type something such as **if (x)**, the next line will automatically be indented an additional level. Figure 7.2 illustrates how **'cindent'** works.

```
Automatic indent  ──────▶   if (flag)
                                do_the_work ( ) ;

Automatic unindent ──▶ if (other_flag) {
Automatic indent  ──────▶      do_file ( ) ;
                               process_file ( ) ;
Automatic unindent ──▶ }
```

Figure 7.2   **cindent**.

When you type something in curly braces ({ }), the text will be indented at the start and unindented at the end.

> **Note**
>
> One side effect of automatic indentation is that it helps you catch errors in your code early. I have frequently entered a } to finish a procedure, only to find that the automatic indentation put it in column 4. This told me that I had accidentally left out a } somewhere in my text.

Different people have different styles of indentation. By default *Vim* does a pretty good job of indenting in a way that 90% of programmers do. There are still people out there with different styles, however; so if you want to, you can customize the indentation style through the use of several options.

   You don't want to switch on the **'cindent'** option manually every time you edit a C file. This is how you make it work automatically: Put the following lines in your .vimrc (UNIX) or _vimrc (Windows) file:

```
:filetype on
:autocmd FileType c,cpp :set cindent
```

The first command (**:filetype on**) turns on *Vim's* file type detection logic. The second, performs the command **:set cindent** if the file type detected is c or cpp. (This includes C, C++, and header files.)

Smartindent

The **'cindent'** mode is not the only indent mode available to *Vim* users. There is also the **'smartindent'** mode. In this mode, an extra level of indentation is added for each { and removed for each }. An extra level of indentation will also be added for any of the words in the **cinwords** option. Lines that begin with "#" are treated specially. If a line starts with "#", all indentation is removed. This is done so that preprocessor directives will all start in column 1. The indentation is restored for the next line. **'smartindent'** is not as smart as **'cindent'**, but smarter than **'autoindent'**.

Autoindent

Structured languages such as a Pascal, Perl, and Python use indentation to help the programmer figure out what the program is doing. When writing these programs, most of the time you want the next line indented at the same level as the preceding one.

To help you do this, the *Vim* editor has an **'autoindent'** option. When on, it causes lines to be automatically indented.

Suppose, for example, that you have autoindent off (**:set noautoident**). To type the following text, you must type four spaces in front of each **printf**:

```
if (true) {
    printf("It is true\n");
    printf("It is really true\n");
}
```

If you have set the **'autoindent'** option using the **:set autoindent** command, the *Vim* editor automatically indents the second **printf** by four spaces (to line up with the preceding line). Figure 7.3 illustrates the operation of the **'autoindent'** option.

Type four spaces for indent; with **'autoindent'** set, the following lines are automatically indented.

```
if (true) {
    printf("It is true\n");
    printf("It is really true\n");
    }
```

That is nice, but when you get ready to enter the } line, the *Vim* editor also indents four spaces. That is not good because you want the } to line up with the **if** statement.

While in insert mode, the **CTRL-D** command will cause *Vim* to back up one shift width (see Figure 7.4). **CTRL-D** moves the } back one shift width.

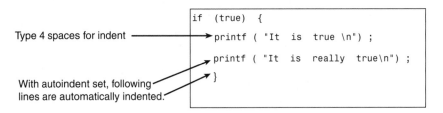

Figure 7.3   **autoindent**.

```
if (true)  {
  printf ( "It  is  true\n");
  printf ( "It  is  really  true\n");
  }
```

CTRL-D moves the } back one shiftwidth

Figure 7.4   **CTRL-D**.

The = Command

The =*motion* command indents the selected text using *Vim*'s internal formatting program. If you want to indent a block of text, for example, you can use the = command to do it. The motion in this case is the **%** (go to matching {}) command. Figure 7.5 shows the results.

```
{
if (strcmp (arg, option1) == 0)
return (1) ;
if (strcmp (arg, option2) == 0)
return (1) ;
return (0) ;
}
```

1) Position cursor on the first "{"
2) Execute the command "=%".

```
{
    if (strcmp (arg, option1) == 0)
        return (1) ;
    if (strcmp (arg, option2) ==0)
        return (1) ;
    return (0) ;
}
```

Figure 7.5   The = command.

Locating Items in a Program

Programmers made the *Vim* editor, so it has a lot of commands that can be used to navigate through a program. These include the following:

[CTRL-I,]CTRL-I	Search for a word under the cursor in the current file and any brought in by **#include** directives.
gd, gD	Search for the definition of a variable.
]CTRL-D, [CTRL-D	Jump to a macro definition.
]d, [d,]D, [D	Display macro definitions.

Instant Word Searches Including *#include* Files ([*CTRL-I,]CTRL-I*)

The [**CTRL-I** command jumps to the word under the cursor. The search starts at the beginning of the file and also searches files brought in by **#include** directives.

The]**CTRL-I** does the same thing, starting at the cursor location.

Jumping to a Variable Definition (*gd, gD*)

The **gd** command searches for the local declaration of the variable under the cursor (see Figure 7.6). This search is not perfect because *Vim* has a limited understanding of C and C++ syntax. In particular, it goes to the wrong place when you ask for the local declaration of a global variable. Most of the time, however, it does a pretty good job.

```
int global_var;

int main()
{
    int local_var;

    global_var = local_var = 5;
    printf("%d %d",
            global_var, local_var);
    return (0);
}
```

gd
Moves cursor from here to here.

Note: hlsearch is set.

Figure 7.6 The **gd** command.

The **gD** command searches for the global definition of the variable under the cursor(see Figure 7.7). Again, this search is not perfect, but most of the time it does the right thing.

```
int global_var;

int main()
{
    int local_var;

    global_var = local_var = 5;
    printf("%d %d",
            global_var, local_var);
    return (0);
}
```

gD
Moves cursor from here to here.

Note: hlsearch is set.

Figure 7.7 The **gD** command.

Jump to Macro Definition (*[CTRL-D,]CTRL-D*)

The **[CTRL-D** command searches for the first definition of the macro whose name is under the cursor. The **]CTRL-D** command searches for the next definition of the macro. These commands search not only the file you are editing, but also all files that are **#included** from this file. Figure 7.8 shows the **[CTRL-D** and **]CTRL-D** commands.

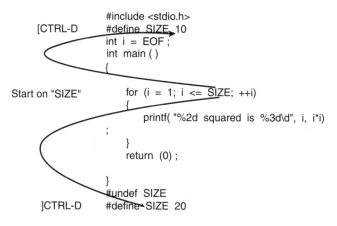

Figure 7.8   **[CTRL-D** and **]CTRL-D**.

Displaying Macro Definitions (*[d,]d, [D,]D*)

The **[d** command displays the first definition of the macro whose name is under the cursor. The **]d** command does the same thing only it starts looking from the current cursor position and finds the next definition. Figure 7.9 shows the result of **[d**.

```
#include <stdio.h>
#define SIZE 10
int i = EOF;
int main()
{
    for (i = 1; i <= SIZE; ++i)
    {
        printf("%2d squared is %3d\n", i, i*i);
    }
    return (0);
}
#undef SIZE
#define SIZE 20
~
~
~
#define SIZE 10
```

Results of
[d

Figure 7.9   **[d** command.

Again, **#include** files are searched as well as the current one.

The **]D** and **[D** commands list all the definitions of a macro. The difference between the two is that **[D** starts the list with the first definition, whereas **]D** starts the list with the first definition after the cursor. Figure 7.10 shows the results of a **[D** command.

Results of
[D

```
int main()
{
    for (i = 1; i <= SIZE; ++i)
    {
        printf("%2d squared is %3d\n", i, i*i);
    }
    return (0);
}
#undef SIZE
#define SIZE 20
~
~
~
test.c
  1:    2 #define SIZE 10
  2:   13 #define SIZE 20
Press RETURN or enter command to continue█
```

Figure 7.10   **[D** command.

Matching Pairs

The **%** command is designed to match pairs of (), {}, or []. Place the cursor on one, type **%** and you will jump to the other. Figure 7.11 shows how the **%** command works.

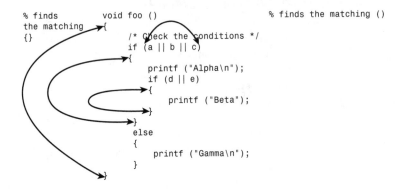

Figure 7.11   % command.

The **%** command will also match the ends of C comments (see Figure 7.12). (For you non-C programmers, these begin with /* and end with */.)

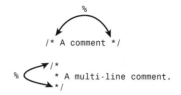

Figure 7.12 % and comments.

Also the % command will match **#ifdef** with the corresponding **#endif**. (Same goes for **#ifndef** and **#if**.)

For **#if**, **#else**, and **#endif** sets, the % command will jump from the **#if** to the **#else**, and then to the **#endif** and back to the **#if**.

Figure 7.13 shows how % works with preprocesser directives.

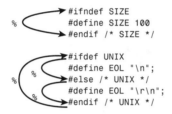

Figure 7.13 % and the **#if**/**#else**/**#endif**.

> **Note**
>
> The *Vim* editor is smart about matching pairs of operators. It knows about strings, and {} or [] will be
> ignored inside a string.

Shifting a Block of Text Enclosed in {}

Suppose that you want to indent the text encoded in {} one level. Position the cursor on the first (or last) {.

Execute the command >%. This shifts the text right to where the motion takes you. In this case, % takes you to the matching {}.

Figure 7.14 shows how these commands work.

```
                int flag;              int flag;
                int main ()            int main ()
       % >      {                      {
                    if (flag)              if (flag)
       Scope           {                      {
       of %            printf ("Flag set/n");     printf ("Flag set/n");
                       do_it () ;             do_it ();
                       }                      }
                    return (0) ;           return (0);
                }                      }
```

Figure 7.14 Shifting a block of text.

Unfortunately this shifts the {} in addition to the text. Suppose you just want to shift what is in the {}. Then you need to do the following:

1. Position the cursor on the first {.
2. Execute the command **>i{**.

This shift right command (**>**) shifts the selected text to the right one shift width. In this case, the selection command that follows is **i{**, which is the "inner {} block" command.

Figure 7.15 shows the execution of these commands.

```
int flag;                              int flag;
int main ()                            int main ()
{                                      {
    if (flag)          >i{                 if (flag)
    {                                      {
    printf ("Flag set/n");                     printf ("Flag set/n");
    do_it ();                                  do_it ();
    }                  Scope               }
    return (0);        of i{           return (0);
}                                      }
```

Figure 7.15 Shifting a block of text (better method).

Indenting a Block Using Visual Mode

To indent a block using visual mode, follow these steps:

1. Position the cursor on the left or right curly brace.
2. Start visual mode with the **v** command.
3. Select the inner {} block with the command **i}**.
4. Indent the text with **>**.

Finding the *man* Pages

The **K** command runs a UNIX **man** command using the word under the cursor as a subject. If you position the cursor on the word *open* and press **K**, for example, the man page for *open* will display.

On Microsoft Windows, the **K** command does the equivalent of performing a **:help** on the word under the cursor. You can also use the visual **K** command to do the same thing.

The format of the **man** command is as follows:

```
$ man [section] subject
```

The **K** command gets the *subject* from the word under the cursor. But what if you need to select the section number? It is simple; the **K** command takes a count argument. If specified, this is used as the section number. Therefore, if you position the **K** over the word *mkdir* and execute the **2K**, you will get the mkdir(2) page.

You can customize the **K** command. It runs the program specified by the **'keywordprg'** option. By default, on UNIX this is man.

Solaris has a non-standard *man* command. Sections must be specified with the -s switch. So the **'keywordprg'** option defaults to *man* -s on Solaris. The *Vim* editor is smart enough to know that if no section is specified, that it must drop the -s.

On Microsoft Windows, there is no *man* command, so **'keywordprg'** defaults to nothing (""). This tells *Vim* to use the internal **:help** command to handle the **K** command.

Finally, the definition of what the **K** command considers a word is defined by the **'iskeyword'** option.

Tags

The *Vim* editor can locate function definitions in C and C++ programs. This proves extremely useful when you are trying to understand a program.

The location of function definitions (called *tags* in *Vim* terminology) is stored in a table of contents file generated by the program *ctags*. (This program comes with *Vim*.). To generate the table of contents file, which is named tags, use the following command:

```
$ ctags *.c
```

Now when you are in *Vim* and you want to go to a function definition, you can jump to it by using the following command:

```
:tag function
```

This command will find the function even if it is another file.

The **CTRL-]** command jumps to the tag of the word that is under the cursor. This makes it easy to explore a tangle of C code.

Suppose, for example, that you are in the function **write_block**. You can see that it calls **write_line**. But what does **write_line** do? By putting the cursor on the call to **write_line** and typing **CTRL-]**, you jump to the definition of this function (see Figure 7.16).

The **write_line** function calls **write_char**. You need to figure out what it does. So you position the cursor over the call to **write_char** and press **CTRL-]**. Now you are at the definition of **write_char** (see Figure 7.17).

```
                                              :tag write_block
                                              positions us here
void write_block(char line_set[])
{
    int i;
    for (i = 0; i < N_LINES; ++i)
        write_line(line_set[i]);
}
```

```
void write_line(char line[])          CTRL-] goes to the definition
{                                      of write_line (switching files
    int i;                             if needed).
    for (i = 0; line[0] != '\0')
        write_char(line[i]);
}
~
"write_line.c" 6L, 99C
```

Figure 7.16   Tag jumping with CTRL-].

```
                                      CTRL-] while positioned on
void write_char(char ch)              write_char (see previous
{                                     figure), gets us here.
    write_raw(ch);
}
~
~
~
"write_char.c" 4L, 48C
```

Figure 7.17   Jumping to the write_char tag.

The :tags command shows the list of the tags that you have traversed through (see Figure 7.18).

```
~
:tags
  # TO tag          FROM line   in file/text
  1  1 write_block         1    write_block.c
  2  1 write_line          5    write_block.c
  3  1 write_char          5    write_line.c
>
Press RETURN or enter command to continue
```

Figure 7.18   The :tags command.

Now to go back. The CTRL-T command goes the preceding tag. This command takes a count argument that indicates how many tags to jump back.

So, you have gone forward, and now back. Let's go forward again. The following command goes to the tag on the list:

   :tag

You can prefix it with a count and jump forward that many tags. For example:

   :3tag

Figure 7.19 illustrates the various types of tag navigation.

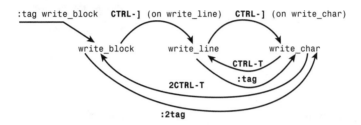

Figure 7.19   Tag navigation.

Help and Tags

The help system makes extensive use of tags. To execute a "hyperlink jump," you press **CTRL-]** (jump to tag). You can return to a preceding subject with **CTRL-T** (jump to preceding tag) and so on.

Windows and Tags

The **:tag** command replaces the current window with the one containing the new function. But suppose you want to see not only the old function but also the new one? You can split the window using the **:split** command followed by the **:tag** command. But *Vim* has a shorthand command that is shorthand for both commands:

   :stag *tag*

Figure 7.20 shows how this command works.

```
void write_block(char line_s      void write_char(char ch)
{                                  {
    int i;                             write_raw(ch);
    for (i = 0; i < N_LINES;       write_char.c
        write_line(line_set[           for (i = 0; i < N_LINES; ++i)
}                                          write_line(line_set[i]);
                                   write_block.c
                                   "write_char.c" 4L, 48C
```

   :stag write_char

Figure 7.20   The **:stag** command.

The **CTRL-W]** command splits the current window and jumps to the tag under the cursor in the upper window (see Figure 7.21). If a *count* is specified, the new window will be *count* lines high.

```
void write_block(char line_s        void write_line(char line[])
{                                    {
    int i;                               int i;
    for (i = 0; i < N_LINES;         write_line.c
        write_line(line_set[             for (i = 0; i < N_LINES; ++i)
}                                            write_line(line_set[i]);
                                     write_block.c
                                     "write_line.c" 6L, 99C
```

CTRL-WCTRL-[—While position on write_line

Figure 7.21   **CTRL-W]**.

Finding a Procedure When You Only Know Part of the Name

Suppose you "sort of" know the name of the procedure you want to find? This is a common problem for Microsoft Windows programmers because of the extremely inconsistent naming convention of the procedures in the Windows API. UNIX programmers fare no better. The convention is consistent; the only problem is that UNIX likes to leave letters out of system call names (for example, creat).

You can use the **:tag** command to find a procedure by name, or it can search for a regular expression. If a procedure name begins with /, the **:tag** command assumes that the name is a regular expression.

If you want to find a procedure named "something write something," for example, you can use the following command:

```
:tag /write
```

This finds all the procedures with the word *write* in their names and positions the cursor on the first one.

If you want to find all procedures that begin with *read*, you need to use the following command:

```
:tag /^read
```

If you are not sure whether the procedure is **DoFile**, **do_file**, or **Do_File**, you can use this command:

```
:tag /DoFile\|do_file\|Do_File
```

or

```
:tag /[Dd]o_\=[Ff]ile
```

These commands can return multiple matches. You can get a list of the tags with the following command:

:tselect {*name*}

Figure 7.22 shows the results of a typical **:tselect** command.

```
~
  # pri kind tag            file
> 1 F C f    write_char        write_char.c
             void write_char(char ch)
  2 F   f    write_block       write_block.c
             void write_block(char line_set[])
  3 F   f    write_line        write_line.c
             void write_line(char line[])
  4 F   f    write_raw         write_raw.c
             void write_raw(char ch)
Enter nr of choice (<CR> to abort): █
```
Results of
:tselect

Figure 7.22   :tselect command.

The first column is the number of the tag.

The second column is the Priority column. This contains a combination of three letters.

F   Full match (if missing, a case-ignored match)

S   Static tag (if missing, a global tag)

C   Tag in the current file

The last line of the **:tselect** command gives you a prompt that enables you to enter the number of the tag you want. Or you can just press Enter (**<CR>** in *Vim* terminology) to leave things alone. The **g]** command does a **:tselect** on the identifier under the cursor.

The **:tjump** command works just like the **:tselect** command, except if the selection results in only one item, it is automatically selected. The **g CTRL-]** command does a **:tjump** on the word under the cursor.

A number of other related commands relate to this tag selection set, including the following:

:count	**tnext**	Go to the next tag
:count	**tprevious**	Go to the previous tag
:count	**tNext**	Go to the next tag
:count	**trewind**	Go to the first tag
:count	**tlast**	Go to the last tag

Figure 7.23 shows how to use these commands to navigate between matching tags of a **:tag** or **:tselect** command.

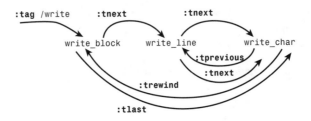

Figure 7.23   Tag navigation.

Shorthand Command

The command **:stselect** does the same thing as **:tselect**, except that it splits the window first. The **:stjump** does the same thing as a **:split** and a **:tjump**.

The Care and Feeding of Makefiles

The UNIX *make* command is designed to manage the compilation and building of programs. The commands to make are stored in a file called *Makefile*.

The format of this file, although simple, is a little tricky to work with. In the following file, for example, the first command works, whereas the second contains an error:

```
alpha.o: alpha.c
        gcc -c alpha.c

beta.o: beta.c
        gcc -c beta.c
```

You may have a little difficulty seeing the problem from this listing. The problem is that the indent for the first command is a tab, whereas the indent on the second one uses eight spaces. This difference is impossible to see onscreen; so how do you tell the difference between the two versions?

The following command puts *Vim* in list mode:

:set list

In this mode, tabs show up as **^I**. Also the editor displays **$** at the end of each line (so you can check for trailing spaces). Therefore, if you use the following command

:set list

your example looks like this:

```
alpha.o: alpha.c$
^Igcc -c alpha.c$
$
beta.o: beta.c$
        gcc -c beta.c$
```

From this it is easy to see which line contains the spaces and which has a tab. (You can customize list mode by using the `'listchars'` option.)

If the `'expandtab'` option is set, when you type a tab, *Vim* inserts spaces. This is not good if you are editing a Makefile. To insert a real tab, no matter what the options are, type in **CTRL-V<Tab>** in insert mode. The **CTRL-V** tells *Vim* not to mess with the following character.

> **Note**
>
> If you have syntax coloring turned on, the *Vim* editor will highlight lines that begin with spaces in red, whereas lines that start with <Tab> display normally.

Sorting a List of Files

Frequently in a Makefile, you will see a list of files:

```
SOURCES = \
            time.cpp         \
            set_ix.cpp       \
            rio_io.cpp       \
            arm.cpp          \
            app.cpp          \
            amem.cpp         \
            als.cpp          \
            aformat.cpp      \
            adump.cpp        \
            rio.cpp          \
            progress.cpp     \
            add.cpp          \
            acp.cpp          \
            rio_glob.cpp
```

To sort this list, execute the following:

1. Position the cursor on the start of the list.

2. Mark this location as a by using the command **ma**.

3. Go to the bottom of the list.

4. Run the block through the external program sort using the command **!'a sort**.

   ```
   SOURCES = \
               acp.cpp          \
               add.cpp          \
               adump.cpp        \
               aformat.cpp      \
               als.cpp          \
               amem.cpp         \
               app.cpp          \
               arm.cpp          \
               progress.cpp     \
   ```

```
rio.cpp           \
rio_glob.cpp
rio_io.cpp        \
set_ix.cpp        \
time.cpp          \
```

> **Warning**
>
> All the lines, except the last one, must end with a backslash (\). Sorting can disrupt this pattern. Make sure that the backslashes are in order after a sort. Figure 7.24 shows how you might need to fix the source list.

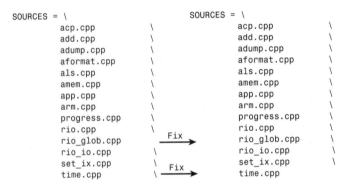

Figure 7.24   Fixing the source list.

Sorting a List in Visual Mode

To sort a list using visual mode, you need to execute the following commands:

1. Move to the top of the text to be sorted.
2. Start line visual mode with the command **v**.
3. Move to the bottom of the text to be sorted.
4. Execute the command **!sort**. The **!** tells *Vim* to pipe the selected text through a command. The command in this case is **sort**. (This command has an implied **<Enter>** at the end.)

Making the Program

The *Vim* editor has a set of commands it calls the *quick-fix mode*. These commands enable you to compile a program from within *Vim* and then go through the errors generated fixing them (hopefully). You can then recompile and fix any new errors that are found until finally your program compiles without error.

:make

The following command runs the program make (supplying it with any argument you give) and captures the results:

`:make arguments`

If errors were generated, they are captured and the editor positions you where the first error occurred.

Take a look at a typical **:make** session. (Typical **:make** sessions generate far more errors and fewer stupid ones.) Figure 7.25 shows the results. From this you can see that you have errors in two files, main.c and sub.c.

When you press Enter (what *Vim* calls Return), you see the results shown in Figure 7.26.

The editor has moved you to the first error. This is line 6 of main.c. You did not need to specify the file or the line number, *Vim* knew where to go automatically. The following command goes to where the next error occurs (see Figure 7.27):

:cnext

```
:!make  |& tee /tmp/vim215953.err
gcc -g -Wall -o prog main.c sub.c
main.c: In function 'main':
main.c:6: too many arguments to function 'do_sub'
main.c: At top level:
main.c:10: parse error before ']'
sub.c: In function 'sub':
sub.c:3: 'j' undeclared (first use in this function)
sub.c:3: (Each undeclared identifier is reported only once
sub.c:3: for each function it appears in.)
sub.c:4: parse error before ']'
sub.c:4: warning: control reaches end of non-void function
make: *** [prog] Error 1

2 returned
"main.c" 11L, 111C
(3 of 12): too many arguments to function 'do_sub'
Press RETURN or enter command to continue█
```

Figure 7.25   **:make** output.

```
int main()
{
    int i=3
    █o_sub("foo");
    ++i;
    return (0);
}
}
~
(3 of 12):  too many arguments to function do_sub
```

Figure 7.26   The first error.

Note

If you are a Visual-C++ user, the make program supplied by Microsoft is called *nmake*. You might need to customize *Vim* using the **'makeprg'** option so that it uses this program rather than the default make (as discussed later in this chapter).

```
int main()
{
    int 1=3
    do_sub("foo");
    ++i;
    return (0);
}
]
~
(5 of 12):  parse error before `}´
```

Figure 7.27   `:cnext`.

The command `:cprevious` or `:cNext` goes to the previous error. Similarly, the command `:clast` goes to the last error and `:crewind` goes to the first. The `:cnfile` goes to first error message for the next file (see Figure 7.28).

If you forget what the current error is, you can display it using the following command:

`:cc`

To see a list of errors, execute this command:

`:clist`

Figure 7.29 shows the output of a `:clist` command.

If you want to list only a subset of the errors, you can give `:clist` a range of errors to list. For example:

```
:clist 3,5    (List errors 3 through 5)
:clist ,5     (List errors 1-5)
:clist 5,     (List errors 5 to the end)
```

The *Vim* editor suppresses all informational messages. If you want everything, use the following command:

`:clist!`

The override option (`!`) tells *Vim* to not suppress anything.

```
int sub(int i)
{
    return (i * j)
}
~
~
~
~
~
(7 of 12):  'j' undeclared (first use in this function)
```

Figure 7.28   `:cnfile` command.

```
~
~
:clist
 3 main.c:6:  too many arguments to function 'do_sub'
 5 main.c:10:  parse error before '}'
 7 sub.c:3:  'j' undeclared (first use in this function)
 8 sub.c:3:  (Each undeclared identifier is reported only once
 9 sub.c:3:  for each function it appears in.)
10 sub.c:4:  parse error before '}'
11 sub.c:4:  warning: control reaches end of non-void function
Press RETURN or enter command to continue█
```

Figure 7.29   **:clist** command.

If you have already run make and generated your own error file, you can tell *Vim* about it by using the **:cfile** *error-file* command. *error-file* is the name of the output of the **make** command or compiler. If the *error-file* is not specified, the file specified by the **'errorfile'** option is used.

Finally the following command exits *Vim* like **:quit** but exits with an error status (exit code=1):

:cquit

This is useful if you are using *Vim* in an integrated development environment and a normal exit would cause a recompilation.

The *'errorfile'* Option

The **'errorfile'** option defines the default filename used for the **:clist** command as well as the **-q** command-line option. (This file is not used for the **:make** command's output.)

If you want to define your default error file, use the following command:

:set errorfile=error.list

Searching for a Given String

The **:grep** command acts much like **:make**. It runs the external program grep and captures the output. (This command does not work all that well on Microsoft Windows because it does not have a *grep* command. You can get one from the GNU people (see `http://www.gnu.org`).

To find all occurrences of the variable *ground_point*, for example, you use this command:

:grep -w ground_point *.c

The **-w** flag tells *grep* to look for full words only. *ground_point* is the variable you are looking for. Finally, there is the list of files to search through (*****.c). Figure 7.30 shows the results.

```
    ++i;
    return (0);
}
}
:!grep -n -w i *.c |& tee /tmp/vim215956.err
main.c:5:    int i=3;
main.c:7:    ++i;
sub.c:1:int sub(int i)
sub.c:3:    return (i * j)
(1 of 4): :    int i=3;
Press RETURN or enter command to continue█
```

Figure 7.30   :grep output.

Note

The *grep* program knows nothing about C syntax, so it will find *ground_point* even it occurs inside a string or comment.

You can use the **:cnext**, **:cprevious**, and **:cc** commands to page through the list of matches. Also **:crewind** goes to the first error and **:clast** to the last.

Finally, the following command goes to the first error in the next file:

    :cnfile

Other Interesting Commands

The *Vim* editor can use different options for different types of files through the use of the **:autocommand** command. See Chapter 13, "Autocommands," for more information.

You can also customize your options on a per-file basis by putting something called a *modeline* in each file. The *Vim* editor scans your file looking for these lines and sets things up based on their content.

8

Basic Abbreviations, Keyboard Mapping, and Initialization Files

THE *VIM* EDITOR HAS SOME FEATURES THAT enable you to automate repetitive tasks. One of these is abbreviation, which enables you to type in part of a word and let *Vim* type the rest. Another is the ability to remap the keyboard. You can easily redefine a key to be a whole set of commands. After you design your customizations, you can save them to an initialization file that will automatically be read the next time you start *Vim*.

This chapter discusses the most common and useful subset of these commands. For a more complete reference, see Chapter 24, "All About Abbreviations and Keyboard Mapping."

Abbreviations

An *abbreviation* is a short word that takes the place of a long one. For example, *ad* stands for *advertisement*. The *Vim* editor enables you to type in an abbreviation and then will automatically expand it for you. To tell *Vim* to expand the abbreviation *ad* into *advertisement* every time you type it, use the following command:

```
:abbreviate ad advertisement
```

Now, when you type *ad*, the whole word *advertisement* will be inserted into the text.

What Is Entered	What You See
I saw the a	I saw the a
I saw the ad	I saw the ad
I saw the ad<space>	I saw the advertisement<space>

It is possible to define an abbreviation that results in multiple words. For example, to define *JB* as *Jack Benny*, use the following command:

```
:abbreviate JB Jack Benny
```

As a programmer, I use two rather unusual abbreviations:

```
:abbreviate #b /**************************************
:abbreviate #e <space>**************************************/
```

These are used for creating boxed comments. The comment starts with **#b**, which draws the top line. I then put in the text and use **#e** to draw the bottom line.

The number of stars (★) in the abbreviations is designed so that the right side is aligned to a tab stop.

One other thing to notice is that the **#e** abbreviation begins with a space. In other words, the first two characters are space-star. Usually *Vim* ignores spaces between the abbreviation and the expansion. To avoid that problem, I spell space as seven characters: "<", "s", "p", "a", "c", "e", ">".

Listing Your Abbreviations

The command **:abbreviate** lists all your current abbreviations. Figure 8.1 shows a typical execution of this command.

```
~
~
! #j          Jack Benny Show
! #l          /*-----------------------------------------------------*/
! #e          *******************************************************/
! #b          /*******************************************************/
! #i          #include
! #d          #define
Press RETURN or enter command to continue█
```

Figure 8.1   **:abbreviate**.

> **Note**
>
> The abbreviation is not expanded until after you finish the word by typing a space, tab, or other whitespace. That is so that a word such as *addition* won't get expanded to *advertisementdition*.

Mapping

Mapping enables you to bind a set of *Vim* commands to a single key. Suppose, for example, that you need to surround certain words with curly braces. In other words, you need to change a word such as *amount* into *{amount}*.

With the `:map` command, you can configure *Vim* so that the F5 key does this job. The command is as follows:

```
:map <F5> i{<Esc>ea}<Esc>
```

Let's break this down:

<F5>	The F5 function key. This is the trigger key that causes the command to be executed as the key is pressed. (In this example, the trigger is a single key; it can be any string.)
i{<ESC>	Insert the { character. Note that we end with the *<Esc>* key.
e	Move to the end of the word.
a}<ESC>	Append the } to the word.

After you execute the `:map` command, all you have to do to put {} around a word is to put the cursor on the first character and press F5.

> **Note**
>
> When entering this command, you can enter **<F5>** by pressing the F5 key or by entering the characters <, *F*, *5*, and >. Either way works. However, you must enter **<Esc>** as characters. That is because the **<Esc>** key tells *Vim* to abort the command. Another way of entering an **<Esc>** key is to type **CTRL-V** followed by the **<Esc>** key. (The **CTRL-V** tells *Vim* literally instead of acting on it.)

> **Warning**
>
> The `:map` command can remap the *Vim* commands. If the trigger string is the same as a normal *Vim* command, the `:map` will supersede the command in *Vim*.

Listing Your Mappings

The `:map` command (with no arguments) lists out all your current mappings (see Figure 8.2).

```
~
~
~
    <F5>          i {<Esc>ea}<Esc>
    <xHome>       <Home>
    <xEnd>        <End>
    <S-xF4>       <S-F4>
    <S-xF3>       <S-F3>
    <S-xF2>       <S-F2>
    <S-xF1>       <S-F1>
    <xF4>         <F4>
    <xF3>         <F3>
    <xF2>         <F2>
    <xF1>         <F1>
Press RETURN or enter command to continue█
```

Figure 8.2 `:map` command.

Fixing the Way Delete Works

On most terminals, the Backspace key acts like a backspace character and the Delete key sends a delete character. Some systems try to be helpful by remapping the keyboard and mapping the Backspace key to Delete.

If you find that your keyboard has the Backspace and Delete keys backward, you can use the following command to swap them:

```
:fixdel
```

It does this by modifying the internal *Vim* definitions for backspace (**t_kb**) and delete (**t_kD**).

This command affects only the *Vim* keyboard mappings. Your operating system may have its own keyboard mapping tables. For example, Linux users can change their keyboard mapping by using the *loadkeys* command. For further information, Linux users should check out the online documentation for *loadkeys*.

The X Window system also has a keyboard mapping table. If you want to change this table, you need to check out the *xmodmap* command. Check the X Window system documentation for details on how to use this command.

Controlling What the Backspace Key Does

The `'backspace'` option controls how the <Backspace> key works in insert mode. For example, the following command tells *Vim* to allow backspacing over autoindents:

```
:set backspace=indent
```

The following command enables you to backspace over the end of lines:

```
:set backspace=eol
```

In other words, with this option set, if you are positioned on the first column and press <Backspace>, the current line will be joined with the preceding one.

The following command enables you to backspace over the start of an insert:

```
:set backspace=start
```

In other words, you can erase more text than you entered during a single insert command.

You can combine these options, separated by commas. For example:

```
:set backspace=indent,eol,start
```

Earlier versions of *Vim* (5.4 and prior) use the following option values. These still work but are deprecated.

0	""	(No special backspace operations allowed)
1	"indent,eol"	
2	"indent,eol,start"	

Saving Your Setting

After performing all your **:map**, **:abbreviate**, and **:set** commands, it would be nice if you could save them and use them again.

The command **:mkvimrc** writes all your settings to a file. The format of this command is as follows:

```
:mkvimrc file
```

file is the name of the file to which you want to write the settings.

You can read this file by using the following command:

```
:source file
```

During startup, the *Vim* editor looks for an initialization file. If it is found, it is automatically executed. (Only the first file found is read.)

The initialization files are as follows:

UNIX

$HOME/.vimrc

$HOME/_vimrc

$HOME/.exrc

$HOME/_exrc

MS-DOS

$HOME/_vimrc

$HOME/.vimrc

$VIM/_vimrc

$VIM/.vimrc

$HOME/_exrc

$HOME/.exrc

$VIM/_exrc

$VIM/.exrc

When you are running the GUI version, some other files are also read. The gvimrc file is found in the same location as the vimrc files mentioned in the list. The $VIMRUNTIME/menu.vim is read too.

One way you can find out which initialization files are read is to use the **:version** command:

```
:version
```

In the middle of all the junk it lists out is a list of the initialization files (see Figure 8.3).

```
:version
VIM - Vi IMproved 5.5 (1999 Sep 19, compiled Nov 27 1999 06:02:50)
Compiled by sdo@www.oualline,com. with (+) or without (-):
+autocmd +browse +builtin_terms +byte_offset +cindent +cmdline_compl
+cmdline_info +comments +cryptv -cscope +dialog_con_gui + digraphs -emacs_tags
+eval +ex_extra +extra_search -farsi +file_in_path -osfiletype +find_in_path
+fork() +GUI_GTK -hangul_input +insert_expand -langmap +linebreak +lispindent
+menu +mksession +modify_fname +mouse -mouse_dec -mouse_gpm -mouse_netterm
+mouse_xterm -multi_byte -perl +quickfix -python -rightleft +scrollbind
+smartindent -sniff +statusline +syntax +tag_binary +tag_old_static
-tag_any_white -tcl +terminfo +textobjects +title +user_commands +visualextra
+viminfo +wildmenu +wildignore +writebackup +X11 -xfontset -xim
+xterm_clipboard -xterm_save
    system vimrc file: "$VIM/vimrc"
      user vimrc file: "$HOME/.vimrc"
       user exrc file: "$HOME/.exrc"
   system gvimrc file: "$VIM/gvimrc"
     user gvimrc file: "$HOME/.gvimrc"
     system menu file: "$VIMRUNTIME/menu.vim"
   fall-back for $VIM: "/usr/local/share/vim"
Compilation: gcc -c -I. -Iproto -DHAVE_CONFIG_H -DUSE_GUI_GTK -I/usr/X11R6/inc
lude -I/usr/lib/glib/include -g -o2 -Wall -I/usr/X11R6/include
Linking: gcc -o vim -L/usr/lib -L/usr/X11R6/lib -lgtk -lgdk -rdynamic -lgmodul
-- More --█
```

Figure 8.3   Locating the initialization files with **:version**.

One other initialization file has not yet been discussed: .exrc. The old *Vi* editor used this file for initialization. This is only read if *Vim* cannot find any other initialization file. Because the old *Vi* program does not understand many of the *Vim* commands, you will probably want to put everything in the .vimrc file.

The **:mkexrc** command writes the mappings to the .exrc file. If you want to use all the power of *Vim*, however, you must use the **:mkvimrc** command instead.

My *.vimrc* File

My .vimrc file contains the following:

```
:syntax on
:autocmd FileType *       set formatoptions=tcql
    \ nocindent comments&
:autocmd FileType c,cpp  set formatoptions=croql
    \ cindent comments=sr:/*,mb:*,ex:*/,://
:set autoindent
:set autowrite
:ab #d #define
:ab #i #include
:ab #b /*******************************
:ab #e <Space>*******************************/
:ab #l /*----------------------------------- */
:ab #j Jack Benny Show
:set shiftwidth=4
:set hlsearch
:set incsearch
:set textwidth=70
```

The file starts with a command to turn syntax coloring on:

```
:syntax on
```

The next thing is an autocommand executed every time a file type is determined (on file load). In this case, set the formatting options to **tcql**, which means autowrap text (**t**), autowrap comments (**c**), allow **gq** to format things (**q**), and do not break long lines in insert mode (**1**).

I also turn off C-style indenting (**nocindent**) and set the `'comments'` option to the default (**comments&**):

```
:autocmd FileType *      set formatoptions=tcql
    \ nocindent comments&
```

If a C or C++ file is loaded, the following autocommand is executed. It defines some additional format options, namely adding the comment header for new lines (**r**) and new lines opened with an **o** command (**o**). It also turns on C indentation and defines the "comments" option for C- and C++-style comments.

Because this autocommand comes after the one for all files, it is executed second (but only for C and C++ files). Because it is executed second, its settings override any set by a previous autocommand:

```
:autocmd FileType c,cpp  set formatoptions=croql
    \ cindent comments=sr:/*,mb:*,ex:*/,://
```

The next options turn on automatic indentation (indent each line the same as the preceding one) and autowriting (write files when needed). Note that because the autocommands execute when the file type is determined, any settings they have override these:

```
:set autoindent
:set autowrite
```

What follows is a set of abbreviations useful to programmers and a collector of old Jack Benny radio shows:

```
:ab #d #define
:ab #i #include
:ab #b /**************************************
:ab #e <Space>**************************************/
:ab #l /*----------------------------------------------*/
:ab #j Jack Benny Show
```

The indentation size is set to **4**, a value that studies have shown is best for programming:

```
:set shiftwidth=4
```

The next two options turn on fancy searching:

```
:set hlsearch
:set incsearch
```

When working with text, I like a 70-column page:

```
:set textwidth=70
```

9

Basic Command-Mode Commands

THIS *VIM* EDITOR IS BASED ON AN older editor called *Vi*. The *Vi* editor was based on a command-line editor called *ex*. The *ex* editor was made before screen-oriented editors were popular. It was designed for the old printing terminals that were standard at that time.

Even though it was line oriented, the *ex* editor was an extremely versatile and efficient editor. It is still very useful today. Even with *Vim's* tremendous command set, a few things are still better done with *ex*-style commands. So the people who created *Vim* give you access to all the *ex* commands through the use of command-line mode. Any command that begins with a colon is considered an *ex*-style command.

This chapter shows how *ex*-mode commands are structured and also discusses the most useful ones, including the following:

- Printing text lines
- Substitution
- Shell (command prompt) escapes

Entering Command-Line Mode

If you want to execute a single command-line-mode command, just type a colon (:) followed by the command. For example, the command **:set number** is actually a command-mode command. A discussion of command-mode commands makes more sense with line numbering turned on. Therefore, the first command-mode command you enter for this example is as follows:

```
:set number
```

After this command has been executed, the editor returns to normal mode.

Switch to command-line mode by executing the command **:ex**. The **Q** command also performs this operation. To switch back to normal mode (visual mode), use the **:visual** command.

The Print Command

The **:print** command (short form **:p**) prints out the specified lines. Without arguments, it just prints the current line:

```
:print
      1 At one university the computer center was
```

Ranges

The **:print** command can be made to print a range of lines. A simple *range* can be something like 1,5. This specifies lines 1 through 5. To print these lines, use the following command:

```
:1,5 print
        1 At one university the computer center was
        2 experiencing trouble with a new type of computer
        3 terminal. Seems that the professors loved to
        4 put papers on top of the equipment, covering
        5 the ventilation holes. Many terminals broke
```

Strictly speaking, you do not have put a space between the **5** and the **print**, but it does make the example look nicer.

If you want to print only line 5, you can use this command:

```
:5 print
        5 the ventilation holes. Many terminals broke
```

You can use a number of special line numbers. For example, the line number **$** is the last line in the file. So to print the whole file, use the following command:

```
:1,$ print
        1 At one university the computer center was
```

...

```
      36 Notice:
      37
      38 If your computer catches fire, please turn it
      39 off and notify computing services.
```

The **%** range is shorthand for the entire file (**1,$**). For example:

```
:% print
         1 At one university the computer center was
...
        36 Notice:
        37
        38 If your computer catches fire, please turn it
        39 off and notify computing services.
```

The line number (.) is the current line. For example:

```
:. print
        39 off and notify computing services.
```

You can also specify lines by their content. The line number /pattern/ specifies the next line containing the *pattern*. Let's move up to the top with **:1 print**, and then print the lines from the current line (.) to the first line containing the word *trouble*:

```
:1 print
         1 At one university the computer center was
:1,/trouble/print
         1 At one university the computer center was
         2 experiencing trouble with a new type of computer
```

Similarly, **?pattern?** specifies the first previous line with *pattern* in it. In the following example, we first move to the end of the file with **:39 print** and then print the last line with the word *Notice* in it to the end of the file:

```
:39 print
        39 off and notify computing services.
:?Notice:?,39 print
        36 Notice:
        37
        38 If your computer catches fire, please turn it
        39 off and notify computing services.
```

Marks

Marks can be placed with the normal-mode **m** command. For example, the **ma** command marks the current location with mark *a*.

You can use marks to specify a line for command-mode commands. The line number **'a** specifies the line with mark *a* is to be used.

Start in normal mode, for example, and move to the first line of the file. This is marked with *a* using the command **ma**. You then move to line 3 and use the command **mz** to mark line as *z*. The command

```
:'a, 'z print
```

is the same as the following command:

```
:1,3 print
```

Visual-Mode Range Specification

You can run a command-mode command on a visual selection. The first step is to enter visual mode and select the lines you want. Then enter the command-mode command to execute. Figure 9.1 shows that the first three lines of the text have been selected.

```
    1 At one university the computer center was
    2 experience trouble with a new type of computer
    3 terminal. Seems that the professors loved to█
    4 put papers on top of the equipment, covering
    5 the ventilation holes. Many terminals broke
    6 down because they became so hot that the solder
-- VISUAL --
```

Figure 9.1   Visual-mode selection.

Next, enter the `:print` command to print these lines. The minute you press `:`, *Vim* goes to the bottom of the screen and displays the following:

```
:'<,'>
```

The special mark `<` is the top line of the visual selection and the mark `>` is the bottom. Thus, *Vim* is telling you that it will run the command on the visual selection. Because `<` is on line 1, and `>` is on line 3, a `:print` at this point prints lines 1 to 3. The full command, as it appears onscreen, looks like this:

```
:'<,'>print
```

Substitute Command

The `:substitute` command enables you to perform string replacements on a whole range of lines. The general form of this command is as follows:

```
:range substitute /from/to/ flags
```

(Spaces were added for readability.)

This command changes the *from* string to the *to* string. For example, you can change all occurrences of *Professor* to *Teacher* with the following command:

```
:% substitute /Professor/Teacher/
```

> **Note**
>
> The `:substitute` command is almost never spelled out completely. Most of the time, people use the abbreviated version `:s`. (The long version is used here for clarity.)

By default, the `:substitute` command changes only the first occurrence on each line. For example, the preceding command changes the line

```
Professor Smith criticized Professor Johnson today.
```

to

```
Teacher Smith criticized Professor Johnson today.
```

If you want to change every occurrence on the line, you need to add the **g** (global) flag. The command

```
:% substitute /Professor/Teacher/g
```

results in

```
Teacher Smith criticized Teacher Johnson today.
```

Other flags include **p** (print), which causes the **:substitute** command to print out each line it changes.

The **c** (confirm) flag tells the **:substitute** to ask you for confirmation before it performs each substitution. When you enter the following

```
:1,$ substitute /Professor/Teacher/c
```

the *Vim* editor displays the text it is about to change and displays the following prompt:

```
Professor:     You mean it's not supposed to do that?
replace with Teacher (y/n/a/q/^E/^Y)?
```

At this point, you must enter one of the following answers:

y	Make this replacement.
n	Skip this replacement.
a	Replace all remaining occurrences without confirmation.
q	Quit. Don't make any more changes.
CTRL-E	Scroll one line up.
CTRL-Y	Scroll one line down.

How to Change Last, First to First, Last

Suppose you have a file containing a list of names in the form last, first, and you want to change it to first, last. How do you do it?

You can use the **:substitute** command to do it in one operation. The command you need is shown in Figure 9.2.

The *to* string takes the first name (**\2**) and last name (**\1**) and puts them in order.

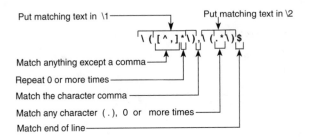

Figure 9.2   Changing last, first to first, last.

Reading and Writing Files

The **:read** *filename* command (short form **:r**) reads in a file and inserts it after the current line.

The **:write** command (short form **:w**) writes out the file. This is a way of saving your work. You can write a different file (prog.c.new, for example) by giving **:write** a filename as an argument:

```
:write prog.c.new
```

> **Warning**
>
> If you exit using the emergency abort command :q!, the file reverts to the last written version.

The **:write** command usually does not overwrite an existing file. The force (!) option causes it to ignore this protection and to destroy any existing file.

The **:write** command proves extremely useful when it comes to exporting portions of a large file to a smaller one—for example, if you have a collection of jokes and want to write one out to a file to send to a friend.

To export a single joke, first highlight it in visual mode. Then use the following command to write it out to the file file.txt:

```
:'<,'> write joke.txt
```

The *:shell* Command

The **:shell** command takes you to the command prompt. You can return to *Vim* by executing the **exit** command.

For example:

```
:shell
$ date
Mon Jan 17 18:55:45 PST 2000
$ exit
-- vim window appears --
```

In this example, we are on UNIX, so we get the UNIX prompt (**$**). If we were using the UNIX version of *gvim*, *Vim* would start a shell in the GUI window.

On MS-DOS, the *Vim* command acts just like UNIX when a **:shell** command is executed. If you are using the GUI, however, the **:shell** command causes an MS-DOS prompt window to appear.

10

Basic GUI Usage

The *Vim* editor works well inside a windowing environment. This *graphical user interface* (GUI) provides you with not only all of *Vim*'s keyboard commands, but also a number of menus and other options. This chapter shows you how to start *Vim* in GUI mode and how to make use of the special GUI features.

Starting *Vim* in GUI Mode

To start *Vim* in windowing mode, use the following command:

```
$ gvim file
```

This command starts up a *Vim* window and begins to edit *file*.

The actual appearance of the screen depends on which operating system you are using. On UNIX it also depends on which X Window system toolkit (Motif, Athena, GTK) you have. Figures 10.1, 10.2, and 10.3 show the various types of GUIs.

Figure 10.1 UNIX with the GTK toolkit.

Figure 10.2   UNIX with the Motif toolkit.

Figure 10.3   Microsoft Windows.

If you have a choice of UNIX GUIs to choose from, it is recommended that you use the GTK version.

Mouse Usage

Standards are wonderful. In Microsoft Windows, you can use the mouse to select text in a standard manner. The X Window system also has a standard system for using the mouse. Unfortunately, these two standards are not the same.

Fortunately, you can customize *Vim*. You can make the behavior of the mouse look like an X Window system mouse or a Microsoft Windows mouse. The following command makes the mouse behave like an X Window mouse:

```
:behave xterm
```

The following command makes the mouse look like a Microsoft Windows mouse:

```
:behave mswin
```

The default behavior of the mouse on UNIX systems is xterm. The default behavior on a Microsoft Windows system is selected during the installation process.

In addition to controlling the behavior of the mouse, the **:behave** command affects the following options:

Option	Setting for **:behave mswin**	Setting for **:behave xterm**
'selectmode'	mouse,key	(empty)
'mousemodel'	popup	extend
'keymodel'	startsel,stopsel	(empty)
'selection'	exclusive	inclusive

X Mouse Behavior

When xterm behavior is enabled, the mouse behavior is as follows:

\<Left Mouse>	Move the cursor.
Drag with **\<Left Mouse>**	Select text in visual mode.
\<Right Mouse>	Extend select from cursor location to the location of the mouse.
\<Middle Mouse>	Paste selected text into the buffer at the mouse location.

Microsoft Windows Mouse Behavior

When mswin behavior is enabled, the mouse behavior is as follows:

\<Left Mouse>	Move the cursor.
Drag with **\<Left Mouse>**	Select text in select mode.
\<S-Left Mouse>	Extend selection to the cursor location.
\<S-Right Mouse>	Display pop-up menu.
\<Middle Mouse>	Paste the text on the system Clipboard into file.

Special Mouse Usage

You can issue a number of other special commands for the mouse, including the following

\<S-Left Mouse>	Search forward for the next occurrence of the word under the cursor.
\<S-Right Mouse>	Search backward for the preceding occurrence of the word under the cursor.
\<C-Left Mouse>	Jump to the tag whose name is under the cursor.
\<C-Right Mouse>	Jump to the preceding tag in the stack.

Tear-Off Menus

The menus in *Vim* (all GUI versions except Athena) have an interesting feature: "tear-off" menus. If you select the first menu item (the dotted lines), you can drag the menu to another location on the screen. Figure 10.4 shows how to tear off a menu.

> **Note**
>
> If you execute a command that requires a motion, such as d*motion*, you can use the left mouse button for the *motion*.

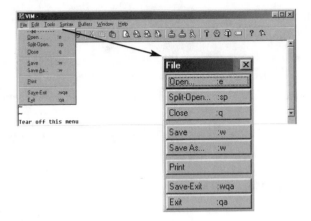

Figure 10.4   Tear-off menus.

When torn off, the menu remains as its own window until you close it using the normal window close command.

Figure 10.5   Toolbar.

Toolbar

A toolbar appears in the GTK and MS-Windows versions of the GUI. It looks something like Figure 10.5.

The icons perform the following functions:

 Open. Brings up a File Open dialog box.

 Save. Saves the current file.

 Save All. Save all the open files in all windows and buffers.

 Print. Print to system printer.

 Undo.

 Redo.

Cut. (Actually "delete.")

 Copy. (Actually "yank.")

 Paste.

 Search. Brings up a dialog box so that you can enter a pattern.

 Find Next.

 Find Previous.

 Replace. Brings up a Search-and-Replace dialog box.

 Make Session. Brings up a dialog box so that you can enter the name of a session file to write to.

 Load Session. Brings up a dialog box so that you can select the session file to load.

 Script. Brings up a dialog box so that you can select a script to run.

 Make. Performs a **:make**.

 Shell. Does a **:shell**.

 Make Tags. Does a **:!ctags -R .** command.

 Tag. Jumps to the definition of the tag under the cursor.

 Help. Brings up the general help screen.

 Help Search. Brings up a dialog box so that you can enter a help topic to be displayed. This button is slightly misnamed because it does not do a general search of the help documents, but only looks for tags.

11

Dealing with Text Files

DESPITE THE PROLIFERATION OF WORD PROCESSING tools such as Microsoft Word, StarOffice, and such, people still use plain-text files for documentation because this type of file is the most easily read.

In this chapter, you learn about the following:

- Automatic text wrapping
- Text formatting command
- Text formatting options
- Dealing with different file formats
- Troff-related commands
- The rot13 algorithm

Automatic Text Wrapping

The *Vim* editor has a number of functions that make dealing with text easier. By default, the editor does not perform automatic line breaks. In other words, you have to press **<Enter>** yourself. This is extremely useful when you are writing programs where you want to decide where the line ends. It is not so good when you are creating documentation and do not want to have to worry about where to break the lines.

If you set the `'textwidth'` option, *Vim* automatically inserts line breaks. Suppose, for example, that you want a very narrow column of only 30 characters. You need to execute the following command:

```
:set textwidth=30
```

Now you start typing (ruler added):

```
         1         2         3
12345678901234567890123456789012345
I taught programming for a while
```

The word *while* makes the line longer than the 30-character limit. When *Vim* sees this, it inserts a line break and you get the following:

```
I taught programming for a
while
```

Continuing on, you can type in the rest of the paragraph:

```
I taught programming for a
while. One time, I was stopped
by the Fort Worth police
because my homework was too
hard. True story.
```

You do not have to type newlines; *Vim* puts them in automatically.

You can specify when to break the line in two different ways. The following option tells *Vim* to break the line 30 characters from the left side of the screen:

```
:set textwidth=30
```

If you use the following option, you tell *Vim* to break the lines so that you have *margin* characters from the right side of the screen.:

```
:set wrapmargin=margin
```

Therefore, if you have a screen that is 80 characters wide, the following commands do the same thing:

```
:set wrapmargin=10
:set textwidth=70
```

The *Vim* editor is not a word processor. In a word processor, if you delete something at the beginning of the paragraph, the line breaks are reworked. In *Vim* they are not; so if you delete some words from the first line, all you get is a short line:

```
I taught for a
while. One time, I was stopped
by the Fort Worth police
because my homework was too
hard. True story.
```

Note

The `'textwidth'` option overrules `'wrapmargin'`.

This does not look good; so how do you get the paragraph into shape? There are several ways. The first is to select the paragraph as part of a visual selection:

```
I taught for a
while. One time, I was stopped
by the Fort Worth police
because my homework was too
hard. True story.
```

Then you execute the **gq** command to format the paragraph.

```
I taught for a while. One
time, I was stopped by the
Fort Worth police because my
homework was too hard. True
story.
```

Another way to format a paragraph is to use the **gq***motion* command. Therefore to format 5 lines, you use the command **gq4j**. (The **4j** tells **gq** to format this line and the next 4–5 lines total.)

The move forward paragraph command (**}**)also proves useful in such cases. To format a paragraph, for example, position the cursor on the first line of the paragraph and use the command **gq}**. It is much easier to use this command than to count the lines.

The command **gqip** formats the current paragraph. (The **gq** formats the selected text and the **ip** selects the "inner paragraph.") This is easier than **gq}** because you don't have to put the cursor on the beginning of a paragraph.

Finally, to format a line, use the **gqgq** command. You can shorten this to **gqq**.

Text Formatting Command

To center a range of lines, use the following command:

```
:range center width
```

If a width is not specified, it defaults to the value of **'textwidth'**. (If **'textwidth'** is 0, the default is 80.) For example:

```
:1,5 center 30
```

results in the following:

```
    I taught for a while. One
    time, I was stopped by the
    Fort Worth police because my
    homework was too hard. True
              story.
```

Similarly, the command **:right** right-justifies the text. So,

```
:1,5 right 30
```

gives results in the following:

```
        I taught for a while. One
       time, I was stopped by the
       Fort Worth police because my
       homework was too hard. True
                              story.
```

Finally there is this command:

```
:range left margin
```

Unlike **:center** and **:right**, however, the argument to **:left** is not the length of the line. Instead it is the left margin. If this is 0, the text will be put against the left side of the screen. If it is 5, the text will be indented 5 spaces.

For example, these commands

```
:1 left 5
:2,5 left 0
```

result in the following::

```
        I taught for a while. One
time, I was stopped by the
Fort Worth police because my
homework was too hard. True
story.
```

Justifying Text

The *Vim* editor has no built-in way of justifying text. However, there is a neat macro package that does the job. To use this package, execute the following command:

```
:source $VIMRUNTIME/macros/justify.vim
```

This macro file defines a new visual command **_j**. To justify a block of text, highlight the text in visual mode and then execute **_j**.

Fine-Tuning the Formatting

A number of options enable you to fine-tune and customize your spaces.

The *joinspaces* Option

The **J** command joins two lines putting in one space to separate them. If the **'joinspaces'** option is set, when the first line ends with a punctuation mark (period, question mark, or exclamation point), two spaces are added.

Input the following (= represents a space):

```
This=is=a=test.
Second=line.
```

When the **'joinspaces'** option is turned off with the following command

```
:set nojoinspaces
```

the result of a **J** on the first line is as follows:

```
This=is=a=test.=Second=line.
```

If the option is set using this command

```
:set joinspaces
```

the result is as follows:

```
This=is=a=test.==Second=line.
```

The *formatoptions* Option

`'formatoptions'` controls how *Vim* performs automatic wrapping. The *Vim* editor is smart about comments and does a proper job of formatting them. With `'formatoptions'` you can control both how text and comments are wrapped.

The format of this option is as follows:

```
:set formatoptions=characters
```

where *characters* is a set of formatting flags. The following list identifies the formatting flags.

t	Automatically wrap text.
c	Automatically wrap comments. Insert the comment leader automatically.
r	Insert comment leader in a comment when a new line is inserted.
o	Insert comment leader in a comment when a new line is created using the **O** and **o** command.
q	Allow **gq** to format comments.
2	Format based on the indent of the second line, not the first.
v	Do old-style *Vi* text wrapping. Wrap only on blanks that you enter.
b	Wrap only on blanks you type, but only if they occur before `'textwidth'`.
l	Do not break line in insert mode. Only let **gq** break the lines.

Take a look at how these flags affect the formatting.

The **t** flag must be on for normal text to be wrapped. The **c** flag must be on for comments to be wrapped. Therefore, setting the `'formatoptions'` option using the following command is good for programming:

```
:set formatoptions=c
```

Long lines inside a comment are automatically wrapped. Long lines of code (*Vim* calls them *text*) are not wrapped. Actually you want to set this option:

```
:set formatoptions=cq
```

This tells *Vim* to not only wrap comments, but also to reformat comments as part of a **gq** command.

Vim is smart about comments. When it wraps a line in the middle of a C-style command, it automatically adds the comment header in front of the line. Suppose, for example, that you enter the following command:

```
/* This is a test of a long line.
```

This line is longer than the '**textwidth**', so it wraps. Because it is in a comment, *Vim* automatically puts in an asterisk (*). Therefore, although you typed everything on one line, the result is as follows:

```
/* This is a test of a long
 * line.
```

But suppose you actually type **<Enter>**? By default, *Vim* does not insert the asterisk. This means that if you type a two-line comment, you get the following:

```
/* Line 1
Line 2
```

If you put an **r** flag in the '**formatoptions**', however, *Vim* automatically supplies the comment leader (*) when you press Return:

```
/* Line 1
 * Line 2
```

If you want to have this done for the **O** and **o** commands, you need to put in the **o** flag as well.

Text Formatting Options

The **2** option tells *Vim* to format based on the second line of the text rather than the first. For example, the original example text is displayed in Figure 11.1.

If you do not have the **2** flag in the **formatoptions** and you reformat the paragraph with **gq}**, you get the results shown in Figure 11.2.

```
    The first Centronics Printer manual had a whole
chapter devoted to how to open up the packing
crate and find the manual. (What did they think we
were reading anyway?)
~
~
~
~
~
```

Figure 11.1   The original text.

```
    The first Centronics Printer manual
    had a whole chapter devoted to how
    to open up the packing crate and
    find the manual. (What did they
    think we were reading anyway?)
~
~
~
```

Figure 11.2   Formatted text (no 2 flag).

If you go back to the original paragraph, however, set the **2** flag with the following

```
:set formatoptions += 2
```

and reformat using **gq}**, you will get the results shown in Figure 11.3.

The **v** flag character controls where a line will be split. Suppose that you have the following line:

```
This is a test of the very long line wrapping
```

Now add the word **logic** to the end of the sentence. Without the **v** flag, the result is as follows:

```
This is a test of the very
long line wrapping logic.
```

With **v** in '**formatoptions**', you get the following:

```
This is a test of the very long line wrapping
logic.
```

Even though the existing line is much longer than '**textwidth**', with **v** set, *Vim* will not break the line in the existing text. Instead it breaks only things in the text you add.

If the *l* character is present in the '**formatoptions**', *Vim* will break only the line if the space you type is less than the '**textwidth**'. If you add the word **logic** to the preceding example, you get the following:

```
This is a test of the very long line wrapping logic.
```

If you were to type this line from scratch, however, you would get the following:

```
This is a test of the very
long line wrapping logic.
```

Using an External Formatting Program

By default, *Vim* uses its internal formatting logic to format the text. If you want, however, you can run an external program to do the job. On UNIX, the standard program *fmt* does a good job of doing the work. If you want to use this command for the **gq** work, set the following option:

```
:set formatprg=fmt
```

```
     The first Centronics Printer manual
had a whole chapter devoted to how to
open up the packing crate and find the
manual. (What did they think we were
reading anyway?)
~
~
~
~
```

Figure 11.3 Formatted text (**2** set).

Even without this option, however, you can always use the filter (!) command to format text. To run a paragraph through the program `fmt`, for example, use the command `!}fmt`. The ! starts a filter command, the } tells *Vim* to filter a paragraph, and the rest (`fmt`) is the name of the command to use.

File Formats

Back in the early days, the old Teletype machines took two character times to do a newline. If you sent a character to the machine while it was moving the carriage back to the first position, it tried to print it on-the-fly, leaving a smudge in the middle of the page.

The solution was to make the newline two characters: **<Return>** to move the carriage to column 1, and **<Line Feed>** to move the paper up.

When computers came out, storage was expensive. Some people decided that they did not need two characters for end-of-line. The UNIX people decided they could use **<Line Feed>** only for end-of-line. The Apple people standardized on **<Return>**. The MS-DOS (and Microsoft Windows) folks decided to keep the old **<Return>** **<Line Feed>**.

This means that if you try to move a file from one system to another, you have line problems. The *Vim* editor automatically recognizes the different file formats and handles things properly behind your back.

The option `'fileformats'` contains the various formats that will be tried when a new file is edited. The following option, for example, tells *Vim* to try UNIX format first and MS-DOS format second:

```
:set fileformats=unix,dos
```

The detected file format is stored in the `'fileformat'` option. To see which format you have, execute the following command:

```
:set fileformat?
```

You can use the `'fileformat'` option to convert from one file format to another. Suppose, for example, that you have an MS-DOS file named `readme.txt` that you want to convert to UNIX format.

Start by editing the MS-DOS format file:

```
$ vim README.TXT
```

Now change the file format to UNIX:

```
:set fileformat=unix
```

When the file is written, it will be in UNIX format.

> **Note**
> If you are an old *Vi* user and tried to edit an MS-DOS format file, you would have found that each line ended with a ^M character. (^M is <Return>.) Fortunately, *Vim* handles both UNIX and MS-DOS file formats automatically.

Changing How the Last Line Ends

The *Vim* editor assumes that your file is made up of lines. This means that *Vim* assumes that the last line in the file ends in an *<EOL>* character. Sometimes you will encounter a strange file that contains an incomplete line. When *Vim* encounters this type of file, it sets the `'noendofline'` option. (If your file ends in a complete line, the `'endofline'` option is set.)

If you want to change whether or not your file ends in an *<EOL>*, use the command

```
:set endofline
```

(Last line ends in *<EOL>*.)

or

```
:set noendofline
```

(Last line does not have an *<EOL>*.) This option only works when the `'binary'` option is set.

Troff-Related Movement

A number of commands enable you to move through text. The **)** command moves forward one sentence. The **(** command does the same thing backward.

The **}** command moves forward one paragraph, and **{** moves one paragraph backward.

Figure 11.4 shows how these commands work.

At one time the troff program was the standard UNIX word processor. It takes as input a text file with processing directives in it and formats the text. Although troff is rarely used these days, the *Vim* editor still contains an option for dealing with this formatter.

The troff program uses macros to tell it what to do. Some of these macros start paragraphs. In the following example, for instance, the macro .LP starts each paragraph:

```
.LP
This is a test of the \fItroff\fP text processor.
It takes encode text and typesets it.
.LP
This is the second paragraph.
```

Figure 11.4   } command.

Because troff uses lots of different macro packages, *Vim* needs to know which macros start a paragraph. The **'paragraphs'** option does this. The format of this option is as follows:

```
:set paragraphs="macromacromacro..."
```

Each macro is the two-character name of a troff macro. For example:

```
:set paragraphs="P<Space>LP"
```

tells *Vim* that the macros .P and .LP start a paragraph. (Note that you use P<Space> to indicate the .P macro.) By default, the **'paragraphs'** option is as follows:

```
:set paragraphs=IPLPPPQPP LIpplpipbp
```

This means that the following macros

.IP	.LP	.PP	.QP	.P	.LI
.pp	.lp	.ip	.bp		

start a new paragraph.

Section Moving

The **[[** and **[]** commands move a section backward. A section is defined by any text separated by a page break character (**CTRL-L**). The reason there are two movement commands is that these commands also move forward and backward through procedures. (Chapter 7, "Commands for Programmers," contains information on programming commands.)

The **]]** and **][** commands perform the forward movements as seen in Figure 11.5.

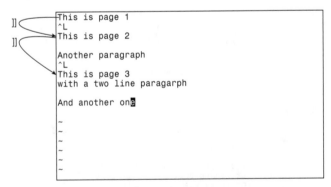

Figure 11.5 The]] command.

Defining Sections

You can also define a section using troff macros. The '**sections**' option acts much like the '**paragraph**' option, except that it defines the macros that separate sections rather than paragraphs. The default is as follows:

```
:set section=SHNHH HUnhsh
```

Encrypting with rot13

If you want to encrypt a block of text with the rot13 algorithm, use the **g?***motion* command. The *rot13 encryption* is an extremely weak encryption scheme designed to obscure text. It is frequently used in news posting for potentially offensive material.

Naturally **g?g?** or **g??** encrypts the current line.

You can decrypt the rot13 encryption by encrypting the text twice.

12

Automatic Completion

THE *VIM* EDITOR CAN AUTOMATICALLY COMPLETE words on insertion. This is where you type the first part of a word, press **CTRL-P**, and *Vim* guesses at the rest. How it decides what to use for completion is both simple and flexible. This chapter covers every aspect of this function.

This chapter discusses the following:

- Automatic completion
- How to customize the automatic completion feature
- How to use different types of completions

Automatic Completion

When you are entering text, *Vim* can assist you to complete words. Suppose, for example, that you are creating a C program and want to type in the following:

```
total = ch_array[0] + ch_array[1] + ch_array[2];
```

You start by entering the following:

```
total = ch_array[0] + ch_
```

At this point, you tell *Vim* to complete the word using the command **CTRL-P**. This command tells *Vim* to search a word to complete. In this case, it is the word *ch_array*. So typing **CTRL-P** gives you the following:

```
total = ch_array[0] + ch_array
```

After a little more typing, you get this:

```
total = ch_array[0] + ch_array[1] +
```

If you now type **CTRL-P** again, *Vim* will search again for a word that completes the word before the cursor. (In this case, it is "".) The first word that matches is *ch_array*.

Typing **CTRL-P** again gives you the next word that matches (in this case, *total*). A third **CTRL-P** causes the editor to run out of words, so it returns to the original entry: " ". A fourth **CTRL-P** causes the editor to start over again with *ch_array*.

How *Vim* Searches for Words

The *Vim* editor goes through a lot of effort to find words to complete. By default, it uses the following search algorithm:

1. Current file
2. Files in other windows
3. Other file in the currently loaded buffers
4. Files in unloaded buffers
5. The current "tags" list
6. All files **#included** by the current file

You can customize the search order. (This is described in the section "Customization of Completion.")

Searching Forward

When you type **CTRL-P**, *Vim* searches backward for a word to complete. The **CTRL-N** command searches forward. Other than the direction, it acts just like the **CTRL-P** command.

Customization of Completion

The **'ignorecase'** option tells the editor to try all words regardless of case:

```
:set ignorecase
```

Therefore, if you have the option on, when you try to complete the string *ins*, *Vim* will consider *INSERT*, *Inside*, and *instep*, all as candidates (assuming that they appear in the text).

When you match words in this way, the completed word takes on the case of the matched word. Therefore, the completion list for *ins* is as follows:

instep

Inside

INSERT

What if you want to match *INSERT*, but put the word *insert* (lowercase) in your text. You must tell *Vim* to infer the case of the new word from what is typed, not what is matched. You can set the following option:

```
:set infercase
```

Then the match list is as follows:

instep

inside

insert

Automatic Completion Details

For the most part, the *Vim* editor does the right thing when it comes to automatic completion. At times, however, you might want to fine-tune your completions.

The **'complete'** option controls where *Vim* searches for words. The form of this option is as follows:

```
:set complete=key,key,key
```

key is a key letter (and possible argument). The possible key values are as follows:

.	Current file
b	Files in loaded buffers, not in a window
d	Definitions in the current file and in files included by a **#include** directive
i	Files included by the current file through the use of a **#include** directive
k	The file defined by the **'dictionary'** option (discussed later in this chapter)
kfile	The file named {*file*}
t	The "tags" file. (The **]** character can be used as well.)
u	Unloaded buffers
w	Files in other windows

The Include Path

Vim uses the **'path'** option to tell it where to look for files that were included in the current file. (Note that the **'path'** option also is used for other commands such as **:find**.)

Specifying a Dictionary

The following option

```
:set dictionary=file,file,...
```

defines a file to be searched when you press **CTRL-P** and **CTRL-N** to match words. To use on Linux, for example, the dictionary file is in /usr/dict/words. Therefore, to add this file to the list of dictionaries searched for, use the following command:

```
:set dictionary=/usr/dict/words
```

If you have a local list of words, you can search this too:

```
:set dictionary=/home/oualline/words,/usr/doc/words
```

You can also specify a dictionary by putting the file after the **k** (*key*). For example:

```
:set complete=k/usr/oualline/words
```

You can use the **k** flag multiple times, each with a different file:

```
:set complete=k/usr/dict/words,k/usr/share/words
```

Controlling What Is Searched For

CTRL-P and **CTRL-N** enable you to perform a wide variety of searches. What if you want to restrict yourself to just one type of search, however? For that you use the **CTRL-X** command. When you type **CTRL-X**, you enter the **CTRL-X** submode. You can then fine-tune your search using one of the commands:

CTRL-D	Macro definitions
CTRL-F	Filenames
CTRL-K	Dictionary
CTRL-I	Current files and **#included** files
CTRL-L	Whole lines
CTRL-]	Tags
CTRL-P	Same as **CTRL-P** without the **CTRL-X** (find previous match)
CTRL-N	Same as **CTRL-N** without the **CTRL-X** (find next match)

The **CTRL-X CTRL-D** command searches for a **#define** macro definition. It will search included files as well. After typing this command, you can type **CTRL-N** to search for the next definition and **CTRL-P** for the previous.

Take a look at how this works on the following test file.

File include.h

```
#define MAX(x, y) ((x) < (y) ? (y) : (x))
#define MIN(x, y) ((x) < (y) ? (x) : (y))
int sum(int i1, int i2)
{return(i1+i2);}
```

File main.c

```
#include "include.h"
#define MORE "/usr/ucb/more"
```

You can start by editing main.c. If you type **CTRL-X**, you enter **CTRL-X** mode. The editor now displays a mini-prompt at the bottom of the screen (see Figure 12.1).

Suppose that you want to look for a macro definition. You would now type **CTRL-D**. The screen briefly displays the fact that there are three matches, and then displays a new menu (see Figure 12.2).

At this point, **CTRL-N** searches for the next match (and **CTRL-P** searches for the previous one). The **CTRL-D** key acts just like **CTRL-P**. Using these keys, you can cycle through the list of definitions until you find the one that you want.

Tag Search

The **CTRL-X CTRL-]** searches for the next tag. A *tag* is a C function definition. The program ctags generates a list of C function definitions (tags) and stores them in the tags file. We have generated our tags file using the following command:

```
$ ctags *.c *.h
```

Now when we enter **CTRL-X CTRL-]** in insert mode, we get what is shown in Figure 12.3.

```
#include "include.h"
#define MORE "/usr/ucb/more"
▌
~
~
~
-- ^X mode (^E/^Y/^L/^]/^F/^I/^K/^D/^N/^P) --
```

Figure 12.1 **CTRL-X** mode.

```
#include "include.h"
#define MORE "/usr/ucb/more"
MAX▌
~
~
~
-- Definition completion (^D/^N/^P) --
```

Figure 12.2 **CTRL-X CTRL-D**.

```
#include "include.h"
#define MORE "/usr/ucb/more"
MORE█
~
~
~
-- Tag completion (^]/^N/^P) --
```

Figure 12.3 **CTRL-X CTRL-]**.

The result of typing **CTRL-P** a couple of times is shown in Figure 12.4.

By default, the *Vim* editor just displays the name alone. If you execute the following command, the entire tag (the function prototype) displays:

```
:set showfulltag
```

If you repeat your matching commands with this option enabled, you get the results shown in Figure 12.5.

Finding Filenames

If you use the **CTRL-X CTRL-F** command, the *Vim* editor will match a filename. It scans the current directory for files and displays each one that matches the word in front of the cursor.

Suppose, for example, that you have the following files in the current directory:

```
main.c   sub_count.c   sub_done.c   sub_exit.c
```

Now enter insert mode and start typing:

```
The exit code is in the file sub
```

At this point, you enter the command **CTRL-X CTRL-F**. The editor now completes the current word *sub* by looking at the files in the current directory. The first match is *sub_count.c*. This is not the one you want, so you match the next file by typing **CTRL-N**. This match is *sub_done.c*. Typing **CTRL-N** again takes you to *sub_exit.c*.

```
#include "include.h"
#define MORE "/usr/ucb/more"
sum█
~
~
~
-- Tag completion (^]/^N/^P) --
```

Figure 12.4 Finding previous completions.

```
#include "include.h"
#define MORE "/usr/ucb/more"
int sum(int i1, int i2)█
~
~
~
-- Tag completion (^]/^N/^P) --
```

Figure 12.5 The results.

The results:

```
The exit code is in the file sub_exit.c
```

Line Mode

All the commands discussed so far work on words only. The **CTRL-X CTRL-L** command works on lines. If you enter **CTRL-X CTRL-L** in the example, for instance, you get the results shown in Figure 12.6.

You can now use **CTRL-N** and **CTRL-P** to go up and down lines.

```
#include "include.h"
#define MORE "/usr/ucb/more"
#define MORE "/usr/ucb/more"█
~
~
~
-- Whole line completion (^L/^N/^P) --
```

Figure 12.6 **CTRL-X CTRL-L**.

Adjusting the Screen

There are two more **CTRL-X** commands which suprisingly don't do completion.

After typing **CTRL-X**, you can move the screen up and down a little. The **CTRL-Y** command scrolls down, whereas the **CTRL-E** scrolls up.

13

Autocommands

ONE OF THE NICE ATTRIBUTES OF THE *Vim* editor is its flexibility. One of the features that makes it so flexible is the autocommand. An *autocommand* is a command executed automatically in response to some event, such as a file being read or written or a buffer change.

Through the use of autocommands, for example, you can train *Vim* to edit compressed files. (You define an autocommand that uncompresses the file on read and another one to compress the file on write. See the file $VIMRUNTIME/vimrc_example.vim in your *VIM* installation.)

In this chapter, you learn about the following:

- Basic autocommands
- Autocommand groups
- Listing and removing autocommands

Basic Autocommands

Suppose you want to put a date stamp on the end of a file every time it is written. One way you could do this is to define a function:

```
:function DateInsert()
:    $read !date      " Insert the date at the end ($)
:                     " of the file.
:endfunction
```

Now when you want to write the file all you have to do is to call this function:

```
:call DateInsert()
```

Then you write the file.

That may be a little difficult, so you can map this to a key:

```
:map <F12> :call DateInsert()<CR> \¦ :write<CR>
```

This makes things "easy" because now you just have to press **<F12>** every time you want to write the file.

If you forget, however, and use the normal *Vim* file writing commands, you screw things up. It would be nice if you could do things automatically. That is where autocommands come in.

The command

```
:autocmd FileWritePre * :call DateInsert()<CR>
```

causes the command **:call DateInsert()** to be executed for all files (*****) just before writing the file (FileWritePre). You do not need to put in a **:write** command because this autocommand is executed just before each **:write**. In other words, with this command enabled, when you do a **:write**, *Vim* checks for any **FileWritePre** autocommands and executes them, and then it performs the **:write**.

The general form of the **:autocmd** command is as follows:

```
:autocmd group events file_pattern nested command
```

The *group* name is optional. It is used in managing and calling the commands (more on this later). The *events* parameter is a list of events (comma separated) that trigger the command. (A complete list of events appears later in this chapter.) The *file_pattern* is a filename (including wildcards). The *nested* flag allows for nesting of autocommands, and finally, the *command* is the command to be executed.

Groups

The **:augroup** command starts the definition of a group of autocommands. The group name is just a convenient way to refer to the set of autocommands. For example:

```
:augroup cprograms
:    autocmd FileReadPost *.c :set cindent
:    autocmd FileReadPost *.cpp :set cindent
:augroup END
```

Because the **:autocmd** definitions are inside the scope **:augroup**, they are put in the cprograms group.

The commands in this group are executed after reading a file that ends in .c or .cpp. If you want to add another command to this group for headers, you can use the **:augroup** command or just include a group name in your specification:

```
:autocmd cprograms FileReadPost *.h :set cindent
```

Now suppose you are editing a file called sam.cx that you would like treated as a C program. You can tell *Vim* to go through all the cprograms autogroup commands and execute the ones that match *.c for the **FileReadPost** event. The command to do this is as follows:

```
:doautocmd cprograms FileReadPost foo.c
```

The general form of the **:doautocmd** command is this:

```
:doautocmd group event file_name
```

This executes the autocommand *group* pretending that the current file is *file_name* rather than the current one. If the *group* is omitted, all groups are used and if *file_name* is left off, the current filename is used. The *event* must be specified and is the event that *Vim* pretends has just happened.

The following command does the same thing as **:doautocmd** except it executes once for each buffer:

```
:doautoall group event file_name
```

(Note: Do not use this to trigger autocommands that switch buffers, create buffers, or delete them. In other words, when using this command, leave the buffers alone.)

Events

You can use the following events to trigger an autocommand:

BufNewFile		Triggered when editing a file that does not exist.
BufReadPre	**BufReadPost**	Triggered before (**BifReadPre**) / after (**BufReadPost**) reading a buffer
	BufRead	Alias for **BufReadPost**.
BufFilePre	**BufFilePost**	Before / after changing the name of a buffer with the **:file** command.
FileReadPre	**FileReadPost**	Before / after reading a file with the **:read** command. For **FileReadPost**, the marks '**[** and '**]** will be the beginning and end of the text read in.
FilterReadPre	**FilterReadPost**	Before / after reading a file with a filter command.

`FileType`		When the **filetype** option is set.
`Syntax`		When the **syntax** option is set.
`StdinReadPre`	`StdReadPost`	Before / after reading from the standard input. (The editor must have been started as **vim-**.)
`BufWritePre`	`BufWritePost`	Before / after writing the entire buffer to a file.
`BufWrite`		Alias for **BufWritePre**.
`FileWritePre`	`FileWritePost`	Before / after writing part of a buffer to a file.
`FileAppendPre`	`FileAppendPost`	Before / after appending to a file.
`FilterWritePre`	`FilterWritePost`	Before / after writing a file for a filter command.
`FileChangedShell`		This is triggered when *Vim* runs a shell command and then notices that the modification time of the file has changed.
`FocusGained`	`FocusLost`	Triggered when *Vim* gets or loses input focus. This means that *Vim* is running in GUI mode and becomes the current window or something else becomes the current window.
`CursorHold`		Occurs after the user pauses typing for more than the timeout specified by the **updatetime** option.
`BufEnter`	`BufLeave`	When a buffer is entered or left.
`BufUnload`		Triggered just before a buffer is unloaded.
`BufCreate`	`BufDelete`	Just after a buffer is created or just before it is deleted.
`WinEnter`	`WinLeave`	Going into or out of a window.
`GuiEnter`		The GUI just started.
`VimEnter`		The *Vim* editor just started and the initialization files have been read.
`VimLeavePre`		The *Vim* editor is exiting, but has not written the .viminfo file.
`VimLeave`		The *Vim* editor is exiting, and the .viminfo file has been written.

FileEncoding	The **fileencoding** option has just been set.
TermChanged	The **term** option changed.
User	Not a real event, but used as a fake event for use with **:doautocmd**.

When writing a file, *Vim* triggers only one pair of the following events:

BufWritePre	BufWritePost
FilterWritePre	FilterWritePost
FileAppendPre	FileAppendPost
FileWritePre	FileWritePost

When reading a file, one of the following set of events will be triggered:

BufNewFile	
BufReadPre	BufReadPost
FilterReadPre	FilterReadPost
FileReadPre	FileReadPost

File Patterns

The filename pattern matching uses the UNIX standard system. The following list identifies the special characters in the file matching patterns.

*	Match any characters, any length
?	Match any single character
,	Separates alternate patterns
	one, two, three
	Match the string *one*, *two*, or *three*.
\?	The **?**.
\,	The **,**.
\character	Treat character as a search pattern character. For example, **a\+** matches a, aa, aaa, and so on.

Nesting

Generally, commands executed as the result of an autocommand event will not trigger any new events. If you read a file in response to a **Syntax** C, for example, it will not trigger a **FileReadPre** event. If you include the keyword **nested**, these events will be triggered. For example:

```
:autocmd FileChangedShell *.c nested e!
```

Listing Autocommands

The following command lists all the autocommands:

```
:autocmd
```

For example:

```
:autocmd
—· Auto·Commands —·
filetype  BufEnter
      *.xpm      if getline(1) =~ "XPM2"¦set ft=xpm2¦endif
      *.xpm2     set ft=xpm2
...
FileType
      *          set formatoptions=tcql nocindent comments&
      c          set formatoptions=croql cindent
...
filetype  StdinReadPost
      *          if !did_filetype()¦so scripts.vim¦endif
Syntax
      OFF        syn clear
      abc        so $VIMRUNTIME/syntax/abc.vim
```

(Listing truncated.)

From this, you can see a number of commands under the group filetype. These command are triggered by the **BufEnter** and **StdinReadPost** events. There are also a couple of commands with no group name triggered by the **FileType** event.

If you want a subset of all the commands, try the following:

```
:autocmd group event pattern
```

If *group* is specified, only the commands for that group are listed. *Event* can be one of the previously defined events or * for all events. The *pattern* specifies an optional file matching pattern. Only the commands that match are listed.

For example:

```
:autocmd filetype BufEnter *.xpm
—· Auto·Commands —·
filetype  BufEnter
      *.xpm      if getline(1) =~ "XPM2"¦set ft=xpm2¦endif
```

Removing Commands

The command **:autocmd!** removes autocommands. The matching rules are the same for listing commands, so the following removes all the autocommands:

```
:autocmd!
```

To remove the commands for a specific group, execute this command:

```
:autocmd! group
```

You can also specify events and patterns for the group, as follows:

```
:autocmd! group event pattern
```

Again, *event* can be * to match all events.

You can use the **:autocmd!** command to remove existing commands and define a new one in one command. The syntax for this is as follows:

```
:autocmd! group event pattern nested command
```

This is the equivalent of the following:

```
:autocmd! group event pattern
:autocmd group event pattern nested command
```

Ignoring Events

At times, you will not want to trigger an autocommand. The **eventignore** option contains a list of events that will be totally ignored. For example, the following causes all Window **Enter** and **Leave** events to ignored:

```
:set eventignore=WinEnter,WinLeave
```

To ignore all events, use the following command:

```
:set eventignore=all
```

14

File Recovery and Command-Line Arguments

THE *VIM* EDITOR IS DESIGNED TO SURVIVE system crashes with minimum losses of data. This chapter discusses how to use *Vim's* crash recovery procedures.

In this chapter, you learn about the following:

- Command-line arguments for file recovery
- Encryption
- Batch files and scripts
- Additional command-line arguments
- Backup file options
- How to do file recovery
- Advanced swap file management

Command–Line Arguments

There are several useful command-line arguments. The most useful is **--help**, which displays a short help screen listing all the command-line arguments:

```
$ vim --help
VIM - Vi IMproved 5.6 (2000 Jan 16, compiled Jan 20 2000 17:35:46)
usage: vim [options] [file ..]     edit specified file(s)
       or: vim [options] -           read text from stdin
       or: vim [options] -t tag      edit file where tag is defined
       or: vim [options] -q [errorfile]  edit file with first error


Options:
       --                     End of options
       -g                     Run using GUI (like "gvim")
   — lots of other help —
```

To find out which version of *Vim* you have as well as to list the compilation options, use the following command:

```
$ vim --version
VIM - Vi IMproved 5.6 (2000 Jan 16, compiled Jan 20 2000 17:35:46)
Compiled by oualline@www.oualline.com, with (+) or without (-):
+autocmd +browse +builtin_terms +byte_offset +cindent +cmdline_compl
+cmdline_info +comments +cryptv -cscope +dialog_con_gui
+digraphs -emacs_tags +eval +ex_extra +extra_search
-farsi +file_in_path -osfiletype +find_in_path +fork() +GUI_GTK
-hangul_input +insert_expand -langmap +linebreak +lispindent
+menu +mksession +modify_fname +mouse -mouse_dec -mouse_gpm
-mouse_netterm +mouse_xterm -multi_byte -perl +quickfix -python
-rightleft +scrollbind +smartindent -sniff +statusline +syntax
+tag_binary +tag_old_static -tag_any_white -tcl +terminfo +textobjects
+title +user_commands +visualextra +viminfo +wildignore +wildmenu
+writebackup +X11 -xfontset -xim +xterm_clipboard -xterm_save
       system vimrc file: "$VIM/vimrc"
           user vimrc file: "$HOME/.vimrc"
           user exrc file: "$HOME/.exrc"
       system gvimrc file: "$VIM/gvimrc"
       user gvimrc file: "$HOME/.gvimrc"
       system menu file: "$VIMRUNTIME/menu.vim"
       fall-back for $VIM: "/usr/local/share/vim"
Compilation: gcc -c -I. -Iproto -DHAVE_CONFIG_H   -DUSE_GUI_GTK
-I/usr/X11R6/include -I/usr/lib/glib/include -g -O2 -Wall
-I/usr/X11R6/include
Linking: gcc  -o vim -L/usr/lib -L/usr/X11R6/lib -lgtk -lgdk -rdynamic
-lgmodule -lglib -ldl -lXext -lX11 -lm -L/usr/X11R6/lib -lXt -lX11
-lncurses
```

To view a file, you can "edit" it in read-only mode by using the **-R** command:

```
$ vim -R file.txt
```

On most systems, the following command does the same thing:

```
$ view file.txt
```

Encryption

The **-x** argument tells *Vim* to encrypt the file. For example, create a file that contains something you want to keep secret:

```
$ vim -x secret.txt
```

The editor now prompts you for a key used for encrypting and decrypting the file:

```
Enter encryption key:
```

You can now edit this file normally and put in all your secrets. When you finish editing the file and tell *Vim* to exit, the file is encrypted and written.

If you try to print this file using the *cat* or *type* commands, all you get is garbage.

Switching Between Encrypted and Unencrypted Modes

The option **'key'** contains your encryption key. If you set this option to the empty string (""), you turn off encryption:

```
:set key=
```

If you set this to a password, you turn on encryption. For example:

```
:set key=secret    (Not a good idea!)
```

Setting the encryption key this way is not a good idea because the password appears in the clear. Anyone shoulder surfing can read your password.

To avoid this problem, the **:X** command was created. It asks you for an encryption key and sets the **key** option to whatever you type in. (Note that the password will not be echoed. Instead ★ is printed for each character entered.)

```
:X
Enter encryption key:
```

Limits on Encryption

The encryption algorithm used by *Vim* is weak. It is good enough to keep out the casual prowler, but not good enough keep out a cryptology expert with lots of time on his hands. Also you should be aware that the swap file is not encrypted; so while you are editing, people with superuser privileges can read the unencrypted text from this file.

One way to avoid letting people read your swap file is to avoid using one. If the **-n** argument is supplied on the command line, no swap file is used (instead, *Vim* puts everything in memory). For example, to edit the encrypted file file.txt and to avoid swap file problems use the following command:

```
$ vim -x -n file.txt
```

Note

If you use the –n argument, file recovery is impossible.

Also while the file is in memory, it is in plain text. Anyone with privilege can look in the editor's memory and discover the contents of the file. If you use a session file, be aware that the contents of text registers are written out in the clear as well.

If you really want to secure the contents of a file, edit it only on a portable computer not connected to a network, use good encryption tools, and keep the computer locked up in a big safe when not in use.

Executing *Vim* in a Script or Batch File

Suppose you have a lot of files in which you need to change the string **- person -** to **Jones**. How do you do that? One way is to do a lot of typing. The other is to write a shell script or batch file to do the work.

The *Vim* editor does a superb job as a screen-oriented editor when started in normal mode. For batch processing, however, it does not lend itself to creating clear, commented command files; so here you will use ex mode instead. This mode gives you a nice command-line interface that makes it easy to put into a batch file.

The ex mode commands you need are as follows:

```
:%s/ — person — /Jones/g
:write
:quit
```

You put these commands in the file change.vim. Now to run the editor in batch mode, use this command:

```
$ vim -es file.txt <change.vim
```

This runs the *Vim* editor in ex mode (**-e** flag) on the file file.txt and reads from the file change.vim. The **-s** flag tells *Vim* to operate in silent mode. In other words, do not keep outputting the **:** prompt, or any other prompt for that matter.

Additional Command-Line Arguments

A number of command-line arguments are designed to control the behavior of the editor. For example, you may want to restrict what you can do in *Vim*. The arguments to support this are as follows:

-R   Open the file for read-only.

-m   Modifications are not allowed. This argument is more of a recommendation than a restriction because all it does is set the **'nowrite'** option. It does not prevent you from setting the **'write'** option and modifying the file.

-Z   Restricted mode. This prevents the user from using **:shell** or other commands to run an external shell. It does not prevent the user from trying to edit another file using the **:vi** *file* command.

The other arguments enable you to choose which initialization files you read:

-u *file* Use *file* rather than `.vimrc` for initialization. If the filename is NONE, no initialization file is used.

-U *file* Use *file* rather than `.gvimrc` for initialization. If the filename is NONE, no initialization file is used.

-i *file* Use *file* rather than the `.viminfo` file.

In UNIX, the *Vim* editor is actually one file with several different names (links). The editor starts in different modes, depending on with which name it is started. The names include the following:

vim Start *Vim* in console mode. (Edits inside the current window.)

gvim Start *Vim* in GUI mode. (The editor creates its own window for editing.)

ex Start in ex mode.

view Start in normal mode, read-only.

gview Start in GUI mode, read-only.

rvim Start in console mode, restricted.

rview Start in console mode, read-only, restricted.

rgvim Start in GUI mode, restricted.

rgview Start in GUI mode, read-only, restricted.

vi Linux only. Alias for **vim**.

You can use command-line arguments to set the initial mode as well:

-g Start *Vim* in GUI mode (same as using the command **gvim**).

-v Start *Vim* in visual mode (same as using the command **vim**).

-e Start *Vim* in ex mode (same as using the command **ex** on most systems).

You can use a number of command-line arguments to debug and test, including the following:

-V*number* Display extra messages letting you know what is going inside the editor. The higher the number, the more output you get. This is used for debugging your *Vim* scripts.

-f Foreground. Do not start a GUI in the background. This proves useful when *gvim* is run for another program that wants to wait until the program finishes. It is also extremely useful for debugging.

-w *script* Write all characters entered by the user into the *script* file. If the *script* file already exists, it is appended to.

-W *script* Like **-w**, but overwrite any existing data.

-s *script* Play back a script recorded with **-w**.

-**T** *terminal*   Set the terminal type. On UNIX, this overrides the value of the
$TERM environment variable. (Of course, if the $TERM environment is wrong, lots of other programs will be screwed up as well.)

You also have compatibility arguments. These are of use only if you really want *Vim* to act like *Vi*.

-**N**   Non-compatible mode. This argument makes *Vim* act like *Vim* rather than *Vi*. This argument is set by default when a `.vimrc` file is present.

-**C**   Compatible. This turns off many of the *Vim* special features and makes the editor look as much like *Vi* as possible.

-**l**   Lisp mode. This mode is an obsolete holdover from the old *Vi* days. It sets the `'lisp'` and `'showmatch'` options. The *Vim* file-type-related commands do a much better job of handling Lisp programs, and they do it automatically.

Finally, you have a few arguments that cannot be classified any other way:

-**d** *device*   Amiga only. Open the given device for editing.

-**b**   Binary mode. Sets `noexpandtab`, `textwidth=0`, `nomodeline`, and `binary`.

Foreign Languages

The *Vim* editor can handle a variety of languages. Unfortunately, to edit these languages, you do not only need a *Vim* editor with the language features compiled in, but you also need special fonts and other operating system support. This means that unfortunately foreign language support is beyond the scope of this book.

But the command-line arguments for the foreign languages are as follows:

-**F**   Farsi

-**H**   Hebrew

Backup Files

Usually *Vim* does *not* produce a backup file. If you want to have one, all you need to do is execute the following command:

```
:set backup
```

The name of the backup file is the original file with a "~" added to the end. If your file is named `data.txt`, for example, the backup file name is `data.txt~`.

If you do not like the fact that the backup files end with ~, you can change the extensions by using the following:

```
:set backupext=string
```

If `'backupext'` is `.bak`, `data.txt` is backed up to `data.txt.bak`.

The *Vim* editor goes you one better when it comes to the backup file. If you set the `'patchmode'` option, *Vim* backs up the file being edited to a file with the same name, but with the `'patchmode'` string appended to it. This will be done only if the file does not exist.

For example, suppose you execute this command:

```
:set patchmode=.org
```

Now you edit the existing file `data.txt` for the first time. When you exit *Vim* checks to see whether the file `data.txt.org` exists. It does not, so the old file is saved under that name. The next time you edit, the file does exist; so the backup is written to `data.txt~`. The file data.txt.org is not used from now on. Instead, all backups will go to `data.txt~`.

Usually *Vim* puts the backup file in the same directory as the file itself. You can change this with the `'backupdir'` option. For example, the following causes all backup files to be put in the `~/tmp` directory:

```
:set backupdir=~/tmp/
```

This can create problems if you edit files of the same name in different directories. That is because their backup files will all go to the `~/tmp` directory and the name collision will cause the old backup files to disappear.

The `'backupdir'` option can actually take a series of directories, separated by comma. The editor puts the backup file in the first directory where a backup file can be created.

Controlling How the File Is Written

Generally when *Vim* writes a file, the following operations are performed:

1. *Vim* checks to see whether the file has been changed outside of *Vim*. For example, someone could have overwritten the file with a new one. If this happens, a warning is issued and the editor asks if you want to continue.

2. If the `'writebackup'` or `'backup'` option is set, any old backup file is removed. The current file is then copied to the backup file.

3. The buffer is written out to the file.

4. If the `'patchmode'` option is set and no patch file exists, the backup file is renamed to become the patch file.

5. If the `'backup'` option is not set, and `'writebackup'` is set, remove the backup file.

The reason that *Vim* overwrites the existing file is to preserve any hard links that you might have on a UNIX system. On non-UNIX systems the backup is created by renaming the original file instead of making a copy.

> **Note**
> If you set the `'nobackup'` and `'nowritebackup'` options, *Vim* just overwrites the existing file. This can cause loss of data if the disk fills up during the file update.

By default, the `'writebackup'` option is set. This means that the system *Vim* uses to write a file makes it very difficult to lose data.

By using this method, there is no chance you will lose your file if the disk fills up. You may not be able to write out the new version of the file, but at least you do not lose the old one.

Basic File Recovery

Suppose that you want to edit a file called `sample.txt`. You start *Vim* with the following command:

```
$ gvim sample.txt
```

The editor now creates a swap file to temporarily hold the changes you make until you write the file. When you finish editing, the swap file is deleted.

If the editor is aborted during mid-edit, however, it does not get a chance to delete the swap file. This means that if you are in the middle of *Vim* sessions and your system locks, forcing a reboot, the swap file will not be deleted.

When *Vim* first starts editing a file, it checks for a swap file. If it finds one, that means that either another editing session is in progress or another editing session was started and the editor got aborted. Therefore, *Vim* issues a warning (see Figure 14.1), and gives you a chance to decide what to do.

```
~
~
~
~
~
ATTENTION
Found a swap file by the name ".sample.txt.swp"
          dated: Thu Feb 17 22:44:00 2000
       owned by: sdo
      file name: /tmp/sample.txt
       modified: no
      host name: www.oualline.com
      user name: sdo
     process ID: 8449 (still running)
While opening file "sample.txt"
          dates: Thu Feb 17 22:45:33 2000

(1) Another program may be editing the same file.
    If this is the case, be careful not to end up with two
    different instances of the same file when making changes.
    Quit, or continue with caution.

(2) An edit session for this file crashed.
    If this is the case, use ":recover" or "vim -r sample.txt"
    to recover the changes (see ":help recovery").
    If you did this already, delete the swap file ".sample.txt.swp"
    to avoid this message.
█
```

Figure 14.1   File in use warning.

At this point, you have four options:

Open Read-Only   This option causes *Vim* to open the file read-only. You should choose this option if you want to look at the file and there is another editing session still running.

Edit anyway	A.K.A. Damn the torpedoes, full steam ahead. If you select this option, you can edit the file. Do not choose this option unless you really know what you are doing. Note that if you have two or more edit sessions running on a single file, the last session to write the file wins.
Recover	If you were editing the file and the editor got aborted due to a system crash or some other reason, choose this option. It examines the swap file for changes and attempts to restart you session from where you left off. It usually comes close, but examine your file carefully because the last few edits may have disappeared.
Quit	Forget about trying to change this file.

After selecting one of these options, you can edit normally. Be careful if you choose Recover, because all your changes may not have been saved.

Recovering from the Command Line

If you know the name of the file you were editing when your editing session was aborted, you can start *Vim* in recovery mode using the **-r** argument. If you were editing the file commands.c when you were rudely interrupted, for example, you can recover with the following command:

```
$ vim -r commands.c
```

If you want to get a list of recoverable editor sessions, use this command:

```
$ vim -r
```

This causes *Vim* to check for swap files in the current directory and the standard temporary directories. For example:

```
$ vim -r
Swap files found:
    In current directory:
          -- none --
     In directory ~/tmp:
          -- none --
     In directory /var/tmp:
          -- none --
     In directory /tmp:
1.   .script.txt.swp
              dated: Fri Feb 18 19:48:46 2000
              owned by: sdo
          file name: /tmp/script.txt
              modified: no
         host name: www.oualline.com
         user name: sdo
         process ID: 26473 (still running)
```

In this example, you see that there is a swap file for the file /tmp/script.txt. The process number of the editor that created the swap file is 26473. The process is still running, so you probably do not want to try to edit or recover the file using this edit session. You probably want to find the window for process 26473 and use it instead.

Several options and other commands affect file recovery. See the section "Advanced File Recovery" for more information.

Advanced Swap File Management

The *Vim* editor goes to a great deal of trouble *not* to overwrite any old swap files. The first time a file is edited, the swap file name is `.file.txt.swp`. If the editor is aborted and you start editing again, the next swap file is called `.file.txt.swo`, and then `.file.txt.swn`, and so on.

You can tell *Vim* to recover using a specific swap file by specifying the name of the swap file with the command:

```
$ vim -r file.txt.swo
```

To find out the name of the swap file you are currently using, execute the following command:

```
:swapname
```

This displays the name of the swap file.

Controlling When the Swap File Is Written

Usually the swap file is written every 4 seconds or when you type 200 characters. These values are determined by the `'updatecount'` and `'updatetime'` options. To change the amount of time *Vim* waits before writing the swap file to 23 seconds, for example, use the following command:

```
:set updatetime=23000
```

To change the number of characters you have to type before *Vim* writes stuff to the swap file to 400, for instance, use this command:

```
:set updatecount=400
```

If you change the `'updatecount'` to 0, the swap file will not be written.

However, the decision whether to write a swap file is better controlled by the `'swapfile'` option. If you have this option set, a swap file will be created (the default):

```
:set swapfile
```

If you do not want a swap file, use the following command:

```
:set noswapfile
```

This option can be set/reset for each edited file. If you edit a huge file and don't care about recovery, set `'noswapfile'`. If you edit a file in another window, it will still use a swap file.

> **Note**
>
> The `'updatetime'` is specified in milliseconds.

On UNIX and Linux, when you "write" a file, the data usually goes into a memory buffer and is actually written to the disk when the operating system "thinks" it is appropriate. This usually takes only a few seconds. If you want to make sure that the data gets to disk, however, you want to use the following command:

```
:set swapsync
```

This command tells *Vim* to perform a sync operation after each writing of the swap file to force the data onto the disk. The **'swapsync'** option can be empty, **'fsync'**, or **'sync'**, depending on what system call you want to do the writing.

Controlling Where the Swap File Is Written

Generally, *Vim* writes the swap file in the same directory as the file itself. You can change this by using the **'directory'** option. For example, the following tells *Vim* to put all swap files in **/tmp**:

```
:set directory=/tmp              (Not a good idea)
```

This is not a good idea because if you try to edit the file readme.txt in two different directories at the same time, you encounter a swap file collision.

You can set the **'directory'** option to a list of directories separated by a comma (,). It is highly recommended that you use a period (.) as the first item it this list. The swap file will be written to the first directory in the list in which *Vim* can write the file. For example, the following tells *Vim* to write the swap file in the current directory, and then to try */tmp*:

```
:set directory=.,/tmp
```

Saving Your Work

Suppose you have made a bunch of changes and you want to make sure they stick around even if *Vim* or the operating system crashes. One way to save your changes is to use the following command to write out the file:

```
:write
```

However, this command overwrites your existing file with all your changes.

The following is a related command:

```
:preserve
```

This command writes all the edits to the swap file. The original file remains unchanged and will not be changed until you do a **:write** or exit with **ZZ**. If the system crashes, you can use the swap file to recover all your edits. Note that after a **:preserve**, you can recover even if the original file is lost. Without this command, you need both the original file and the swap file to recover.

The *:recover* Command

The following command tries to recover the file named file.txt:

```
:recover file.txt
```

It is just like this command:

```
$ vim -r file.txt
```

If the file you are trying to recover is currently being edited this command fails. If no filename is specified, it defaults to the file in the current buffer.

If you want to discard any changes you have made to the file and attempt to recover, use the following command:

```
:recover! file.txt
```

MS-DOS Filenames

If you are on an MS-DOS or Windows 3.1 machine, you are stuck with very limited filenames. The *Vim* editor detects this and limits the swap filename to something that can be used on this type of machine. Whereas the normal swap file for `foo.txt` is `.foo.txt.swp`, for example, if you are in short name mode, it is `foo_txt.swp`.

You can set the `'shortname'` option to force *Vim* to use this convention. This is useful if have a Linux or other system and are editing files on an MS-DOS partition. In this case, the operating system (Linux) supports long filenames, but the actual disk you are working on (MS-DOS format) does not. Therefore, you need to tell *Vim* to use the short swap names by giving it the following command:

```
:set shortname
```

This option is not available for the MS-DOS version of *Vim* because it would be always on. Instead, it is used when you are cross-platform editing.

readonly and *modified* Options

The `'modified'` flag is set if the buffer has been modified. You probably do not want to set this option yourself because it is handled automatically. You can use the value of this option in macros, however.

The `'readonly'` flag is also set automatically if the file is read-only. In only one circumstance should you reset this: when you are using a source control system that normally leaves files in read-only mode. You want to edit the file, so you start *Vim*.

The editor warns you that the file is read-only and sets the `'readonly'` option. At this point, you realize that you forgot to tell the source control system that you want to edit the file. So you use `:shell` to go to the command prompt and execute the commands needed to tell the system that you want to edit the file. The RCS system uses the `co -l` command to do this, for example; the SCCS system uses `sccs edit`.

After getting permission to edit the file, you use the **exit** command to return to *Vim*, where you execute the following command to mark the file as editable:

```
:set noreadonly
```

15

Miscellaneous Commands

THIS CHAPTER DISCUSSES ALL THE COMMANDS that do not quite fit in any other chapter. In this chapter, you learn about the following:

- Getting character number information
- How to go to a specific byte in the file
- Redrawing the screen
- Sleeping
- Terminal control
- Suspending the editor
- Reshowing the introduction screen

Printing the Character

The command `:ascii` or `ga` prints the number of the character under the cursor. The output looks like this:

```
<*>  42,  Hex 2a,  Octal 052
```

If editing a multibyte (Japanese or Chinese for example) file, and the character under the cursor is a double-byte character, the output shows both bytes.

Going to a Specific Character in the File

The `countgo` command goes to byte number *count* of the file. The command `g` `CTRL-G` displays the current byte number of a file (along with the current line, column, and other information).

The command `:goto` `offset` also positions the cursor to a given byte location within the file.

The `gg` command acts much like the `G` command. It goes to the line specified by its count. For example, `5gg` goes to line 5. The difference between `gg` and `G` is that if no count is specified, `gg` goes to the first line and `G` goes to the last.

Screen Redraw

The `CTRL-L` command redraws the screen. This proves useful when you are on a terminal and some system message or other text screws up your screen. With the advent of the dedicated GUI, the need for this command is greatly diminished.

Sleep

The `:sleep` `time` command does nothing for the specified number of seconds. If *time* ends in *m*, it is specified in milliseconds. This command proves useful when you want to pause during the execution of a macro.

The `countgs` command also sleeps for *count* seconds.

Terminal Control

On most terminals, the `CTRL-S` command stops output. To restart it again, you type `CTRL-Q`. These commands are not part of *Vim*; to avoid keyboard conflicts, however, they are not used by any *Vim* commands.

You should not try to use these commands in a `:map` command because your terminal might interpret them and they might never get to *Vim*.

Suspending the Editor

If you are on UNIX in terminal mode, you can suspend the editor with the normal-mode command `CTRL-Z`. To continue editing, use the shell command `fg`. This works only on shells that have job control. The `:suspend` command does the same thing.

> **Note**
> `CTRL-Z` in insert mode inserts the character *CTRL-Z*; it does not suspend the editor.

General Help

The :help, <F1> and <Help> commands all display the general help screen.

Window Size

The **z height** <CR> command resizes the current window to *height*. If there is only one window open, *Vim* will desplay only *height* lines. (The rest will be blank.) This is useful for slow terminals.

Viewing the Introduction Screen

If you start *Vim* without a filename, you will see an introductory flash screen. This screen disappears when you type the first character. If you want to see it again, issue the following command:

    :intro

Open Mode

The *Vim* editor has all the capabilities of the *Vi* editor except one: open mode. This mode is *Vi*'s way of coping with terminals it does not understand. It is difficult to get into this mode, difficult to use it, and the fact that *Vim* does not have it is no great loss.

   Vim does have a command to enter open mode, but when you issue the command

    :open

all you get is an error message.

16

Cookbook

THIS CHAPTER PRESENTS A COOKBOOK FULL OF short recipes for doing some common (and not so common) *Vim* editing.

The "recipes" include the following:

- Character twiddling
- Replacing one word with another using one command
- Interactively replacing one word with another
- Moving text
- Copying a block of text from one file to another
- Sorting a section
- Finding a procedure in a C program
- Drawing comment boxes
- Reading a UNIX man page
- Trimming the blanks off an end-of-line
- Oops, I left the file write-protected
- Changing Last, First to First Last
- How to edit all the files containing a given word
- Finding all occurrences of a word

Character Twiddling

If you type fast, your fingers can easily get ahead of your mind. Frequently people transpose characters. For example, the word *the* comes out *teh*.

To swap two characters (for example, *e* with *h*), put the cursor on the *e* and type **xp**.

The **x** command deletes a character (the *e*), and the **p** pastes it after the cursor (which is now placed over the *h*).

Replacing One Word with Another Using One Command

Suppose you want to make all *idiots* into *managers*.

Execute the following command:

```
:1,$s/idiots/managers/g
```

The colon (**:**) indicates that you are going to execute an ex type command. All ex commands begin with range of line numbers on which the command operates. In this case, the whole document is chosen, from line 1 to the last line (**$**). The shorthand for **1,$** is simply **%** as shown previously.

The **:s** (abbreviation for **:substitute**) command performs a substitution. The old text follows enclosed in slashes (**/idiots/**). The replacement text comes next, also delimited by the slashes (**/managers/**). The **g** flag tells the editor that this is a global change and so if the word *idiots* appears more than once on a line, to change them all.

> ### The Virgin What!?
>
> A church just bought its first computer and was learning how to use it. The church secretary decided to set up a form letter to be used in a funeral service. Where the person's name was to be, she put in the word *name*. When a funeral occurred, she would change this word to the actual name of the departed.
>
> One day, there were two funerals, first for a lady named Mary, and then later one for someone named Edna. So the secretary used global replace to change *name* to *Mary*. So far, so good. Next, she generated the service for the second funeral by changing the word *Mary* to *Edna*. That was a mistake
>
> Imagine the minister's surprise when he started reading the part containing the Apostles' Creed and saw, "Born of the Virgin Edna."

Interactively Replacing One Word with Another

Suppose you want to replace every occurrence of the word *idiot* with the word *manager*, but you want the chance to review each change before you do it.

To do so, follow these steps:

1. Use **1G** to go to the top of the document.

2. Execute **/idiot** to find the first occurrence of the word *idiot*.

3. Issue the command **cwmanager<Esc>**.

4. Change the word (**cw**) to *manager*.

5. Use the **n** command to repeat the last search (find the next *idiot*).

6. Execute the **.** command to repeat the last edit (change one word to *manager*). If you do not want to change the word, skip this step.

7. Repeat steps 4 and 5 until you have replaced all occurrences of *idiot* to *manager*.

Alternate Method

Execute the following command:

```
:%s/idiot/manager/cg
```

This starts an ex-mode command **:substitute** (abbreviated **:s**). The **%** tells *Vim* to apply this command to every line in the file. You change *idiot* to *manager*. The **c** flag tells **:substitute** to get confirmation before each change. The **g** flag tells the command to change all occurrences on the line. (The default is to change just the first occurrence.)

Moving Text

Suppose you want to move a bunch of paragraphs from the top of the document to the bottom.

To do so, follow these steps:

1. Move the cursor to the top of the paragraph you want to move.

2. Use **ma** to place a mark named *a* at this location.

3. Move the cursor to the bottom of the paragraph to be moved.

4. Execute **d'a** to delete to mark *a*. This puts the deleted text in a register.

5. Move the cursor to the line where the text is to go. The paragraph will be placed after this one.

6. Use the **p** command to paste the text below the cursor.

Another method consists of the following steps:

1. Select the first line as in the previous list; make it mark *a*.

2. Move to the bottom of the paragraph (use the **}** command). Mark *b*.

3. Move to the line above where you want to put the text, and type the command:

```
:'a,'b move .
```

Copying a Block of Text from One File to Another

The old *Vi* editor did not handle multiple files very well. Fortunately, *Vim* does a superb job of dealing with more than one file. There are lots of different ways to copy text from one to another. If you are used to the traditional *Vi*-style commands, you can use a method based around that style. On the other hand, *Vim* has a very nice visual mode. You can use it as well. Finally, *Vim* can make use of the system Clipboard to move text from one *Vim* program to another. All these methods work, and work well. Which one you should use is a matter of taste.

Method: Two Windows with Traditional *Vi*-Style Commands

To copy a block of text between files, follow these steps:

1. Edit the first file.
2. Execute `:split` *second_file* to go to the second file. Opens another window and starts editing the second file in it.
3. Use **CTRL-W p** to go to the "previous" window, the one with the original file.
4. Go to the top line to be copied.
5. Mark this line as mark *a* by using the **ma** command.
6. Go to the bottom line to be copied
7. Execute **y'a** to yank (copy in Microsoft parlance) the text from the current cursor location to mark *a* (**'a**) into the default register.
8. Use **CTRL-W p** to go to the file that will receive the text.
9. Go to the line where the insert is to occur. The text will be placed before this line.
10. Issue the **P** command to put (paste in Microsoft terminology) the text in the default register above the current line.

Method: Two Windows Using Visual Mode

To copy a block of text between files, follow these steps:

1. Edit the first file.
2. Execute `:split` to edit the second file.
3. Use **CTRL-W p** to go to the "previous" window, the one with the original file.
4. Go to the start of the text to be copied.
5. Issue the **v** command to start visual mode.
6. Go to the end of the text to be copied. The selected text will be highlighted.
7. Execute **y** to yank (Copy in Microsoft parlance) the text into the default register.

8. Use **CTRL-W p** to go to the file that will receive the text.

9. Go to the line where the insert is to occur. The text will be placed before this line.

10. Issue the **P** command to put (paste in Microsoft terminology) the text in the default register above the current line.

Method: Two Different *Vim* Programs

In this method, you start up two *Vim* programs and copy text from one to another. You do this by using the system Clipboard register (**"***).

1. Edit the first file.

2. Start another *Vim* program to edit the second file.

3. Go to the window with the first file in it.

4. Go to the start of the text to be copied.

5. Issue the **v** command to start visual mode.

6. Go to the end of the text to be copied. The selected text will be highlighted.

7. Use the **"*y** command to yank (copy in Microsoft parlance) the text into the system Clipboard register (**"***).

8. Change to the other editing command. (Make that editor your active window.)

9. Go to the line where the insert is to occur. The text will be placed before this line.

10. Issue the command **"*P** to put (paste in Microsoft terminology) the text in the system Clipboard register (**"***) above the current line.

> **Note**
>
> This method enables you to not only move text between two *Vim* applications, but also to "yank" and "put" between *Vim* and other applications as well. For example, you can select text in an xterm window using the mouse and paste it into a *Vim* editing using "*P. Or you can copy text into the system register in a *Vim* session and paste it into a Microsoft Word document using the Edit, Paste commands.

Sorting a Section

Frequently you will be editing a file with a list of names in it (for example, a list of object files that make up a program). For example:

```
version.o
pch.o
getopt.o
util.o
getopt1.o
inp.o
patch.o
backupfile.o
```

This list would be nice in alphabetic order (or at least ASCII order). To alphabetize this list, follow these steps:

1. Move the cursor to the first line to be sorted.

2. Use the command **ma** to mark the first line as mark *a*.

3. Move to the bottom of the text to be sorted.

4. Execute the **!'asort** command. The **!** command tells *Vim* to run the text through a UNIX command. The **'a** tells the editor that the text to be worked on starts at the current line and ends at mark *a*.

The command that the text is to go through is **sort**.
The result looks like this:

```
backupfile.o
getopt.o
getopt1.o
inp.o
patch.o
pch.o
util.o
version.o
```

Visual Method

1. Move the cursor to the first line to be sorted.

2. Issue the **v** command to enter visual mode.

3. Move to the bottom of the text to be sorted. The text will be highlighted.

4. Execute the **!sort** command. The **!** command tells *Vim* to run the highlighted text through the UNIX command **sort**.

Warning

In actual practice, what you see in most Makefiles (files used by UNIX to control compilation) looks more like this:

```
OBJS = \
        version.o       \
        pch.o           \
        getopt.o        \
        util.o          \
        getopt1.o       \
        inp.o           \
        patch.o         \
        backupfile.o
```

Notice that the backslash (\) is used to indicate a continuation line. After sorting this looks like the following:

```
OBJS = \
        backupfile.o
        getopt.o        \
        getopt1.o       \
        inp.o           \
        patch.o         \
        pch.o           \
        util.o          \
        version.o       \
```

The names are in order, but the backslashes are wrong. Do not forget to fix them using normal editing before continuing:

```
OBJS = \
        backupfile.o    \
        getopt.o        \
        getopt1.o       \
        inp.o           \
        patch.o         \
        pch.o           \
        util.o          \
        version.o
```

Finding a Procedure in a C Program

The *Vim* program was designed by programmers for programmers. You can use it to locate procedures within a set of C or C++ program files.

First, however, you must generate a table of contents file called a *tags file*. (This file has been given the obvious name *tags*.) The **ctags** command generates this table of contents file.

To generate a table of contents of all the C program files in your current working directory, use the following command:

```
$ ctags *.c
```

For C++, use this command:

```
$ ctags *.cpp
```

If you use an extension other than .cpp for your C++ files, use it rather than .cpp.

After this file has been generated, you tell *Vim* that you want to edit a procedure and it will find the file containing that procedure and position you there. If you want to edit the procedure **write_file**, for example, use the following command:

```
$ gvim -t write_file
```

Now suppose as you are looking at the **write_file** procedure that it calls **setup_data** and you need to look at that procedure. To jump to that function, position the cursor at the beginning of the word *setup_data* and press **CTRL-]**. This tells *Vim* to jump to the definition of this procedure. This repositioning occurs even if *Vim* has to change files to do so.

> **Note**
>
> If you have edited the current file and not saved it, *Vim* will issue a warning and ignore the CTRL-] command.

A number of tag-related commands enable you to jump forward/backward through tags, split the windows and put the called procedure in the other window, find inexact tags, and many more things.

Drawing Comment Boxes

I like to put a big comment box at the top of each of my procedures. For example:

```
/*******************************************************
 * Program — Solve it — Solves the worlds problems.  *
 *    All of them. At once. This will be a great     *
 *    program when I finish it.                      *
 *******************************************************/
```

Drawing these boxes like this is tedious at best. But *Vim* has a useful feature called *abbreviations* that makes things easier.

First, you need to create a *Vim* initialization file called ~/.vimrc. The ~/.vimrc file must contain the following lines:

```
:ab #b /***********************************
:ab #e <Space>***********************************/
```

These commands define a set of *Vim* abbreviations. Abbreviations were discussed in Chapter 8, "Basic Abbreviations, Keyboard Mapping, and Initialization Files."

To create a comment box, enter **#b<Enter>;**. The screen looks like this:

```
/***********************************************
```

Enter the comments, including the beginning and ending * characters. Finally, end the comment by typing **#e<Enter>**. This causes the ending comment to be entered.

Another (better) option is to use an external program like *boxes* (see http://www.vim.org), which generates all kinds of ASCII art boxes and can be customized.

Here, one might visually select the text and then issue the command **:'<,'>
!boxes -r** ,which would remove an existing box and put a new box around the text.

> **Note**
>
> This page was written in *Vim*. So how did we enter the #b and #e? Easy, we typed in #bb and the deleted a character. (We could not enter #b or it would have been expanded.) The actual command was i#bb<Esc>x.

Another good tool for this sort of thing is *tal*, which lines up the final character (the
*, here) so it looks nice.

Reading a UNIX man Page

You can use the *Vim* editor to browse through text files. One of the most useful sets
of files to browse through is the man pages. Unfortunately, man pages try to simulate
formatting by underlining characters using a sequence such as **_<BS>x** for **x**. This make
viewing of the man page in *Vim* difficult. If you try to read a man page directly, you
will see something like this:

```
N^HNA^HAM^HME^HE
        date - print or set the system date and time
```

To get rid of these characters, use the standard UNIX command **ul -i**. This is a
formatting program that removes the hard-to-read control characters. The result looks
like this:

```
NAME
!!!!
        date - print or set the system date and time
```

Now all that is needed is to put three commands together: the **man** command to get
the manual page, the **ul -i** command to fix the formatting, and **vim** to read the page.
The resulting command is as follows:

```
$ man date ¦ ul -i ¦ vim -
```

Another technique is to use *Vim*:

```
:%s/.\b//g
```

This will remove all characters followed by the backspace (\b), rendering the file
readable.

Trimming the Blanks off an End-of-Line

Some people find spaces and tabs at the end of a line useless, wasteful, and ugly. To
remove whitespace at the end of every line, execute the following command:

```
:%s/\s*$//
```

The colon (**:**) tells *Vim* to enter command mode. All command-mode commands start
with a line range; in this case, the special range **%** is used, which represents the entire
file.

The first set of slashes encloses the "from text." The text is "any whitespace" (**\s**),
repeated zero or more times (*****), followed by "end-of-line" (**$**). The result is that this
pattern matches all trailing whitespace.

The matching text is to be replaced by the text in the next set of slashes. This text
is nothing, so the spaces and tabs are effectively removed.

Oops, I Left the File Write-Protected

Suppose you are editing a file and you have made a lot of changes. This is a very important file and to preserve it from any casual changes, you write-protected it, even against yourself.

The *Vim* editor enables you to edit a write-protected file with little or no warning. The only trouble is that when you try to exit using **ZZ** you get the following error:

```
file.txt    File is read-only
```

And *Vim* does not exit.

So what can you do? You do not want to throw away all those changes, but you need to get out of *Vim* so that you can turn on write permission.

Use the command **:w!** to force the writing of the file.

Another option: Use the **:w otherfilename** command to save your work in a different file so you can fix the file permissions if that is what is required.

Changing Last, First to First, Last

You have a list of names in the following form:

```
Last, First
```

How do you change them to

```
First, Last
```

You can do so with one command:

```
:1,$s/\([^,]*\), \(.*$\)/\2 \1/
```

The colon (**:**) tells *Vim* that this is an ex-style command.

The line range for this command is the whole file, as indicated by the range **1,$**.

The **s** (abbreviations for **:substitute**) tells *Vim* to perform a string substitution.

The old text is a complex regular expression. The **\(. . . \)** delimiters are used to inform the editor that the text that matches the regular expression inside the parentheses is to be remembered for later use.

The text in the first **\(. . . \)** is assigned to **\1** in the replacement text. The second set of text inside **\(. . . \)** is assigned **\2**, and so on.

In this case, the first regular expression is any bunch of characters that does not include a comma. The **[^,]** means anything but a comma, and the ***** means a bunch (zero or more characters). Note: This means that all leading spaces will also be matched, which may not be what is desired.

The second expression matches anything (**.*** up to the end-of-line: **$**).

The result of this substitution is that the first word on the line is assigned to **\1** and the second to **\2**. These values are used in the end of the command to reverse the words.

The following example shows the relationship between the \(\) enclosed strings and the \1, \2 markers.

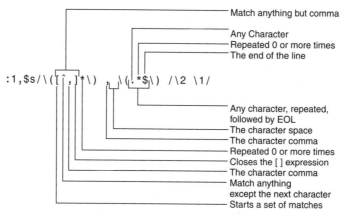

```
:1,$s/\([^,]*\) ,\(.*$\) /\2 \1/
```

Match anything but comma

Any Character
Repeated 0 or more times
The end of the line

Any character, repeated, followed by EOL
The character space
The character comma
Repeated 0 or more times
Closes the [ ] expression
The character comma
Match anything except the next character
Starts a set of matches

The next example breaks out the various parts of the regular expressions used in this illustration:

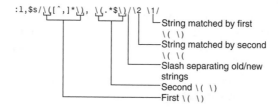

```
:1,$s/\([^,]*\), \(.*$\)/\2 \1/
```

String matched by first \(\)
String matched by second \(\(
Slash separating old/new strings
Second \(\)
First \(\)

How to Edit All the Files that Contain a Given Word

If you are a UNIX user, you can use a combination of *Vim* and *grep* to edit all the files that contain a given word. This is extremely useful if you are working on a program and want to view or edit all the files that contain a specified variable.

For example, suppose you want to edit all the C program files that contain the word frame_counter. To do this you use the command:

```
$ vim `grep -l 'frame_counter' *.c`
```

Let's look at this command in detail. The *grep* command searches through a set of files for a given word. Because the *-l* option is specified, the command will only list the files containing the word and not print the line itself. The word it is searching for is *frame_counter*. Actually, this can be any regular expression. (Note: What *grep* uses for regular expressions is not as complete or complex as what *Vim* uses.)

The entire command is enclosed in backticks (`). This tells the UNIX shell to run this command and pretend that the results were typed on the command line. So what happens is that the *grep* command is run and produces a list of files, these files are put on the *Vim* command line. This results in *Vim* editing the file list that is the output of *grep*. You can then use the commands **:n** and **:rewind** to browse through the files.

Why show this here? This is a feature of the UNIX shell (such as 'bash'), and isn't part of *Vim*'s repertoire. The way to accomplish something similar within *Vim*, and which works on Win32 as well is:

```
:args `grep -l 'frame_counter' *.c`
```

which will set the 'argument list', in other words, the files "on the command line."

Finding All Occurrences of a Word Using the Built-in Search Commands

The *Vim* editor has a built-in **:grep** command that you can use to search a set of files for a given string. If you want to find all occurrences of *error_string* in all C program files, for example, enter the following command:

```
:grep error_string *.c
```

This causes *Vim* to search for a string (**error_string**) in all the specified files (***.c**).

The editor will now open the first file where a match is found. Position the file on the first matching line. To go to the next matching line (no matter what file), use the **:cnext** command. To go to the previous match, use the **:cprev** command.

Note: The *Vim* grep command uses the external *grep* (on Unix) or *findstr* (on Windows) commands. You can change the external command used by setting the option **'grepprg'**.

17

Topics Not Covered

THE *VIM* EDITOR HAS A TREMENDOUSLY RICH set of features. Unfortunately, a few areas are beyond the scope of this book, and therefore are not covered here. These include support for commercial applications that I do not have access to and foreign languages. This chapter briefly describes the commands omitted from the rest of the book.

Interfaces to Other Applications

The *Vim* editor is designed to interface with many common commercial packages as well as a few Open Source packages. Because I do not have these packages installed, I could not examine and test these commands. Some brief documentation appears here.

Cscope

The **cscope** command is designed to examine a set of C or C++ programs and produce a database containing information about the location of functions and variables in the programs. You can then use the Cscope program to query this database to locate where an identifier is defined or used. Cscope is available from `http://cscope.sourceforge.net`.

For full information use the following command:

`:help cscope`

Cscope–Related Command Reference

`:cs` *arguments*	
`:cscope` *argument*	Handle various activities associated with the Cscope program.
`:cstag` *procedure*	Go to the tag in the CScope database named *procedure*.
`:set csprg=`*program*	
`:set cscopeprg=`*program*	Define the name of the Cscope program (Default=cscope).
`:set cst`	
`:set cscopetag`	
`:set nocst`	
`:set nocscopetag`	If set, this option causes the commands that do tag navigation (`:tags`, `CTRL-]`, and so on) to use the Cscope database rather than tags.
`:set csto=`*flag*	
`:set cscopetagorder=`*flag*	Define the search order for the CScope tag-searching commands. If flag is 0, the default, search the CScope database, followed by tags. If flag is 1, search tags first.
`:set csverb`	
`:set cscopeverbose`	
`:set nocsverb`	
`:set nocscopeverbose`	If set, output error messages occur when *Vim* looks for a CScope database and fails to find it. This proves useful when debugging initialization files that try to load a set of databases (default=nocscopeverbose).

OLE

The OLE system is a method by which programs running under Microsoft Windows can communicate with each other. The *Vim* editor can act as an OLE server. This means that you can write Microsoft Windows programs that interface to it. For those of you who know how to write Visual Basic or other Microsoft-based applications, you can find more information by using the command:

`:help ole-interface`

Perl

The Perl interface enables you to execute **perl** command from *Vim* and also gives the Perl programs an interface that they can use to access some of *Vim*'s functions. For a complete description of what is available, execute the following command:

```
:help perl
```

Perl Interface Command Reference

:pe *command*

:perl *command*   Execute a single **perl** command.

*:range***perld** *command*

*:range***perldo** *command*   Execute a **perl** command on a range of lines. The perl variable **$_** is set to each line in *range*.

Python

The Python interface enables you to execute Python statements and programs from within *Vim*. Like Perl, the Python interface provides you with lots of functions and objects that enable you to access parts of the *Vim* editor. For complete help, execute the following:

```
:help python
```

Python Interface Command Reference

*:range***py** *statement*

*:range***python** *statement*   Execute a single Python statement.

*:range***pyf** *file*

*:range***pyfile** *file*   Execute the Python program contained in *file*.

Sniff+

Sniff+ is a commercial programming environment. The *Vim* editor enables you to interface with this program.

To get complete help on using this programming tool, execute the following command:

```
:help sniff
```

Sniff+ Interface Command Reference

`:sni` *command*

`:sniff` *command*   Perform a command using the interface to Sniff+. If no command is present, list out information on the current connection.

Tcl

Tcl is another scripting language. As usual, *Vim* provides you with a way to execute Tcl scripts as well as an interface for accessing parts of *Vim* from within Tcl. For full information, use the following command:

`:help tcl`

Tcl Interface Command Reference

`:tc` *command*

`:tcl` *command*   Execute a single Tcl command.

`:range`tcld *command*

`:range`tcldo *command*   Execute a Tcl command once for each line in the range. The variable *line* is set to the contents of the line.

`:tclf` *file*

`:tclfile` *file*   Execute the Tcl script in the given file.

Foreign Languages

The *Vim* editor can handle many different types of foreign languages. Unfortunately, the author cannot. Here is a very short listing of the commands available to you for editing in other languages. For complete information, you need to consult the *Vim* documentation and as well as the documentation that came with your computer system.

Although *Vim* contains many language-specific options, a few are fairly generic.

`<F8>`   Toggle between left-to-right and right-to-left modes.

`:set rl`

`:set rightleft`

`:set norl`

`:set norightleft`   When set, indicates that the file is displayed right to left rather than left to right (default=norightleft).

`:set ari`

`:set allowrevins`

`:set noari`

`:set noallowrevins`   When set, let **CTRL-_** toggle the **revins** option.
This enables you to input languages that run from
right to left rather than left to right.

`:set ri`

`:set revins`

`:set nori`

`:set norevins`   When set, insert mode works right to left rather
than left to right. The **CTRL-_** command toggles
this option if the option allowrevins is set.

`:set gfs=f1,f2`

`:set guifontset=f1,f2`   Define a font *f1* for English and another *f2* for a
foreign language.

                         This works only if *Vim* was compiled with the
fontset enabled and only applies on UNIX
systems.

`:set lmap=ch1ch2,ch1ch2`

`:set langmap=ch1ch2,ch1ch2`   Define a keyboard mapping for a foreign
language.

Chinese

Written Chinese is a beautiful pictographic language where one character can convey
a world of meaning. Unfortunately typing that one character can be extremely difficult given the limits of a computer keyboard.

Chinese can be written left to right, right to left, or up to down. The *Vim* editor
supports right to left and left to right. It also supports both traditional Chinese characters as well as simplified Chinese.

Note

The *Vim* documentation does not contain help on the subject of Chinese input. That is operating system
dependent.

Chinese-Related Command Reference

`:set fe=`*encoding*

`:set fileencoding=`*encoding*   Set the file encoding to be used for this file. For the Chinese language, this can be **taiwan** for the traditional Chinese character set or **prc** for simplified Chinese.

Farsi

The Farsi language is supported, although you must explicitly enable Farsi when you compile the editor. It is not enabled by default. To edit in a Farsi file, start *Vim* in Farsi mode by using the **– F** option. For example:

```
$ vim —F file.txt
```

You can get complete information on Farsi editing by executing the following command:

```
:help farsi
```

Farsi-Related Command Reference

`:set fk`

`:set fkmap`

`:set nofk`

`:set nofkmap`   If set, this option tells *Vim* that you are using a Farsi keyboard (default=nofkmap).

`:set akm`

`:set altkeymap`

`:set noakm`

`:set noaltkeymap`   When **altkeymap** is set, the alternate keyboard mapping is Farsi. If **noaltkeymap** is set, the default alternate keyboard mapping is Hebrew (default=noaltkeymap).

`CTRL-_`   Toggle between Farsi and normal mode (insert-mode command).

`<F9>`   Toggles the encoding between ISIR-3342 standard and *Vim* extended ISIR-3342 (supported only in right-to-left mode).

Hebrew

Hebrew is another language that goes right to left. To start editing a Hebrew file, use the following command:

```
$ vim —H file.txt
```

To get help editing in this language, execute the following command:

```
:help hebrew
```

Hebrew–Related Command Reference

`:set hk`	
`:set hkmap`	
`:set nohk`	
`:set nohkmap`	Turn on (or off) the Hebrew keyboard mapping (default=nohkmap).
`:set hkp`	
`:set hkmapp`	
`:set nohkp`	
`:set nohkmapp`	When set, this option tells *Vim* that you are using a phonetic Hebrew keyboard, or a standard English keyboard (default=nohkmapp).
`:set al=number`	
`:set aleph=number`	Define the numeric value of the first character in the Hebrew alphabet. The value used depends on how your system encodes the Hebrew characters. (Default: Microsoft DOS: 128. Other systems: 224)
`CTRL-_`	Toggle between reverse insert and normal insert modes. Hebrew is usually inserted in reverse, like Farsi.
`:set akm`	
`:set altkeymap`	
`:set noakm`	
`:set noaltkeymap`	If `altkeymap` is set, the alternate keyboard mapping is Farsi. If `noaltkeymap` is set, the default alternate keyboard mapping is Hebrew (default=noaltkeymap).

Japanese

Japanese-encoded files are supported. Unfortunately there is no specific online help for Japanese.

Japanese-Related Command Reference

`:set fe=japan`

`:set fileencoding=japan`   Tells *Vim* that the current file is encoded using the Japanese character set.

Korean

To edit in Korean, you need to tell *Vim* about your keyboard and where your fonts reside. You can obtain information on how to do this by executing the following command:

`:help hangul`

Korean-Related Command Reference

`:set fe=korea`

`:set fileencoding=korea`   Tells *Vim* that the current file is encoded using the Korean character set.

Binary Files

Editing binary files using a text editor is tricky at best and suicidal at worst. If you have the right combination of expertise and desperation, you can use *Vim* to edit binary files.

`:set bin`

`:set binary`

`:set nobin`

`:set nobinary`   If set, then set things up for editing a binary file.

> **Note**
>
> I realize that some people out there need to edit a binary file and that you know what you are doing. For those of you in that situation, *Vim* is an excellent editor.
>
> Fortunately for those who need to, *Vim* comes with a great utility, 'xxd' which allows one to edit binary files almost painlessly. See the online docs for more information:
>
> `:help xxd`

Modeless (Almost) Editing

If you enable the '**insertmode**' option, insert mode is the default. If you want to switch to normal, use the **CTRL-O** command to execute a normal-mode command. This option is for people who do not like modes and are willing to deal with the confusing setting it generates.

> `:set im`
>
> `:set insertmode`
>
> `:set noim`
>
> `:set noinsertmode`   Make insert mode the default.
>
> `CTRL-L`   Leave insert mode if '**insertmode**' is set.

Operating System File Modes

Some operating systems keep file type information around on the file. The two operating systems covered in this book do not have this feature. If the OS does determine the file type, the result will be saved in the '**osfiletype**' option.

> `:set osf=`*type*
>
> `:set osfiletype=`*type*   This is set to the file type detected by an OS capable of doing so.
>
> `:set st=`*type*
>
> `:set shelltype=`*type*   Define the shell type for an Amiga.

II

The Details

18

Complete Basic Editing

IN CHAPTER 2, "EDITING A LITTLE FASTER," you were introduced to some of the basic editing commands. You can do 90% of most common edits with these commands. If you want to know everything about basic editing, however, read this chapter.

Chapter 2, for example, discussed the **w** command to move forward one word. This chapter devotes a page to discussing in detail how to define exactly what a word is. Chapter 2 described how to use two commands (**CTRL-D** and **CTRL-U**) to move screen up and down through the text. There are actually six commands to do this, with options, and that does not include the other dozen or so positioning commands. This chapter discusses the complete command list.

Generally you will not use all the commands in this chapter. Instead you will pick out a nice subset you like and use them. Chapter 2 presented one subset. If you prefer to pick your own, however, read this chapter and have fun.

Word Movement

The *Vim* editor has many different commands to enable you move to the beginning or end of words. But you can also customize the definition of a word through the use of some of the *Vim* options. The following sections explore in depth the word-movement commands.

Move to the End of a Word

The **w** command moves forward one word. You actually wind up on the beginning of the next word. The **e** command moves forward one word, but leaves you on the end of the word.

The **ge** command moves backward to the end of the preceding word.

Figure 18.1 shows how the various word-movement commands work.

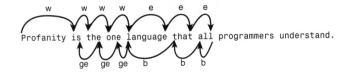

Figure 18.1   Word movement commands.

Defining What a Word Is

So what is a word, anyway? There are two answers to this question:

1. The *Vim* editor does a good job of defining a sane answer to this question. (Skip to the next section.)

2. If you want to know the details, read the rest of this section.

Your first answer to "What is a word?" might be the easy answer: It is a series of letters. However, a C programmer might consider something like *size56* to be word. Therefore, another answer might be to use the C identifier definition: the letters, digits, and the underscore.

But LISP programmers can use the dash (–) in a variable name. They consider the word *total-size* a single word. C programmers consider it two words. So how do you resolve this conflict?

The *Vim* solution is to create an option that defines what is in a word and what is not. The following command defines the characters that belong in a word:

```
:set iskeyword=specification
```

To see what the current value of this option is, use this command:

```
:set iskeyword?
```

The following represents a typical value:

```
iskeyword=@,48-57,_,192-255
```

This is all the letters (**@**), the digits (ASCII characters numbered **48-57** or 0-9), the underscore (**_**) and the international letters (**192-255**, à through Ÿ).

The specification consists of characters separated by commas. If you want the word characters to be exclusively vowels, for instance, use this command:

```
:set iskeyword=a,e,i,o,u
```

You can specify a range of characters by using a dash. To specify all the lowercase letters, for example, issue the following command:

```
:set iskeyword=a-z
```

For characters that cannot be specified directly (such as comma and dash), you can use a decimal number. If you want a word to be the lowercase letters and the dash (character #45), use the following command:

```
:set iskeyword=a-z,45
```

The @ character represents all characters where the C function `isalpha()` returns true. (This might vary, depending on the setting of the C locale, and also depending on the C compiler and OS you are using to build *Vim*!)

To exclude a character or set of character, precede it with a circumflex (^). The following command defines a word as all the letters except lowercase *q*:

```
:set iskeyword=@,^q
```

The @ character is represented by `@-@`.

Special Characters for the *iskeyword* Option

a	Character *a*.
a–z	Character range (all characters from *a* to *z*).
45	Character number 45 (in this case, -).
@	All letters (as defined by `isalpha()`).
@-@	The character @.
^x	Exclude the character *x*.
^a–c	Exclude the characters in the range *a* through *c*.

Note
You can abbreviate the `'iskeyword'` option as `isk`.

Other Types of Words

The 'iskeyword' option controls what is and is not a keyword. Other types of characters are controlled by similar options, including the following:

'isfname' Filenames

'isident' Identifiers

'isprint' Printing characters

The 'isfname' option is used for commands such as the gf command, which edits the
file whose name is under the cursor. (See Chapter 23, "Advanced Commands for
Programmers," for more information on this command.)

The 'isident' option is used for commands such as [d, which searches for the
definition of a macro whose identifier is under the cursor. (See Chapter 7,
"Commands for Programmers," for information on this command.)

The 'isprint' option defines which characters can be displayed literally on the
screen. Careful: If you get this wrong the display will be messed up. This is also used
by the special search pattern \p, which stands for a printable character. (See Chapter
19, "Advanced Searching Using Regular Expressions," for information on search
patterns.)

There Are "words," and Then There Are "WORDS"

So now you know what words are, right? Well, the *Vim* editor also has commands that
affect WORDS. These two terms, *WORDS* and *words*, represent two different things.
(Only a programmer could think up terms that differ only by case.)

The term *word* means a string of characters defined by the 'iskeyword' option. The
term *WORD* means any sequence of non-whitespace characters. Therefore

```
that-all
```

is two words, but it is one WORD.

The W command moves forward WORDS and the B command moves backward
WORDS. The complete list of WORD-related commands is as follows:

<C-Left>

[count] B   Move *count* WORDS backward.

[count] E   Move *count* WORDS forward to the end of the WORD.

[count] gE   Move *count* WORDS backward to the end of the WORD.

<C-Right>

[count] W   Move *count* WORDS forward.

Note: <C-Left> is the same as CTRL<LEFT>. See Appendix B for a list of <> key names.

Beginning of a Line

The ˆ command moves you to the first non-blank character on the line. If you want to go to the beginning of the line, use the **0** command. Figure 18.2 shows these commands.

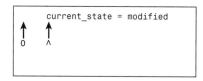

Figure 18.2   ˆ and **0** commands.

Repeating Single-Character Searches

The **fx** command searches for the first *x* after the cursor on the current line. To repeat this search, use the **;** command. As usual, this command can take an argument that is the number of times to repeat the search.

The **;** command continues the search in the same direction as the last **f** or **F** command. If you want to reverse the direction of the search, use the **,** command. Figure 18.3 shows several typical searches.

Figure 18.3   Repeat single-character search.

Moving Lines Up and Down

The − command moves up to the first non-blank character on the preceding line. If an argument is specified, the cursor moves up that many lines.

The + command moves down to the beginning of the next line. If an argument is specified, the cursor moves down that number of lines.

Figure 18.4 shows these commands.

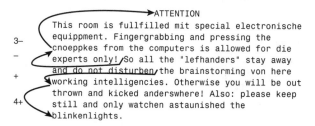

Figure 18.4   The + and - commands.

The _ command moves to the first non-blank character of the line. If a count is specified, it moves the first character of the *count* − 1 line below the cursor.

Cursor-Movement Commands

Several commands enable you to move to different parts of the screen. The **H** command moves to the top of the screen. If a count is specified, the cursor will be positioned to the *count* line from the top. Therefore, **1H** moves to the top line, **2H** the second line, and so on.

The **L** command is just like **H** except that the end of the screen is used rather than the start.

The **M** command moves to the middle of the screen.

Figure 18.5 summarizes the cursor-positioning commands.

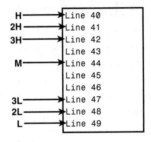

Figure 18.5 Cursor-positioning commands.

Jumping Around

The *Vim* editor keeps track of where you have been and enables you to go back to previous locations. Suppose, for example, that you are editing a file and execute the following commands:

1G   Go to line 1

10G   Go to line 10

20G   Go to line 20

Now, you execute this command:

```
:jumps
```

You get the following:

```
    jump line  col file/text
    2     1    0 Dumb User Stories
    1    10    0 ventilation holes. Many terminals
>
```

From this you see that you have recorded as jump 1, line 10, column 0, the "ventilation holes" line. Jump 2 is at line 1, column, the "Dumb User Stories" line.

Line 20 is not recorded in the jump list yet, because you are on it. The jump list records only things after you jump off of them. The > points to the current item in the list; in this case, it points to the blank line at the end indicating an unrecorded location.

Now that you know what the jump list is, you can use it. The **CTRL-O** command jumps back one line. Executing this command takes you back to line 10. The jump list now looks like this:

```
  jump line  col file/text
    2    1     0 Dumb User Stories
>   0   10     0 ventilation holes. Many terminals
    0   20     0
```

The > has moved up one line. If you use the **CTRL-O** command again, you move to line 1. The **CTRL-I** or **<TAB>** command moves you to the next jump in the list. Thus you have the following:

1G	Go to line 1.
10G	Go to line 10.
20G	Go to line 20.
CTRL-O	Jump to previous location (line 10).
CTRL-O	Jump to previous location (line 1).
<TAB>	Jump to next location (line 10).

Using these commands, you can quickly navigate through a series of jumping off points throughout your file.

Controlling Some Commands

Normally *Vim* stops any left or right movement at the beginning or end of the line. The **'whichwrap'** option controls which characters are allowed to go past the end and in which modes. The possible values for this option are as follows:

Character	Command	Mode(s)
b	**<BS>**	Normal and visual
s	**<Space>**	Normal and visual
h	**h**	Normal and visual
l	**l**	Normal and visual
<	**<Left>**	Normal and visual
>	**<Right>**	Normal and visual
~	**~**	Normal
[	**<Left>**	Insert and replace
]	**<Right>**	Insert and replace

Figure 18.6 shows how `'whichwrap'` affects cursor movement.

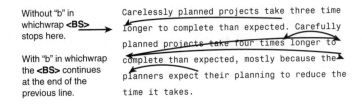

Without "b" in whichwrap **<BS>** stops here.

With "b" in whichwrap the **<BS>** continues at the end of the previous line.

Carelessly planned projects take three time longer to complete than expected. Carefully planned projects take four times longer to complete than expected, mostly because the planners expect their planning to reduce the time it takes.

Figure 18.6   Effects of the `'whichwrap'` option.

Where Am I, in Detail

The **CTRL-G** command displays summary information at the bottom of the screen telling you where you are in the file (see Chapter 2). However, you can get more detailed information if you ask. The basic **CTRL-G** output looks like this:

```
"c02.txt" [Modified] line 81 of 153 —52%— col 1
```

To get more information, give **CTRL-G** a count. The bigger the count, the more detailed information you get. The **1CTRL-G** command gives you the full path of the file, for example:

```
"/usr/c02.txt" [Modified] line 81 of 153 —52%— col 1
```

The **2CTRL-G** command lists a buffer number as well. (You can read more on buffers in Chapter 5, "Windows.")

```
buf 1: "/usr/c02.txt" [Modified] line 81 of 153 —52%— col 1
```

The **gCTRL-G** command displays another type of status information indicating the position of the cursor in terms of column, line, and character:

```
Col 1 of 0; Line 106 of 183; Char 3464 of 4418
```

If you are interested in having the current cursor location displayed all the time, check out the `'ruler'` option in Chapter 28, "Customizing the Appearance and Behavior of the Editor."

Scrolling Up

As discussed in Chapter 2, the **CTRL-U** command scrolls up half a screen.

To be precise, the **CTRL-U** command scrolls up the number of lines specified by the `'scroll'` option. You can explicitly set this option with a `:set` command:

```
:set scroll=10
```

You can also change the value of this option by giving an argument to the **CTRL-U** command. For example, **2CTRL-U** changes the scroll size to 2 and moves up 2 lines. All subsequent **CTRL-U** commands will only go up 2 lines at a time, until the scroll size is changed. Figure 18.7 shows the operation of the **CTRL-U** command.

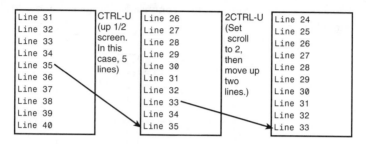

Figure 18.7   The **CTRL-U** command.

To scroll the window up one line at a time, use the **CTRL-Y** command. This command can be multiplied by an argument. For example, **5CTRL-Y** scrolls up 5 lines (see Figure 18.8).

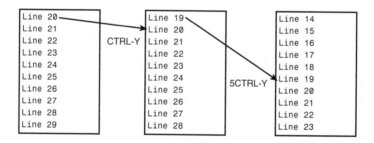

Figure 18.8   The **CTRL-Y** command.

The **CTRL-B** command scrolls up an entire screen at a time (see Figure 18.9).

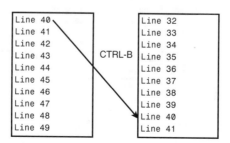

Figure 18.9   The **CTRL-B** command.

You can specify this command as **<PageUp>** or **<S-Up>**. (**<S-Up>** is the *Vim* notation for the Shift+up-arrow key.)

Scrolling Up Summary

Figure 18.10 illustrates the various scrolling commands. Commands move the top line to the indicated location.

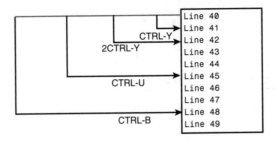

Figure 18.10   Scrolling commands.

Scrolling Down

There are similar commands for moving down as well, including the following:

CTRL-D   Move down. The amount is controlled by the **'scroll'** option.

CTRL-E   Move down one line.

CTRL-F   Move down one screen of data (also **<PageDown>** or **<S-Down>**).

Figure 18.11 summarizes the scrolling commands.

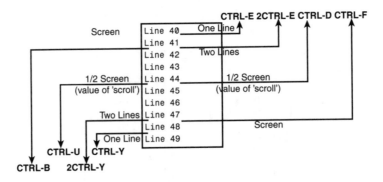

Figure 18.11   More scrolling commands.

Define How Much to Scroll

When you move the cursor off the top or bottom, the window scrolls. The amount of the scrolling is controlled by the **'scrolljump'** option. By default this is a single line; if you want more scrolling, however, you can increase this to a jump of 5, as follows:

```
:set scrolljump=5
```

The **'sidescroll'** option does the same thing, except in the horizontal direction.

Usually the cursor must reach the top or bottom line of the screen for scrolling to occur. If you want to add a little padding to this margin, you can set the **'scrolloff'** option. To make sure that there are at least 3 lines above or below the cursor, use the following command:

```
:set scrolloff=3
```

Adjusting the View

Suppose you want a given line at the top of the screen. You can use the **CTRL-E** (up one line) and **CTRL-Y** (down one line) commands until you get the proper line at the top. Or you can position the cursor on the line and type the command **z<Enter>**. Figure 18.12 shows how this command changes the screen.

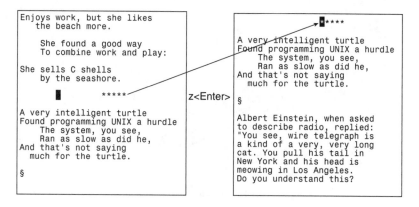

Figure 18.12 The **z<Enter>** command.

If you supply an argument to this command, it will use that line rather than the current one. **z<Enter>** positions the current line at the top of the screen, for instance, whereas **88z<Enter>** positions line 88 at the top.

The **z<Enter>** command not only positions the line at the top of the screen, it also moves the cursor to the first non-blank character on the line. If you want to leave the cursor where it is on the line, use the command **zt**. (If you change the current line by giving the command an argument, *Vim* will try to keep the cursor in the same column.) Figure 18.13 shows the **zt** command.

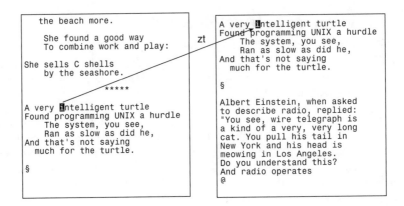

Figure 18.13   The **zt** command.

If you want to position a line to the end of the screen, use the **zb** or **z-** command. The **z-** positions the cursor on the first non-blank column, whereas **zb** leaves it alone. Figure 18.14 shows the effects of these commands.

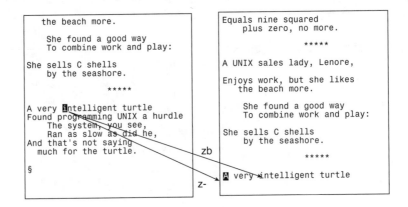

Figure 18.14   The **zb** and **z-** commands.

Finally, the **zz** and **z.** commands position the line at the center of the window. The **zz** command leaves the cursor in its current column, and **z.** moves it to the first non-blank column. Figure 18.15 shows what these commands do.

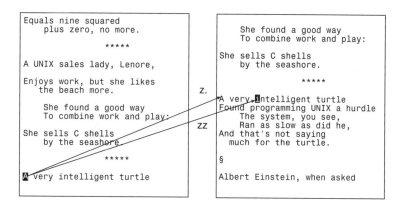

Figure 18.15   The **z.** and **zz** commands.

Delete to the End of the Line

The **D** command deletes to the end of the line. If preceded by a count, it deletes to the end of the line and *count* − 1 more lines. (The **D** command is shorthand for **d$**.) See Figure 18.16 for some examples of this command.

```
                  ATTENTION
This room is fullfilled mit special electronische D
equippment. Fingergrabbing and pressing the
cnoeppkes from the computers is allowed for die
experts only! So all the "lefhanders" stay away  3D
and do not disturben the brainstorming von here
working intelligencies. Otherwise you will be out
thrown and kicked anderswhere! Also: please keep
still and only watchen astaunished the
blinkenlights.
```

Figure 18.16   The **D** command.

The *C* Command

The **C** command deletes text from the cursor to the end of the line and then puts the editor in insert mode. If a count is specified, it deletes an additional *count* − 1 lines. In other words, the command works like the **D** command, except that it puts you in insert mode.

The *s* Command

The **s** (substitute) command deletes a single character and puts the editor in insert mode. If preceded by a count, then *count* characters are deleted. Figure 18.17 illustrates this command.

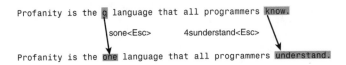

Figure 18.17 The **s** command.

The *S* Command

The **s** command deletes the current line and puts the editor in insert mode. If a count is specified, it deletes *count* lines. This differs from the **C** command in that the **C** command deletes from the current location to the end of the line, whereas the **S** command always works on the entire line. Figure 18.18 illustrates the use of the **S** command.

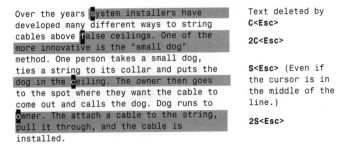

Figure 18.18 The **s** command.

Deleting Text

The `"register count` **x** command deletes characters starting with the one under the cursor moving right. The **X** command deletes characters to the left of the cursor. Figure 18.19 shows how these two commands work.

```
1 is equal to 2 for sufficiently large values of 1.
                        │ 3x
                        ▼
1 is equal to 2 for suffintly large values of 1.


1 is equal to 2 for sufficiently large values of 1.
                       / 3X
                      ✗
1 is equal to 2 for suciently large values of 1.
```

Figure 18.19   The x and X commands.

Insert Text at the Beginning or End of the Line

The **I** command inserts text like the **i** command does. The only difference is that the **I** command inserts starting at the beginning of the line. (In this case, "beginning" means at the first non-blank character.) To insert at the first character of the line (space or not), use the **gI** command. The **A** command appends text like the **a** command, except the text is appended to the end of the line.

Arithmetic

The *Vim* editor can perform simple arithmetic on the text. The **CTRL-A** command increments the number under the cursor. If an argument is specified, that number is added to the number under the cursor. Figure 18.20 shows how various types of numbers are incremented.

```
123          0177         0x1E         123
 │ CTRL-A     │ CTRL-A     │ CTRL-A     │ CTRL-A
124          0200         0x1F         128
```

Figure 18.20   Incrementing.

If a number begins with a leading 0, it is considered an octal number. Therefore, when you increment the octal number 0177, you get 0200. If a number begins with 0x or 0X, it is considered a hexadecimal number. That explains 0x1E to 0x1F.

The *Vim* editor is smart about number formats, so it will properly increment decimal, hexadecimal, and octal.

The **CTRL-X** command works just like the **CTRL-A** command, except the number is decremented; or if an argument is present, the number is subtracted from the number. Figure 18.21 shows how to decrement numbers.

```
123                0120              0x1E              123
 │ CTRL-X           │ CTRL-X          │ CTRL-X          │ 5 CTRL-X
124                0117              0x1F              118
```

Figure 18.21 Decrementing.

By default, *Vim* recognizes the octal and hexadecimal numbers. Which formats are recognized is controlled by the **nrformats** option. If you want to recognize decimal and octal numbers, for instance, execute the following command:

```
:set nrformats=""
```

If you want to recognize just octal numbers, use this command:

```
:set nrformats=octal
```

The default recognizes decimal, hexadecimal, and octal:

```
:set nrformats=octal,hex
```

> **Note**
>
> Decimal is always recognized. Unlike hexadecimal and octal, there is no way to turn off decimal recognition.

The *Vim* editor can do more sophisticated calculations. See Chapter 27, "Expressions and Functions," for information on the "= register.

Joining Lines with Spaces

The **J** command joins the current line with the next one. A space is added to the end of the first line to separate the two pieces that are joined. But suppose you do not want the spaces. Then you use the **gJ** command to join lines without spaces (see Figure 18.22). It works just like the **J** command, except that no space is inserted between the joined parts.

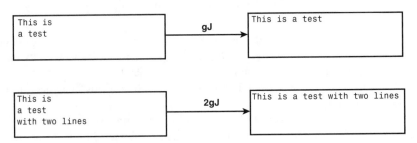

Figure 18.22 The **gJ** command.

> **Note**
>
> If the first line ends with some trailing spaces, the **gJ** command will not remove them.

Replace Mode

The **R** command causes *Vim* to enter replace mode. In this mode, each character you type replaces the one under the cursor. This continues until you type **<Esc>**. Figure 18.23 contains a short example.

Figure 18.23   The **R** command.

If a count is specified, the command will be repeated *count* times (see Figure 18.24).

Figure 18.24   **R** command with a count.

You may have noticed that this command replaced 12 characters on a line with only 5 left on it. The **R** command automatically extends the line if it runs out of characters to replace.

Virtual Replace Mode

One of the problems with replace comes when you have a <Tab> in the text. If you are sitting on a <Tab> and execute the command **rx**, the <Tab> will be replaced by *x*. This can shift your line around (see Figure 18.25).

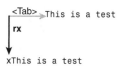

Figure 18.25   Simple non-virtual replace.

If you use the virtual replace command, **gr***character*, you replace the "virtual character" under the cursor (see Figure 18.26). If the real character under the cursor is part of a tab, only the space representing the tab jumped over is replaced.

Figure 18.26   Virtual replacement.

The **gR** command enters virtual replace mode. Each character you type will replace one character in screen space until you finish things off with **<Esc>**.

Digraphs

As learned in Chapter 2, executing **CTRL-K** *character1 character2* inserts a digraph. You can define your own digraphs by using the following command:

```
:digraphs character1 character2 number
```

This tells *Vim* that when you type **CTRL-K** *character1 character2* that you should insert the character whose character number is *number*.

If you are entering a lot of digraphs, you can turn on the **'digraph'** option by using this command:

```
:set digraph
```

This means that you can now enter digraphs by using the convention *character1***<BS>***character2*. (**<BS>** is the backspace character.)

This mode has its drawbacks, however. The digraph **c<BS>0** is the copyright character (©). If you type **x** but want to type **y**, you can correct your mistake by typing **x** (oops), **<BS>**, and **y**. If you do that with **c** and **0**, however, it does not erase the *c* and put in the *0*; instead, it inserts ©.

Therefore, you need to type **c** (oops), **<BS>**, **0** (darn, © appeared), **<BS>**, and **0**.

To turn off digraph mode, use the following command:

```
:set nodigraph
```

Changing Case

The ~ command changes a character's case. The behavior of the ~ command depends on the value of the **'tildeop'** option. With the option unset, the command behaves normally:

```
:set notildeop
```

If you set the following option, however, the syntax of the command changes to *~motion*:

```
:set tildeop
```

For example the command *~fq* changes the case of all the characters up to and including the first *q* on the line. Figure 18.27 shows some examples.

```
      now is the time. . . .            NOW IS the TIME. . . .

3~l   |                          ~fM   |
      v                                v
      Now is the time. . . .           Now is THE time. . . .
```

Figure 18.27   `~motion` commands.

The **g**-*motion* command changes the case of the indicated characters. It is just like the *~motion* command except that it does not depend on the **tildeop** option. Figure 18.28 shows some examples.

```
      now is the time. . . .            NOW IS the TIME. . . .

3g~l  |                          g~fm  |
      v                                v
      Now is the time. . . .           Now is THE time. . . .
```

Figure 18.28   The **g~** command.

A special version of this command, **g~~** or **g~g~**, changes the case of the entire line (see Figure 18.29).

```
      Now IS the Time. . . .

g~~   |
      v
      nOW IS THE TIME. . .  ■
```

Figure 18.29   The **g~~** command.

Other Case-Changing Commands

The **gU**motion command makes the text from the cursor to *motion* all uppercase. The command **gUU** or **gUgU** works on a single line. If *count* is specified, *count* lines are changed.

The **gu**motion, **guu**, and **gugu** act just like their **gU** counterparts, except that they make the text lowercase.

Figure 18.30 illustrates these commands.

Figure 18.30   Case-changing commands.

Undo Level

You can execute only so many undo commands. This limit is set by the **undolevels** option. To set this limit to 5,000 changes, use the following command:

```
:set undolevels=5000
```

Getting Out

The **ZQ** command is an alias for the **:q!** or **:quit!** command. The command exits and discards all changes.

The **:write** command writes out the file. The **:quit** command exits. You can use a shorthand for these commands:

```
:wq
```

This command can take a filename as an argument. In this case, the edit buffer will be written to the file and then *Vim* will exit. To save your work under a new filename and exit, for instance, use the following command:

```
:wq count.c.new
```

This command will fail with an **error** message if the file count.c.new exists and is read-only. If you want *Vim* to overwrite the file, use the override option (**!**):

```
:wq! count.c.new
```

Finally, you can give the **:wq** command a line-range argument. (See Chapter 25, "Complete Command-Mode Commands" for more on ranges.) If a line range is present, only those lines are written to the file. To write out only the first 10 lines of a file and exit, for example, execute the following command:

```
:1,10wq count.c.new
```

The :xit command acts much like the :wq command except that it only writes the file if the buffer has been modified.

19

Advanced Searching Using Regular Expressions

VIM HAS A POWERFUL SEARCH ENGINE THAT enables you to perform many different types of searches. In this chapter, you learn about the following:

- Turning on and off case sensitivity
- Search options
- Instant word searching
- How to specify a search offset
- A full description of regular expressions

Searching Options

This section describes some of the more sophisticated options that you can use to fine-tune your search. `'hlsearch'` has been turned on to show you how these options affect the searching.

Case Sensitivity

By default, *Vim*'s searches are case sensitive. Therefore, *include, INCLUDE,* and *Include* are three different words and a search will match only one of them. The following example searched for *include*. Notice that *INCLUDE, Include* and *iNCLude* are *not* highlighted. Figure 19.1 shows the result of an /`include` command.

```
*        Report the speed of a cd-rom                         *
*                     (Also works on hard drives and other    *
*                     devices)                                *
*                                                             *
* Usage:                                                      *
*     cd-speed <device>                                       *
*                                                             *
***************************************************************/
#Include <iostream.h>
#INCLUDE <iomanip.h>
#Include <unistd.h>
#iNCLude <stdlib.h>
/include
```

Figure 19.1   Case-sensitive search.

Now let's turn on the '**ignorecase**' option by entering the following command:

```
:set ignorecase
```

Now when you search for *include*, you will get all four flavors of the word as (see Figure 19.2).

```
*        Report the speed of a cd-rom                         *
*                     (Also works on hard drives and other    *
*                     devices)                                *
*                                                             *
* Usage:                                                      *
*     cd-speed <device>                                       *
*                                                             *
***************************************************************/
#Include <iostream.h>
#INCLUDE <iomanip.h>
#Include <unistd.h>
#iNCLude <stdlib.h>
```

Figure 19.2   Non-case-sensitive search.

To turn on case sensitivity, use this command:

```
:set noignorecase
```

(Technically what you are doing is turning off case insensitivity, but it tortures the English language too much to say it this way.)

If you have '**ignorecase**' set, *word* matches *word*, *WORD*, and *Word*. It also means that *WORD* will match the same thing. If you set the following two options, any search string typed in lowercase is searched, ignoring the case of the search string:

```
:set ignorecase
:set smartcase
```

If you have a string with at least one uppercase character, however, the search becomes case sensitive.

Thus you have the following matches:

String	Matches
word	word, Word, WORD, worD
Word	Word
WORD	WORD
WorD	WorD

Wrapping

By default, a forward search starts searching for the given string starting at the current cursor location. It then proceeds to the end of the file. If it does not find the string by that time, it starts from the beginning and searches from the start of the file to the cursor location. Figure 19.3 shows how this works.

```
                              1
                              2 // Read at most 10MB
                              3 const. unsigned int MAX_READ = (10 * 1024 *1024
    Start                     4 ▮
                              5 // Size of a buffer
                              6 const unsigned int BUF_SIZE = (62 * 1024);
    1) /unsigned              7
    2) n                      8 // Buffer to be written
                              9 static unsigned char buffer[BUF_SIZE];
    3) n                     10
```

Figure 19.3   Wrapping.

This example starts by searching for *unsigned*. The first search goes to line 6. The next search moves to line 9. When trying to search again, you reach the end of the file without finding the word. At this point, the search wraps back to line 1 and the search continues. The result is that you are now on line 3.

Turning Off Search Wrapping

To turn off search wrapping, use the following command:

```
:set nowrapscan
```

Now when the search hits the end of the file, an error message displays (see Figure 19.4).

```
#include <sys/fcntl.h>
#include <sys/time.h>
#include <errno.h>

// Read at most 10MB
const unsigned int MAX_READ = (10 * 1024 *1024);
// Size of a buffer
const unsigned int BUF_SIZE = (62 * 1024);

// Buffer to be written
static unsigned char buffer[BUF_SIZE];

search hit BOTTOM without match for: unsigned
```

Figure 19.4   nowrapscan.

To go back to normal wrapping searches, use the following command:

```
:set wrapscan
```

Interrupting Searches

If you are in the middle of a long search and want to stop it, you can type **CTRL-C** on a UNIX system or **CTRL-BREAK** on Microsoft Windows. On most systems, unless you are editing a very large file, searches are almost instantaneous.

Instant Word Searches

The * command searches for the word under the cursor. For example, position the cursor on the first *const*. Pressing * moves the cursor to the next occurrence of the word, specifically line 26. Figure 19.5 shows the results.

```
19 #include <sys/fcntl.h>
20 #include <sys/time.h>
21 #include <errno.h>
22
23 // Read at most 10MB
24 Const. unsigned int MAX_READ = (10 * 1024 *1024);
25 // Size of a buffer
26 const unsigned int BUF_SIZE = (62 * 1024);
27
28 // Buffer to be written
29 static unsigned char buffer[BUF_SIZE];
```

Figure 19.5   * command.

The **#** or **£** command does an instant word search in the backward direction. These commands work on whole words only. In other words, if you are on *const* and conduct a * search, you will not match *constant*. The **g*** command performs an instant word search, but does not restrict the results to whole words. So whereas * will not match constant, the **g*** command will match it.

The **g#** command does the same thing in the reverse direction.

Search Offsets

By default, the search command leaves the cursor positioned on the beginning of the pattern. You can tell *Vim* to leave it some other place by specifying an *offset*. For the forward search command (*/*), the offset is specified by appending a slash (/) and the offset, as follows:

```
/const/2
```

This command searches for the pattern *const* and then moves to the beginning of the second line past the pattern. Figure 19.6 shows how this works.

/const/2

Find const

Move to the
start of the
pattern +2 lines

```
19 #include <sys/fcntl.h>
20 #include <sys/time.h>
21 #include <errno.h>
22
23 // Read at most 10MB
24 const unsigned int MAX_READ = (10 * 1024 *1024);
25 // Size of a buffer
26 const unsigned int BUF_SIZE = (62 * 1024);
27
28 // Buffer to be written
29 static unsigned char buffer[BUF_SIZE];
```

Figure 19.6 Search offsets.

If the offset is a simple number, the cursor will be placed at the beginning of the offset line from the match. The offset number can be positive or negative. If it is positive, the cursor moves down that many lines; if negative, it moves up.

If the offset begins with **b** and a number, the cursor moves to the beginning of the pattern, and then travels the "number" of characters. If the number is positive, the cursor moves forward, if negative, backward. The command **/const/b2** moves the cursor to the beginning of the match, for instance, and then two characters to the right (see Figure 19.7).

```
const unsigned int BUF_SIZE = (62 * 1024);
```

2 characters to the right

pattern

Results of
/const/b2

Figure 19.7 **/const/b2**.

Note

The **b** offset is a synonym for **s**. Therefore, you can use **b** (begin), and **s** (start) for the first character of the match.

The **e** offset indicates an offset from the end of the match. Without a number it moves the cursor onto the last character of the match. The command **/const/e** puts the cursor on the *t* of *const*. Again, a positive number moves the cursor to the right, a negative number moves it to the left (see Figure 19.8).

```
const unsigned int BUF_SIZE = (62 * 1024);
```

pattern end

3 characters to the left

Results of
/const/e-3

Figure 19.8 **/const/e-3**.

Finally, there is the null offset. This is the empty string. This cancels the preceding offset.

Specifying Offsets

To specify an offset on a forward search (/ command), append /*offset* to the command, as follows:

```
/const/e+2
```

If you want to repeat the preceding search with a different offset, just leave out the pattern and specify the new offset:

```
//5
```

To cancel an offset, just specify an empty offset.

```
//
```

For example:

/const/e+2	Search moves to the end of the pattern, and then to the right two characters.
/	Repeats last search, with the preceding offset.
//	Repeats the last search with no offset. (Cursor will be placed on the first character of the pattern.)

To specify an offset for a reverse search (**?** command), append **?***offset* to the command, as follows:

```
?const?b5
```

To repeat with the same pattern and a new offset, use the following:

```
??-2
```

To remove the offset and repeat the search with the preceding pattern, use the following:

```
??
```

One thing to remember when using search offsets, the search always starts from the current cursor position. This can get you into trouble if you use a command such as this:

```
/const/-2
```

This command searches for *const* and then moves up two lines. If you then repeat the search with the **n** command, it goes down two lines, finds the *const* you just found, and then moves the cursor back up two lines for the offset. The result is that no matter how many times you type **n**, you go nowhere.

Complete Regular Expressions

The search logic of *Vim* uses regular expressions. You saw some simple ones in Chapter 3, "Searching," but this chapter goes into them in extreme detail. Regular expressions enable you to search for more than simple strings. By specifying a regular expression in your search command, you can search for a character pattern, such as "all words that begin with *t* and end in *ing*" (regular expression = **\<t[^]*ing\>**).

However, the power of regular expressions comes with a price. Regular expressions are quite cryptic and terse. It may take some time for you to get used to all the ins and outs of this powerful tool.

While learning regular expressions, you should execute the following command:

```
:set hlsearch
```

This causes *Vim* to highlight the text you matched with your last search. Therefore, when you search for a regular expression, you can tell what you really matched (as opposed to what you thought you matched).

A regular expression consists of a series of atoms. An *atom* is the smallest matching unit in a regular expression. Atoms can be things like a single character, such as **a** (which matches the letter *a*), or a special character, such as **$** (which matches the end of the line). Other atoms, such as **\<** (word start, see the following section), consist of multiple characters.

Beginning (\<) and End (\>) of a Word

The atom **\<** matches the beginning of a word. The atom **\>** matches the end of a word.

For example, a search for the expression **for** finds all occurrences of *for*, even those in other words, such as *Californian* and *Unfortunately*. Figure 19.9 shows the results of this search.

If you use the regular expression **\<for\>**, however, you match only the actual word *for*. Figure 19.10 contains the results of this refined search.

```
Calls and letters to the company failed to correct
this problem.  Finally the fellow just gave up and
wrote a check for $0.00 and the bills ceased.


A Californian who loved sailing went down and applied
for a personalized license plate. He filled in his
three choices as 1)SAIL 2)SAILING and 3)NONE. He got
a new plate labeled "NONE."

Unfortunately, when the police write out a ticket
/for
```

Figure 19.9 Search for /**for**.

```
Calls and letters to the company failed to correct
this problem.  Finally the fellow just gave up and
wrote a check for $0.00 and the bills ceased.



A Californian who loved sailing went down and applied
for a personalized license plate. He filled in his
three choices as 1)SAIL 2)SAILING and 3)NONE. He got
a new plate labeled "NONE."

Unfortunately, when the police write out a ticket
/\<for\>
```

Figure 19.10   Search for /\<for\>.

Modifiers and Grouping

The modifier * is used to indicate that an atom is to be matched 0 or more times. The match is "greedy." In other words, the editor will try to match as much as possible. Thus, the regular expression **te*** matches *te*, *tee*, *teee*, and so on.

The expression **te*** also matches the string **t**. Why? Because **e*** can match a zero-length string of *e*'s. And **t** is the letter *t* followed by zero *e*'s.

Figure 19.11 shows the results of the search for **te***.

```
This is a test.

te tee teee teee
~
~
/te*
```

Figure 19.11   Search for /te*.

The \+ modifier indicates that the atom is to be matched one or more times. Therefore, **te\+** matches *te*, *tee*, and *teee*, but not *t*. (**te\+** is the same as **tee***.). Figure 19.12 illustrates what is matched for the search /te\+.

```
This is a test.

te tee teee teee
~
~
/te\+
```

Figure 19.12   Search for /te\+.

Finally, there is the \= modifier. It causes the preceding atom to be matched zero or one time. This means that **te\=** matches *t* and *te*, but not *tee*. (Although it will match the first two characters of *tee*.) Figure 19.13 shows a typical search.

```
This is a test.
te tee teee teee
~
~
/te\=
```

Figure 19.13 Search for /**te**\=.

Special Atoms

A number of special escaped characters match a range of characters. For example, the **a** atom matches any letter, and the **d** option matches any digit. The regular expression **a****a****a** matches any three letters.

Now try a search for any four digits. Figure 19.14 displays the results.

```
   1
   2 // Read at most 10MB
   3 const unsigned int MAX_READ = (10 * 1024 *1024);
   4
   5 // Size of a buffer
   6 const unsigned int BUF_SIZE = (62 * 1024);
   7
   8 // Buffer to be written
   9 static unsigned char buffer[BUF_SIZE];
  10
/\d\d\d\d
```

Figure 19.14 Search for /**d****d****d****d**.

Now try a search for any three letters followed by an underscore. Figure 19.15 displays the results.

```
   1
   2 // Read at most 10MB
   3 const unsigned int MAX_READ = (10 * 1024 *1024);
   4
   5 // Size of a buffer
   6 const unsigned int BUF_SIZE = (62 * 1024);
   7
   8 // Buffer to be written
   9 static unsigned char buffer[BUF_SIZE];
  10
/\a\a\a_
```

Figure 19.15 Search for /**a****a****a**.

Character Ranges

The **a** atom matches all the letters (uppercase and lowercase). But suppose you want to match only the vowels. The range operator enables you to match one of a series of characters. For example, the range **[aeiou]** matches a single lowercase vowel. The string **t[aeiou]n** matches *tan*, *ten*, *tin*, *ton* and *tun*.

You can specify a range of characters inside the brackets ([]) by using a dash. For example, the pattern **[0-9]**, matches the characters 0 through 9. (That is 0,1,2,3,4,5,6,7,8,9.)

You can combine ranges with other characters. For example, **[0-9aeiou]** matches any digit or lowercase vowel.

The ^ character indicates a set of characters that match everything *except* the indicated characters. To match the constants, for example, you can specify **[^aeioAEIOU]**.

> **Note**
>
> To match the ^, you need to escape it. For example, [\^$.] matches any one of the three symbols ^, $, or ..

Pattern	Matches
one[\-]way	one-way, but not one way or one+way
2\^4	2^4
2[\^*]4	2^4, 2*4

Character Classes

Suppose you want to specify all the uppercase letters. One way to do this is to use the expression **[A-Z]**. Another way is to use one of the predefined character classes. The class **[:upper:]** matches the uppercase characters. Therefore, you can write **[A-Z]** as **[[:upper:]]**.

You can write the entire alphabet, upper- and lowercase, **[[:upper:][:lower:]]**. There are a large number of different character classes.

> **Note**
>
> You cannot use the special atoms like \a and \d in a range. For example, [\a\d] matches the characters \, a, \, and d. It does not match the letters (\a) and digits (\d).

Repeat Modifiers

You can specify how many times an atom is to be repeated. The general form of a repeat is as follows:

```
\{minimum, maximum}
```

For example, the regular expression a\{3,5} will match 3 to 5 *a*'s. (that is, *aaa, aaaa,* or *aaaaa.*) By default, the *Vim* editor tries to match as much as possible. So **a\{3,5}** will match as many *a*'s as it can (up to 5).

The *minimum* can be omitted, in which case it defaults to zero. Therefore, **a,\{,5}** matches 0–5 repeats of the letter. The *maximum* can be omitted as well, in which case it defaults to infinity. So **a\{3,}** matches at least 3 *a*'s, but will match as many *a*'s as you have got on the line.

If only one number is specified, the atom must match exactly that number of times. Therefore, **a\{5}** matches 5 *a*'s, exactly.

Repeating as Little as Possible

If you put a minus sign (-) before any of the numbers, the *Vim* editor tries to match as *little* as possible.

Therefore, **a\{-3,5}** will match 3 to 5 *a*'s, as little as possible. Actually if this expression is by itself, it will always match just three *a*'s. That is because even if you have the word *aaaaa*, the editor will match as little as possible.

The specification **a\{-3,}** matches 3 or more *a*'s, as little as possible. The expression **a\{-,5}** matches 0–5 letters.

The expression **a\{-}** matches 0 to infinity number of characters, as little as possible. Note that this pattern by itself will always match zero characters. It only makes sense when there is something after it. For example: **[a-z]\{-}x** will match *cx* in *cxcx*. Using **[a-z]*x** would have matched the whole *cxcx*.

Finally, the specification **a\{-5}** matches exactly 5 *a*'s, as little as possible. Because as little as possible is exactly 5, the expression **a\{-5}** acts just like **a\{5}**.

Grouping (\(\))

You can specify a group by enclosing it in a **\(** and **\)**. For example, the expression **a*b** matches b, *ab*, *aab*, *aaab*, and so on. The expression **a\(XY\)*b** matches ab, *aXYb*, *aXYXYb*, *aXYXYXYb*, and so on.

When you define a group using **\(\)**, the first enclosed string is assigned to the atom **\1**. To match the string **the the**, for instance, use the regular expression **\(the\) \1**. To find repeated words, you can get a bit more general and use the expression **\(\<\a\+\>\) \1**. Figure 19.16 breaks this into its components.

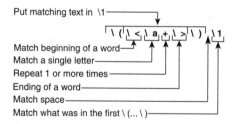

Put matching text in \1

Match beginning of a word
Match a single letter
Repeat 1 or more times
Ending of a word
Match space
Match what was in the first \(...\)

Figure 19.16 The repeat (\1) expression.

The first group is assigned to **\1**, the second **\2**, and so on.

The Or Operator (\|)

The \| operator enables you to specify two or more possible matches. The regular expression **foo\|bar** matches *foo* or *bar*.

For example, the search

```
/procedure\|function
```

searches for either procedure or function.

Putting It All Together

Let's create a regular expression to match California license plate numbers. A sample license plate looks like 1MGU103. The pattern is one digit, three uppercase letters, and three digits. There are several ways of doing this.

Start by specifying the digit as **[0-9]**, now add the uppercase letter: **[0-9][A-Z]**. There are three of them, so you get **[0-9][A-Z]\{3}**. Finally, you add the three digits on the end, resulting in **[0-9][A-Z]\{3}[0-9]\{3}**.

Another way to do this is to recognize that **\d** represents any digit and **\u** any uppercase character. The result is **\d\u\{3}\d\{3}**.

The experts tell us that this form is faster than using the [] form. If you are editing a file where this speed up makes a difference, however, your file might be too big.

You can accomplish this without repeats as well: **\d\u\u\u\d\d\d**.

Finally, you can use the character classes, yielding

[[:digit:]][[:upper:]]\{3}[[:digit:]]\{3}.

All four of these expressions work. Which version should you use? Whichever one you can remember. You should remember this old adage: The simple way you can remember is much faster than the fancy way you can't.

The *magic* Option

The expressions discussed so far assume that the **'magic'** option is on. When this option is turned off, many of the symbols used in regular expressions lose their magic powers. They only get them back when escaped.

Specifically, if you execute the command

```
:set nomagic
```

the ★, ., [, and] characters are not treated as special characters. If you want to use the ★ for "0 or more repeats," you need to escape it: \★.

You should keep the **'magic'** option on (the default) for portability and macro files.

Offset Specification Reference

[num]	
+[num]	Down [num] lines. Cursor is placed at the beginning of the line.
-[num]	Up [num] lines. Cursor is placed at the beginning of the line.
e	End of the match.
e[num]	End of the match, the move [num]. If [num] is positive, move right, negative, move left.
b	
s	Start of the match.
b[num]	
s[num]	Start of the match, then move [num]. If [num] is positive, move right; negative, move left.

Regular Expressions Reference

The following table assumes that the 'magic' option is on (the default).

Simple Atoms

x	The literal character x.
^	Start of line.
$	End of line.
.	A single character.
\<	Start of a word.
\>	End of word.

Range Atoms

[abc]	Match either a, b, or c.
[^abc]	Match anything except a, b, or c.
[a-z]	Match all characters from a through z.
[a-zA-Z]	Match all characters from a through z and A through Z.

Character Classes

[:alnum:]	Match all letters and digits.
[:alpha:]	Match letters.
[:ascii:]	Match all ASCII characters.
[:backspace:]	Match the backspace character (<BS>).

`[:blank:]`	Match the space and tab characters.
`[:cntrl:]`	Match all control characters.
`[:digit:]`	Match digits.
`[:escape:]`	Matches the escape character (**<Esc>**).
`[:graph:]`	Match the printable characters, excluding space.
`[:lower:]`	Match lowercase letters.
`[:print:]`	Match printable characters, including space.
`[:punct:]`	Match the punctuation characters.
`[:return:]`	Matches the end-of-line (carriage return, **<Enter>**, **<CR>**, **<NL>**).
`[:space:]`	Match all whitespace characters.
`[:tab:]`	Match the tab character (**<Tab>**).
`[:upper:]`	Match the uppercase letters.
`[:xdigit:]`	Match hexadecimal digits.

Patterns (Used for Substitutions)

`\(pattern\)`	Mark the pattern for later use. The first set of `\(\)` marks a subexpression as `\1`, the second `\2`, and so on.
`\1`	Match the same string that was matched by the first subexpression in `\(` and `\)`. For example: `\([a-z]\).\1` matches *ata*, *ehe*, *tot*, and so forth.
`\2`	Like `\1`, but uses second subexpression,
`\9`	Like `\1`, but uses ninth subexpression.

Special Character Atoms

`\a`	Alphabetic character (A–Za–z).
`\A`	Non-alphabetic character (any character except A–Za–z).
`\b`	**<BS>**.
`\d`	Digit.
`\D`	Non-digit.
`\e`	**<Esc>**.
`\f`	Any filename character as defined by the **isfname** option.
`\F`	Any filename character, but does not include the digits.
`\h`	Head of word character (A–Za–z_).
`\H`	Non-head of word character (any character except A–Za–z_).
`\i`	Any identifier character as defined by the **isident** option.
`\I`	Any identifier character, but does not include the digits.

`\k`	Any keyword character as defined by the **iskeyword** option.
`\K`	Any keyword character, but does not include the digits.
`\l`	Lowercase character (a-z).
`\L`	Non-lowercase character (any character except a-z).
`\o`	Octal digit (0-7).
`\O`	Non-octal digit.
`\p`	Any printable character as defined by the **isprint** option.
`\P`	Any printable character, but does not include the digits.
`\r`	**<CR>**.
`\s`	Whitespace (**<Space>** and **<Tab>**).
`\S`	Non-whitespace character. (Any character except **<Space>** and **<Tab>**).
`\t`	**<Tab>**.
`\u`	Uppercase character (A-Z).
`\U`	Non-uppercase character (any character except A-Z).
`\w`	Word character (0-9A-Za-z_).
`\W`	Non-word character (any character except 0-9A-Za-z_).
`\x`	Hexadecimal digit (0-9 a-f A-F).
`\X`	Non-hexadecimal digit.
`\~`	Matches the last given substitute string.

Modifiers

`*`	Match the previous atom 0 or more times. As much as possible.
`\+`	Match the previous atom 1 or more times. As much as possible.
`\=`	Match the previous atom 0 or 1 times.
`\{}`	Match the previous atom 0 or more times. (Same as the `*` modifier.)
`\{n}`	
`\{-n}`	Match the previous atom n times.
`\{n,m}`	Match the previous atom n to m times.
`\{n,}`	Match the previous atom n or more times.
`\{,m}`	Match the previous atom from 0 to m times.
`\{-n,m}`	Match the previous atom n to m times. Match as little as possible.
`\{-n,}`	Match the previous atom at least n times. Match as little as possible.

`\{-,`*m*`}`	Match the previous atom up to m times. Match as little as possible.
`\{-}`	Match the previous atom 0 or more times. Match as little as possible.
str1\¦str2	Match str1 or str2.

20

Advanced Text Blocks
and Multiple Files

THE *VIM* EDITOR HAS LOTS OF DIFFERENT ways of doing things. Chapter 4, "Text Blocks and Multiple Files," presented a representative subset of the commands dealing with text blocks and multiple files and described them. It is entirely possible for you to edit efficiently using only those commands.

This chapter shows you all the other ways of doing things. If you find that you do not like the limitations of the commands in Chapter 4, read this one; you should find a way to get around your annoyances.

For example, you learned how to yank and put (cut and paste) using a single register to hold the text. That is fine if you are dealing with a single block of text. If you want to deal with more, however, check out how to use multiple registers later in this chapter.

This chapter covers the following:

- Different ways to yank and put
- How to use special registers
- How to edit all the files containing a specific string
- Advanced commands for multiple files
- Global marks
- Advanced insert–mode commands
- How to save and restore your setting by using a VIMINFO file
- Dealing with files that contain lines longer than the screen width

Additional Put Commands

When inserting lines, **p** and **P** commands do not move the cursor. The **gp** command works just like the **p** command, except that the cursor is left at the end of the new text. The **gP** command does the same things for the **P** command. Figure 20.1 shows the effects of these commands.

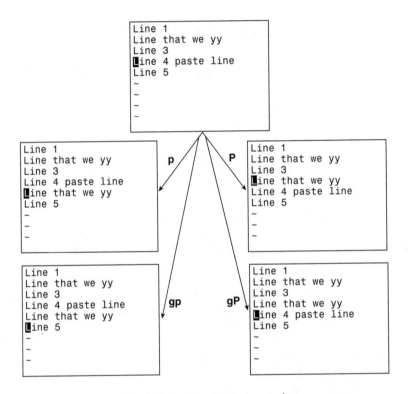

Figure 20.1 Paste (put) commands.

Special Marks

Vim has a number of special built-in marks. The first one is the single quotation (') mark. It marks the location of the cursor before the latest jump. In other words, it is your previous location (excluding minor moves such as up/down and so on).

Other special marks include the following:

]   The beginning of the last inserted text

[The end of the last inserted text

"   The last place the cursor was resting when you left the file

Multiple Registers

So far, you have performed all your yanks and deletes without specifying which register to use. If no register is specified, the unnamed register is used. The characters that denote this register are two double quotation marks (""). The first double quote denotes a register; the second double quote is the name of the register. (Therefore, for example, **"a** means use register a.)

You can specify which register the deleted or yanked text is to go into by using a register specification before the command. The format of a register specification is **"register**, where *register* is one of the lowercase letters. (This gives you 26 registers to play around with.)

Therefore, whereas **yy** puts the current line into the unnamed register, the command **"ayy** places the line in the a register, as seen in Figure 20.2. (The text also goes into the unnamed register at the same time.)

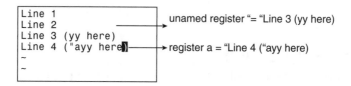

Figure 20.2   Using the a register for yank and put.

Unnamed Register

It seems a bit silly to name the unnamed register, "The Unnamed Register," because this gives it a name. The name is a misnomer, because the unnamed register is named "The Unnamed Register." So, in fact, the unnamed register has a name even though it calls itself "The Unnamed Register."

Persons understanding the preceding paragraph have demonstrated aptitude for writing programs and are urged to enroll in their nearest engineering college.

To get an idea of what the registers contain, execute the following command:

```
:registers
```

Figure 20.3 shows the results of this command.

```
~
:registers
--- Registers ---
""   Line 3 (yy here)^J
"0   Line 3 (yy here)^J
"1   We will tdelete he word in the middle
"2   /* File for bad names */^J
"3   Line 2^J
"4   To err is human --^J     to really scre
"5   ^J
"6   ^J
"7       to really screw up, you need a com
"a   Line 4 ("ayy here)^J
"-   to be yy'ed)
".   "ayy here)
":   registers
"%   test.txt
"#   tmp.txt
Press RETURN or enter command to continue█
```

Figure 20.3 `:registers` command.

This illustration shows that the unnamed register (") contains **Line 3 (yy here)**.

The a register contains **Line 4 ("ayy here)**.

The alphabetic registers are the normal ones used for yanking and pasting text. Other, special registers are described in the following sections.

You can display the contents of specific registers by giving them as an argument to the **:registers** command. For example, the following command displays the contents of registers a and x:

```
:registers ax
```

Appending Text

When you use a command such as **"ayy**, you replace the text in the register with the current line. When you use the uppercase version of a register, say **"Ayy**, you append the text to what is already in the register (see Figure 20.4).

Note that the result is two lines, "Line 3" and "Line 2". (The ^J in the register indicates end of line.)

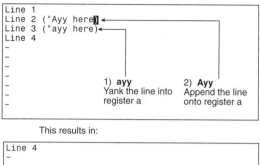

```
Line 1
Line 2 ("Ayy here)
Line 3 ("ayy here)
Line 4
~
~
~
~
~
~
~
                    1) ayy              2) Ayy
                    Yank the line into  Append the line
                    register a          onto register a
```

This results in:

```
Line 4
~
~
~
~
~
~
~
:register a
--- Registers ---
"a   Line 3 ("ayy here)^JLine 2 ("Ayy here)^J
Press RETURN or enter command to continue
```

Figure 20.4 Appending text to a register.

Special Registers

Vim has a number of special registers. The first is the unnamed register, whose name is double quote (").

Others include the registers 1 through 9. Register 1 contains the last text you deleted; register 2 the next to last, and so on.

(Back in the bad old days of *Vi*, these registers were a lifesaver. You see, *Vi* had only one level of undo. So if you deleted three lines by executing **dd** three times, you were out of luck if you wanted to undo the delete using the **u** command. Fortunately, the three lines were stored in registers 1, 2, and 3, so you could put them back with **"1P"2P"3P**. You can also use the command **""P..** (**""**P and two dots).

Other special registers include the following:

Register	Description	Writeable
0	The last yanked text	Yes
-	The last small delete	No
.	The last inserted text	No
%	The name of the current file	No
#	The name of the alternate file	No
/	The last search string	No
:	The last ":" command	No
_	The black hole (more on this later)	Yes
=	An expression (see next page)	No
*	The text selected with the mouse	Yes

The Black Hole Register (_)

Placing text into the black hole register causes it to disappear. You can also "put" the black hole register, but this is pretty much useless because the black hole register always contains nothing.

The black hole register is useful when you want to delete text without having it go into the 1 through 9 registers. For example, **dd** deletes a line and stores it in 1. The command **"_dd** deletes a line and leaves 1 alone.

The Expression Register (=)

The expression register (=) is designed so that you can enter expressions into text. When you enter a command beginning with an expression register specification, the *Vim* editor displays the prompt = at the end of the screen. This gives you an opportunity to type in an expression such as **38*56**, and you can then put the result into the text with the **p** command. For example **"=38*56<Enter>p** gives you 2128. Figure 20.5 shows this register in action.

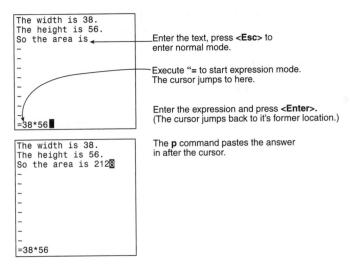

```
The width is 38.
The height is 56.
So the area is
~
~
~
~
~
~
=38*56
```
Enter the text, press **<Esc>** to enter normal mode.

Execute "= to start expression mode. The cursor jumps to here.

Enter the expression and press **<Enter>**. (The cursor jumps back to it's former location.)

```
The width is 38.
The height is 56.
So the area is 2128
~
~
~
~
~
~
=38*56
```
The **p** command pastes the answer in after the cursor.

Figure 20.5   The expression register.

An expression can contain all the usual arithmetic operators (*, +, -, /, and so on) as well as a ton of specialized *Vim* functions and operators. If you are doing more than simple arithmetic, you will want to check the full expression documentation.

You can specify the value of an environment variable, for example, by using the expression $*NAME* (for instance, **$HOME**). You can determine the value of a *Vim* variable by just specifying the variable (**LineSize**, for instance).

The Clipboard Register (*)

The clipboard register (*) enables you to read and write data to the system clipboard. This can be the X selection (UNIX) or the Microsoft Windows Clipboard. This enables you to cut and paste text between the *Vim* editor and other applications.

How to Edit All the Files That Contain a Given Word

If you are a UNIX user, you can use a combination of *Vim* and *Grep* to edit all the files that contain a given word. This proves extremely useful if you are working on a program and want to view or edit all the files that contain a specified variable.

Suppose, for example, that you want to edit all the C program files that contain the word *frame_counter*. To do this, you use the following command:

```
$ vim `grep -l 'frame_counter' *.c`
```

Consider this command in detail. The **grep** command searches through a set of files for a given word. Because the **-l** option is specified, the command will list only the files containing the word and not print the line itself. The word it is searching for is *frame_counter*. Actually, this can be any regular expression. (Note that what *Grep* uses for regular expressions is not as complete or complex as what *Vim* uses.)

The entire command is enclosed in backticks (`). This tells the UNIX shell to run this command and pretend that the results were typed on the command line. So what happens is that the **grep** command is run and produces a list of files; these files are put on the *Vim* command line. This results in *Vim* editing the file list that is the output of *Grep*.

You might be asking, "Why show this here?" This is a feature of the UNIX shell (for example, **bash**), and is not part of *Vim*'s repertoire. The way to accomplish something similar within *Vim*, and which works on Win32 as well, is as follows:

```
:arg `grep -l 'frame_counter' *.c`
```

This command sets the argument list (for example, the files "on the command line," as it were).

> **Note**
>
> The *Vim* command **:grep** can perform a similar function.

Editing a Specific File

To edit a specific file in this list (file 2, for instance), you need the following command:

```
:argument 2
```

This command enables you to specify a file by its position in the argument list.

Suppose, for instance, that you start *Vim* with this command:

```
$ gvim one.c two.c three.c four.c five.c six.c seven.c
```

The following command causes you to be thrown into the file **four.c**.

```
:argument 4
```

Changing the File List

The file list is initially set to the list of files you specify on the command line. You can change this list by specifying a new list to the **:args** command. For example:

```
:args alpha.c beta.c gamma.c
```

After executing this command, you start editing `alpha.c`; the next file is `beta.c` and so on. (The previous file list is lost.)

> **Note**
>
> The **:next** *file-list* command will do the same thing.

The *+cmd* Argument

Suppose that you want to start editing a file at line 97. You can start *Vim* and execute a **97G**, or you can tell *Vim* to start editing with the cursor on line 97. You can do this by using the option *+linenumber* on the command line. For example:

```
$ gvim +97 file.c
```

You can also use the *+cmd* to search for a string by using *+/string* on the command line. To start editing a file with the cursor positioned on the first line containing **#include**, for instance, use this command:

```
$ vim +/#include file.c
```

Finally, you can put any command-mode command after the plus sign (+).

You can specify the *+cmd* argument in a number of commands. For example, the general form of the **:vi** command is as follows:

```
:vi [+cmd] {file}
```

These other commands can take a *+cmd*:

```
:next [+cmd]
:wnext [+cmd]
:previous [+cmd]
:wprevious [+cmd]
:Next [+cmd]
:wNext [+cmd]
:rewind [+cmd]
:last [+cmd]
```

Global Marks

The marks a–z are local to the file. In other words, you can place a mark a in file one.c and another mark a in file two.c. These marks are separate and have nothing to do with each other. If you execute a go-to-mark command, such as 'a, you will jump within that file to the given mark.

The uppercase marks (A–Z) differ. They are global. They mark not only the location within the file, but also the file itself.

Take a look at an example. You are editing the file one.c and place the mark A in it. You then go on to edit file two.c. When you execute the jump-to-mark-A command ('A), the *Vim* editor will switch you from file two.c to file one.c and position the cursor on the mark.

For example, you are editing a bunch of C files named alpha.c, beta.c, and gamma.c. You execute the following commands:

1. **/#include**   Find the first **#include** (in **alpha.c**).

2. **mi**   Mark it with the mark **i**.

```
                    ┌───────────────────────────┐
mark "i" ─────────► │ /* alpha.c */             │
                    │ #include <stdio.h>        │
                    │                           │
                    │ int alph(void)            │
                    │ {                         │
                    │     printf("In alpha\n"); │
                    │ }                         │
                    └───────────────────────────┘
```

3. **:next**   Go to file beta.c.

4. **n**   Find the first include.

5. **mi**   Mark it with the mark i.

6. **/magic_function**   Find the magic function.

7. **mF**   Mark it with the mark F.

```
                    ┌──────────────────────────────┐
mark "i" ─────────► │ /* beta.c */                 │
                    │ #include <stdio.h>           │
                    │                              │
mark "F" ─────────► │ int magic_function(void)     │
                    │ {                            │
                    │     printf("In beta\n");     │
                    │ }                            │
                    │ "beta.c" 8L, 88C             │
                    └──────────────────────────────┘
```

8. **:next** Go to file gamma.c.

9. **/#include** Find the first include.

10. **mi** Mark it with the mark i.

```
                        /* gamma.c */
mark "i" ─────────────▶ ▓include <stdio.h>

                        int gamma(void)
                        {
                            printf("In gamma\n");
                        }
                        "gamma.c" 8L, 81C
```

After executing these commands, you have three local marks, all named i. If you execute the command **'i**, you jump to the mark in your buffer. The mark F is global because it is uppercase.

Currently you are in file gamma.c. When you execute the command to go to mark F (**'F**), you switch files to beta.c.

Now you use the following command to go to alpha.c.

```
:rewind
```

Place the F mark there because this is a global mark (you can put it in only one place), the mark named F in the file **beta.c** disappears.

Advanced Text Entry

When you are entering text in insert mode, you can execute a number of different commands. For example, the **<BS>** command erases the character just before the cursor. **CTRL-U** erases the entire line (or at least the part you just inserted). **CTRL-W** deletes the word before the cursor.

Movement

Even though you are in insert mode, you can still move the cursor. You cannot do this with the traditional *Vim* keys **h**, **j**, **k**, and **l**, because these would just be inserted. But you can use the arrow keys **<Left>**, **<Right>**, **<Up>**, and **<Down>**. If you hold down the Control key, you can move forward and backward words. In other words, execute **<C-Left>** to go backward one word, and **<C-Right>** forward.

The **<Home>** command moves the cursor to the beginning of a line, and **<End>** moves to the end. The key **<C-Home>** moves to the beginning of the file, and **<C-End>** moves to the end.

The **<PageUp>** moves one screen backward, and **<PageDown>** a screen forward.

Inserting Text

If you type **CTRL-A**, the editor inserts the text you typed the last time you were in insert mode.

Assume, for example, that you have a file that begins with the following:

```
"file.h"
/* Main program begins */
```

You edit this file by inserting **#include** at the beginning of the first line:

```
#include "file.h"
/* Main program begins */
```

You go down to the beginning of the next line using the command **j^**. You now start to insert a new line that contains a new **include** line. So you type **iCTRL-A**. The result is as follows:

```
#include "file.h"
#include /* Main program begins */
```

The **#include** was inserted because **CTRL-A** inserts the contents of the previous insert. Now you type **"main.c"<Enter>** to finish the line:

```
#include "file.h"
#include "main.h"
/* Main program begins */
```

The **CTRL-@** command does a **CTRL-A** and then exits insert mode.

The **CTRL-V** command is used to quote the next character. In other words, any special meaning the character has, it will be ignored. For example, **CTRL-V<Esc>** inserts an escape. You can also use the command **CTRL-V***digits* to insert the character number *digits*. For example, the character number 64 is **@**. So **CTRL-V64** inserts **@**. The **CTRL-V***digits* uses "decimal" digits by default, but you can also insert the "hex" digits. For example,

```
CTRL-V123
```

and

```
CTRL-Vx7b
```

both insert the **{** character.

The **CTRL-Y** command inserts the character above the cursor. This is useful when you are duplicating a previous line.

One of my favorite tricks is to use ASCII art to explain complex things such as regular expressions. For example:

```
[0-9]*[a-z]*
|||||||||||+—— Repeat 0 or more times
||||||+++++—— Any lower case letter
|||||+——————— Repeat 0 or more times
+++++—————————· Any digit
```

Take a look at how you can use **CTRL-Y** to create this file. You start by entering the first two lines:

```
[0-9]*[a-z]*
¦¦¦¦¦¦¦¦¦¦¦¦¦+-— Repeat 0 or more times
```

Now you type **CTRL-Y** six times. This copies the ¦ from the previous line down six times:

```
[0-9]*[a-z]*
¦¦¦¦¦¦¦¦¦¦¦¦¦+-— Repeat 0 or more times
¦¦¦¦¦¦
¦¦¦¦¦¦
```

The **CTRL-E** command acts like **CTRL-Y** except it inserts the character below the cursor.

Inserting a Register

The command **CTRL-R***register* inserts the text in the register. If it contains characters such as **<BS>** or other special characters, they are interpreted as if they had been typed from the keyboard. If you do not want this to happen (you really want the **<BS>** to be inserted in the text), use the command **CTRL-R CTRL-R** *register*.

First you enter the following line:

```
All men^H^H^Hpeople are created equal
```

> **Note**
>
> To enter the backspace characters (which show up as **^H**), you need to type **CTRL-V<BS>** or **CTRL-V CTRL-H**.

Now you dump this into register a with the command **"ayy**.

Next you enter insert mode and use **CTRL-Ra** to put the text into the file. The result is as follows:

```
All men^H^H^Hpeople are created equal    (original line)
All people are created equal             (CTRL-Ra line)
```

Notice that *Vim* put the contents in as if you had typed them. In other words, the **<BS>** character (**^H**) deletes the previous character.

Now if you want to put the contents of the register in the file without interpretation, you could use **CTRL-R CTRL-R a**. This results in the following:

```
All men^H^H^Hpeople are created equal    (original line)
All people are created equal             (CTRL-Ra line)
All men^H^H^Hpeople are created equal    (CTRL-R CTRL-R a)
```

Leaving Insert Mode

The command **CTRL-\ CTRL-N** ends insert mode and goes to normal mode. In other words, it acts like **<Esc>**. The only advantage this has over **<Esc>** is that it works in all modes.

Finally, **CTRL-O** executes a single normal-mode command and goes back to insert mode. If you are in insert mode, for instance, and type **CTRL-Odw**, the *Vim* editor goes into normal mode, deletes a word (**dw**), and then returns to insert mode.

The *viminfo* File

The problem with global marks is that they disappear when you exit *Vim*. It would be nice if they stuck around.

The `viminfo` file is designed to store information on marks as well as the following:

- Command-line history
- Search-string history
- Input-line history
- Registers
- Marks
- Buffer list
- Global variables

The trick is that you have to enable it. This is done through the following command:

```
:set viminfo=string
```

The string specifies what to save.

The syntax of this string is an option character followed by an argument. The option/argument pairs are separated by commas.

Take a look at how you can build up your own `viminfo` string.

First, the ' option is used to specify how many files for which you save local marks (a–z). Pick a nice even number for this option (1000, for instance). Your **viminfo** option now looks like this:

```
:set viminfo='1000
```

The **f** option controls whether global marks (A–Z 0–9) are stored. If this option is 0, none are stored. If it is 1 or you do not specify an **f** option, the marks are stored. You want this feature, so now you have this:

```
:set viminfo='1000,f1
```

The **r** option tells *Vim* about removable media. Marks for files on removable media are not stored. The idea here is that jump to mark is a difficult command to execute if the file is on a floppy disk that you have left in your top desk drawer at home. You can specify the **r** option multiple times; therefore, if you are on a Microsoft Windows system, you can tell *Vim* that floppy disks A and B are removable with the **r** option:

```
:set viminfo='1000,f1,rA:,rB:
```

UNIX has no standard naming convention for floppy disks. On my system, however, the floppy disk is named /mnt/floppy; therefore, to exclude it, I use this option:

```
:set viminfo='1000,f1,r/mnt/floppy
```

Note

There is a 50-character limit on the names of the removable media.

The \" option controls how many lines are saved for each of the registers. By default, all the lines are saved. If 0, nothing is saved. You like the default, so you will not be adding a \" specification to the **viminfo** line.

The : option controls the number of lines of : history to save. 100 is enough for us:

```
:set viminfo='1000,f1,r/mnt/floppy,:100,
```

The / option defines the size of the search history. Again 100 is plenty:

```
:set viminfo='1000,f1,r/mnt/floppy,:100,/100
```

Note that *Vim* will never store more lines than it remembered. This is set with the **'history'** option.

Generally, when *Vim* starts, if you have the **'hlsearch'** option set, the editor highlights the previous search string (left over from the previous editing sessions). To turn off this feature, put the **h** flag in your **'viminfo'** option list. (Or you can just start *Vim*, see the highlighting, and decide you do not like it and execute a **:nohlsearch**.)

The **'@'** option controls the number of items to save in the input-line history. (The input history records anything you type as result of an **input** function call.) For this example, let this default to the size of the input-line history.

If the **'%'** option is present, save and restore the buffer list. The buffer list is restored only if you do not specify a file to edit on the command line:

```
:set viminfo='1000,f1,r/mnt/floppy,:100,/100,%
```

The **'!'** option saves and restores global variables. (These are variables whose names are all uppercase.)

```
:set viminfo='1000,f1,r/mnt/floppy,:100,/100,%,!
```

Finally, the **n** option specifies the name of the viminfo file. By default, this is $HOME/.viminfo on UNIX. On Microsoft Windows, the file is as follows:

```
$HOME\_viminfo          if $HOME is set
$VIM\_viminfo           if $VIM is set
C:\_viminfo             otherwise
```

The **'n'** option must be the last option parameter. Because we like the default filename, we leave this option off. Therefore, the full **viminfo** line is this:

```
:set viminfo='1000,f1,r/mnt/floppy,:100,/100,%,!
```

You can put this command and other initializations into a `vimrc` initialization file. The `viminfo` file is automatically written when the editor exits, and read upon initialization. But you may want to write and read it explicitly.

The following command writes the `viminfo` file:

`:wviminfo[!] [file]`

If a file is specified, the information is written to that file.

Similarly, you can read the `viminfo` file using this command:

`:rviminfo [file]`

This reads all the settings from *file*. If any settings conflict with currently existing settings, however, the file settings will not be used. If you want the information in the `viminfo` file to override the current settings, use the following command:

`:rviminfo! [file]`

Dealing with Long Lines

Sometimes you will be editing a file that is wider than the number of columns in the window. When that occurs, *Vim* wraps the lines so that everything fits on the screen (see Figure 20.6).

If you set the `'nowrap'` option, each line in the file shows up as one line on the screen. Then the ends of the long lines disappear off the screen to the right (see Figure 20.7).

Wrapped line

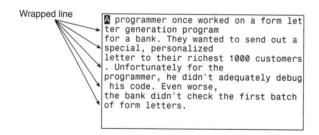

Figure 20.6 Text wrapping.

```
A programmer once worked on a form let
for a bank. They wanted to send out a
letter to their richest 1000 customers
programmer, he didn't adequately debug
the bank didn't check the first batch

The result: the wealthiest 1000 custom
that began, "Dear Rich Bastard."
~
~
~
:set nowrap
```

Figure 20.7 `:set nowrap`.

By default, *Vim* does not display a horizontal scrollbar on the GUI. If you want to enable one, as shown in Figure 20.8, use the following command:

```
:set guioptions+=b
```

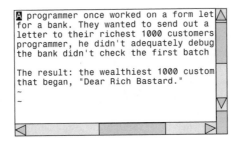

Figure 20.8 Horizontal scrollbar.

This window can be scrolled horizontally. All you have to do is position the cursor on a long line and move to the right using the **l** or **$** command. Figure 20.9 shows what happens when you do a little horizontal scrolling.

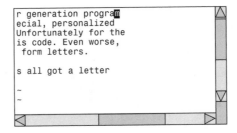

Figure 20.9 Horizontal scrolling.

The **^** command moves to the first non-blank character of the line. The **g^** command moves to the first non-blank character on the screen. If there is text to the left of the window, it is ignored. There are a number of similar **g**-type commands:

Command	Command	Meaning (When nowrap Set)
^	g^	Leftmost non-blank character on the screen
<Home>	g<Home>	
0	g0	Leftmost character on the screen
<End>	g<End>	
$	g$	Rightmost character on the screen
	gm	Move to the middle of the screen

Figure 20.10 shows how these commands work.

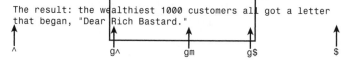

```
A programmer once worked on a form letter generation program
for a bank. They wanted to send out a special, personalized
letter to their richest 1000 customers. Unfortunately for the
programmer, he didn't adequately debug his code. Even worse,
the bank didn't check the first batch of form letters.

The result: the wealthiest 1000 customers all got a letter
that began, "Dear Rich Bastard."

    ^             g^           gm          g$            $
```

Figure 20.10 Line-movement commands.

The [count]| command goes to the count column on the screen.

The [count]**zh** command scrolls the screen [count] characters left while the **zl** command does the same thing to the right.

The **zL** command scrolls half a screen to the left and the **zR** command scrolls half screen to the right.

The **j** or **<Down>** command moves down a line. These command move down lines in the file. Take a look at Figure 20.11.

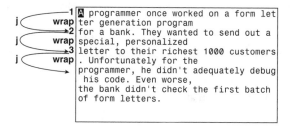

Figure 20.11 The **j** (down) command.

In this case, line 3 has wrapped. Now you start with the cursor on line 2. Executing a **j** command moves you to the beginning of line 3. Another **j** and you are down to the beginning of line 4. Note that although you have moved down a line in text space, you have moved down two lines in screen space.

Typing a **gj** or **g<Down>** command moves one line down in screen space. Therefore, if you start at the beginning of line 3 and type **gj**, you wind up one line down in screen space (see Figure 20.12). This is halfway between line 3 and line 4. (In file space, you are on the middle of line 3.)

The **gk** and **g<Up>** commands do the same thing going up.

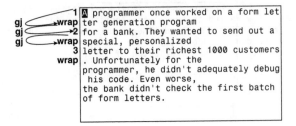

Figure 20.12   The **gj** (down screen line) command.

Wrapping

By default, the *Vim* editor wraps long lines. It does this by putting as much of the line as possible on the first screen line, and then to breaking it, and putting the rest on the next line.

You can to turn this off by setting the following option:

```
:set nowrap
```

With this option set, long lines just disappear off the right side of the screen. When you move the cursor along them, the screen scrolls horizontally and you can see what you are doing.

You can customize wrapping by setting some *Vim* options.

First of all, you can tell *Vim* to break lines at nice places by setting the option:

```
:set linebreak
```

Figure 20.13 shows how this option affects the screen.

```
A programmer once worked on a form
 letter generation program
for a bank. They wanted to send ou
t a special, personalized
letter to their richest 1000 custo
mers. Unfortunately for the
programmer, he didn't adequately d
ebug his code. Even worse,
the bank didn't check the first ba
tch of form letters.
```
:set nolinebreak

```
A programmer once worked on a
form letter generation program
for a bank. They wanted to send
out a special, personalized
letter to their richest 1000
customers. Unfortunately for the
programmer, he didn't adequately
debug his code. Even worse,
the bank didn't check the first
batch of form letters.
:set linebreak
```
:set linebreak

Figure 20.13   The **linebreak** option.

But what defines a "nice" place on the line. The answer is the characters in the **'breakat'** option. By default, these are ^ **I** ! @ * - + _ ; : , . / **?**. Now suppose you do not want to break words with _ in them. You need to remove _ from the list of **'breakat'** characters, so you execute the following command:

```
:set breakat -=_
```

Usually when lines are broken, nothing is put at the beginning of the continuation lines. You can change this, however, by defining the `'showbreak'` option. For example:

```
:set showbreak="——>"
```

Finally, there is the question of what to do if you need to break a line at the end of the screen. You have two choices: First, you can refuse to display half of a line. The *Vim* editor will display an @ at the bottom of the screen to indicate "there is a long line here that we cannot fit it on the screen. Second, you can display half the line.

The *Vim* default is method one. If you want to use method two, execute this command:

```
:set display=lastline
```

21

All About Windows and Sessions

I N CHAPTER 5, "WINDOWS," YOU LEARNED THE basic commands for using windows. But there are a lot more window-related commands. This chapter discusses many different commands for selecting and arranging windows. You will also learn how to customize the appearance of the windows.

Finally, this chapter discusses session files. These files enable you to save and restore all your editing and window settings so that you can return to editing where you left off.

The topics covered in this chapter include the following:

- Moving between windows
- Moving windows up and down
- Performing operations on all windows
- Editing the "alternate" file
- Split searches
- Shorthand operators
- Advanced buffer commands
- Session files

Moving Between Windows

As previously discussed, **CTRL-Wj** goes to the next window and **CTRL-Wk** goes to the preceding one. The following commands also change windows.

CTRL-Wt	Go to the top window.
CTRL-Wb	Go to the bottom window.
CTRL-Wp	Go to the window you were in before you switched to this one. (Go to the preceding window.)

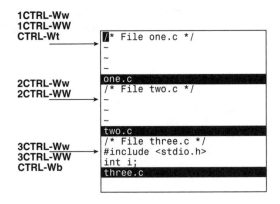

Figure 21.1 Window selection commands.

*count***CTRL-Ww** Go down a window. If at the bottom, wrap. If *count* is specified, go to the window number *count*.

*count***CTRL-WW** Go up a window. If at the top, wrap. If *count* is specified, go to the window number *count*.

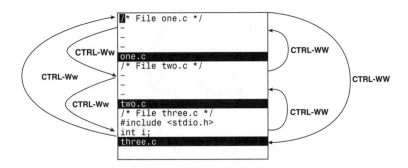

Figure 21.2 More window selection commands.

Moving Windows Up and Down

The **CTRL-Wr** command rotates the windows downward (see Figure 21.3).

The **CTRL-Wr** command takes a *count* argument, which is the number of times to perform the rotate down.

The **CTRL-WR** command rotates the windows upward (see Figure 21.4).

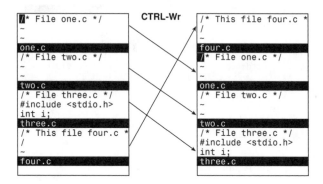

Figure 21.3 Rotating a window down.

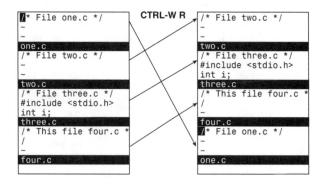

Figure 21.4 Rotating a window up.

The **CTRL-Wx** command exchanges the current window with the next one (see Figure 21.5). If the current window is the bottom window, there is no next window, so it exchanges the current window with the previous one.

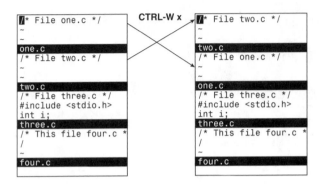

Figure 21.5   Exchanging a window.

Performing Operations on All Windows

The **:write** command writes out the current file. If you want to write all the files that have been modified (including hidden buffers), use the following command:

```
:wall
```

The quit command (**:quit**) closes the current window. (If this is the last window for a file, the file is closed.) If you have multiple windows up, you can quit them all using this command:

```
:qall
```

If some of the files have been modified, and the changes have not been saved, the **:qall** command fails. If you want to abandon the changes you have made, use the force option (**!**), which gives you this command:

```
:qall!
```

(Use this with caution because you can easily discard work you wanted to keep.)

If you want to perform a combination of **:wall** and **:qall**, use this command:

```
:wqall
```

Other Window Commands

The **CTRL-Wo** command makes the current window the only one on the screen. As Figure 21.6 shows, all the other windows are closed. (The system pretends that you did a **:quit** in each of them.)

If you have specified multiple files on the command line or through the **:argument** *file-list* command, the **:all** command opens up a window for each file (see Figure 21.7).

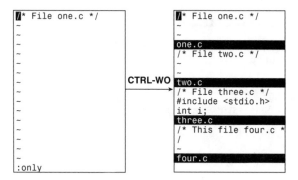

Figure 21.6   The CTRL-Wo command.

Figure 21.7   :all.

A variation of the :all command opens a new window for each hidden buffer:

```
:unhide
```

This command can take an argument that limits the number of windows that can be opened at one time. To unhide all the buffers but put no more than five windows onscreen, for example, use the following command:

```
:unhide 5
```

Editing the Alternate File

You can split the window and edit the alternate file with the command CTRL-W CTRL-^. Figure 21.8 shows the results.

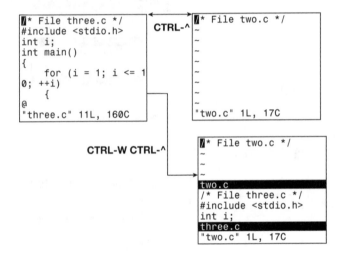

Figure 21.8   CTRL-W CTRL-^.

Split Search

The CTRL-W CTRL-I command splits the window, and then searches for the first occurrence of the word under the cursor. This search goes through not only the current file, but also any #include files.

If you position the cursor of the printf on *Hello World* and press CTRL-W CTRL-I, you get a screen that looks like Figure 21.9.

```
extern int fprintf _P ((FILE *_restrict _stream,
                        _const char *_restrict _format, ...));
/* Write formatted output to stdout. */
extern int printf _P ((_const char *_restrict _format, ...));
/* Write formatted output to S. */
extern int sprintf _P ((char *_restrict _s,
                        const char _* restrict _format, ...));
/usr/include/stdio.h [RO]
#include <stdio.h>
int main()
{
    printf("Hello World!\n");
    return (0);
}
/tmp/hello.c
```

Figure 21.9   The CTRL-W CTRL-I command.

Shorthand Commands

The *Vim* editor contains some shorthand commands that do the work of multiple commands, including the following:

:*count*snext	:split followed by :*count*next
:*count*sprevious	:split followed by :*count*previous
:*count*sNext	:split followed by :*count*Next
:srewind	:split followed by :rewind
:slast	:split followed by :last
:sargument	:split followed by :argument
CTRL-W CTRL-D	:split followed by]CTRL-D
CTRL-W f	:split followed by a :find
CTRL-Wg]	:split followed a CTRL-]

One nice thing about these commands is that they do not open a new window if they fail.

Advanced Buffers

The following sections discuss adding, deleting, and unloading buffers.

Adding a Buffer

The *Vim* editor maintains a list of buffers. Usually you put a file on the list by editing it. But you can explicitly add it with the following command:

:badd *file*

The named file is merely added to the list of buffers. The editing process will not start until you switch to the buffer. This command accepts an argument:

```
:badd +lnum file
```

When you open a window for the buffer, the cursor will be positioned on *lnum*.

Deleting a Buffer

The **:bdelete** command deletes a buffer. You can specify the buffer by name:

```
:bdelete file.c
```

Or by number:

```
:bdelete 3
:3 bdelete
```

You can also delete a whole range of buffers, as follows:

```
:1,3 bdelete
```

If you use the override (!) option, any changes to the buffer are discarded:

```
:bdelete! file.c
```

Unloading a Buffer

The command **:bunload** unloads a buffer. The buffer is unloaded from memory and all windows for this buffer are closed. However, the file remains listed in the buffer list. The **:bunload** command uses the same syntax as the **:bdelete**.

Opening a Window for Each Buffer

The **:ball** command opens a window for each buffer.

Windowing Options

The **'laststatus'** option controls whether the last window has a status line. (See Figure 21.10.) The three values of this option are as follows:

0   The last window never has a status line.

1   If there is only one window on the screen, do not display the status line. If there are two or more, however, display a status line for the last window. (default).

2   Always display a status line even if there is only one window onscreen.

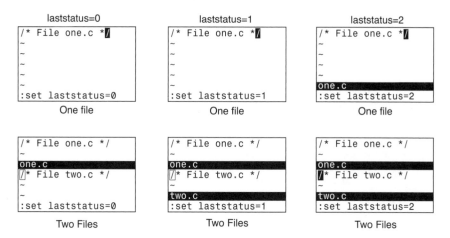

Figure 21.10 `'laststatus'` option.

The `'winheight'` option sets the minimum number of lines for a window. This is not a hard limit; if things get too crowded, *Vim* will make smaller windows.

When the `'equalalways'` option is enabled (the default), *Vim* will always split the screen into equal-size windows. When off, splits can result in windows of different sizes. Figure 21.11 shows the effect of this option.

The `'winheight'` option is the minimum height of the current window. The `'winminheight'` option controls how small any other window can be.

Generally a `:split` command opens a window above the current window. The `'splitbelow'` option causes a new window to appear below the current one.

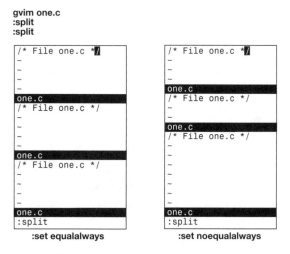

Figure 21.11 `'equalalways'` option.

Sessions

Suppose you are editing along, and it is the end of the day. You want to quit work and pick up where you left off the next day. You can do this by saving your editing session and restoring it the next day.

A *Vim* session contains all the information about what you are editing. This includes things such as the file list, windows, marks, registers, and other information. (Exactly what is controlled by the `'sessionoptions'` option is described later in the section "Specifying What Is Saved in a Session.")

The following command creates a session file:

```
:mksession file
```

For example:

```
:mksession vimbook.vim
```

Later if you want to restore this session, you can use this command:

```
:source vimbook.vim
```

If you want to start *Vim* and restore a specific session, you can use the following command:

```
$ vim -c ":source vimbook.vim"
```

(This tells *Vim* to execute a specific command on startup (`-c`). The command is `:source vimbook.vim`, which loads the session `vimbook.vim`.)

Specifying What Is Saved in a Session

The `'sessionoption'` option controls what is saved in a session file. It is a string of keywords separated by commas. For example, the default `'sessionoptions'` setting is as follows:

```
:set sessionoptions=buffers,winsize,options,help,blank
```

The various keywords are

`buffers`	Saves all buffers. This includes the ones on the screen as well as the hidden and unloaded buffers.
`globals`	Saves the global variables that start with an uppercase letter and contain at least one lowercase letter.
`help`	The help window.
`blank`	Any blank windows on the screen.
`options`	All options and keyboard mapping.
`winpos`	Position of the GUI *Vim* window.
`resize`	Size of the screen.

winsize   Window sizes (where possible).

slash   Replace backslashes in filenames with forward slashes. This option is useful if you share session files between UNIX and Microsoft Windows. (You should set UNIX as well.)

unix   Write out the file using the UNIX end-of-line format. This makes the session portable between UNIX and Microsoft Windows.

Note

If you enable both the **slash** and **unix** options, the session files are written out in a format designed for UNIX. The Microsoft Windows version of *Vim* is smart enough to read these files.

Unfortunately, the UNIX version of *Vim* is not smart enough to read Microsoft Windows format session files. Therefore, if you want to have portable sessions, you need to force *Vim* to use the UNIX format.

22

Advanced Visual Mode

I N CHAPTER 6, "BASIC VISUAL MODE," YOU LEARNED HOW TO perform the simple
visual commands. Now you can take a look at many of the other visual-related commands. Many of these commands have a limited audience; but read on, that audience
may include you.

In this chapter, you learn about the following:

- Using visual mode with text registers
- Using the **$** selection command
- Reselecting text
- Additional highlighting commands
- Miscellaneous editing commands
- Select mode

Visual Mode and Registers

Chapter 4, "Text Blocks and Multiple Files," showed you how to use the yank, put,
and delete commands with registers. You can do similar things with the visual-mode
commands.

To delete a block of text, for instance, highlight in visual mode and then use the **d**
command. To delete the text into a register, use the command **"*register* d**.

To yank the text into a register, use the **y** command.

The **D** and the **Y** commands act like their lowercase counterparts, except they work on entire lines, whereas **d** and **y** work on just the highlighted section.

The $ Command

In block visual mode, the **$** command causes the selection to be extended to the end of all the lines in the selection. Moving the cursor up or down extends the select text to the end of the line. This extension occurs even if the new lines are longer than the current ones. Figure 22.1 shows what happens when you *don't* use the **$** command, and Figure 22.2 shows what happens when this command is used.

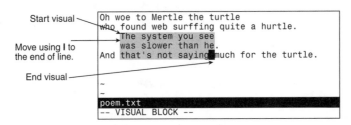

Figure 22.1   Block visual mode without **$** command.

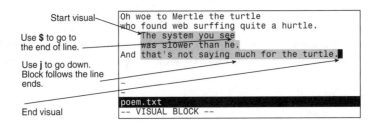

Figure 22.2   Block visual mode with the **$** command.

Repeating a Visual Selection

The **gv** command repeats the preceding visual mode selection. If you are already in visual mode, it selects the preceding selection. Repeated **gv** commands toggle between the current and preceding selection. Figure 22.3 shows the effects of these commands. The steps are as follows:

1. First visual selection.

2. Finished with visual.

3. **gv** reselects the old visual.

4. Define new visual.

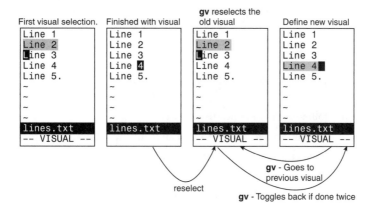

Figure 22.3 The **gv** command.

Selecting Objects

A number of commands in visual mode are designed to help you highlight the text you want.

The **aw** command, for example, highlights the next word. Actually it highlights not only the word, but also the space after it. At first this may seem a bit useless. After all, the **w** command moves you forward one word, so why not just use it?

That is because when you perform a selection, the text selected is from the old cursor location to the new one *inclusive*. Now if you use the **w** command to move, the result is that the cursor is placed on the first character of the next word. Therefore if you delete the text, you not only get the words you selected, but the first character of the next word.

The **aw** command leaves the cursor positioned just before the first character of the next word. In other words, it selects the word and the spaces beyond it, but not the next word.

Another reason to use **aw** rather than **w** is that **aw** selects the whole word, no matter which part of the word the cursor is on, whereas **w** just selects from the current location to the end of the word.

If you want to just select the word, and nothing but the word, use the **iw** (inner word) command. Figure 22.4 shows how **iw** and **aw** work.

```
This is a test of some commands such as aw and iw
```

Figure 22.4   **iw** and **aw** commands.

You can use the following commands to select text:

*count***aw**	Select a word and the space after it.
*count***iw**	Select a word only (inner word).
*count***aW**	Select a WORD and the space after it.
*count***iW**	Select inner WORD (the word only)
*count***as**	Select a sentence (and spaces after it.)
*count***is**	Select the sentence only.
*count***ap**	Select a paragraph and the following space.
*count***ip**	Select a paragraph only.
*count***a(**	From within text enclosed in (), select the text up to and including the ().
*count***i(**	Like **ab**, except the () characters are not selected.

```
for (i = 0; i < 100; ++1)       for (i = 0; i < 100; ++1)
     a(                              i(
```

Figure 22.5   **a(** and **i(** commands.

*count***a<**	Select matching <> pair, include the <>.
*count***i<**	Select matching <> pair, excluding the <>.
*count***a[**	Select matching [] pair, including the [].
*count***i[**	Select matching [] pair, excluding the [].
*count***a{**	Select matching {} pair, including the {}.
*count***i{**	Select matching {} pair, excluding the {}.

Moving to the Other End of a Selection

The **o** command moves the cursor to the other end of a selection (see Figure 22.6). You can then move back to the other end (where you came from) with another **o**.

```
#include <stdio.h>
int i;
int main()
{
    for (i = 1; i <= 10; ++i) {
        printf("%2d squared is %3d\n", i, i*i);
    }
    return (0);
}
three.c [+]
-- VISUAL --
```

o
Toggle between
the two ends of
a selection.

Figure 22.6   The **o** command.

The **O** command moves the cursor to the other corner of the selection in block visual
mode (see Figure 22.7). In other words, the **O** command moves to the other end of the
selection on the same line.

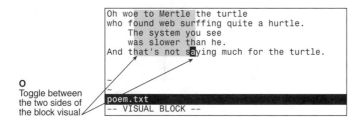

O
Toggle between
the two sides of
the block visual

```
Oh woe to Mertle the turtle
who found web surffing quite a hurtle.
    The system you see
    was slower than he.
And that's not saying much for the turtle.

~
~
~
poem.txt
-- VISUAL BLOCK --
```

Figure 22.7   The **O** command.

Case Changes

The ~ command inverts the case of the selection. The **U** command makes the text
uppercase and the **u** command turns the text into lowercase. Figure 22.8 illustrates
how the various case-changing commands work. The figures show initial selection, ~,
U, and **u**, respectively.

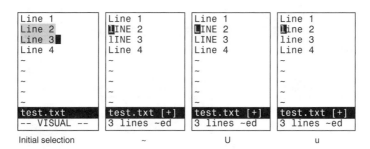

Figure 22.8   Case-changing commands.

Joining Lines

The **J** command joins all the highlighted lines into one long line. Spaces are used to separate the lines.

If you want to join the lines without adding spaces, use the **gJ** command.

Figure 22.9 shows how the **J** and **gJ** commands work.

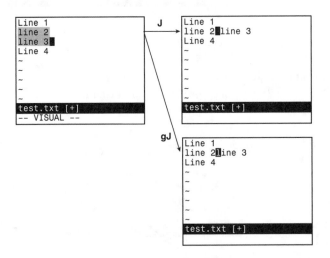

Figure 22.9 **J** and **gJ** commands.

Formatting a Block

The **gq** command formats the text (see Figure 22.10).

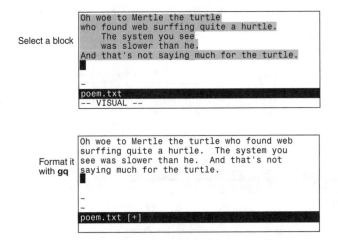

Figure 22.10 The **gq** command.

The Encode (*g?*) Command

The **g?** command encodes or decodes the highlighted text using the rot13 encoding. (This primitive encoding scheme is frequently used to obscure potentially offensive Usenet news postings.)

With rot13, if you encode something twice, you decode it. Therefore if the text is encoded, **g?** decodes it. If it is in plain text, **g?** encodes it. Figure 22.11 shows how this encryption works.

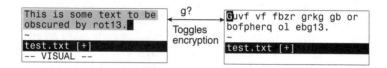

Figure 22.11   The g? command.

The Colon (*:*) Commands

The **:** command starts a command-mode command with a range already specified. If you want to write a block to a file, for example, select the text using visual mode, and then execute the following command:

```
:write block.txt
```

This writes the text to the file **block.txt**.
Note: The **:** command only works on whole lines.

Pipe (*!*) Command

The **!** command pipes a region of text through an external program. For example, the **!sort** pipes the selection through the UNIX sort program. Figure 22.12 shows the visual **!** command used to sort a range of lines.

Figure 22.12   The ! (pipe) command.

> **Note**
> The ! command always works on lines even if you are in character visual mode or visual block mode.

Select Mode

Select mode is yet another visual mode that allows for quick deletion or replacement of the selected text. The way you use select mode is simple. You highlight the text and then type **<BS>** to delete it. Or you can highlight the text, and then replace it by just typing the replacement.

How does select mode compare with visual mode? With visual mode, you highlight the text and then perform an operation. In other words, you need to end the visual mode operation with a command. With select mode, the commands are limited to **<BS>** (for delete) and printable characters (for replacement). This makes things faster because you do not need to enter a command, but it is much more limited than visual mode.

You can choose from three select-mode flavors. The commands to start the various flavors of the select mode are as follows:

gh	Start characterwise selection.
gH	Start linewise selection.
gCTRL-H	Start block selection.

Moving the cursor in select mode is a little more difficult than moving it in normal visual mode because if you type any printable character, you delete the selected text and start inserting. Therefore, to select text, you must use the arrow, CTRL, and function keys.

You can also use the mouse to select text if you set the **'selectmode'** option to **mouse**, as follows:

```
:set selectmode=mouse
```

(Without this option, the mouse performs a visual selection rather than a select-mode selection.)

You can also use the **'selectmode'** option to let the shifted cursor keys enter select mode.

Deleting the Selection

The backspace command (**<BS>** or **CTRL-H**) deletes the selected text (see Figure 22.13).

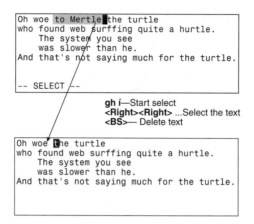

Figure 22.13 Deleting text in select mode.

Replacing Text

Typing any printable character causes the selected text to be deleted and throws *Vim* into insert mode (see Figure 22.14).

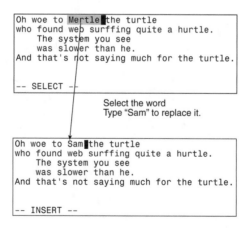

Figure 22.14 Replacing text in select mode.

Switching Modes

The **CTRL-O** command switches from selection mode to visual mode for one command. The **CTRL-G** command switches to visual mode without returning. To switch from visual mode to select mode, use the **CTRL-G** command.

Avoiding Automatic Reselection

Usually when you select text, the text remains selected. Even if you execute a command, the selection remains. The **gV** command causes the selection to disappear after the command is executed. This proves extremely useful for macros that make a selection, do something with it, and then want it to disappear.

23

Advanced Commands for Programmers

T HE *VIM* EDITOR WAS WRITTEN BY PROGRAMMERS who wanted a good text editor. Because of that, *Vim* includes a lot of commands you can use to customize and enhance it to make editing programs easier.

Consider, for example, the problem of the **<Tab>** character. You can deal with this character in many different ways. You can set the tab stops to the indentation size, leave them at the default eight characters, or eliminate them altogether (force everyone to use spaces). The *Vim* editor supports all these types of editing. This chapter shows you how to use each of them.

Previously, you saw how to turn on C indent mode. This chapter describes, in detail, how to customize this mode.

You have learned how to turn syntax highlighting on as well. This chapter takes you a step further, showing you how to customize it.

This chapter discusses the following:

- Removing autoindents
- Inserting registers and indent
- Indentation program options
- Tabbing options
- Customizing C indentation

- Comparing two files
- Using the preview window
- Matching options
- Additional motion commands for programmers
- Commands for editing files in other directories
- Advanced **:make** options
- Customizing the syntax highlighting

Removing an Automatic Indentation

Suppose you are editing a program. You have **'autoindent'** set and are currently indenting in about three levels. You now want to put in a comment block. This is a big block, and you want to put it in column 1, so you need to undo all the automatic indents. One way to this is to type **CTRL-D** a number of times. Or you can use **0CTRL-D**.

The **0CTRL-D** command in insert mode removes all the automatic indentation and puts the cursor in column 1. (Note that when you type the 0, it appears on the screen—at this point, *Vim* thinks you are trying to insert a 0 into the text. When you type in the **CTRL-D**, it realizes you are executing a **0CTRL-D** command and the 0 disappears.)

When you use **0CTRL-D**, the cursor returns to column 1 (see Figure 23.1). The next line also starts in column 1 (normal autoindent behavior).

Suppose, however, that you are typing in a label or an **#ifdef** directive and want to go to column 1 for one line only. In this case, you want the **^CTRL-D** command. This places you in column 1 for the current line only. When you enter the next line, the indent is automatically restored (see Figure 23.2).

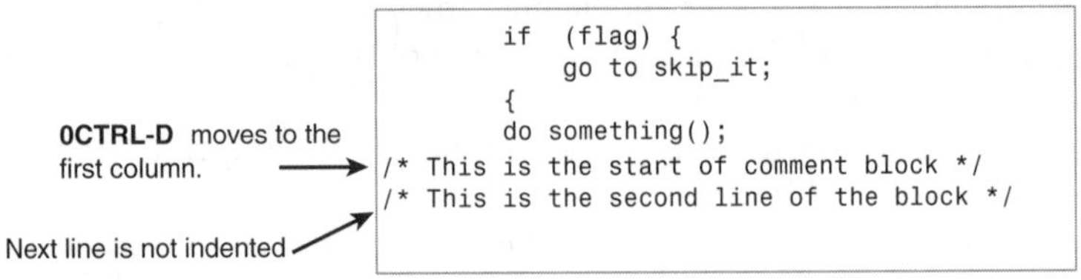

Figure 23.1 The **0CTRL-D** command.

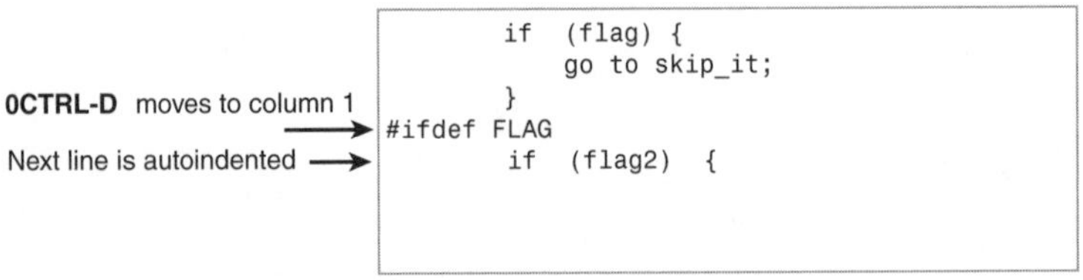

Figure 23.2 The **^CTRL-D** command.

Inserting Indent

The **CTRL-T** command is like a **<Tab>**, except that it inserts an indent the size of the **'shiftwidth'** option. If you use a **'shiftwidth'** of 4, for instance, pressing **<Tab>** moves you to the next 8-column boundary (a **'tabstop'**, assuming that you have the default setting of **'tabstop=8'**). But pressing **CTRL-T** moves us you to the next 4-column boundary.

The **CTRL-T** and **CTRL-D** commands work at any point on the line (not just the beginning). Therefore, you can type some text and then use **CTRL-T** and **CTRL-D** to adjust the indentation.

Inserting Registers

Generally when you use **CTRL-R** to insert the contents of a register, the contents are autoindented. If you do not want this to happen, use the command **CTRL-R CTRL-O** *register*. On the other hand, if you want to insert a register and have *Vim* "do the right thing," use the **CTRL-R CTRL-P** *register* command.

Take a look at how this works. Assume that you are editing a file that contains the following:

```
1 int main()
2 {
3     if (x)
4     {
5         y();
6     }
```

The following settings have been made:

```
:set number
:set cindent
:set shiftwidth=4
```

You start on line 3 and do a **V** to enter line visual mode. Going down to line 6, you highlight the entire **if** block. You dump this in register **a** with the command **"ay**.

Next you add two lines at the end to start another **if**. Your text now looks like this:

```
1 int main()
2 {
3     if (x)
4     {
5         y();
6     }
7     if (z)
8     {
```

Register **a** contains the following:

```
if (x)
{
    y();
}
```

Next you go into insert mode and insert the contents of register a using the command **CTRL-R a**. The result is ugly:

```
 1 int main()
 2 {
 3     if (x)
 4     {
 5      y();
 6     }
 7     if (z)
 8     {
 9             if (x)
10                     {
11                                 y();
12                                 }
```

So what happened? Register **a** contains indented lines. But *Vim* has indenting turned on. Because you inserted the register indent and all, you wound up with double indentation. That was not what you wanted.

Go back to where you were (**CTRL-Ou**, undo) and execute a **CTRL-R CTRL-O a**. The result is as follows:

```
 1 int main()
 2 {
 3     if (x)
 4     {
 5         y();
 6     }
 7     if (z)
 8     {
 9     if (x)
10     {
11         y();
12     }
```

This is better. You do not have the double indents. Trouble is, you still do not have the right indent. The problem is that *Vim* kept the old indent from the original text. Because this line is under the **if (z)** statement, however, it should be indented an extra level.

So you go back and try **CTRL-R CTRL-P a**. The result is as follows:

```
 1 int main()
 2 {
 3     if (x)
 4     {
 5         y();
 6     }
 7     if (z)
 8     {
 9         if (x)
10         {
11             y();
12         }
```

Now *Vim* correctly indented the text by recalculating the indent of each line as it was put in.

In normal mode, the `"register`**p** command inserts the text in the specified register into the buffer. The `"register`**]p** command does the same thing, except each line has its indent adjusted. Similarly, the `"register`**]P** command acts like the `"register`**P** command with indent adjustment.

To Tab or Not to Tab

Back in the early days, B.C. (*before computers*), there existed a communication device called a Teletype. Some models of Teletype could do tabs. Unfortunately, tab stops were set at every eight spaces. When computers came along, their first consoles were Teletypes. Later, when more modern devices (such as video screens) replaced Teletypes, the old tab size of eight spaces was kept for backward compatibility.

This decision has caused programmers no end of trouble. Studies have shown that the most readable indentation size is four spaces. Tab stops are normally eight spaces. How do we reconcile these two facts? People have chosen several ways. The three main ones are as follows:

1. Use a combination of spaces and tabs in your program to enter code. If you need an indentation of 12, for example, use a tab (8) and four spaces (4).

2. Tell the machine that tab stops are only 4 spaces and use tabs everywhere. (This is one solution I personally frown upon, because I do not use the special setting and the text appears to be over-indented.)

3. Throw up your hands and say that tabs are the work of the devil and always use spaces.

The *Vim* editor, thank goodness, supports all three methods.

Spaces and Tabs

If you are using a combination of tabs and spaces, you just edit normally. The *Vim* defaults do a fine job of handling things.

But you can make life a little easier by setting the '**softtabstop**' option. This option tells *Vim* to make the Tab key look and feel as if tabs were set at the value of '**softtabstop**', but use a combination of tabs and spaces to fake things (see Figure 23.3).

After you execute the following command, every time you press the Tab key the cursor moves to the next 4-column boundary:

```
:set softtabstop=4
```

The first time you press it, however, you get 4 spaces inserted in your text. The second time, *Vim* takes out the 4 spaces and puts in a tab (thus taking you to column 8).

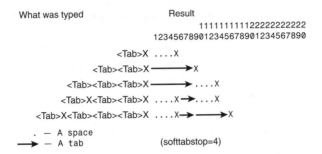

Figure 23.3 Soft tabs.

Smart Tabs

Another related option is the `'smarttab'` option. With this option on (`:set smarttab`), tabs inserted at the beginning of a line are treated like soft tabs. The tab size used in this case is defined the `'shiftwidth'` option.

But tabs inserted elsewhere in the text act just like normal tabs. Note that you must have soft tabs off (`:set softtabstop=0`) for this option to work. Figure 23.4 shows sample results.

Smart indenting is a combination of soft tabs and normal tabs. When you execute the following command, *Vim* treats tabs at the beginning of a line differently:

```
:set smarttab
```

Suppose, for example, that you have the following settings:

```
:set shiftwidth=4
:set tabstop=8
:set smarttabs
```

Tab stops are every eight spaces and the indentation size is four spaces. When you type **<Tab>** at the beginning of a line, the cursor will move over the indentation size (four spaces). Doing a double **<Tab>** moves over two indention sizes (eight spaces [4*2]).

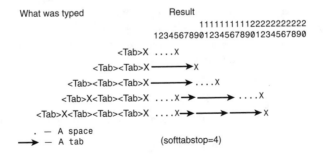

Figure 23.4 Smart tabs.

The following table shows you what happens if you type certain things at the beginning of the line.

You Type	What Is Inserted
`<Tab>`	Four spaces
`<Tab><Tab>`	One tab
`<Tab><Tab><Tab>`	One tab, four spaces
`<Tab><Tab><Tab><Tab>`	Two tabs

When you type `<Tab>` anywhere else in the line, however, it acts like a normal tab.

Using a Different Tab Stop

The following command changes the size of the tab stop to **4**:

```
:set tabstop=4
```

You can actually change it to be any value you want. Figure 23.5 shows what happens when `'tabstop'` is set to **4**.

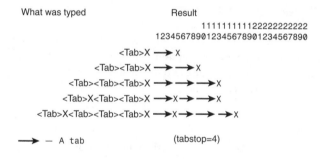

Figure 23.5 **tabstop** set at 4.

> **Note**
>
> Just because you change it in *Vim* does not mean that it will change in your terminal window, that your printing program will not still use eight-character tab stops, or that other editors will use the new setting. Therefore, your type and print commands might require special options to handle things.

No Tabs

If you want absolutely no tabs in your file, you can set the `'expandtab'` option. When this option is set, the Tab key inserts a series of spaces. (Note that setting `'expandtab'` does not affect any existing tabs. In other words, any tabs in the document remain tabs. If you want to convert tabs to spaces, use the `:retab` command, which is explained later.)

> **Note**
>
> If you really want to insert a tab when this option is on, type **CTRL-V\<Tab\>**. The **CTRL-V** command tells *Vim* that you really want to insert this **\<Tab\>** as a tab and not a bunch of spaces.

The *:retab* Command

The **:retab** command transforms text with tab stops at one setting to tab stops with another. You can use it to turn tabs into a series of spaces as well, or a series of spaces into tabs. The **:retab** command transforms text with tab stops at one setting to tap stops with another. For example, suppose that you have a file that was created with tab stops of 4 (**:set tabstop=4**). This is a non-standard setting, and you want to change things so that the tab stops are 8 spaces. (You want the text to look the same, just with different tab stops.)

To change the tap stop in the file from 4 to 8, first execute the command

```
:set tabstop=4
```

The text should appear on the screen correctly. Now execute the command

```
:%retab 8
```

This changes the tab stops to 8. The text will appear unmodified, because *Vim* has changed the white space to match the new value of **'tabstop'**.

For another example, suppose that you are required to produce files with no tabs in them. First, you set the **'expandtabs'** option. This causes the **\<Tab\>** key to insert spaces on any new text you type. But the old text still has tabs in it. To replace these tabs with spaces, execute the command

```
:%retab
```

Because you didn't specify a new tabstop, the current value of **'tabstop'** is used. But because the option **'expandtabs'** is set, all tabs will be replaced with spaces.

Modelines

One of the problems with all these tabbing options is that people use them. Therefore, if you work with files created by three different people, you can easily have to work with many different tab settings. One solution to this problem is to put a comment at the beginning or end of the file telling the reader what tab stops to use. For example:

```
/* vim:tabstop=8:expandtabs:shiftwidth=8 */
```

When you see this line, you can establish the appropriate *Vim* settings, if you want to. But *Vim* is a smart editor. It knows about comments like this and will configure the settings for you. A few restrictions apply. The comment must be formatted in this manner and it must appear in the first or last five lines of the program (unless you change the setting of **'modelines'**).

This type of comment is called a *modeline*.

Shift Details

Suppose that you are typing with a shift width of 4 and you enter a line with 3 spaces in front of it. What should the **>>** command do? Should it add 4 spaces in front of the line or move it to the nearest shift width. The answer depends on the value of the `'shiftround'` option.

Usually this option is not set, so **>>** puts in 4 spaces. If you execute the following command, **>>** moves the indent to the next shift-width boundary:

```
:set shiftround
```

Figure 23.6 shows how this works.

(Note "shiftwidth=4")
With "noshiftround">>moves
the text over 4 spaces

```
12345678901234567890
  size = 20;
    size = 20;
```

With "shiftround">>moves
the text to the next "shiftwidth"
boundary. (In this case, column 4.)

```
12345678901234567890
  size = 20;
    size = 20;
```

Figure 23.6 The `'shiftround'` option.

Specifying a Formatting Program

You can define the program *Vim* uses when executing the **=** command, by setting the `'equalprg'` option. If this option is not set (and you are not editing a lisp program), the *Vim* editor uses its own built-in indentation program that indents C or C++ programs. If you want to use the GNU indent program (available from www.gnu.org), for instance, execute this command:

```
:set equalprg=/usr/local/bin/indent
```

Formatting Comments

One of the great things about *Vim* is that it understands comments. You can ask *Vim* to format a comment and it will do the right thing.

Suppose, for example, that you have the following comment:

```
/*
 * This is a test.
 * Of the text formatting.
 */
```

You then ask *Vim* to format it using the following commands:

1. Position the cursor to the start of the comment.

2. Press **v** to start visual mode.

3. Go to the end of the comment.

4. Format the visual block with the command **gq**.

The result is as follows:

```
/*
 * This is a test. Of the text formatting.
 */
```

Note that *Vim* properly handled the beginning of each line.

(For deciding what is and is not a comment, *Vim* uses the '**comments**' option, described in the following section.)

The **gq**{*motion*} command accomplishes the same thing.

Defining a Comment

The '**comments**' option defines what is a comment. This option is a series of *flag*:*string* pairs.

The possible flags are as follows:

b	Blank must follow. This means the character begins a comment only if followed by a blank or other whitespace.
f	Only the first line has the comment string. Do not repeat the string on the next line, but preserve indentation.
l	When used on part of a three-piece comment, make sure that the middle lines up with the beginning or end. This must be used with either the **s** or **e** flag.
n	Indicates a nested comment.
r	Same as **l**, only right-justify.
x	Tells *Vim* that a three-part comment can be ended by typing just the last character under the following circumstances:

1. You have already typed in the beginning of the comment.

2. The comment has a middle.

3. The first character of the end string is the first character on the line.

For three-part comments, the following flags apply:

s	Start of three-piece comment.
m	Middle of a three-piece comment.
e	End of a three-piece comment.
number	Add the *number* of spaces (can be negative) to the indentation of a middle part of a three-part comment.

A C comment starts with **/***, has a middle of ***, and ends with ***/**, as follows:

```
/*
 * This is a comment
 */
```

This results in the '**comments**' option specification of

```
s1:/*,mb:*,ex:*/
```

The **s1** indicates that this is the start of a three-part comment (**s**) and the other lines in the command need to be indented an extra space (**1**). The comment starts with the string /*.

The middle of the comment is defined by the **mb:*** part. The **m** indicates a middle piece, and the **b** says that a blank must follow anything that is inserted. The text that begins the comment is *.

The ending is specified by **ex:*/**. The **e** indicates the end, and the **x** indicates that you have only to type the last character of the ending to finish the comment. The end delimiter is */.

Take a look at how this definition works. First, you need to set the following option:

```
:set formatoptions=qro
```

The following options prove useful for formatting text (see Chapter 11, "Dealing with Text Files," for complete details):

q   Allow formatting of comments using **gq**.

r   Automatically insert the middle of a comment after pressing **<Enter>**.

o   Automatically insert the middle of a comment when a line inside a comment is opened with an **O** or **o** command.

Now start typing in comments. You start with a line containing the comment header, /*, as follows:

```
/*
```

When you type **<Enter>**, because **r** is in the format options, you get the following:

```
/*
 *
```

The *Vim* editor automatically inserted the * surrounded by a space on each side to make the comment look good. Now enter a comment and a new line:

```
/*
 * This is an example
 *
```

Now you need to end the comment. But *Vim* has already typed a space after the asterisk. How can you enter */? The answer is that *Vim* is smart and will end the comment properly if you just type /. The cursor moves back, the slash is inserted, and you get the following:

```
/*
 * This is an example
 */
```

You can use a number of different formatting commands to format text or comments. For more information on these, see Chapter 11 and Chapter 20, "Advanced Text Blocks and Multiple Files."

Customizing the C Indentation

The C indentation process is controlled by the following options:

`cinkeys`	Defines the keys that trigger an indent event
`cinoptions`	Defines how much to indent
`cinwords`	Defines the C and C++ keywords

The `'cinkeys'` option defines which keys cause a change to indentation. The option is actually a set of *type-char key-char* pairs.

The *type-chars* are as follows:

!   The following key is not inserted. This proves useful when you want to define a key that just causes the line to be re-indented. By default, **CTRL-F** is defined to effect re-indentation.

*   The line will be re-indented before the key is inserted.

0   The key causes an indentation change only if it is the first character typed on the line. (This does not mean that it is the first character on the line, because the line can be autoindented. It specifies the first typed character only.)

The *key-chars* are as follows:

`<name>`	The named key. See Appendix B, "The < > Key Names," for a list of names.
`^X`	Control character (that is, **CTRL-X**).
`o`	Tells *Vim* to indent the line when you use an **o** command to open a new line.
`O`	Line **o**, but for the **O** command.
`e`	Re-indent the line when you type the final *e* in *else*.
`:`	Re-indent the line when you type a colon after a label or case statement.
`<^>, <<>, <>>, <o>, <e>, <O>`	The literal character inside the angle brackets.

The default value for this the `'cinkeys'` option is as follows:

```
0{,0},:,0#,!^F,o,O,e
```

Figure 23.7 shows how the `'cinkeys'` option works.

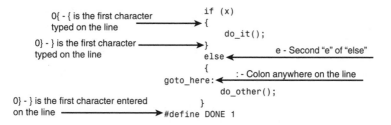

Figure 23.7   The '`cinkeys`' option.

The *'cinoptions'* Options

The '`cinoptions`' option controls how much *Vim* indents each line. This option consists of a series of *key indent* pairs. The *key* is a single letter that controls what part of the program is affected (see the following table and Figures 23.8 and 23.9). The *indent* tells the program how much indentation to use. This can be a number of spaces (for example, 8), or a negative number of spaces (–8). It can also be a multiple of the '`shiftwidth`' option that is specified as **s**. For example, **1s** is a shift width, **0.5s** is half a shift width, and **–1s** un-indents a shift width.

Key	Default	Description
>	s	Normal shift used for indents not covered by another letter.
e	0	Extra indent added to lines following a line with a curly brace that ends a line (or more technically, one that does not begin a line).
n	0	Extra indent added to single lines not inside curly braces after an **if**, **while**, and so on.
f	0	Extra indent added to a function body. Includes the outermost {} that define the function.
{	0	Spaces to be added to opening {.
}	0	Spaces to be added to closing }.
^	0	Spaces to be added to text inside a set of {} that start in column 1. For example, a value of **-1s** causes the body of a function to be pushed one shift width to the left.
:	s	Amount to indent a case inside a switch statement.
=	s	Extra indent for statements after the case statement.
g	s	Indentation for C++ protection keywords (public, private, protected).
h	s	Indentation for statements that follow a protection keyword.
p	s	Shift for K&R-style parameters.

t	s	Indent the type declaration for a function if it is on a separate line.
+	s	Indent for continuation lines (the **2-n** lines of a statement).
c	3	Indent the middle of a multiline comment (if no middle * is present).
(	2s	Indent for a line in the middle of an expression. Actually, the indent for a line that breaks in the middle of a set of ().
u	s	Indent for a line that breaks in the middle of a nested set of () (like **(**, but one level deeper).
)	20	Specify the number of lines to search for closing ().
*	30	Specify the number of lines to search for unclosed comment.

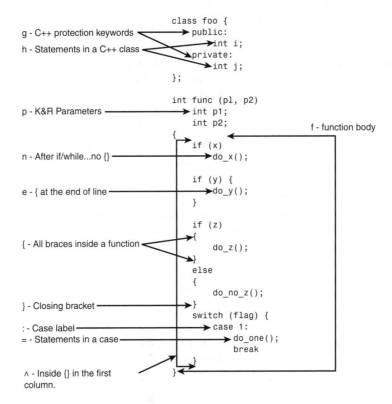

Figure 23.8 Indentation options (part 1).

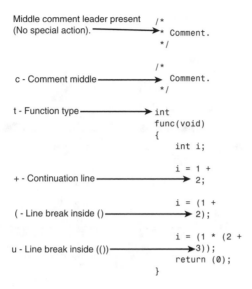

Figure 23.9   Indentation options (part 2).

The *'cinwords'* Option

The '`cinwords`' option defines what words cause the next C statement to be indented one level in the Smartindent and Cindent mode. The default value of this option is as follows:

```
:set cinwords=if,else,while,do,for,switch
```

Comparing Two Files

Suppose you want to compare two files that differ by a just a few edits. To do this, start by opening two windows, one for each edit. Next, execute the following command in each window:

```
:set scrollbind
```

Now when one window scrolls, so does the other. Figure 23.10 demonstrates how this command works. (Go down to line 14 in the first window; the second window scrolls.)

As you scroll through both windows, you might encounter a place where you must move one window without moving the other. To do so, all you have to do is execute the following command in the window you want to move and move it:

```
:set noscrollbind
```

Then to synchronize scrolling, you execute this command:

```
:set scrollbind
```

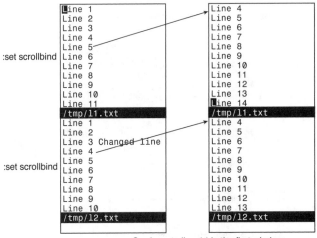

Go down to line 14 in the first window.
The second window scrolls.

Figure 23.10 `'scrollbind'`.

The `'scrollopt'` option controls how `'scrollbind'` works. It is a set of the following keywords:

ver Vertical scrolling

hor Horizontal scrolling

jump When switching between windows, make sure the offsets are 0.

Finally, the following command synchronizes the two windows:

```
:syncbind
```

Suppose, for example, that you have been looking at two versions of a file, moving both around. To look at some things, you turned off `'scrollbind'`. Now the files point at two different places.

You want to go back to synchronized scrolling. You could synchronize the windows by going to each and moving it to the right location; you let *Vim* do the work. In this case, you set scrollbind in both windows and then execute the following:

```
:syncbind
```

Vim then synchronizes the two files.

The Preview Window

Suppose you are going through a program and find a function call that you do not understand. You could do a **CTRL-]** on the identifier and jump to the location represented by the tag. But there is a problem with this. The current file disappears because the file with the function definition replaces it.

A solution to this is to use a special window called the "preview" window. By executing the following command, you open a preview window and display the function definition:

```
:ptag {function}
```

(If you already have a preview window up, it is switched to the definition of the function.) Figure 23.11 shows a typical example. Assume that you have just executed the following command:

```
:ptag copy_p_date
```

After you have finished with the preview window, execute the following command:

```
:pclose
```

(**CTRL-Wz** or **ZZ** accomplishes the same thing.)

A whole set of commands is designed to manipulate the file in the preview window. The commands are as follows:

:ppop	Do a **:pop** command in the preview window.
:ptselect {*identifier*}	Open a preview window and do a **:tselect**.
:ptjump {*identifier*}	Open a preview window and do a **:tjump**.
:[*count*] **ptnext**	Do a **:**[*count*] **tnext** in the preview window.
:[*count*] **ptprevious**	Do a **:**[*count*] **tprevious** in the preview window.
:[*count*] **ptrewind**	Do a **:**[*count*] **trewind** in the preview window.
:ptlast	Do a **:tlast** in the preview window.
CTRL-W}	Do a **:ptag** on the word under the cursor.
CTRL-Wg}	Do a **:ptjump** on the word under the cursor.

```
    assert((*the_data->n_data_ptr) <1000);
    return (result);
}

/* Create data from a db data record */
void copy_p_data(
    struct p_data *the_data,
    const datum db_data
) {
    the_data->n_data_ptr = (int *)&the_data->raw_data[0];
    set_datum(the_data, db_data);
}
/mnt/sabina/sdo/tools/local/proto/p_data.c [Preview]

    copy_p_data(&cur_entry, cur_value);

pq.c
```

Figure 23.11   **:ptag** example.

Match Options

The `'matchpairs'` option controls what characters are matched by the `%` command. The default value of this option is as follows:

```
:set matchpairs = (:),{:},[:]
```

This tells *Vim* to match pairs of `()`, `[]`, and `{}`.

To match `<>` (useful if you are editing HTML documents), for example, use the following command:

```
:set matchpairs=<:>
```

This matches just `<>` pairs. If you want to match `<>` in addition to the other characters, you need this command:

```
:set matchpairs=(:),{:},[:],<:>
```

This is a little long and awkward to type. The `+=` flavor of the `:set` command adds characters to an option. Therefore, to add `<>` to the match list, use the following command:

```
:set matchpairs+=<:>
```

Showing Matches

If you execute the following command, when you enter any type of bracket (`(`, `)`, `[`, `]`, `{`, `}`), *Vim* will cause the cursor to jump to the matching bracket briefly when entering:

```
:set showmatch
```

Generally this jump lasts only for a half second, but you can change it with the `'matchtime'` option. If you want to make it 1.5 seconds, for instance, use the following command:

```
:set matchtime=15
```

The value of this option is 1/10 second.

Finding Unmatched Characters

The `[{` command finds the previous unmatched `{` (see Figure 23.12). The `]{` command finds the next unmatched `{`. Also, `[}` finds the next unmatched `}`, whereas `]}` finds the previous unmatched `}`.

```
            int main()
            {
       [{        if  (flag)
                      do_part2();
                      do_part1();

                  return (0) ;
            }
```

Figure 23.12 The `[{` command.

The **]}** command finds the next unmatched **)**. **The [(** finds the previous unmatched **(**. The command **[#** finds the previous unmatched **#if** or **#else** (see Figure 23.13). The command **]#** finds the next unmatched conditional.

```
                          #ifdef FOO
                          #   define SIZE 1
                          #else /* FOO */
[# moves up to  ─────→    #   ifdef BAR  ◄─────
here.                     #     define SIZE 20     )
                          #   else /* BAR */  ◄──
                          #     define SIZE 30
                          #   endif /* BAR */
                          #endif
```

Figure 23.13   The **[#** command.

These commands are not that reliable because matching by mechanical means is impossible. It is possible to tell that you have three { and two }, but *Vim* can only guess at which { is missing a }.

Method Location

The following commands move to the beginning or end of a Java method:

[m   Search backward for the start of a method.

[M   Search backward for the end of a method.

]m   Search forward for the start of a method.

]M   Search forward for the end of a method.

Movement

Several movement commands are designed to help programmers navigate through their text.

The first set finds the characters { and } in column 1. (This usually indicates the start of a procedure, structure, or class definition.)

The four curly brace–related movement commands are as follows:

[count] **[[**   Move backward to the preceding { in column 1.

[count] **[]**   Move backward to the preceding } in column 1.

[count] **]]**   Move forward to the next { in column 1.

[count] **][**   Move forward to the next } in column 1.

Figure 23.14 shows how these commands work.

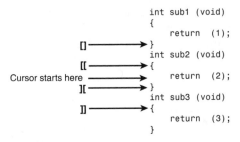

Figure 23.14   Curly brace movement commands.

Comment Moves

The commands **[/** and **[*** move you backward to the start of the first C comment it can find. The commands **]/** and **]*** move you forward to the end of the next C comment it can find. Figure 23.15 illustrates some simple comment motions.

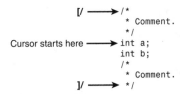

Figure 23.15   Comment motions.

Dealing with Multiple Directories

As programming projects grow larger and larger, you might find it convenient to organize things in different directories. Take a look at a small project. You have a main directory that contains `main.c` and `main.h`. The other directory is `lib` and it contains `lib.c` and `lib.h`. (This naming has no imagination, but it does make a good example.) Figure 23.16 shows this example organization.

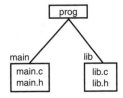

Figure 23.16   File layout.

You start editing in the directory main. The first thing you need to do is tell *Vim* about your new directory. You use the **:set** ^= command to put the directory at the top of the search path with the following command:

```
:set path ^= ../lib
```

Suppose you are editing the file main.c. The file looks like this:

```
#include "main.h"
#include "lib.h"

int main(int argc, char *argv[])
```

Now you need to check out a subroutine declaration in lib.h. One way of going to that file is to execute the following command:

```
:vi ../lib/lib.h
```

This assumes you know where lib.h resides. But there is a better way. First, you position the cursor over the filename in the following line:

```
#include "lib.h"
```

Now you execute the command **gf**. The *Vim* editor tries to edit the filename which is under the cursor. The editor searches for the file in each directory in the *path* variable.

Suppose, however, that you want to edit the file lib.c. This name does not appear in the text, so you cannot use the **gf** command. Instead, you execute the following command:

```
:find lib.c
```

This acts just like the **:vi** command, except the editor searches for the file along the path. The following command does the same thing, but it splits the window and then does a **:find**:

```
:sfind lib.c
```

The **gf** command acts like a **:find** command but use the word under the cursor as the name of the file to edit. If there is more than one file along the '**path**' that matches the given file name, then you can select which one *Vim* edits by giving the **gf** command a count.

In other words if you position the cursor on the name param.h and execute the command **2gf**, *Vim* will edit the second param.h file it finds looking through the directories specified by the '**path**' option.

The **]f** and **[f** command are older, depreciated versions of the **gf** command.

The *include* Path

The **path** option is used by *Vim* to tell it where to look for files that were included in the current file. The format of this option is as follows:

```
:set path=directory,directory,...
```

Directory is a directory to search. For example:

```
:set path=/usr/include,/usr/X11R6/include
```

You can use wildcards (*) in any directory of the path specification:

```
:set path=/usr/include,/usr/include/*
```

There are a number of special directories:

** Match an entire tree. For example:

```
:set path=/usr/include/**
```

This command searches `/usr/include` and all its subdirectories. The following path specification searches the files in any directory that starts with
`/home/oualline/progs` and ends with include:

```
:set path=/home/oualline/progs/**/include
```

"" The empty string indicates the current directory. (For example, the middle
directory of the trio "first,, last".)

. The directory in which the file being edited resides.

For example, the following command tells *Vim* to search `/usr/include` and all it is
subdirectories, the directory in which the file resides (.), and the current directory
(,,).

```
:set path=/usr/include/**,.,,
```

Checking the Path

To make sure that you can find all the **#include** files, you can execute the following
command:

```
:checkpath
```

This command works not only on the **#include** directives in the file you are editing,
but also on any files that they **#include** and so on. The result is that all **#include** files
are checked.

Figure 23.17 shows how this command works.

In this case, a number of files include the files stddef.h and stdarg.h. But *Vim*
cannot find these files. If you want to tell *Vim* to search the Linux-specific include
directory, you can execute the following command:

```
:set path+=/usr/include/linux
```

```
                get_rel_name(&cur_entry, i),
                get_full_name(&cur_entry, i));
        }

        if (gdbm_errno != 0) {
--- Included files not found in path ---
/usr/include/stdio.h -->
  <stddef.h>
  <stdarg.h>
  /usr/include/bits/types.h -->
    <stddef.h>
  /usr/include/libio.h -->
    /usr/include/_G_config.h -->
      <stddef.h>
      <stdarg.h>
    /usr/include/bits/stdio-lock.h -->
      /usr/include/pthread.h -->
        /usr/include/sched.h -->
          /usr/include/time.h -->
            <stddef.h>
/usr/include/stdlib.h -->
  <stddef.h>
  /usr/include/sys/types.h -->
    <stddef.h>
  /usr/include/alloca.h -->
    <stddef.h>
/usr/include/string.h -->
  <stddef.h>
Press RETURN or enter command to continue█
```

Figure 23.17   The :checkpath command.

Now do another:

:checkpath

Figure 23.18 shows the results.

```
        for (i = 0; i < *cur_entry.n_data_ptr; i++) {
            printf("\t%d %s (%s)\n",
                (int)get_flags(&cur_entry, i),
                get_rel_name(&cur_entry, i),
                get_full_name(&cur_entry, i));
        }

        █f (gdbm_errno != 0) {
All included files were found
```

Figure 23.18   :checkpath with all files found.

This command lists only the files that cannot be found. If you want to list all **#include** files, use this command:

:checkpath!

Figure 23.19 shows the results.

```
--- Included files in path ---
<stdio.h>
/usr/include/stdio.h -->
  <features.h>
  /usr/include/features.h -->
    <sys/cdefs.h>
    /usr/include/sys/cdefs.h -->
      <features.h>   (Already listed)
    <gnu/stubs.h>
  <stddef.h>
  <stdarg.h>
  <bits/types.h>
  /usr/include/bits/types.h -->
    <features.h>   (Already listed)
    <stddef.h>   (Already listed)
    <bits/pthreadtypes.h>
    /usr/include/bits/pthreadtypes.h -->
      <bits/sched.h>
  <libio.h>
  /usr/include/libio.h -->
-- More --█
```

Figure 23.19   The `:checkpath!` command.

Defining a Definition

The *Vim* editor knows about C and C++ macro definitions. But what about other languages? The option `'define'` contains the regular expression that *Vim* uses when it looks for a definition. To have *Vim* look for macros that start with the string **function**, for instance, use the following command:

    :set define=function

Locating *include* Files

The `'include'` option defines what an **include** directive looks like. This option is used for the **]CTRL-I**, **[CTRL-I**, **]d**, and **[d** searches that look through **#include**'d files.

This option is used for the `:checkpath` command as well. Like the `'define'` option, the value of this option is a regular expression.

The **[i** command searches for the first occurance of the word under the cursor. Text inside comments is ignored.

The **]i** command searches for the next occurance of the word under the cursor. Again, text inside comments is ignored.

The **[I** command lists all the lines which contain the keyword under the cursor. (Comments ignored.) The **]I** command does the same thing starting at the current cursor location.

Multiple Error Lists

The `:make` file generates an error list. The *Vim* editor remembers the results of your preceding 10 `:make` or `:grep` commands. To go to a previous error list, use the following command:

    :colder

To go to a newer one, use this command:

```
:cnewer
```

Customizing the *:make* Command

The name of the program to run when the **:make** command is executed is defined by the **'makeprg'** option. Usually this is set to **make**, but Visual C++ users should set this to **nmake** by executing the following command:

```
:set makeprg=nmake
```

The **:make** command redirects the output of *Make* to an error file. The name of this file is controlled by the **'makeef'** option. If this option contains the characters **##**, the **##** will be replaced by a unique number. The default value for this option depends on the operating system you are on. The defaults are as follows:

Amiga	**t:vim##.Err**
UNIX:	**/tmp/vim##.err**
Microsoft Windows and others	**vim##.err**

You can include special *Vim* keywords in the command specification. The **%** character expands to the name of the current file. So if you execute the command

```
:set makeprg=make\ %
```

and you do a

```
:make
```

it executes the following command:

```
$ make file.c
```

File.c is the name of the file you are editing. This is not too useful, so you will refine the command a little and use the **:r** (root) modifier:

```
:set makeprg=make\ %:r.o
```

Now if you are editing *file.c*, the command executed is as follows:

```
$ make file.o
```

The Error Format

The option **'errorformat'** controls how *Vim* parses the error file so that it knows the filename and line number where the error occurred.

The format of this option is as follows:

```
:set errorformat={string},{string},{string}
```

The string is a typical error message with the special character **%** used to indicate special operations (much like the standard C function **scanf**). The special characters are as follows:

%f	Filename
%l	Line number
%c	Column
%t	Error type (a single character)
%n	Error number
%m	Error message
%r	Matches the remainder of the line
%*{*char*}	Matches (and skips) any **scanf** conversion specified by {*char*}.
%%	The character **%**

When compiling a program, you might traverse several directories. The GNU *make* program prints a message when it enters and leaves a directory. A sample make log looks like this:

```
make[1]: Entering directory `/usr/src/linux-2.2.12'
make -C kernel fastdep
make[2]: Entering directory `/usr/src/linux-2.2.12/kernel'
/usr/src/linux/scripts/mkdep sysctl.c time.c > .depend
make[2]: Leaving directory `/usr/src/linux-2.2.12/kernel'
make -C drivers fastdep
make[2]: Entering directory `/usr/src/linux-2.2.12/drivers'
/usr/src/linux/scripts/mkdep  > .depend
make[3]: Entering directory `/usr/src/linux-2.2.12/drivers'
make -C block fastdep
make[4]: Entering directory `/usr/src/linux-2.2.12/drivers/block'
/usr/src/linux/scripts/mkdep xd.c xd.h xor.c z2ram.c > .depend
make _sfdep_paride _FASTDEP_ALL_SUB_DIRS=" paride"
make[5]: Leaving directory `/usr/src/linux-2.2.12/drivers/block'
make[4]: Leaving directory `/usr/src/linux-2.2.12/drivers/'
```

To get the filename right *Vim* needs to be aware of this change. The following error format specifications are used to tell *Vim* about directory changes:

%D	Specifies a message printed on entering a directory. The **%f** in this string indicates the directory entered.
%X	Specifies the leave directory message. The **%f** in this string specifies the directory that make is done with.

Some compilers, such as the GNU *GCC* compiler, output very verbose error messages. The *GCC* error message for an undeclared variable is as follows:

```
tmp.c: In function `main':
tmp.c:3: `i' undeclared (first use in this function)
tmp.c:3: (Each undeclared identifier is reported only once
tmp.c:3: for each function it appears in.)
```

If you use the default *Vim* `'errorformat'` settings, this results in three error messages. This is really annoying. Fortunately, the *Vim* editor recognizes multiline error messages. The format codes for multiline error misusages are as follows:

%A   Start of a multiline message (unspecified type)

%E   Start of a multiline error message

%W   Start of a multiline warning message

%C   Continuation of a multiline message

%Z   End of a multiline message

%G   Global; useful only in conjunction with **+** or **-**

%O   Single-line file message: overread the matched part

%P   Single-line file message: push file **%f** onto the stack

%Q   Single-line file message: pop the last file from stack

A **+** or **-** can precede any of the letters. These signify the following

%-*letter*   Do not include the matching line in any output.

%+*letter*   Include the whole matching line in the **%m** error string.

Therefore, to define a format for your multiline error message, you begin by defining the start message. This matches the following:

```
tmp.c:3: 'i' undeclared (first use in this function)
%E%f:%l:\ %m\ undeclared\ (first\ use\ in\ this\ function)
```

Note the use of \ to tell *Vim* that the space is part of the string. Now you have a problem. If you use this definition, the **%m** will match just `'i'`. You want a longer error message. So you use **+** to make *Vim* put the entire line in the message:

```
%+E%f:%l:\ %m\ undeclared\ (first\ use\ in\ this\ function)
```

The middle matches this:

```
tmp.c:3: (Each undeclared identifier is reported only once
%-C%f:%l:\ (Each\ undeclared\ identifier\ is\ reported\ only\ once
```

Note the use of the **-** modifier to keep this message out of the list of messages. The end of the error is as follows:

```
tmp.c:3: for each function it appears in.)
%-Z%f:%l:\ for\ each\ function\ it\ appears\ in.)
```

So you add these three lines to the error format:

```
%+E%f:%l:\ '%*\k*'\ undeclared\ (first\ use\ in\ this\ function),
%-C%f:%l:\ (Each\ undeclared\ identifier\ is\ reported\ only\ once,
%-Z%f:%l:\ for\ each\ function\ it\ appears\ in.)
```

Now this works, but there is a slight problem. When the GNU compiler encounters the second undefined variable, it does not output the three-line message. Instead, it outputs just the first line. (It figures you have already seen the stuff in parenthesis, so why output it again.)

Unfortunately, your error specification tries to match all three lines. Therefore, you need a different approach. The solution is to globally tell *Vim* to forget about the second two lines:

```
%-G%f:%l:\ (Each\ undeclared\ identifier\ is\ reported\ only\ once
%-G%f:%l:\ for\ each\ function\ it\ appears\ in.)
```

Now all you have to do is to add this option to your vimrc file. You can just add them on to the `'errorformat'` option by using the following command:

```
" This will not work
:set errorformat+=
\%-G%f:%l:\ (Each\ undeclared\ identifier\ is\ reported\ only\ once,
\%-G%f:%l:\ for\ each\ function\ it\ appears\ in.)
```

Note that in *Vim*, continuation lines *start* with a backslash (\). Also, you have added a comma at the end of the first error message to separate it from the second.

There is only one problem with this technique: It doesn't work. The problem is that *Vim* goes through the list of strings in `'errorformat'` in order, stopping on the first one that matches.

The error string for the GNU compiler (`%f:%l:%m`) is matched first, and therefore you never get to your two new error messages. You need to put the more specific matches (your two new messages) at the beginning. This is accomplished with the following command:

```
" This will work
:set errorformat ^=
\%-G%f:%l:\ (Each\ undeclared\ identifier\ is\ reported\ only\ once,
\%-G%f:%l:\ for\ each\ function\ it\ appears\ in.)
```

Remember, the `:set` `^=` operator adds the string to the beginning of the list.

The '*switchbuf*' Option

Normally when you do a :make and errors occur, Vim will display the offending file in the current window. If you set the `'switchbuf'` option to split, then the editor will split the current window displaying the bad file in the new window. Note the `'switchbuf'` option can have the values: "'(nothing), 'split,' 'useopen' and 'split,useopen'." For a description of the "useopen" argument see Chapter 5, "Windows."

```
$ gvim Makefile                              :set switchbuf=""
                                             :make
```

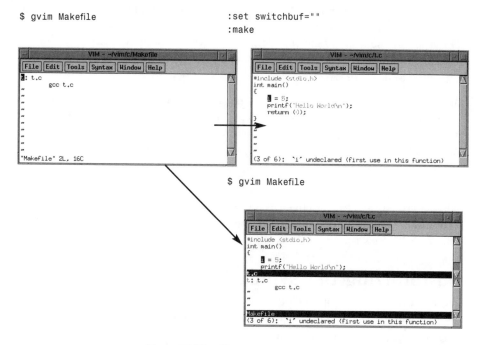

$ gvim Makefile

Figure 23.20   The '**switchbuf**' option.

Customizing *:grep*

The **:grep** command runs the program specified by the '**grepprg**' option. This option contains the command line to use. The **#** and **%** characters will be expanded to be the names of the current and alternate file.

Also the string **$*** will be replaced by any arguments to the **:grep** command.

Note that on UNIX, the '**grepprg**' defaults to **grep -n**. On Microsoft Windows, it defaults to **findstr/s**. The capabilities of these two programs differ vastly.

The **:grep** command uses the '**grepformat**' option to tell *Vim* how to parse the output of *Grep*. (It uses the same format as the '**errorformat**' option.)

Defining How a Tag Search Is Done

Usually *Vim* does a binary search for a given tag name. This makes things quick if the tag file is sorted. Otherwise, a linear search is performed.

To force a linear search, use this command:

```
:set notagbsearch
```

The '**notagbsearch**' option is useful if your tag file is not sorted.

Some systems limit the number of characters you can have in a function name. If you want this limit to be reflected in *Vim*, you can set the `'taglength'` option to the maximum length of your function names.

You specify the name of the tags file with the `'tags'` option. This can be made to point to a file in another directory. For example:

```
:set tags+=/home/oualline/tools/vim/tags
```

But this causes a little confusion. Did you start in the current directory and tell `ctags` to put the tag file in the directory /home/oualline/tools/vim or did you execute the `ctags` command in this directory? The *Vim* editor solves this problem with yet another option. If you set the following, all tags are relative to the directory that contains the tag file:

```
:set tagrelative
```

Otherwise, they are relative to the current directory.

With the `'tagstack'` option set, the `:tag` and `:tjump` commands build a tag stack. Otherwise, no stack is kept.

Customizing the Syntax Highlighting

The *Vim* editor enables you to customize the colors used for syntax hightlighting. The *Vim* editor recognizes three different types of terminals:

term   A normal black-and-white terminal (no color)

cterm   Color terminal, such as xterm or the Microsoft Windows MS-DOS window

gui   A window created by *Gvim*

Black-and-White Terminals

To change the highlighting for a normal terminal, use this command:

```
:highlight group-name term=attribute
```

The *group-name* is the name of the syntax group to be highlighted. This is the name of a syntax-matching rule set used by *Vim* to tell what part of the program to highlight. A list of the standard group names can be found later in this section.

The *attribute* is a terminal attribute. The terminal attributes for a normal black-and-white terminal are as follows:

bold   **underline reverse** (also called inverse)

italic   **standout**

You can combine attributes by separating them with commas, as follows:

```
:highlight Keyword term=reverse,bold
```

Suppose, however, that you have a terminal that has very unusual terminal codes. You can define your own attributes with the **start** and **stop** highlight options. These define a string to be sent to start the color and one to stop it. For example:

```
:highlight Keyword start=<Esc>X stop=<Esc>Y
```

With this definition, when *Vim* displays keywords (for example, **if**, it will output
<Esc>Xif<Esc>Y).

If you are familiar with the terminal definition files used on UNIX (called termcap
or terminfo files), you can use terminal codes. The termcap entry **us** defines the
underline start code, for example, and **ue** is the exit underline-mode string. To specify
these in a highlight entry, you use the following command:

```
:highlight Keyword start=t_us stop=t_ue
```

Color Terminals

The color entries are defined by the **cterm** settings. You can set them using
cterm=*attribute* just like a normal term entry.

But there are additional options for a color terminal. The setting **ctermfg=***color-
number* defines the foreground color number. The **ctermbg=***color-number* defines the
background.

Color names are recognized rather than color numbers.

The following tells *Vim* to display comments in red on blue, underlined:

```
:highlight Comment cterm=underline ctermfg=red ctermbg=blue
```

(Incidentally, this looks really ugly.)

GUI Definition

The GUI terminal uses the option **gui=***attribute* to display the attributes of a syntax
element in the GUI window. The options **guifg** and **guibg** define the colors. These
colors can be named. If the name contains a space, the color name should be enclosed
in single quotation marks. To keep things portable, the *Vim* people suggest you limit
your color names to the following.

Black	Blue	Brown	Cyan
DarkBlue	DarkCyan	DarkGray	DarkGreen
DarkMagenta	DarkRed	Gray	Green
LightBlue	LightCyan	LightGray	LightGreen
LightMagenta	LightRed	LightYellow	Magenta
Orange	Purple	Red	SeaGreen
SlateBlue	Violet	White	Yellow

You can define the color as well by using the standard X11 color numbers. (This
works on all systems, regardless of whether you are using X11.) These are of the form
#rrggbb, where **rr** is the amount of red, **bb** is the amount of blue, and **yy** is the
amount of yellow. (These three numbers are in hexadecimal.)

Under Microsoft Windows, the following colors are available:

Black	Blue	Brown	Cyan

DarkBlue	DarkCyan	DarkGray	DarkGreen
DarkMagenta	DarkRed	Green	LightBlue
LightCyan	LightGray	LightGreen	LightMagenta
LightRed	Magenta	Red	Sys_3DDKShadow
Sys_3DFace	Sys_3DHighlight	Sys_3DHilight	Sys_3DLight
Sys_3DShadow	Sys_ActiveBorder	Sys_ActiveCaption	Sys_AppWorkspace
Sys_BTNFace	Sys_BTNHighlight	Sys_BTNHilight	Sys_BTNShadow
Sys_BTNText	Sys_Background	Sys_CaptionText	Sys_Desktop
Sys_GrayText	Sys_Highlight	Sys_HighlightText	Sys_InactiveBorder
Sys_InactiveCaption	Sys_InactiveCaptionText	Sys_InfoBK	Sys_InfoText
Sys_Menu	Sys_MenuText	Sys_ScrollBar	Sys_Window
Sys_WindowFrame	Sys_WindowText	White	Yellow

You can use the **font=***x-font* as well to define which font to use. This is not for the faint of heart, because X11 font names are complex. For example:

```
:highlight Comment font=
\font=-misc-fixed-bold-r-normal—14-130-75-75-c-70-iso8859-1
```

Microsoft Windows fonts can be used as well:

```
:highlight Comment font=courier_helv:h12
```

Combining Definitions

You can define colors for multiple terminals on a single highlight line. For example:

```
:highlight Error term=reverse
        \ cterm=bold  ctermfg=7  ctermbg=1
```

Syntax Elements

The syntax elements are defined by the macros in `$VIMRUNTIME/syntax`. To make things easier, however, the following names are generally used.

Boolean	**Character**	**Comment**	**Conditional**
Constant	Debug	Define	Delimiter
Error	Exception	Float	Function
Identifier	Include	Keyword	Label
Macro	Number	Operator	PreCondit
PreProc	Repeat	Special	SpecialChar
SpecialComment	Statement	StorageClass	String
Structure	Tag	Todo	Type
Typedef			

In addition to these syntax elements, *Vim* defines the following for the various things it generates:

`Cursor`	The character under the cursor.
`Directory`	Directory names (and other special names in listings).
`ErrorMsg`	Error messages displayed on the bottom line.
`IncSearch`	The result of an incremental search.
`ModeMsg`	The mode shown in the lower-left corner (for example, `--INSERT--`).
`MoreMsg`	The prompt displayed if *Vim* is displaying a long message at the bottom of the screen and must display more.
`NonText`	The *Vim* editor displays ~ for lines past the end of the file. It also uses @ to indicate a line that will not fit on the screen. (See Chapter 20.) This syntax element defines what color to use for these elements.
`Question`	When *Vim* asks a question.
`SpecialKey`	The `:map` command lists keyboard mapping. This defines the highlight to use for the special keys, such as `<Esc>`, displayed.
`StatusLine`	The status line of current window.
`StatusLineNC`	Status lines of the other windows.
`Title`	Titles for output from `:set all`, `:autocmd`, and so on.
`Visual`	This color is used to highlight the visual block.
`VisualNOS`	Visual-mode selection when *Vim* is "Not Owning the Selection." This works only on X Windows Systems.
`WarningMsg`	Warning messages displayed on the last line of the window.
`WildMenu`	Current match in `'wildmenu'` completion.
`LineNr`	Line number for `:number` and `:#` commands, and when the `'number'` option is set.
`Normal`	Normal text.
`Search`	The results of the last search when the `'hlsearch'` option is enabled.
`User1` through `User9`	The `'statusline'` option enables you to customize the status line. You can use up to nine different highlights on this line, as defined by these names.
`Menu`	Menu color for the GUI.
`Scrollbar`	Scrollbar color for the GUI.

Color Chart

If you want to see what the various colors look like on your terminal, you can use *Vim*'s color chart. To access this chart, either pull down the Syntax|Color test menu (*Gvim*) or follow these steps:

1. Edit the file `$VIMRUNTIME/syntax/colortest.vim`. Your directories might be different if you install *Vim* in a different place.
2. Execute the following command:

   ```
   :source %
   ```

3. Browse the color list (in the third column).

Figure 23.20 shows the results. Unfortunately, this book is in black and white, but you can imagine what it would look like in color.

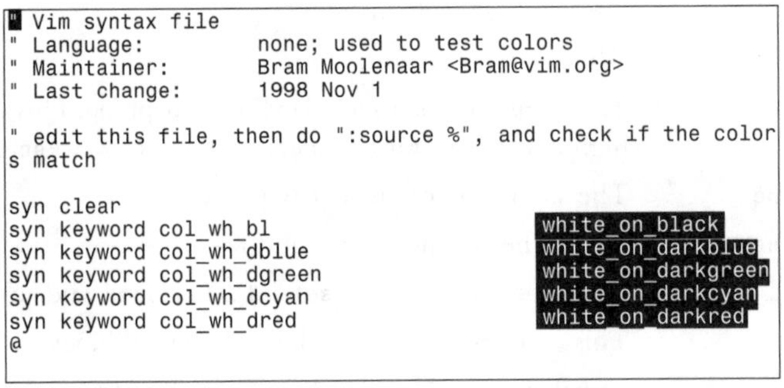

```
" Vim syntax file
" Language:         none; used to test colors
" Maintainer:       Bram Moolenaar <Bram@vim.org>
" Last change:      1998 Nov 1

" edit this file, then do ":source %", and check if the color
s match

syn clear
syn keyword col_wh_bl                              white_on_black
syn keyword col_wh_dblue                           white_on_darkblue
syn keyword col_wh_dgreen                          white_on_darkgreen
syn keyword col_wh_dcyan                           white_on_darkcyan
syn keyword col_wh_dred                            white_on_darkred
@
```

Figure 23.21 Color test.

The *'syntax'* Option

The **'syntax'** option contains the name of the current language used for syntax highlighting. You can turn syntax highlighting off by entering the command:

```
:set syntax=off
```

To turn it back on, use this command:

```
:set syntax=on
```

24

All About Abbreviations
and Keyboard Mapping

IN CHAPTER 8, "BASIC ABBREVIATIONS, KEYBOARD MAPPING, and Initialization Files," you learned about abbreviations and keyboard mappings, but that discussion focuses on only the most useful subset of the commands. This chapter examines things in complete detail. These commands have a lot of different variations, and this chapter covers them all.

In this chapter, you learn about the following:

- How to remove an abbreviation
- Creation of mode-specific abbreviations
- Listing abbreviations
- How to force abbreviation completion in insert mode
- Mode-specific mappings
- Clearing and listing mappings
- Other mapping options

Removing an Abbreviation

To remove an abbreviation, use the command **:unabbreviate**. Suppose you have the following abbreviation, for example:

```
:abbreviate @a fresh
```

You can remove it with this command:

```
:unabbreviate @a
```

To clear out all the abbreviations, use the following command:

```
:abclear
```

> **Note**
>
> One problem with this command is that the abbreviation **@a** is expanded on the command line. *Vim* is smart, however, and it will recognize that **fresh** is really **@a** expanded and will remove the abbreviation for **@a**.

Abbreviations for Certain Modes

The **:abbreviate** command defines abbreviations that work for both insert mode and command-line mode. If you type the abbreviation **@a** in the text, for example, it will expand to **fresh**. Likewise, if you put it in a command-mode (**:**) command, it will also expand.

Normal mode	**i@a\<ESC>**	Inserts **fresh**
Command mode	**:s/xx/@a/**	Executes **:s/xx/fresh/**

If you want to define an abbreviation that works only in insert mode, you need the **:iabbreviate** command, as follows:

```
:iabberviate @a fresh
```

This means that in command mode, **@a** is just **@a**. The **noremap** version of this command is **:inoreabbrev**. To unabbreviate an insert-mode abbreviation, use the command **:iunabbreviate**. To clear out all the insert abbreviations, use the following command:

```
:iabclear
```

If you want an abbreviation defined just for command mode, use the **:cabbreviate** command. The **noremap** version of this command is **:cnoreabbrev**. To remove a definition, use the **:cunabbreviate** command; and to clear out the entire abbreviation list, use the command **:cabclear**.

Listing Abbreviations

You can list all abbreviations by using the **:abbreviate** command with no arguments (see Figure 24.1).

```
~
~
~
c  r           :rewind
i  ab          abbreviate
!  h           Help
Press RETURN or enter command to continue█
```

Figure 24.1   **:abbreviate** output.

The first column contains a flag indicating the abbreviation type. The flags are as follows:

c   Command mode

i   Insert mode

!   Both

Forcing Abbreviation Completion

In insert mode, the command **CTRL-]** causes *Vim* to insert the current abbreviation. The command **CTRL-C** causes *Vim* to exit insert mode. The difference between **CTRL-C** and **<Esc>** is that **CTRL-C** does not check for an abbreviation before entering normal mode.

Mapping and Modes

The **map** command enables you to define mappings limited to certain modes. Suppose, for example, that you want to use the F5 key to yank the current visual-mode select into register **v**. You can define the following command:

```
:map <F5> "vy
```

This maps the F5 key for normal, visual, and operator-pending modes. But you want this mapping to be valid only for visual mode. To do that, use a special version of the mapping command:

```
:vmap <F5> "vy
```

The "v" flavor of the **:map** command tells *Vim* that this mapping is valid only for visual mode. Table 24.1 lists seven different flavors of the **:map** command.

Table 24.1 *:map* **Commands**

Command	Normal	Visual	Operator Pending	Insert	Command Line
:map	X	X	X		
:nmap	X				
:vmap		X			
:omap			X		
:map!				X	X
:imap				X	
:cmap					X

> **Note**
>
> Operator-pending mode is the mode that occurs when you enter a command such as **d** that expects a motion to follow. (For example, **dw** deletes a word. The **w** is entered in operator-pending mode.)

Now suppose that you want to define **<F7>** so that the command **d<F7>** deletes the C program block (text enclosed in curly braces, {}). Similarly **y<F7>** would yank the program block into the unnamed register. Therefore, what you need to do is to define **<F7>** to select the current program block. You can do this with the following command:

```
:omap <F7> a{
```

This causes **<F7>** to perform a select block (**a{**) in operator-pending mode. With this mapping in place, when you press the **d** of **d<F7>**, you enter operator-pending mode. Pressing **<F7>** executes the command **a{** in operator-pending mode, selecting the block. Because you are performing a **d** command, the block is deleted.

Other *:map* Commands

A number of commands relate to mapping. The first is this:

```
:map lhs rhs
```

This adds the mapping of *lhs* to *rhs*. Therefore, pressing *lhs* results in the execution of *rhs*.

The **:map** command allows remapping of *rhs*. The following command, however, does not:

```
:noremap lhs rhs
```

For example:

```
:map ^A dd
:map ^B ^A
```

This causes *Vim* to delete a line when you type **CTRL-A**. It also causes the **CTRL-B** command to do the same thing as **CTRL-A**—that is, delete a line. Note: When entering the control characters, you must "quote" them with **CTRL-V**. In other words, you must type

```
:map CTRL-VCTRL-A dd
```

to get:

```
:map ^A dd
```

Suppose you use the following **:noremap** command:

```
:map ^A dd
:noremap ^B ^A
```

When you type **CTRL-B**, you execute a normal **CTRL-A** (not mapped) **CTRL-A** command. Therefore, **CTRL-B** will now increment the value of the number under the cursor.

Undoing a Mapping

The **:unmap** command removes a mapping. To cause a mapped **CTRL-A** command to revert to the default, use the following command:

```
:unmap ^A
```

This also proves useful if you want to map a command for a limited set of modes. To define a command that exists in only normal and visual modes, but not operator-pending mode, for example, use the following commands:

```
:map ^A 3w
:ounmap ^A
```

The first command maps the **CTRL-A** to **3w** in normal, visual, and operator-pending modes. The second removes it from the operating-pending mode map.

Clearing Out a Map

The following command removes all mapping:

```
:mapclear
```

Be careful with this one because it also removes any default mappings you might have.

Listing the Mappings

The **:map** command with no arguments lists out the mappings (see Figure 24.2).

```
~
~
~
      <xHome>        <Home>
      <xEnd>         <End>
      <S-xF4>        <S-F4>
      <S-xF3>        <S-F3>
      <S-xF2>        <S-F2>
      <S-xF1>        <S-F1>
      <xF4>          <F4>
      <xF3>          <F3>
      <xF2>          <F2>
      <xF1>          <F1>
Press RETURN or enter command to continue█
```

Figure 24.2   Output of `:map` command.

The first column lists flags indicating the modes for which the mapping is valid.

Character	Mode
<Space>	Normal, visual, and operator-pending
n	Normal
v	Visual
o	Operator-pending
!	Insert and command line
i	Insert
c	Command line

The second column indicates the various *lhs* of any mappings. The third column is the value of the *rhs* of the mapping. If the *rhs* begins with an asterisk (★),the *rhs* cannot be remapped.

The `:map` command lists all the mappings for normal, visual, and operator-pending modes. The `:map!` command lists all the mappings for insert and command-line mode. The `:imap`, `:vmap`, `:omap`, `:nmap`, and `:cmap` commands list only the mappings for the given modes.

Recursive Mapping

By default, *Vim* allows recursive command mapping. To turn off this feature, execute the following command:

```
:set noremap
```

This may break some scripts. Using `:noremap` will avoid this problem.

The `'suffixes'` option lists a set of file name suffixes that will be given a lower priority when it comes to matching wildcards. In other words if a file has one of these suffixes it will be placed at the end of any wildcard list.

Remapping Abbreviations

Abbreviations can cause problems with mappings. Consider the following settings, for example:

```
:abbreviate @a ad
:imap ad adder
```

Now when you type **@a**, the string **ad** is inserted. Because **ad** is mapped in insert mode to the string **adder**, however, the word *adder* is inserted in the text.

If you use the command **:noreabbrev**, however, you tell *Vim* to avoid this problem. Abbreviations created with this command are not candidates for mapping.

One of the problems with the **:abbreviate** command is that the abbreviations on the right side are expanded when the abbreviations are defined. There is a clumsy way of avoiding this: Type an extra character before the word, type the word, then go back and delete the extra character.

:map Mode Table

The modes are as follows:

N   Normal

V   Visual

O   Operator pending

I   Insert

C   Command line

NVO	N	V	O	IC	I	C
`:map`	`:nm`	`:vm`	`:om`	`:map!`	`:im`	`:cm`
	`:nmap`	`:vmap`	`:omap`		`:imap`	`:cmap`
`:no`	`:nn`	`:vn`	`:ono`	`:no!`	`:ino`	`:cno`
`:noremap!`	`:nnremap`	`:vnoremap`	`:onoremap`	`:noremap!`	`:inoremap`	`:cnoremap`
`:unm`	`:nun`	`:vu`	`:ou`	`:unm!`	`:iu`	`:cu`
`:unmap`	`:nunmap`	`:vunmap`	`:ounmap`	`:unmap!`	`:iunmap`	`:cunmap`
`:mapc`	`:nmapc`	`:vmapc`	`:omapc`	`:mapc!`	`:imapc`	`:cmapc`
`:mapclear`	`:nmapclear`	`:vmapclear`	`:omapclear`	`:mapclear!`	`:imapclear`	`:cmapclear`

25

Complete Command-Mode (:) Commands

Aᴌᴛʜᴏᴜɢʜ ᴛʜᴇ *Vɪᴍ* ᴇᴅɪᴛᴏʀ ɪs sᴜᴘᴇʀʙ when it comes to doing things visually, sometimes you need to use command mode. For example, command-mode commands are much easier to use in scripts. Also, a number of other specialized commands are found only in command mode.

Being expert in the command-mode command means that you are a *Vim* power user with the ability to execute a number of amazing high-speed editing commands.

Editing Commands

The `:delete` command deletes a range of lines. To delete lines 1 through 5 (inclusive), for example, use the following command:

```
:1,5 delete
```

The general form of the `:delete` command is as follows:

```
: range delete register count
```

The *register* parameter specifies the text register in which to place the deleted text. This is one of the named registers (a–z). If you use the uppercase version of the name (A–Z), the text is appended to what is already in the *register*. If this parameter is not specified, the unnamed register is used.

The *count* parameter specifies the number of lines to delete (more on this later in this section).

The *range* parameter specifies the lines to use. Consider the following example (spaces added for readability):

```
:1, 3 delete
```

Figure 25.1 shows the results of this command.

```
    1 █ UNIX sales lady, Lenore,
    2 Enjoys work, but she likes the beach more.
    3     She found a good way
    4     To combine work and play:
    5 She sells C shells by the seashore.
~
```

```
    1      █o combine work and play:
    2 She sells C shells by the seashor
~
~
~
3 fewer lines
```

Figure 25.1   **:1,3 delete**.

You have learned how to use search patterns for line specification. For example, the following command deletes starting from the first line with *hello* to the first line that contains *goodbye*.

```
:/hello/,/goodbye/ delete
```

Note: If goodbye comes before hello, the line range will be backwards, and the command will not work.

You can refine the search string specification by adding an offset. For example, **/hello/+1** specifies the line one line after the line with the word *hello* in it. Therefore, the following command results in the screen shown in Figure 25.2.

```
:/beach/+1, /seashore/-1 delete
```

```
    1 A UNIX sales lady, Lenore,
    2 Enjoys work, but she likes the beach more.
    3 █he sells C shells by the seashore.
~
~
: /beach/+1, /seashore/-1 delete
```

Figure 25.2   Results of **:/beach/+1, /seashore/-1 delete**.

You can also use special shorthand operators for patterns, as follows:

\/   Search forward for the last pattern used.

\?   Search backward for the last pattern used.

\&   Search forward for the pattern last used as substitute pattern.

You can also chain patterns. The following command, for example, finds the string **first** and then searches for the string **second**.

```
/first//second/
```

Figure 25.3 shows the result of this command:

```
:/found//work/ delete
```

```
              1 A UNIX sales lady, Lenore,
              2 Enjoys work, but she likes the beach more.
              3     She found a good way
              4 ▉he sells C shells by the seashore.
          ~
          ~
          ~
          :/found//work/ delete
```

Figure 25.3   `:/found//word/delete`.

You can also specify a line number on which to start. To start the search at line 7, for instance, use the following command-line specification:

```
7/first/
```

Other Ways to Specify Ranges

If you execute a **:** command with no count (as most users generally do), the *Vim* editor puts you into command mode and enables you to specify the range. If you give the command a count(**5:**, for example), the range is *count* lines (including the current one). The actual specification of this arrangement is that if you include a *count*, your line range is as follows:

```
:.,count - 1
```

In the example original file, for instance, if you move to the top line and then execute the following command, you get the results shown in Figure 25.4:

```
3:delete
```

```
              1     ▉o combine work and play:
              2 She sells C shells by the seashore.
          ~
          ~
          ~
          ~
          3 fewer lines
```

Figure 25.4   `3:delete`.

Deleting with a Count

Another form of the **delete** command is as follows:

```
:line delete count
```

In this case, the **:delete** command goes to *line* (default = the current line) and then deletes *count* lines.

If you execute the following command on the original example file, for instance, you get the results shown in Figure 25.5:

```
:3 delete 2
```

```
        1 A UNIX sales lady, Lenore,
        2 Enjoys work, but she likes the beach more.
        3 She sells C shells by the seashore.
~
~
~
:3 delete 2
```

Figure 25.5 **:3 delete 2**.

> **Note**
>
> You can specify a line range for this type of command, but the first line is ignored and the second one is used.

Copy and Move

The **:copy** command copies a set of lines from one point to another. The general form of the copy command is as follows:

```
:range copy address
```

If not specified, *range* defaults to the current line. This command copies the line in *range* to the line specified after *address*. Consider the following command, for example:

```
:1,3 copy 4
```

Executed on the original joke, you get the results shown in Figure 25.6.

```
        1 A UNIX sales lady, Lenore,            ,
        2 Enjoys work, but she likes the beach more.
        3     She found a good way
        4     To combine work and play:
        5 A UNIX sales lady, Lenore,
        6 Enjoys work, but she likes the beach more.
        7     She found a good way
        8 She sells C shells by the seashore.
~
3 more lines
```

Figure 25.6 **:1,3 copy 4**.

The :**move** command is much like the :**copy** command, except the lines are moved rather than copied. The following command results in what is shown in Figure 25.7:

```
:1,3 move 4
```

```
    1      To combine work and play:
    2 A UNIX sales lady, Lenore,
    3 Enjoys work, but she likes the beach more.
    4      She found a good way
    5 She sells C shells by the seashore.
~
~
~
~
3 lines moved
```

Figure 25.7   :**1,3 move 4**.

Inserting Text

Suppose that you want to insert a bunch of lines and for some reason you want to use command mode. You need to go to the line above where you want the new text to appear. In other words, you want the text to be inserted after the current line.

Now start the insert by executing the :**append** command. Type the lines that you want to add and finish by typing a line that consists of just a period (.).

The following example illustrates the :**append** command.

```
:% print
A UNIX sales lady, Lenore,
Enjoys work, but she likes the beach more.
     She found a good way
     To combine work and play:
She sells C shells by the seashore.
:1append
This line is appended.
.
:% print
A UNIX sales lady, Lenore,
This line is appended.
Enjoys work, but she likes the beach more.
     She found a good way
     To combine work and play:
She sells C shells by the seashore.
```

The general form of the :**append** command is as follows:

```
:line append
```

The *line* is the line after which to insert the new text.

The **:insert** command also inserts text. It has a similar form:

:line **insert**

It works just like **:append** except that **:append** inserts after and **:insert** inserts before the current line.

Printing with Line Numbers

You do not have to turn on the **number** option to print the text with line numbers. The **:#** command accomplishes the same thing as **:print** but includes line numbers:

```
:1 print
A UNIX sales lady, Lenore,
:1 #
      1 A UNIX sales lady, Lenore,
```

Printing with *list* Enabled

The **'list'** option causes invisible characters to be visible. The **:list** command lists the specified lines, assuming that this option is on:

```
:1,5 list
```

The following example shows the difference between **:print** and **:list**:

```
:100,111 print
open_db(void)
{
      if (proto_db == NULL) {
            proto_db = gdbm_open(proto_db_name, 512, GDBM_READER ,
                                 0666, NULL);
            if (proto_db == NULL) {
                  fprintf(stderr, "Error: Could not open database  %s\n",
                              proto_db_name);
                  exit (8);
            }
      }
}
:100,111 list
open_db(void)$
{$
      if (proto_db == NULL) {$
^Iproto_db = gdbm_open(proto_db_name, 512, GDBM_READER, $
^I^I^I^I0666, NULL);$
^Iif (proto_db == NULL) {$
^I     fprintf(stderr, "Error: Could not open database %s\n", $
^I     ^I^I proto_db_name);$
^I     exit (8);$
^I}$
      }$
}$
```

Print the Text and Then Some

The **:z** command prints a range of lines (the current one being the default) and the lines surrounding them. For example, the following command prints line 100 and then a screen full of data:

```
:100 z
```

The **:z** command takes a count of the number of extra lines to list. For example, the following command lists line 100 and three additional lines:

```
:100 z 3
```

The **:z** command can be followed by a code indicating how much to display. The following table lists the codes:

Code	Listing Start	Listing End	New Current Line
+	Current line	One screen forward	One screen forward
-	One screen back	Current line	Current line
^	Two screens back	One screen back	One screen back
.	One-half screen back	One-half screen forward	One-half screen forward
=	One-half screen back	One-half screen forward	Current line

Substitute

The format of the basic **substitute** command is as follows:

```
:range substitute /from/to/flags count
```

> **Note**
>
> This example uses a slash (/) to separate the patterns. Actually you can use almost any character that does not appear in the patterns. The following, for example, is perfectly valid:
>
> ```
> :substitute +from+to+
> ```
>
> This can prove extremely useful when you are dealing with patterns that contain slashes, such as filenames:
>
> ```
> :1,$ substitute +/home/user+/apps/product+
> ```

Delimiters can be any character except letters, digits, backslash, double quote, or vertical bar.

The *Vim* editor uses a special set of magic characters to represent special things. For example, star (*) stands for "repeat 0 or more times."

If you set the **'nomagic'** option, however, the magic meanings of some of these characters are turned off. (For a complete list of the magic characters and how the **'nomagic'** option affects them, see Chapter 19, "Advanced Searching Using Regular Expressions.")

The **:smagic** command performs a substitute but assumes that the **'magic'** option is set during the command.

For example, start in command mode with a one-line file. You start by printing the entire file:

```
:%print
Test aaa* aa* a*
```

Now set the **'magic'** option and perform a substitution. The **p** flag tells the editor to print the line it changed:

```
:set magic
:1 substitute /a*/b/p
bTest aaa* aa* a*
```

This command made only one change at the beginning of the line. So why did it change Test to b*Test when there is no a around? The answer is that the magic character star (*****) matches *zero* or more times. Test begins with zero a's.

But why did it make only one change? Because the **:substitute** command changes only the first occurrence unless the **g** flag is present. Now undo the change and try again:

```
:undo
:1 substitute /a*/b/pg
bTbebsbtb b*b b*b b*b
```

This time you got what you wanted. Now try it again with the **'nomagic'** option set:

```
:undo
:set nomagic
:1 substitute /a*/b/pg
Test aab ab b
```

Without **'magic'**, a star (*****) is just a star. It is substituted directly.

The **:smagic** command forces magic on the star (*****) and other characters while the substitution is being made, resulting in the following:

```
:undo
:1 smagic /a*/b/pg
bTbebsbtb b*b b*b b*b
```

The **:snomagic** forces **'magic'** off.

```
:undo
:set magic
:1 snomagic /a*/b/pg
Test aab ab b
```

The **&** command repeats the substitution. This enables you to keep your old *from* and *to* strings, but also to supply a different *range* or *flags*. The general form of this command is as follows:

```
:range& flags count
```

For example:

```
:1 substitute /a\+/b/p
Test b* aa* a*
```

The command changes the first occurrence of *from* on the line. You want the entire line, so you repeat the substitution with the **g** option:

```
:&g
```

Of course, this does not print (because the new flags—in this case **g**—replaces the flags and you did not specify **p** or, more specifically, **pg**). Take a look at the result:

```
:1 print
Test b* b* b*
```

This is what you wanted.

The **:&** command and the **:substitute** command with no *from* or *to* specified acts the same.

The normal-mode **&** command repeats the last **:substitute** command. If you were to execute the following command, for instance, you would change the first *manager* on line 5 to an *idiot*:

```
:5 substitute /manager/idiot/
```

Now if you enter normal mode (through the **:vi** command) and execute an **&** command, the next *manager* on this line would change as well. If you were to move down to another line and execute an **&** command, you would change that line as well. If you give **&** a *count*, it will work on that many lines.

The **:~** command acts just like the **&g** command, except that it uses as *from* the last search pattern (used for a **/** or **?** search) rather than the last **:substitute** *from* string. The general form of this command is as follows:

```
:range~ flags count
```

Repeat Substitution

The **&** command repeats the last substitution.

Making *g* the Default

Generally the **:substitute** command changes only the first occurrence of the word unless you use the **'g'** option. To make the **'g'** option the default, use the following command:

```
:set gdefault
```

Note: This can break some scripts you may use.

Global Changes

The command-mode commands covered so far have one limitation: They work only on a contiguous set of lines. Suppose, however, that you want to change just the lines that contain a certain pattern. In such a case, you need the **:global** command. The general form of this command is as follows:

```
:range global /pattern/ command
```

This tells *Vim* to perform the given command on all lines that contain the pattern in the specified range. To print all the lines within a file that contain the word *Professor*, for instance, use the following command:

```
:% global /Professor/ print
Professor:      Yes.
Professor:      You mean it's not supposed to do that?
Professor:      Well there was no Computer Center Bulletin
Professors of mathematics will prove the existence of
```

The `:global!` command applies the command to all the lines that do *not* match the given pattern, as will the `:vglobal` command.

Commands for Programs

The following sections describe some commands for programs.

Include File Searches

The `:ijump` command searches for the given pattern and jumps to the first occurrence of the word in the given range. It searches not only the current file, but all files brought in by `#include` directives. The general form of this command is as follows:

```
:range ijump count [/]pattern[/]
```

If a count is given, jump to the *count* occurrence of the pattern. The pattern is considered literal text unless it is enclosed in slashes (in which case, it is a regular expression).

Consider the file `hello.c`, for example:

```
#include <stdio.h>
int main()
{
    printf("Hello World\n");
    return (0);
}
```

The following command goes to the first line that contains *define EOF*:

```
:ijump /define\s*EOF/
```

In this case, it is in the include file `stdio.h`.

The `:ilist` command acts like `:ijump`, except it lists the lines instead of jumping to them:

```
:ilist EOF
/usr/include/libio.h
    1:    84 #ifndef EOF
    2:    85 # define EOF (-1)
    3:   327         && __underflow (_fp) == EOF ? EOF \
/usr/include/stdio.h
```

```
   4:    83 #ifndef EOF
   5:    84 # define EOF (-1)
   6:   408     null terminator), or -1 on error or EOF. */
/usr/include/bits/stdio.h
   7:   138                          if (__c == EOF)      \
   8:   157 if (_IO_putcun (*__ptr++, __stream) == EOF)   \
```

The **:isearch** command is like **:ilist**, except that the first occurrence is listed:

```
:isearch EOF
#ifndef EOF
```

Finally, the command **:isplit** works like a **:split** and a **:ijump**.

Jumping to Macro Definitions

You learned how to use the command **[CTRL-D]** to jump to the definition of the macro under the cursor. The following command accomplishes the same thing for the macro named *name*:

```
:djump name
```

To jump to the macro MAX, for example, use this command:

```
:djump MAX
```

You do not have to know the full name of the macro to find its definition. If you know only part of a name, you can perform a regular expression search for the definition by enclosing the name in slashes, as follows:

```
:djump /MAX/
```

This command finds the first definition of the macro with the word *MAX* in it.

You can give the **:djump** command a range argument that restricts the search to the given range:

```
:50,100 djump /MAX/
```

This command finds the first definition of any macro containing the word *MAX* in lines 50 through 100.

If you do not want the first definition, but the second, you can add a count to the command. To find the second definition of *MAX*, for instance, use this command:

```
:djump 2 MAX
```


Split the Window and Go to a Macro Definition

The following command is shorthand for **:split** and **:djump**:

```
:range dsplit count [/]pattern[/]
```

Listing the Macros

The **:dlist** command works just like **:djump**, except that instead of moving to the macro definition, the command just lists all the definitions that match:

```
:dlist EOF
/usr/include/libio.h
  1:   85 # define EOF (-1)
/usr/include/stdio.h
  2:   84 # define EOF (-1)
```

Listing the First Definition

The **:dsearch** command works just like **:dlist**, except that it displays only the first definition:

```
:dsearch EOF
# define EOF (-1)
```

Override Option (*!*)

The **:ilist**, **:ijump**, **:djump**, **:dlist**, and **:dsearch** commands take an override option (**!**). If the **!** is present, definitions within comments found as well.

Directory Manipulation

To change the current working directory, use the following command:

```
:cd dir
```

This command acts just like the system **cd** command.

On UNIX, it changes the current working directory to the given directory. If no directory is specified, it goes to the user's home directory.

On Microsoft Windows, it goes to the indicated directory. If no directory is specified, it prints the current working directory.

The following command changes the directory to the previous path:

```
:cd -
```

In other words, it does a **cd** to the last directory you used as the current working directory.

To find out which directory *Vim* is currently using, use this command:

```
:pwd
```

Start deep in the directory tree, for instance:

```
:pwd
/mnt/sabina/sdo/writing/book/vim/book/11
```

You are working on a UNIX system, so go to your $home directory:

```
:cd
:pwd
/home/sdo
```

Jump into another directory:

```
:cd tmp
:pwd
/home/sdo/tmp
```

Return to the previous directory:

```
:cd -
:pwd
/home/sdo
```

Return to the previous directory before this one:

```
:cd -
:pwd
/home/sdo/tmp
```

Current File

The following command prints out the current file and line information:

```
:file
```

If you want to change the name of what *Vim* thinks is the filename, use this command:

```
:file name
```

Suppose, for example, that you start editing a file called `complete.txt`. You get this file just right, so you write it out using the **:write** command. Now you want shorten the file and write it out as `summary.txt`. So now you execute this command:

```
:file summary.txt
```

Now when you continue to edit, any changes are saved to `summary.txt`.

Take a look at how this works. You start by editing the file `star.txt`.

```
:file
"star.txt" line 1 of 1 —100%— col 1
```

The **:write** command with no arguments writes the file to the current filename (in this case, `star.txt`).

```
:write
"star.txt" 1 line, 18 characters written
```

Now you want to change the filename to `new.txt`. The editor tells you that this is a new filename.

```
:file new.txt
"new.txt" [Not edited] line 1 of 1 —100%— col 1
```

The **:write** command is used to write the file. In this case, the current filename differs; it is new.txt.

```
:write
"NEW.TXT" [New File] 1 line, 18 characters written
```

There is another command similar to **:file**; the following command prints the current line number:

```
:=
```

For example:

```
:=
line 1
```

Advanced *:write* Commands

The **:write** command writes the buffer (or a selected range of lines) to a file. It has some additional options. The following command, for example, appends the contents of the file you are editing to the file named **collect.txt**:

```
:write >> collect.txt
```

If the **collect.txt** file does not exist, this command aborts with an error message. If you want to "append" to the file even if does not exist, use the force (**!**) option:

```
:write! >> collect.txt
```

The **:write** command can not only write to a file, but it can also be used to pipe the file to another program. On Linux or UNIX, for instance, you can send the file to a printer by using the following command:

```
:write !lpr
```

> **Warning**
>
> The following two commands are different; the difference being only the spacing:
>
> ```
> :write! lpr
> :write !lpr
> ```
>
> The first writes to the file named *lpr* with the force option in place. The second sends the output to the command lpr.

Updating Files

The **:update** command acts just like the **:write** command, with one exception: If the buffer is not modified, the command does nothing.

Reading Files

The **:read** command reads in a file. The general form of this command is as follows:

```
:line read file
```

The preceding command reads the *file* in and inserts it just after *line*. If no file is specified, the current file is used. If no line is supplied, the current line is used.

Like **:write**, the **:read** command can use a command rather than a file. To read the output of a command and insert it after the current line, use the following command:

```
:line read !command
```

Register Execution

Chapter 2, "Editing a Little Faster," showed you how to record macros in registers. If you want to use these macros in command mode, you can execute the contents of a register with the following command:

```
:line@register
```

This command moves the cursor to the specified line, and then executes the register. This means that the following command executes the previous command line:

```
:@:
```

To execute the previous **:@register** command, use this command:

```
:line@@
```

Simple Edits

The following sections describe simple edits.

Shifting

The **:>** command shifts lines to the right. The **:<** command shifts lines to the left.
    The following command, for example, shifts lines 5 through 10 to the right:

```
:5, 10 >
```

Changing Text

The **:change** command acts just like the **:delete** command, except that it performs an **:insert** as well.

Entering Insert Mode

The **:startinsert** command starts insert mode as if you were in normal mode and were to press **i**.

Joining Lines

The **:join** command joins a bunch of lines (specified by the *range* parameter) together into one line. Spaces are added to separate the lines.

If you do not want the added spaces, use the **:join!** command.

Yanking Text

The following command yanks the specified lines into the *register*:

```
:range yank register
```

If no register is specified, the unnamed register is used.

Putting Text

The **:put** command puts the contents of a register after the indicated line. To dump the contents of register a after line 5, for example, use the following command:

```
:5put a
```

If you want to put the text before the line, use this command:

```
:5put! a
```

Undo/Redo

The **:undo** command undoes a change just like the **u** command does. The **:redo** command redoes a change like **CTRL-R** does.

To mark the beginning of the line, use the

```
:mark {register}
```

command. If a line is specified, that line will be marked. The **:k** command does the same thing, with the exception that you don't have to put a space in front of the register name. The following two commands are equivalent:

```
:100 mark x
:100 ka
```

Miscellaneous Commands

The following sections describe some miscellaneous commands you can use.

The *:preserve* Command

The **:preserve** command writes out the entire file to the "swap" file. This makes it possible to recover a crashed editing session without the original file. (If you do not use this command, you need both the swap file and the original to perform recovery.) See Chapter 14, "File Recovery and Command Line Arguments," for information on recovering crashed sessions.

The Shell Commands

To execute a single shell command, use the following *Vim* command (where *cmd* is the system command to execute):

```
:!cmd
```

To find the current date, for instance, use this command:

```
:!date
```

The following command repeats the last shell command you executed:

```
:!!
```

Finally, the following command suspends *Vim* and goes to the command prompt:

```
:shell
```

You can now enter as many system commands as you want. After you have finished, you can return to *Vim* with the **exit** command.

Shell Configuration

The following several options control the actual execution of a command.

shell	The name of the shell (command processor).
shellcmdflag	Flag that comes after the shell.
shellquote	The quote characters around the command.
shellxquote	The quote characters for the command and the redirection.
shellpipe	String to make a pipe.
shellredir	String to redirect the output.
shellslash	Use forward slashes in filenames (MS-DOS only).

Command History

The **:history** command prints out the current command-mode command history:

```
:history
          #  cmd history
          2  1 print
          3  5
          4  7 print
          5  . print
   >      6  history
```

The *Vim* editor maintains a set of histories for various commands. A code identifies each of these:

Code			History Type
c	cmd	:	Command-line history (command-mode commands)
s	search	/	Search strings (See Chapter 3, "Searching")
e	expr	=	Expression register history
i	input	@	Input line history (data typed in response to an **:input** operator)
a	all		All histories

Therefore, to get a list of all the various history buffers, use the **:history all** command:

```
:history all
          #  cmd history
          2  1 print
          3  5
          4  7 print
          5  . print
          6  history
   >      7  history all
          #  search history
          1  human
          2  uni
          3  comp
          4  Seem
   >      5  \<At\>
          #  expr history
          1  55
          2  2*88
   >      3  5+99
          #  input history
Press Return or enter command to continue
```

The general form of the **:history** command is as follows:

:history *code first* , *last*

If no *first* and *last* are specified, the whole history is listed. The *first* parameter defaults to the first entry in the history, and the *last* defaults to the last. Negative numbers indicate an offset from the end of the history. For example, −2 indicates the next-to-last history entry.

The following command, for example, list history entries 1 through 5 for command-mode commands:

```
:history c 1,5
```

And, this next command lists the last 5 search strings:

```
:history s -5,
```

Setting the Number of Remembered Commands

The `'history'` option controls how may commands to remember for command-mode (: mode) commands. To increase the number of commands to remember (to 50, for instance), use this command:

```
:set history=50
```

Viewing Previous Error Messages

The *Vim* editor keeps track of the last few error and information messages displayed on the last line of the screen. To view the message history, use the following command:

```
:messages
"../joke.txt" 6092 lines, 174700 characters
Entering Ex mode. Type "visual" to go to Normal mode.
search hit BOTTOM, continuing at TOP
Not an editor command: xxxxx
search hit BOTTOM, continuing at TOP
search hit BOTTOM, continuing at TOP
Pattern not found: badbad
Not an editor command: :^H
Invalid address
```

Redirecting the Output

The following command causes all output messages to be copied to the file as well as to appear on the screen:

```
:redir > file
```

To end the copying, execute the following command:

```
:redir END
```

This command proves useful for saving debugging information or messages for inclusion in a book.

You can also use the **:redir** command to append to a file by using this command:

```
:redir >> file
```

Executing a *:normal* Command

The **:normal** command executes a normal-mode command. The following command, for instance, changes the word where the cursor is located to the word *DONE*:

```
:normal cwDONE<Esc>
```

The group of commands is treated as one for the purposes of undo/redo.

The command should be a complete command. If you leave *Vim* hanging (suppose that you executed a command **cwDone**, for instance), the display will not update until the command is complete.

If you specify the '**!**' option, mappings will not be done on the command.

Getting Out

The following command writes the current file and closes the window:

```
:exit
```

When the last window is closed, the editor stops.

If the override flag (**!**) is given, an attempt will be made to write the file even if it is marked read-only.

You can also specify a filename on the command line. The data will be written to this file before exiting. The following command, for example, saves the current file in save-it-it.txt and exits.

```
:exit save-it.txt
```

If you want to save only a portion of the file, you can specify a range of lines to write. To save only the first 100 lines of a file and exit, for example, use this command:

```
:1,100 exit save-it.txt
```

Write and Quit

The following command does the same thing that **:exit** does, except it always writes the file:

```
:range wq! file
```

The **:exit** command writes only if the file has been changed.

26

Advanced GUI Commands

THE *VIM* EDITOR IS HIGHLY CONFIGURABLE. This chapter shows you how to customize the GUI. Among other things, you can configure the following in *Vim*:

- The size and location of the window
- The display of menus and toolbars
- How the mouse is used
- The commands in the menu
- The buttons on the toolbar
- The items in the pop-up menu

The remainder of this chapter introduces you to the commands that enable you to customize all these features.

Switching to the GUI Mode

Suppose you are editing in a terminal window and want to switch to the GUI mode. To do so, use the following command:

```
:gui
```

Window Size and Position

When you first start *gvim (GUI Vim)*, the window is positioned by the windowing system. The size of the window on UNIX is set to the size of the terminal window that started the editor. In other words, if you have a 24×80 *xterm* window and start *gvim*, you get a 24×80 editing window. If you have a larger window, say 50×132, you get a 50×132 editing window.

On UNIX you can tell *gvim* to start at a given location and size by using the **-geometry** flag. The general format of this option is as follows:

```
-geometry width+ x heightx_offset-y_offset
```

The *width* and *height* options specify the width and height of the window (in characters). The *x-offset* and *y-offset* tell the X Windows System where to put the window.

The *x-offset* specifies the number of pixels between the left side of the screen and the right side of the window. If the *x-offset* specification is negative, it specifies the distance between the left edge of the editor and the right side of the screen.

Similarly, the *y-offset* specifies the top margin, or if negative, the bottom margin.

Thus, the **-geometry +0+0** option puts the window in the upper-left corner, whereas **-geometry -0-0** specifies the lower-right corner.

The *width* and *height* parameters specify how big the editing window is to be in lines and columns. To have a 24-by-80 editing window, for example, use the option **-geometry 80x24**.

Figure 26.1 shows how these options work.

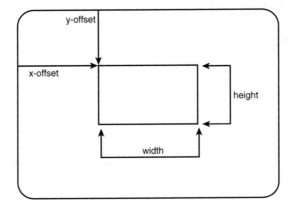

Figure 26.1   **-geometry** option.

Microsoft Windows Size and Position Command-Line Specification

The Microsoft Windows version of *gvim* starts with an editing window of 80×25. The *gvim* editor uses the standard Microsoft Windows command-line option to specify an initial size and position. Because Microsoft Windows does not have a standard option for this value, *gvim* does not have one either.

Moving the Window

The following command displays the current location (in pixels) of the upper-left corner of the window:

    :winpos

If you want to move the window, you can use this command:

    :winpos X Y

To position the screen 30 pixels down and 20 pixels over from the left, for instance, use the following command:

    :winpos 20 30

Window Size

The following command displays the number of lines in the editing window:

    :set lines?

To change this number, use this command:

    :set lines=lines

Lines is the number of lines you want in the new editing window.

To change the number of columns on the screen, use this command:

    :set columns=columns

The *:winsize* Command

Older versions of *Vim* use a **:winsize** command. This command is deprecated because the **:set lines** and **:set columns** commands have superseded it.

The *guioptions*

You can control a number of GUI-based features with the **'guioptions'** option. The general form this command is as follows:

    :set guioptions=options

Options is a set of letters, one per option.

The following options are defined:

a	Autoselect	When set, if you select text in the visual mode, *Vim* tries to put the selected text on the system's global clipboard. This means that you can select text in one *Vim* session and paste it in another using the `"*p` command. Without this option you must use the `"*y` command to copy data to the clipboard.

It also means that the selected text has been put on the global clipboard and is available to other applications. On UNIX, for example, this means that you can select text in visual mode, and then paste it into an xterm window using the middle mouse button.

If you are using Microsoft Windows, any text selected in visual mode is automatically placed on the clipboard. (Just as the Copy ^C menu item does in most other applications.) This means that you can select the text in *Vim* and paste it into a Microsoft Word document.

f	Foreground	On UNIX, the gvim command executes a **fork()** command so that the editor can run in the background. Setting this flag prevents this, which is useful if you are writing a script that needs to run the **gvim** command to let the user edit a file, and that needs to wait until the editing is done. (The **-f** command-line option accomplishes the same thing.)

The **f** flag also proves useful if you are trying to debug the program.

Note

You must set this in the initialization file (because by the time you can set it from the edit window, it is too late).

i	Icon	If set, *gvim* displays an attractive icon when the editor in minimized on an X Windows System. If not present, the program just displays the name of the file being edited with no icon (see Figure 26.2).

Figure 26.2   **i** option

m	Menu	Display menu bar (see Figure 26.3)

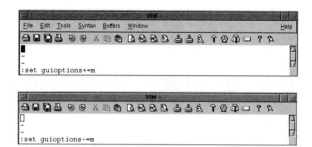

Figure 26.3 m option.

M	No menu	If this option is present during initialization, the system menu definition file $VIMRUNTIME/menu.vim is not read in.

> **Note**
>
> This option must be set in the vimrc file. (By the time givmrc is read, it is too late.)

g	Gray	Turn menu items that cannot be used gray. If not present, these items are removed from the menu (see Figure 26.4).
t	Tear off	Enable tear off menus.

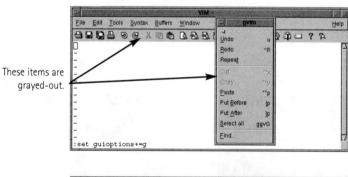

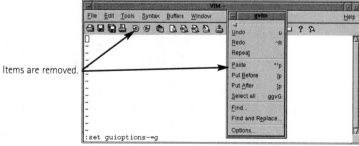

Figure 26.4 g option.

T	Toolbar	Include toolbar (see Figure 26.5)
r	Right scrollbar	Put a scrollbar on the right (see Figure 26.6).

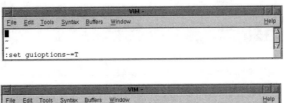

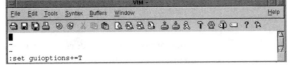

Figure 26.5 **T** option.

l	Left scrollbar	Put a scrollbar on the left (see Figure 26.6).
b	Bottom scrollbar	Put a scrollbar on the bottom (see Figure 26.6).

Figure 26.6 Scrollbars.

v	Vertical dialog boxes	Use vertical alignment for dialog boxes (see Figure 26.7).

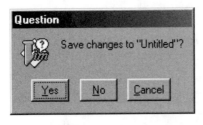 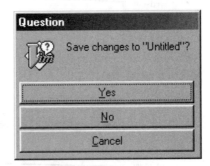

Figure 26.7 **v** option.

p	Pointer callback fix	This option is designed to fix some problems that might occur with some X11 window managers. It causes the program to use pointer callbacks. You must set this in the `gvimrc` file.

Changing the Toolbar

The '**toolbar**' option controls the appearance of the toolbar. It is a set of values:

icon   Display toolbar icons

text   Display text

tooltips   When the cursor hovers over an icon, display a ToolTip.

The default displays ToolTips and icons:

```
:set toolbar=icons,tooltips
```

Figure 26.8 shows how this option affects the screen.

```
:set toolbar=icons,tooltips
```

```
:set toolbar=icons,text,tooltips
```

```
:set toolbar=text,tooltips
```

Figure 26.8   The '**toolbar**' option.

> **Note**
>
> To turn off the toolbar, you *cannot* set this option to the empty string. Instead use the following command:
>
> ```
> :set guioptions -= T
> ```

Customizing the Icon

If you are editing in a terminal window, some terminals enable you to change the title of their window and their icon. If you want *Vim* to try to change the title to the name of the file being edited, set this option:

```
:set title
```

Sometimes the name of the file with its full path name is longer than the room you have for the title. You can change the amount of space used for the filename with the following command:

```
:set title=85
```

In this case, the title text can consume 85% of the title bar.

For example:

```
:set titlelen=45
```

Figure 26.9 shows how 'titlelen' can affect the display.

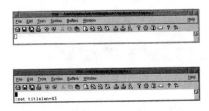

Figure 26.9 'titlelen' option.

If you do not like what *Vim* selects for your title, you can change it by setting the following:

```
:set titlestring=Hello\ World!
```

When you exit *Vim*, it tries to restore the old title. If it cannot restore it (because it is impossible to remember it), the editor sets the title to the string specified by the 'titleold' option. For example:

```
:set titleold=vim\ was\ here!
```

When the window is iconified, the icon option tells *Vim* whether to attempt to put the name of the file in the icon title. If this option is set, *Vim* attempts to change the icon text.

If you do not like the *Vim* default, you can set the 'iconstring' option and that text will be used for the icon string.

The 'icon' option, if set causes the string under the icon to contain the name of the file being edited (or the value of 'iconstring' if set). If the option is turned off, the icons just have the generic title Vim.

Figure 26.10 shows the results of the following command:

```
:set iconstring=Now\ editing\ tutorial
```

:set icon (Editing the file *Makefile*)   :set noicon

Figure 26.10 The 'icon' option.

Mouse Customization

The *Vim* editor is one of the few UNIX text editors that is mouse-aware. That means you can use the mouse for a variety of editing operations. You can customize the utility of the mouse by using the options discussed in the following sections.

Mouse Focus

Generally when you want to move from one *Vim* editing window to another, you must use one of the window change commands such as **CTRL-Wj** or **CTRL-Wk**. If you execute the following command, the current *Vim* editing window is the one where the mouse pointer is located:

```
:set mousefocus
```

Note

This option affects only the windows within a *Vim* session. If you are using the X Windows System, the selection of the current window (X Client window) is handled by the window manager. On Microsoft Windows, the current window selection is handled by Microsoft Windows, which always forces you to use "click to type."

The *'mousemodel'* Option

The **'mousemodel'** option defines what the mouse does. There are three possible modes: extend, popup, and popup_setpos. To set the mouse model, use the following command:

```
:set mousemodel=mode
```

In all modes, the left mouse button moves the cursor, and dragging the cursor using the left button selects the text.

In **extend** mode, the right mouse button extends the text and the middle button pastes it in. This behavior is similar to the way an **xterm** uses the mouse.

In **popup** mode, the right mouse button causes a small pop-up menu to appear. This behavior is similar to what you find in most Microsoft Windows applications.

The **popup_setpos** mode is exactly like **popup** mode, except when you press the right mouse button, the text cursor is moved to the location of the mouse pointer, and then the pop-up menu appears.

The following table illustrates how **'mousemodel'** affects the mouse buttons.

Mouse	extend	popup	popup_setpos
Left	Place cursor	Place cursor	Place cursor
Drag-left	Select text	Select text	Select text
Shift-left	Search word	Extend selection	Extend selection
Right	Extend selection	Pop-up menu	Move cursor, and then pop-up menu
Drag-right	Extend selection		
Middle	Paste	Paste	Paste

Mouse Configuration

The `'mouse'` option enables the mouse for certain modes. The possible modes are as follows:

n   Normal

v   Visual

i   Insert

c   Command-line

h   All modes when in a help file except "hit-return"

a   All modes except the "hit-return"

r   "more-prompt" and "hit-return" prompt

Mouse Mapping

The left mouse button (`<LeftMouse>`) moves the text cursor to where the mouse pointer is located. The `<RightMouse>` command causes *Vim* to enter visual mode. The area between the text cursor and the mouse pointer is selected. The `<MiddleMouse>` acts like the **P** command and performs a put to insert in the unnamed register in the file. If you precede the mouse click with a register specification (such as `"a`, for instance), the contents of that register are inserted.

If you have a wheel on your mouse, the up-wheel (`<MouseUp>`) moves three lines up. Similarly, a down-wheel movement (`<MouseDown>`) moves three lines down. If you press Shift, the screen moves a page. In other words, `<S-MouseUp>` goes up a page and `<S-MouseDown>` goes down a page.

Double-Click Time

The `'mousetime'` option defines the maximum time between the two presses of a double-click. The format of this command is as follows:

```
:set mousetime=time
```

Time is the time in milliseconds. By default, this is half a second (500ms).

Hiding the Mouse Pointer

When you are editing with the GUI, you have a text cursor and a mouse pointer to deal with. If that is too confusing, you can tell *Vim* to turn off the mouse pointer when not in use. To enable this feature, use the following command:

```
:set mousehide
```

When you start typing, the mouse pointer disappears. It reappears when you move the mouse.

Select Mode

The `'selectmode'` option defines when the editor starts select mode instead of visual mode. The following three events can trigger select mode:

mouse   Moving the mouse (see `'mousemode'`, discussed earlier)

key   Using some special keys

cmd   The **v**, **V**, or **CTRL-V** command

The general form of the command is as follows:

```
:set selectmode=mode
```

Mode is a comma-separated list of possible select events (**mouse**, **key**, **cmd**).
    The `'keymodel'` option allows the keys **<Left>**, **<Right>**, **<Up>**, **<Down>**, **<End>**, **<Home>**, **<PageUp>**, and **<PageDown>** to do special things. If you set this option as follows, Shift+*key* starts a selection:

```
:set keymodel=startsel
```

If the option is set as follows, an unshifted *Key* results in the section being stopped:

```
:set keymodel=stopsel
```

You can combine these options as well, as follows:

```
:set keymodel=startsel,stopsel
```

Custom Menus

The menus that *Vim* uses are defined in the file $VIMRUNTIME/menu.vim. If you want to write your own menus, you might first want to look through that file.
    To define a menu item, use the **:menu** command. The basic form of this command is as follows:

```
:menu menu-item command-string
```

(This command is very similar to the **:map** command.)
    The *menu-item* describes where on the menu to put the item. A typical *menu-item* is File.Save, which represents the item Save under the menu File. The ampersand charac-

ter (&) is used to indicate an accelerator. In the *gvim* editor, for instance, you can use **Alt-F** to select File and **S** to select save. Therefore, the *menu-item* looks like **&File.&Save**.

The actual definition of the File.Save menu item is as follows:

```
:menu 10.340 &File.&Save<Tab>:w          :confirm w<CR>
```

The number 10.340 is called the *priority* number. It is used by the editor to decide where it places the menu item. The first number (10) indicates the position on the menu bar. Lower numbered menus are positioned to the left, higher numbers to the right.

The second number (340) determines the location of the item within the pull-down menu. Lower numbers go on top, higher number on the bottom.

Figure 26.11 diagrams the priorities of the current menu items.

The *menu-item* in this example is **&File.&Save<Tab>:w**. This brings up an important point: *menu-item* must be one word. If you want to put spaces or tabs in the name, you either use the **<>** notation (**<space>**, **<tab>**, for instance) or use the backslash (\) escape.

```
:menu 10.305 &File.&Do\ It :exit<CR>
```

In this example, the name of the menu item contains a space (**Do It**) and the command is **:exit<CR>**.

Finally, you can define menu items that exist for only certain modes. The general form of the menu command is as follows:

```
:[mode]menu [priority] menu-item command-string
```

Figure 26.11   Menu item priorities.

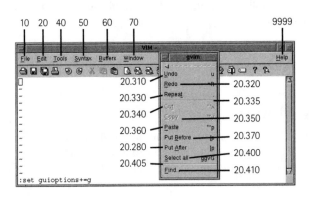

mode is one of the following:

Character	Mode
a	Normal, visual, and operator-pending
n	Normal
v	Visual
o	Operator-pending
i	Insert
c	Command line

Special Menu Names

There are some special menu names. These are

ToolBar   The toolbar (the icons under the menu)

PopUp   The pop-up window that appears when you press the right mouse
            button in the edit window in certain modes

Toolbar Icons

The toolbar uses icons rather than text to represent the command. For example, the
menu-item named ToolBar.New causes the New icon to appear on the toolbar. The
Vim editor has 28 built-in icons. The following table lists these.

Each icon has two names. The New icon, for instance, can be specified as
ToolBar.New or ToolBar.builtin00.

If the icon does not match one of the built-in icons, the editor looks for a file in
the $VIMRUNTIME/bitmaps directory. The name of the icon file is *NAME*.BMP on
Microsoft Windows and *name.xpn* on UNIX. On Microsoft Windows, the icon may be
any size. On UNIX, it must be 20×20 pixels.

Icon	Name	Alternative Name
	New	builtin00
	Open	builtin01
	Save	builtin02
	Undo	builtin03

continues

Icon	Name	Alternative Name
	Redo	builtin04
	Cut	builtin05
	Copy	builtin06
	Paste	builtin07
	Print	builtin08
	Help	builtin09
	Find	builtin10
	SaveAll	builtin11
	SaveSesn	builtin12
	NewSesn	builtin13
	LoadSesn	builtin14
	RunScript	builtin15
	Replace	builtin16
	WinClose	builtin17
	WinMax	builtin18
	WinMin	builtin19

Icon	Name	Alternative Name
	WinSplit	builtin20
	Shell	builtin21
	FindPrev	builtin22
	FindNext	builtin23
	FindHelp	builtin24
	Make	builtin25
	TagJump	builtin26
	RunCtags	builtin27

Toolbar Tips

The toolbar can display a "tip" when the cursor is placed over an icon. To define the tip, issue the following command:

`:tmenu` *menu-item tip*

For example, the following command causes the tip `Open file` to display when the cursor rests over the Open icon (see Figure 26.12):

`:tmenu ToolBar.Open Open file`

Figure 26.12   ToolTip.

Listing Menu Mappings

The following command lists all the menu mappings:

```
:menu
```

```
:menu
— · Menus — ·
1 ToolBar
  10 Open
       n    :browse e<CR>
       v    <C-C>:browse e<CR>
       o    <C-C>:browse e<CR>
  20 Save
       n    :w<CR>
       v    <C-C>:w<CR>
       o    <C-C>:w<CR>
... lots of other lines ...
```

The problem with the **:menu** command is that you get 51 screens of data. That is a lot. To get just the menu items for a specific top-level menu, use the following command:

```
:menu menu
```

For example, the following command lists only the menu items for the File menu:

```
:menu File
```

The next command lists the items for just the File.Save menu:

```
:menu File.Save
```

```
:menu File.Save
— · Menus — ·
340 &Save          :w
       n    :confirm w<CR>
       v    <C-C>:confirm w<CR>
       o    <C-C>:confirm w<CR>
```

The letters at the beginning of each line denote the mode in which the command applies. They correspond to the letters used for the *mode* parameter described earlier.

Executing a Menu Item

The following command executes the *menu-item* as if the user had selected the command from the menu:

```
:emenu menu-item
```

No Remapping Menus

The **:menu** command defines a menu item. If you want to define an item and make sure that no mapping is done on the right side, use the **:noremenu** command.

Removing Menu Items

The command removes an item from the menu:

```
:[mode]unmenu menu-item
```

If you use an asterisk (*) for the *menu-item*, the entire menu is erased.
To remove a ToolTip, use the following command:

```
:tunmenu menu-item
```

Tearing Off a Menu

You can tear off a menu by using the dotted tear-off line on the GUI. Another way to do this is to execute the following command:

```
:tearoff menu-name
```

Special GUI Commands

The *Vim* editor has many commands designed for use in GUI-based menus. These commands are all based around various dialog boxes (such as the file browser connected with the File.Open menu).

The File Browsers

The **:browse** command opens up a file browser and then executes a command on the file selected. For example, the following command opens a file browser and enables the user to select a file (see Figure 26.13):

```
:browse edit
```

The editor then performs an **:edit** *file* command.

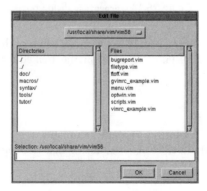

Figure 26.13   File browser.

The general form of the **:browse** command is as follows:

```
:browse command [directory]
```

The *command* is any editor command that takes a filename as an argument. Commands such as **:read**, **:write**, and **:edit** fall into this category.

The [*directory*] parameter, if present, determines the directory in which the browser starts.

If the [*directory*] parameter is not present, the directory for the browser is selected according to the **'browsedir'** option. This option can have one of three values:

last   Use the last directory browsed (default).

buffer   Use the same directory as the current buffer.

current   Always use the current directory.

Therefore, if you always want to start in the current directory, put the following command in your initialization file:

```
:set browsedir=current
```

Finding a String

The following command displays a search dialog box (see Figure 26.14):

```
:promptfind [string]
```

Figure 26.14   **promptfind** dialog box.

If a string is specified, the string is used as the initial value of the Find What field.

When the user presses the Find Next button, the *Vim* editor searches for the given string.

Replace Dialog Box

There is a similar dialog box for the **replace** command.

The following command displays a Replace dialog box (see Figure 26.15):

```
:promptrepl string
```

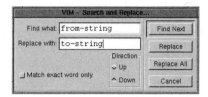

Figure 26.15 `promptrepl` dialog box.

If a string parameter is present, it is used for the Find What parameter.

Finding Help

The following command brings up a dialog box that enables you to type in a subject that will be used to search the help system:

    :helpfind

Confirmation

The '`:confirm`' option executes a command such as `:quit` that has the potential for destroying data. If the execution of the command would destroy data, a confirmation dialog box displays.

For example, the following command on a modified buffer results in the dialog box displayed in Figure 26.16:

    :confirm :quit

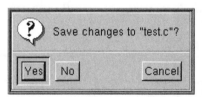

Figure 26.16 Confirmation dialog box.

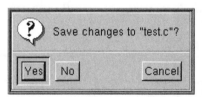

Figure 26.17 Confirmation without a GUI.

> **Note**
>
> This command works for the terminal version of *Vim* as well, but the Confirmation dialog box does not look as nice. This is illustrated in Figure 26.17.

Browsing the Options

The following command opens a window that enables you to browse through the options:

```
:browse set
```

Figure 26.18 shows the screen.

```
Each "set" line shows the current value of an option (on the left).
Hit <CR> on a "set" line to execute it.
           A boolean option will be toggled.
           For other options you can edit the value.
Hit <CR> on a help line to open a help window on this option.
Hit <CR> on an index line to jump there.
Hit <Space> on a "set" line to refresh it.

1 important
2 moving around, searching and patterns
3 tags
4 displaying text
5 syntax and highlighting
6 multiple windows
```

Figure 26.18 **:browse set**.

This window gives you access to all the options. The beginning is a short table of contents, starting with the following:

```
1 important
2 moving around, searching and patterns
```

You can use the cursor commands to position the cursor on one of the items and press Return to get a list of the options for this section. If you were to move the cursor down to the first entry (important) and press Return, for instance, you would get Figure 26.19.

```
1 important

compatible      behave very Vi compatible (not advisable)
set nocp        cp
cpoptions       list of flags to specify Vi compatibility
set cpo=aABceFs
insertmode      use Insert mode as the default mode
set noim        im
paste           paste mode, insert typed text literally
set nopaste     paste
pastetoggle     key sequence to toggle paste mode
set pt=
helpfile        name of the main help file
set hf=/usr/local/share/vim/vim56/doc/help.txt
```

Figure 26.19 **:browse set** detail screen.

The first option in this window is the `'compatible'` option. According to the help text beside it, setting this option causes *Vim* to "behave very *Vi* compatible (not advisable)." The abbreviation for this option is `'cp'`, and the current setting is `'nocp'`.

If you move down to the `'compatible'` line and press Return, you get a full help screen on the option (see Figure 26.20).

```
 ┌────────────────────────────────────────────────────────────────────────┐
 │                        █'compatible'* *'cp'* *'nocompatible'* *'nocp'*   │
 │ 'compatible'  'cp'     boolean (default on, off when a .vimrc file is found)│
 │                        global                                            │
 │                        (not in Vi)                                       │
 │          This option has the function of making Vim either more Vi-compatible,│
 │          or behave in a more useful way. This is a special kind of option,│
 │          because when it's set or reset, other options are also changed as a│
 │          side effect. CAREFUL: Setting or resetting this option can have a lot│
 │          of unexpected effects: Mappings are interpreted in another way, undo│
 │          behaves differently, etc.                                       │
 │          By default this option is on and the Vi defaults are used for the│
 ├─options.txt─[help][RO]───────────────────────────────────────────────────┤
 │ compatible      behave very Vi compatible (not advisable)                 │
 │ option-window                                                            │
 └────────────────────────────────────────────────────────────────────────┘
```

Figure 26.20 **:browse set** help screen.

If you move down to the **set nocp** line and press **<CR>**, the option is toggled. (This works for all Boolean options.)

The next option (**'cpoptions'**) is a string. To change its value, just edit it using the normal *Vim* editing commands, and then press **<Enter>** to set the option to this value.

Using the Clipboard

The **'clipboard'** option controls how *Vim* treats text selected with the mouse. If you use the following command, *Vim* takes all the text that should go in the unnamed register and puts it in the clipboard register:

```
:set clipboard=unnamed
```

This means that the text is placed on the system clipboard and can be pasted into other applications.

Another option is this:

```
:set clipboard=autoselect
```

When this option is set, any text selected in visual mode is put on the system clipboard (if possible). (The **a** flag of the **'guioptions'** option does the same thing.)

The **'autoselect'** option works for both the GUI and console versions of *Vim*.

Coloring

When *Vim* starts the GUI, it tries to figure out whether you have a light or dark background and performs the following command to set the proper value:

:set background=*value*

The syntax files use the value of this option to determine which colors to use.

> **Warning**
>
> When the GUI is started, the value of this option is light. The gvimrc file is then read and processed. After this, the window is created. Only after the window is created can *Vim* tell the color of the background, so it is only after this that the background option is set. This means that anything in the gvimrc that depends on the background being correct will fail.

Selecting the Font

If you do not like the font that *Vim* uses for its GUI, you can change it by using the following option:

```
:set guifont=font
```

Font is the name of a font. On an X Windows System, you can use the command **xlsfonts** to list out the available fonts. On Microsoft Windows, you can get a list of fonts from the Control Panel.

You can also use the following command:

```
:set guifont=*
```

This command causes *Vim* to bring up a font selection window from which you can pick your font.

Customizing Select Mode

The **'selection'** option defines how a selection is handled. The possible values are as follows

- **old**—Does not allow selection for one character past the end of a line. The last character of the selection is included in the operation.

- **inclusive**—The character past the end of the line is included, and the last character of the selection is included in the operation.

- **exclusive**—The character past the end of the line is included, and the last character of the selection is not included in the operation.

Mouse Usage in Insert Mode

Clicking the left mouse button (**<LeftMouse>** in *Vim* terminology) causes the cursor to move to where the mouse pointer is pointing.

If you have a wheel on your mouse, the mouse-wheel commands act just like they do in normal mode.

Microsoft Windows–Specific Commands

By setting the **'winalt keys'** option to "no," *Vim* will take over the entire keyboard. This means that you can use the Alt key for keyboard commands and mappings. However, Microsoft Windows generally uses the Alt key to access menus.

The **:simalt** key simulates the pressing of Alt+*key*. You can use this in the following command, for example:

```
:map <M-f> :simalt f<CR>
```

This command tells *Vim* that when Meta-F (Alt+f in Microsoft Windows terminology) is pressed, the editor is to simulate the pressing of the Alt+f key. This brings down the File menu.

Changing the Appearance of the Cursor

The `'guicursor'` option defines how the cursor looks for the GUI version of *Vim*. The format of this command is as follows:

```
:set guicursor=mode:style[-highlight],mode:style[-highlight],...
```

You can set the *mode* as follows:

n	Normal mode
v	Visual mode
ve	Visual mode with 'selection' *exclusive* (same as **v**, if not specified)
o	Operator-pending mode
i	Insert mode
r	Replace mode
c	Command-line normal (append) mode
ci	Command-line insert mode
cr	Command-line replace mode
sm	`showmatch` in insert mode
a	All modes

You can combine by separating them with hyphens, as follows:

n-v-c   For normal, visual, and command modes

The *style* is as follows:

hor*N*	Horizontal bar, N percent of the character height
ver*N*	Vertical bar, *N* percent of the character width
block	block cursor, fills the whole character
blinkwait*N*	
blinkon*N*	
blinkoff*N*	When these options are specified, the system waits for **blinkwait** milliseconds, and then turns the cursor off for **blinkoff** and on for **blinkon**. The off/on cycle repeats.

And *highlight* is a highlight group name.

The following table describes the default value for this option.

Parameter	Modes	Cursor Type	Highlight Group
`n-v-c:block-Cursor`	Normal Visual Command-line normal	Simple block cursor	Cursor
`ve:ver35-Cursor`	Visual selection exclusive	Vertical bar cursor 35% high	Cursor
`o:hor50-Cursor`	Operator-pending	Horizontal cursor half size	Cursor
`i-ci:ver25-Cursor`	Insert Command insert	Small vertical bar (35% high) block	Cursor
`r-cr:hor20-Cursor`	Replace Command replace	Small horizontal bar (20% width)	Cursor
`sm:block-Cursor-blinkwait175-blinkoff150-blinkon175`	Showmatch	Block cursor with fast blinking	Cursor

X Windows System–Specific Commands

In the X Windows System, the window manager is responsible for the border around the window and other decorations. The `'guiheadroom'` option tells the *Vim* editor how big the margin is around the window (top and bottom) so that when it goes into full screen mode, it can leave room for the border.

Selecting the Connection with :*shell* Commands

What happens when you are using the GUI window and you try to execute a `:shell` command? Usually the system uses a UNIX device called pty to handle the command interface.

If you want to connect using a pipe, set the following option:

```
:set noguipty
```

Otherwise the default is used and a pty connection made between the shell and the GUI:

```
:set guipty
```

MS-DOS-Specific Commands

The following command changes the screen mode of an MS-DOS window:

`:mode mode`

This command is effective only if you are editing inside MS-DOS; it does not work inside a Microsoft Windows GUI.

Mode is an MS-DOS screen mode such as B80, B40, c80, c40, or one of the screen-mode numbers.

27

Expressions and Functions

T HE *VIM* EDITOR CONTAINS A RICH script language. This command language gives you tremendous flexibility when it comes to customizing your editor for specialized tasks.

This chapter covers the following:

- Basic variables and expressions
- The **:echo** statement
- Control statements
- User-defined functions
- A complete list of built-in functions

Basic Variables and Expressions

The *Vim* editor enables you to define, set, and use your own variables. To assign a value to a variable, use the **:let** command. The general form of this command is as follows:

```
:let {variable} = {expression}
```

The *Vim* editor uses the same style variable names as most other languages—that is, a variable begins with a letter or underscore and then consists of a series of letters, digits, and the underscore.

To define the variable *line_size*, for example, use this command:

```
:let line_size = 30
```

To find out what the variable is, use the **:echo** command:

```
:echo "line_size is" line_size
```

When entered, this command results in *Vim* displaying the following on the last line:

```
line_size is 30
```

Variables can contain numbers (such as 30) or strings (such as "foo"). For example:

```
:let my_name = "Steve Oualline"
```

Special Variable Names

The *Vim* editor uses special prefixes to denote different types of variables. The prefixes are as follows:

Name	Use
All uppercase, digits, and underscore	Variable which can be stored in the **viminfo** file. if the **'viminfo'** option contains the "!" flag
Initial uppercase letter	Variable saved by the make session (**:mksession**) command.
Lowercase letter somewhere inside	
`:let Save_this_option = 1` `:let forget_this = "yes"`	`" Options saved in session` `" Discarded between sessions`
All lowercase, digits, and underscore	A variable not stored in any save file.
$environment	Environment variable.
@register	Text register.
&option	The name of an option.
`b:`*name*	The variable is local to the buffer. Each buffer can have a different value of this variable.
`w:`*name*	A variable local to a window.
`g:`*name*	A global variable. (Used inside functions to denote global variables.)
`a:`*name*	An argument to a function.
`v:`*name*	A *Vim* internal variable.

Some examples:

```
" The environment variable $PAGER contains the name of the page viewing command
:let $PAGER = "/usr/local/bin/less"

" Display the value of the last search pattern
:echo "Last search was "@/

" The following two commands do the same thing
:let &autoindent = 1
:set autoindent

" Define the syntax for the current buffer
:let b:current_syntax = c
"Note: This doesn't handle all the side effects associated with "changing the
language of the buffer
```

The internal variables (**v:***name*) are used by *Vim* to store a variety of information. The following table shows the full list of variables.

Variable	Functions
v:*count*	The count given for the last normal-mode command.
v:count1	Like v:count, except that it defaults to 1 if no count is specified.
v:errmsg	The last error message.
v:warningmsg	The last warning message.
v:statusmsg	The last status message.
v:shell_error	Result of the last shell command. If 0, the command worked; if non-0, the command failed.
v:this_session	Full filename of the last loaded or saved session file.
v:*version*	Version number of *Vim*. Version 5.01 is stored as 501.

Constants

The *Vim* editor uses a variety of constants. There are the normal integers:

```
123        " Simple integer
0123       " Octal integer
0xAC       " Hexadecimal
```

There are also string constants:

```
"string"              " A simple string
'string'              " A literal string
```

The difference between a simple string and a literal string is that in a simple string, characters escaped by backslash are expanded, whereas in a literal string a backslash is just a backslash. For example:

```
:echo ">\100<"
>@<
:echo '>\100<'
>\100<
```

> **Note**
>
> The character number octal 100 is @.

Expressions

You can perform a variety of operations on integers. These include the arithmetic operators:

int + *int*	Addition
int − *int*	Subtraction
int ⋆ *int*	Multiplication
int / *int*	Integer divide (and truncate)
int % *int*	Modulo
− *int*	Negation

> **Note**
>
> Strings are automatically converted to integers when used in conjunction with these operators.

In addition, a number of logical operators work on both strings and integers. These return a 1 if the comparison succeeds and 0 if it does not.

var == *var*	Check for equality.
var != *var*	Inequality.
var < *var*	Less than.
var <= *var*	Less than or equal to.
var > *var*	Greater than.
var >= *var*	Greater than or equal to.

In addition, the comparison operators compare a string against a regular expression. For example, the following checks the given string ("word") against the regular expression "\w*" and returns a 1 if the string matches the expression:

```
"word" =~ "\w*"
```

The two regular expression comparison operators are as follows:

string =~ regexp	Regular expression matches.
string !~ regexp	Regular expression does not match.

In addition, strings have the following special comparisons:

`string ==? string`	Strings equal, ignore case.
`string ==# string`	Strings equal, case must match.
`string !=? string`	Strings not equal, ignore case.
`string !=# string`	Strings not equal, case must match.
`string <? string`	Strings less than, ignore case.
`string <# string`	Strings less than, case must match.
`string <=? string`	Strings less than or equal, ignore case.
`string <=# string`	Strings less than or equal, case must match.
`string >? string`	Strings greater than, ignore case.
`string ># string`	Strings greater than, case must match.
`string >=? string`	Strings greater than or equal, ignore case.
`string >=# string`	Strings greater than or equal, case must match.

There are three forms of each operator. The bare form (i.e. ==) honors the `'ignorecase'` option. The "?" form (i.e.==?) always ignores case differences while the "#" form (i.e.==#) never ignores different case characters.

Deleting a Variable

The following command deletes a variable:

```
:unlet[!] {name}
```

Generally, if you try to delete a variable that does not exist, an error result. If the override (!) character is present, no error message results.

Entering Filenames

When you are entering a filename, you can use a number of special words and characters, as follows:

`%`	Current filename
`#`	Alternate filename
`<cword>`	The word under the cursor.
`<cWORD>`	The WORD under the cursor.
`<cfile>`	The filename under the cursor.
`<afile>`	The name of a file being read or written during the execution of a related autocommand. (See Chapter 13, "Autocommands," for more information.)

`<abuf>`	The current buffer number in an autocommand.
`<amatch>`	Like **`<abuf>`**, but when used with a FileType or Syntax event it is not the file name, but the file type or syntax name.
`<sfile>`	The name of the file currently being **`:sourced`**.

You can modify each of these words by one or more of the modifiers listed here (for example, the **`:p`** modifier, which turns a filename into a full pathname). If the name of the file under the cursor is `test.c`, for instance, **`<cfile>`** would be `test.c`. On the other hand, **`<cfile:p>`** would be `/home/oualline/examples/test.c`.

You can use the following modifiers:

`:p`	Turn a filename into a full path. Must appear first if multiple modifiers are used.
`:~`	Turn an absolute path such as `/home/oualline/examples/test.c` into a short version using the ~ notation, such as `~oualline/examples/test.c`.
`:.`	Turn the path into one relative to the current directory, if possible.
`:h`	Head of the filename. For example, `../path/test.c` yields `../path`.
`:t`	Tail of the filename. Therefore, `../path/test.c` yields `test.c`.
`:r`	Filename without extension. Therefore, `../path/test.c` yields `test`.
`:e`	Extension.
`:s?`*`from`*`?`*`to`*`?`	Substitution changing the pattern *from* to the pattern *to*, first occurrence.
`:gs?`*`from`*`?`*`to`*`?`	Substitution changing the pattern *from* to the pattern *to*, all occurrences.

How to Experiment

You can determine how *Vim* will apply modifiers to a filename. First create a text file whose content is the filename on which you want to run experiments. Put the cursor on this filename and then use the following command to test out a modifier:

```
:echo expand("<cword>:p")
```

(Change **`:p`** to whatever modifier you want to check.)

The following sections discuss the **`:echo`** statement and **`expand`** function in more detail.

The :echo Statement

The **:echo** statement just echoes its arguments. For example:

```
:echo "Hello world"
Hello world
```

You can also use it to display the value of a variable:

```
:let flag=1
:echo flag
1
```

The **:echon** command echoes the arguments, but does not output a newline. For example:

```
:echo "aa" ¦ echo "bb"
aa
bb
:echon "aa" ¦ echon "bb"
aabb
```

> **Note**
>
> The bar (|) is used to separate two commands on the same line.

Echoing in Color

You can use the **:echohl** command to change the color of the output **:echo** to a given highlight group. For example:

```
:echohl ErrorMsg
:echo "A mistake has been made"
:echohl None
```

> **Note**
>
> Good programming practice dictates that you always reset the highlighting to None after your message. That way you do not affect other **:echo** commands.

If you want to see what highlight groups are defined, use this command:

```
:highlight
```

Control Statements

The *Vim* editor has a variety of control statements that enable you to change the flow of a macro or function. With these, you can make full use of *Vim*'s sophisticated script language.

The :*if* Statement

The general form of the `:if` statement is as follows:

```
:if {condition}
:    " Statement
:    " Statement
:endif
```

The statements inside the `:if` statement are executed if the *condition* is non-zero. The four-space indent inside the `:if` is optional, but encouraged because it makes the program much more readable.

The `:if` statement can have an **else** clause:

```
:if {condition}
:    " Statement
:    " Statement
:else
:    " Statement
:    " Statement
:endif
```

Finally, the `:elseif` keyword is a combination of `:if` and `:else`. Using it removes the need for an extra `:endif`:

```
:if &term == "xterm"
:    " Do xterm stuff
:elseif &term == "vt100"
:    " Do vt100 stuff
:else
:    " Do non xterm and vt100 stuff
:endif
```

Looping

The `:while` command starts a loop. The loop ends with the `:endwhile` command:

```
:while counter < 30
:    let counter = counter + 1
:    " Do something
:endwhile
```

The `:continue` command goes to the top of the loop and continues execution. The `:break` command exits the loop:

```
:while counter <: 30
:    if skip_flag
:        continue
:    endif
:    if exit_flag
:        break
:    endif
:    "Do something
:endwhile
```

The :*execute* Command

The :**execute** executes the argument as a normal command-mode command:

```
:let command = "echo 'Hello world!'"
:execute command
Hello World
```

Defining Your Own Function

The *Vim* editor enables you to define your own functions. The basic function declaration begins as follows:

```
:function {name}({var1}, {var2}, ...)
```

Note

Function names must begin with a capital letter.

It ends as follows:

```
:endfunction
```

Let's define a short function to return the smaller of two numbers, starting with this declaration:

```
:function Min(num1, num2)
```

This tells *Vim* that the function is named **Min** and it takes two arguments (**num1** and **num2**).

The first thing you need to do is to check to see which number is smaller:

```
:    if a:num1 < a:num2
```

The special prefix **a:** tells *Vim* that the variable is a function argument. Let's assign the variable *smaller* the value of the smallest number:

```
:    if a:num1 < a:num2
:        let smaller = a:num1
:    else
:        let smaller = a:num2
:    endif
```

The variable *smaller* is a local variable. All variables used inside a function are local unless prefixed by a **g:**.

Warning

A variable outside a function declaration is called *var*; whereas inside if you want to refer to the same variable, you need to call it **g:***var*. Therefore, one variable has two different names depending on the context.

You now use the `:return` statement to return the smallest number to the user. Finally, you end the function:

```
:    return smaller
:endfunction
```

The complete function definition is as follows:

```
:function Min(num1, num2)
:    if a:num1 < a:num2
:        let smaller = a:num1
:    else
:        let smaller = a:num2
:    endif
:    return smaller
:endfunction
```

> **Note**
>
> I know that this function can be written more efficiently, but it is designed to be a tutorial of features, not efficiency.

Using a Function

You can now use your function in any *Vim* expression. For example:

```
:let tiny = Min(10, 20)
```

You can also call a function explicitly using the function name with the `:call` command:

```
:[range] call {function}([parameters])
```

If a [*range*] is specified, the function is called for each line, unless the function is a special "range"-type function (as discussed later).

Function Options

If you attempt to define a function that already exists, you will get an error. You can use the force option (`!`) to cause the function to silently replace any previous definition of the function:

```
:function Max(num1, num2)
:    " Code
:endfunction

:function Max(num1, num2, num3)
— error —

:function! Max(num1, num2, num3)
— no error —
```

By putting the **range** keyword after the function definition, the function is considered a **range** function. For example:

```
:function Count_words() range
```

When run on a range of lines, the variables **a:**_firstline_ and **a:**_lastline_ are set to the first and last line in the range.

If the word **abort** follows the function definition, the function aborts on the first error. For example:

```
:function Do_It() abort
```

Finally, *Vim* enables you to define functions that have a variable number of arguments. The following command, for instance, defines a function that *must* have 1 argument (**start**) and can have up to 20 additional arguments:

```
:function Show(start, ...)
```

The variable **a:**_1_ contains the first optional argument, **a:**_2_ the second, and so on. The variable **a:**_0_ contains the number of extra arguments. For example:

```
:function Show(start, ...)
:    let index = 1        " Loop index
:    echo "Show is" a:start
:
:    while (index <= a:0)
:        echo "Arg" index "is " a:index
:        let index = index + 1
:    endwhile
:endfunction
```

Listing Functions

The **:function** command lists all the user-defined functions:

```
:function
function FTCheck_nroff()
function FTCheck_asm()
```

To see what is in a single function, execute this command:

```
:function {name}
```

For example:

```
:function Show
function Show
    let index = 1        " Loop index
    echo "Show is" a:start

    while (index <= a:0)
        echo "Arg" index "is "a:.index
        let index = index + 1
    endwhile
endfunction
```

Deleting a Function

To delete a function, use this command:

```
:delfunction name
```

User-Defined Commands

The *Vim* editor enables you to define your own commands. You execute these commands just like any other command-mode command. To define a command, use the `:command` command, as follows:

```
:command Delete_first :1delete
```

Now when you execute the command

```
:Delete_first
```

the *Vim* editor performs a

```
:1delete
```

which deletes the first line.

> **Note**
>
> User-defined commands must start with a capital letter.

To list out the user-defined commands, execute the following command:

```
:command
```

To remove the definition of a user-defined command, issue the `:delcommand`, as follows:

```
:delcommand Delete_one
```

You can clear all user-defined commands with the following command:

```
:comclear
```

User-defined commands can take a series of arguments. The number of arguments must be specified by the `-nargs` option on the command line. For instance, the example `Delete_one` command takes no arguments, so you could have defined it as follows:

```
:command Delete_first -nargs=0 1delete
```

However, because `-nargs=0` is the default, you do not need to specify it.

The other values of `-nargs` are as follows:

`-nargs=0`	No arguments
`-nargs=1`	One argument
`-nargs=*`	Any number of arguments
`-nargs=?`	Zero or one argument
`-nargs=+`	One or more arguments

Inside the command definition, the arguments are represented by the **<args>** keyword. For example:

```
:command -nargs=+ Say :echo "<args>"
```

Now when you type

```
:Say Hello World
```

the system echoes

```
Hello World
```

Some commands take a range as their argument. To tell *Vim* that you are defining such a command, you need to specify a **-range** option. The values for this option are as follows:

-range	Range is allowed. Default is the current line.
-range=%	Range is allowed. Default is the while file.
-range=count	Range is allowed, but it is really just a single number whose default is *count*.

When a **range** is specified, the keywords **<line1>** and **<line2>** get the values of the first and last line in the range.

For example, the following command defines the **SaveIt** command, which writes out the specified range to the file save_file:

```
:command -range=% SaveIt :<line1>, <line2> write! save_file
```

Some of the other options and keywords are as follows:

-count=number	The command can take a count whose default is *number*. The resulting count is stored in the **<count>** keyword.
-bang	You can use the override (**!**) modifier. If present, a **!** will be stored in the keyword **<bang>**.
-register	You can specify a register. (The default is the unnamed register.) The register specification is put in the **<reg>** (a.k.a. **<register>**) keyword.

The **<f-args>** keyword contains the same information as the **<args>** keyword, except in a format suitable for use as function call arguments. For example:

```
:command -nargs=* DoIt :call AFunction(<f-args>)
:DoIt a b c
```

Execute the following command:

```
:call AFunction("a", "b", "c")
```

Finally, you have the **<lt>** keyword. It contains the character **<**.

Built-In Functions

The *Vim* editor has a number of built-in functions. This section lists all the built-in functions.

append({*line_number*}, {*string*})

What it does:	Appends the *string* as a new line after *line_number*.

Parameters:

line_number	The line number after which the text is to be inserted. A value of 0 causes the text to be inserted at the beginning of the file.
string	The string to be inserted after the given line.
Returns:	Integer flag.
	0 = no error; 1 = error caused by a *line_number* out of range.

argc()

What it does:	Counts the number of arguments in the argument list.
Returns:	Integer.
	The argument count.

argv({*number*})

What it does:	Returns an argument in the argument list.

Parameter:

number	The argument index. Argument 0 is the first argument in the argument list (not the name of the program, as in C programming).
Returns:	String.
	Returns the requested argument.

browse(*save*, *title*, *initial_directory*, *default*)

What it does:	Displays a file browser and lets the user pick a file. This works only in the GUI version of the editor.

Parameters:

save	An integer that indicates whether the file is being read or saved. If *save* is non-0, the browser selects a file to write. If 0, a file is selected for reading.
title	Title for the dialog box.
initial_directory	The directory in which to start browsing.
default	Default filename.
Returns:	String.
	The name of the file selected. If the user selected Cancel or an error occurs, an empty string is returned.

bufexists(*buffer_name*)

What it does:	Checks to see whether a buffer exists.
Parameter:	
buffer_name	The name of a buffer to check for existence.
Returns:	Integer flag.
	Returns true (1) if the buffer exists and false (0) otherwise.

bufloaded(*buffer_name*)

What it does:	Check to see whether a buffer is loaded.
Parameter:	
buffer_name	The name of a buffer to check to see whether it is currently loaded.
Returns:	Integer flag.
	Returns true (1) if the buffer is loaded and false (0) otherwise.

bufname(*buffer_scpecification*)

What it does:	Find the indicated buffer.
Parameter:	
buffer_specification	A buffer number or a string that specifies the buffer. If a number is supplied, buffer number *buffer_specification* is returned. If a string is supplied, it is treated as a regular expression and the list of buffers is searched for a match and the match returned. There are three special buffers: % is the current buffer, # is the alternate buffer, and $ is the last buffer in the list.
Returns:	String.
	String containing the full name of the buffer or an empty string if there is an error or no matching buffer can be found.

bufnr(*buffer_expression*)

What it does:	Obtains the number of a buffer.
Parameter:	
buffer_expression	A buffer specification similar to the one used by the **bufname** function.
Returns:	Integer.
	Number of the buffer, or −1 for error.

bufwinnr(*buffer_expression*)

What it does: Obtains the window number for a buffer.

Parameter:

buffer_expression   A buffer specification similar to the one used by the **bufname** function.

Returns: Integer.
The number of the first window associated with the buffer or −1 if there is an error or no buffer matches the *buffer_expression*.

byte2line(*byte_index*)

What it does: Converts a byte index into a line number.

Parameter:

byte_index   The index of a character within the current buffer.

Returns: Integer.
The line number of the line that contains the character at *byte_index* or −1 if *byte_index* is out of range.

char2nr(*character*)

What it does: Converts a character to a character number.

Parameter:

character   A single character to be converted. If a longer string is supplied, only the first character is used.

Returns: Integer.
The character number. For example, **char2nr("A")** is 65. (The ASCII code for 'A' is 65.)

col(*location*)

What it does: Returns the column of the specified location.

Parameter:

location   Is a mark specification (for example, **''x**) or **"."** to obtain the column where the cursor is located.

Returns: Integer.
The column where the mark or cursor resides, or 0 if there is an error.

```
confirm({message}, {choice_list}, [default], [type])
```

What it does: Displays a dialog box giving the user a number of choices and returns what the user chooses.

Parameters:

{*message*} A prompt message displayed in the dialog box.

{*choice_list*} A string containing a list of choices. The newline ("\n") separates each choice. The ampersand (&) is used to indicate an accelerator character.

[*default*] An index indicating default choice. The first button is #1. If this parameter is not specified, the first button is selected.

[*type*] The type of the dialog box to be displayed. The choices are "Error", "Question", "Info", "Warning", or "Generic". The default is "Generic".

Returns: Integer.

The choice number (starting with 1), or 0 if the user aborted out of the dialog box by pressing **<ESC>** or **CTRL-C**.

Examples:

```
echo confirm("Choose one", "&One\n&Two\n&Three", 2, "Error")
echo confirm("Choose one", "&One\n&Two\n&Three", 1, "Question")
echo confirm("Choose one", "&One\n&Two\n&Three", 1, "Warning")
echo confirm("Choose one", "&One\n&Two\n&Three", 0, "Info")
echo confirm("Choose one", "&One\n&Two\n&Three", 0, "Generic")
```

Figure 27.1 shows the various types of confirmation dialog boxes.

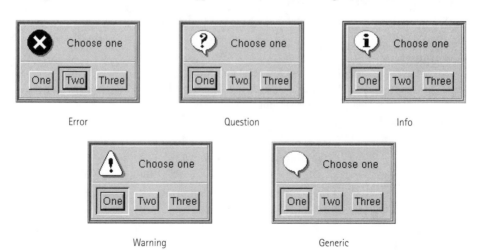

Error   Question   Info

Warning   Generic

Figure 27.1 Dialog box types.

Note

This function works on both the GUI and console version of the editor. The console versions of the dialog boxes do not look as nice:

```
:echo confirm("Hello", "&One\n&Two", 1, "Error")
Hello
[O]ne, (T)wo: O
```

delete({*file_name*})

What it does: Deletes the file.

Parameter:

   {*file_name*}   The name of the file to delete.

Returns: Integer.

   0 means that the file was deleted. Non–0 for error.

did_filetype()

What it does: Checks to see whether the **FileType** event has been done. This command is useful in conjunction with the autocommands.

Returns: Integer.

   Non–0 if autocommands are being executed and at least one **FileType** event has occurred. 0 otherwise.

escape({string}, {character_list})

What it does: Turns a {*string*} of characters into an escaped string. The {*character_list*} specifies the character to be escaped.

Parameters:

   {*string*}   The string you want to escape.

   {*character_list*}   The list of characters in {*string*} that need to have the escape character (\) put in front of them.

Returns: String.

   The escaped string. For example:

```
:echo escape("This is a 'test'.", " '")
This\ is\ a\ \'test\'."
```

`exists({string})`

What it does: Checks to see whether the item specified by [{*string*} exits.

Parameters:

{*string*}   An item to check. This can be used to specify an option
                  (`'&autoindent'`), an environment variable (`'$VIMHOME'`), a
                  built-in function name (`'*escape'`), or a simple variable
                  (`'var_name'`). (Note: The quotation marks are required because
                  you are passing in a string.)

Returns: Integer.
                  Returns 1 if the item exists, 0 otherwise.

`expand({string}, [flag])`

What it does: Returns a list of files that match the {*string*}. This string can
                  contain wildcards and other specifications. For example,
                  expand(`"*.c"`) returns a list of all C files.

Parameters:

{*string*}   A string to be expanded. The string can contain any of the
                  special file characters described earlier. Note: The `'suffixes'`
                  and `'wildignore'` options affect how the expansion is carried
                  out.

                  When a special word such as `'<cfile>'` is expanded, no fur-
                  ther expansion is performed. If the cursor is on the string
                  `'~/.vimrc'`, for example, `'expand('<cfile>')'` results in
                  `'~/.vimrc'`.

                  If you want the full filename, however, you need to expand
                  twice. Therefore, `'expand(expand('<cfile>'))'` returns
                  `'/home/oualline/.vimrc'`.

                  The `'wildignore'` and `'suffixes'` options are honored unless
                  a non-0 [*flag*] argument is supplied.

Returns: String list.
                  A list of filenames that match the {*string*} separated by new-
                  lines. If nothing matches, an empty string is returned.

`filereadable({file_name})`

What it does: Checks to see whether a file is readable.

Parameter:

{*file_name*}   The name of the file to check.

Returns: Integer.
                  Non-0 number is returned when the file exists and can be
                  read. A 0 indicates that the file does not exist or is protected
                  against reading.

`fnamemodify({file_name}, {modifiers})`

What it does: Applies the {*modifiers*} to the {*file_name*} and return the result.

Parameters:
  {*file_name*}   The name of a file.
  {*modifiers*}   Modification flags such as ":r:h".

Returns: String.
  The modified filename.

`getcwd()`

What it does: Obtains the current working directory.

Returns: String.
  The current directory.

`getftime({file_name})`

What it does: Gets the modification time of a file.

Parameter:
  {*file_name*}   The name of the file to check.

Returns: Integer.
  The modification time of the file (in UNIX format, seconds since January 1, 1970), or −1 for error.

`getline({line_number})`

What it does: Gets a line from the current editing buffer.

Parameter:
  {*line_number*}   The line number of the line to get or "." for the line the cursor is on.

Returns: String.
  The text of the line or an empty string if the {*line_number*} is out of range.

`getwinposx() getwinposy()`

What they do: Return the x or y position of the *Vim* GUI window.

Returns: Integer.
  The location in pixels of the x or y position of the GUI window, or −1 when the information is not available.

glob({file_name})

> **What it does:**   Expands the wildcards in the filename and return a list of files.
>
> **Parameter:**
>
>   *{file_name}*   A string representing the filename pattern to match. You can also use an external command enclosed in backticks (`` ` ``). For example **glob("`find . -name '*.c' -print`")**.
>
> **Returns:**   String list.
> The list of files matched (separated by <NL>), or the empty string if nothing matches.

has({feature})

> **What it does:**   Checks to see whether a particular feature is installed.
>
> **Parameter:**
>
>   *{feature}*   A string containing the feature name.
>
> **Returns:**   Integer flag.
> 1 if the feature is compiled in, or 0 if it is not.

histadd({history}, {command})

> **What it does:**   Adds an item to one of the history lists.
>
> **Parameters:**
>
>   *{history}*   Name of the history to use. Names are as follows:

"cmd"	":"	Command history
"search"	"/"	Search pattern history
"expr"	"="	Expressions entered for "=
"input"	"@"	Input line history

> **Returns:**   Integer flag.
> 1 for okay, 0 for error.

histdel({history}, [pattern])

> **What it does:**   Removes commands from a history.
>
> **Parameters:**
>
>   *{history}*   Which history list to use.
>
>   *[pattern]*   A regular expression that defines the items to be removed. If no pattern is specified, all items are removed from the history.
>
> **Returns:**   Integer flag.
> 1 for okay, 0 for error.

`histget({history}, [index])`

What it does: Obtains an item from the history.

Parameters:

{history} Which history list to use.

[index] An index of the item to get. The newest entry is −1, the next newest −2, and so on. The last entry is 1, next to last 2, and so on. If no *[index]* is specified, the last entry is returned.

Returns: String.
The specified item in the history, or an empty string if there is an error.

`histnr({history})`

What it does: Returns the number of the current entry in the given
{history}.

Parameter:

{history} The history to be examined.

Returns: Integer.
The number of the last item in the history or −1 for error.

`hlexists({name})`

What it does: Checks to see whether a syntax highlighting group exists.

Parameter:

{name} Name of the group to check for.

Returns: Integer flag
Non-0, the group exists; 0 it does not.

`hlID({name})`

What it does: Given the name of a syntax highlight group, returns the ID number.

Parameter:

{name} Name of the syntax highlighting group.

Returns: Integer.
The ID number.

`hostname()`

What it does: Gets the name of the computer.

Returns: String.
The hostname of the computer.

input({*prompt*})

> **What it does:**   Asks a question and gets an answer.
>
> **Parameter:**
>
> {*prompt*}   The prompt to be displayed.
>
> **Returns:**   String.
>
> What the user types in as a response.

isdirectory({*file_name*})

> **What it does:**   Tests to see whether {*file_name*} is a directory.
>
> **Parameter:**
>
> {*file_name*}   The name of the item to be checked.
>
> **Returns:**   Integer flag.
>
> 1, it is a directory; 0 it is not a directory or does not exist.

libcall({dll_name}, {function}, {argument})

> **What it does:**   Calls a function in a DLL file. (Microsoft Windows only).
>
> **Parameters:**
>
> {*dll_name*}   Name of a shared library (DLL) file in which the {*function*} is defined.
>
> {*function*}   The name of the function
>
> {*argument*}   A single argument. If this argument is an integer, it will be passed as an integer. If it is a string, it will be passed as "char ★".

Note

The function must return a string or NULL. A function that returns a random pointer might crash *Vim*.

> **Returns:**   String.
>
> Whatever the function returns.

line({*position*})

> **What it does:**   Given a marker or other position indicator, returns the line number.
>
> **Parameter:**
>
> {*position*}   The position marker. This can be a mark: 'x, the current cursor location ".", or the end-of-file "$".
>
> **Returns:**   Integer.
>
> The line number or 0 if the marker is not set or another error occurs.

`line2byte({line_number})`

What it does:	Converts a line number to a byte index.

Parameter:

{line_number}	The line number to be converted. This can also be a mark (`'x'`), the current cursor position (`'.'`) or the last line in the buffer (`'$'`).
Returns:	Integer.
	The byte index of the first character in the line starting with 1. An error results in a return of −1.

`localtime()`

What it does:	Returns the current time in the UNIX standard time format.
Returns:	Integer.
	The number of seconds past January 1, 1970.

`maparg({name}, [mode])`

What it does:	Returns what a key is mapped to.

Parameters:

{name}	The name of a *{lhs}* mapping.
{mode}	The mode in which the string is mapped. This defaults to "".
Returns:	String.
	The resulting mapping string. An empty string is returned if there is no mapping.

`mapcheck({name}, [mode])`

What it does:	Checks to see whether a mapping exists.

Parameters:

{name}	The name of a *{lhs}* mapping.
{mode}	The mode in which the string is mapped. This defaults to "".
Returns:	String.
	This returns *any* mapping that can match *{name}*. This differs slightly from the **maparg** function in that it looks at mappings for conflicting names. If you have a mapping for "ax," for instance, it will conflict with "axx".

For example:

```
:map ax Test
:echo maparg("ax")
Test
:echo maparg("axx")

:echo mapcheck("ax")
Test
:echo mapcheck("axx")
Test
```

`match({string}, {pattern})`

What it does:	Checks to see whether {*string*} matches {*pattern*}. Setting the 'ignorecase' option causes the editor to ignore upper/lowercase difference.
Parameters:	
{*string*}	String to check.
{*pattern*}	Pattern to check it against. This pattern acts like magic was set.
Returns:	Integer. The index of the first character of {*string*} where {*pattern*} occurs. The first character is number 0. If nothing matches, a −1 is returned.

`matchend({string}, {pattern})`

What it does:	Similar to the match function, except that it returns the index of the character of {*string*} just after where {*pattern*} occurs.

`matchstr({string}, {pattern})`

What it does:	Like the match function, but returns the string that matches.
Parameters:	
{*string*}	String to check.
{*pattern*}	Pattern to check it against. This pattern acts like magic was set.
Returns:	String. The part of {*string*} that matches or the empty string if nothing matches.

`nr2char({number})`

What it does:	Turns a number into a character.
Parameter:	The number of an ASCII character.
Returns:	String of length 1. The ASCII character for the number.

`rename({from}, {to})`

What it does:	Renames a file.
Parameters:	
{*from*}	The name of the existing file.
{*to*}	The name to which we want to rename the file.
Returns:	Integer flag. 0 for success, non-0 for failure.

setline({line_number}, {line})

What it does: Replaces the contents of line {*line_number*} with the string {*line*}.

Parameters:

{*line_number*}   The number of the line to change.

{*line*}   The text for the replacement line.

Returns: Integer flag.
0 for no error, non-0 if there was a problem.

strftime({format}, [time])

What it does: Returns the time formatted according to the {*format*} string. The conversion characters that can be put in the string are determined by your system's *strftime* function.

Parameters:

{*format*}   The format string.

[*time*]   The time (in seconds since 1970) to be used. (Default is now).

Returns: String.
The *time* string containing the formatted time.

strlen({string})

What it does: Computes the length of a {*string*}.

Parameter:

{*string*}   The string whose length you want.

Returns: Integer.
The length of the string.

strpart({string}, {start}, {length})

What it does: Returns the substring of {*string*} that starts at index {*start*} and up to {*length*} characters long.

For example:

```
:echo strpart("This is a test", 0, 4)
This
:echo strpart("This is a test", 5, 2)
is
```

If the {*start*} or {*length*} parameters specify non–existent characters, they are ignored. For example, the following **strpart** command starts to the left of the first character:

```
:echo strpart("This is a test", -2, 4)
Th
```

Parameters:

{*string*}	The string from which you want a piece.
{*start*}	The location of the start of the string you want to extract.
{*length*}	The length of the string to extract.

Returns: String.

The substring extracted for {*string*}.

strtrans({*string*})

What it does: Translates the unprintable characters in {*string*} to printable ones.

Parameter:

{*string*} A string containing unprintable characters.

Returns: String.

The resulting string has unprintable characters, such as CTRL-A translated to ^A.

substitute({string}, {pattern}, {replace}, {flag})

What it does: In {*string*}, changes the first match of {*pattern*} with {*replace*}. This is the equivalent of performing the following on a line containing {*string*}:

:. substitute /{*pattern*}/{*replace*}/{*flag*}

Parameters:

{*string*}	The string in which the replacement is to be made.
{*pattern*}	A {*pattern*} used to specify the portion of {*string*} to be replaced.
{*replace*}	The replacement text.
{*flag*}	If the empty string, replace just the first occurrence. If "g", replace all occurrences.

Returns: String.

The string that results from the substitution.

synID({line}, {column}, {transparent_flag})

What it does: Returns the syntax ID of the item at the given {*line*} and {*column*}.

Parameters:

{*line*}, {*column*}	The location of the item in the buffer.
{*transparent_flag*}	If non-0, transparent items are reduced to the items they reveal.

Returns: Integer.

The Syntax ID.

synIDattr({sytnax_id}, {attribute}, [mode])

What it does:	Obtains an attribute of a syntax color element.

Parameters:

{*syntax_id*}   The syntax identification number.

{*attribute*}   The name of an attribute. The attributes are as follows:

"name"	The name of the syntax item
"fg"	Foreground color
"bg"	Background color
"fg#"	Foreground color in #RRGGBB form
"bg#"	Background color in #RRGGBB form
"bold"	"1" if this item is bold
"italic"	"1" if this item is italic
"reverse"	"1" if this item is reverse
"inverse"	Same as "reverse"
"underline"	"1" if this item is underlined

{*mode*}   Which type of terminal to get the attributes for. This can be "gui", "cterm", or "term". It defaults to the terminal type you are currently using.

Returns:	String. The value of the attribute.

synIDtrans({syntax_id})

What it does:	Returns a translated syntax ID.

Parameter:

{*syntax_id*}   The ID of the syntax element.

Returns:	Integer. The translated syntax ID.

system({command})

What it does:	Executes the external command named {*command*} and captures the output. The options '**shell**' and '**shellredir**' apply to this function.

Parameter:

{*command*}   A command to execute.

Returns:	String. Whatever the command output is returned.

tempname()

What it does:	Generates a temporary filename.
Returns:	String. The name of a file that can be safely used as a temporary file.

`visualmode()`

What it does: Gets the last visual mode.

Returns: String.

The last visual mode as a command string. This is either **v**, **V**, or **CTRL-V**.

`virtcol({location})`

What it does: Computes the virtual column of the given {*location*}.

Parameter:

{*location*}   A location indicator such as **.**" (cursor location), **'a** (mark a), or **$**" (end of the buffer).

Returns: Integer.

The location of the virtual column (that is, the column number assuming that tabs are expanded and unprintable characters are made printable).

`winbufnr({number})`

What it does: Gets the buffer number of the buffer that is in a window.

Parameter:

{*number*}   The window number or 0 for the current window.

Returns: Integer.

Buffer number or −1 for error.

`winheight({number})`

What it does: Gets the height of a window.

Parameter:

{*number*}   The window number or 0 for the current window.

Returns: Integer.

Window height in lines or −1 for error.

`winnr()`

What it does: Gets the current window number.

Returns: Integer.

The current window number. The top window is #1.

Obsolete Functions

A few functions are currently obsolete and have been replaced with newer versions; however, you might still find some scripts that use them.

Obsolete Name	Replacement
buffer_exists()	bufexists()
buffer_name()	bufname()
buffer_number()	bufnr()
last_buffer_nr()	bufnr("$")
file_readable()	filereadable()
highlight_exists()	hlexists()
highlightID()	hlID()

28

Customizing the Editor

THE *VIM* EDITOR IS HIGHLY CUSTOMIZABLE. It gives you a huge number of options. This chapter discusses how to use the ones that enable you to customize the appearance and the behavior of your *Vim* editor.

This chapter discusses the following:

- The **:set** command (in extreme detail)
- Local initialization files
- Customizing keyboard usage
- Customizing messages and the appearance of the screen
- Other miscellaneous commands

Setting

The *Vim* editor has a variety of ways of setting options. Generally, to set an option, you use the following command:

    :set option=value

This works for most options. Boolean options are set with this command:

    :set option

They are reset with the following command:

```
:set nooption
```

To display the value of an option, use this command:

```
:set option?
```

If you want to set an option to its default value, use the following command:

```
:set option&
```

Boolean Options

You can perform the following operations on a Boolean option.

Operation	Meaning
:set option	Turn the option on.
:set nooption	Turn the option off.
:set option!	Invert the option.
:set invoption	Invert the option.
:set option&	Set the option to the default value.

For example:

```
:set list
:set list?
list
:set nolist
:set list?
nolist
:set list!
:set list?
list
:set list&
:set list?
nolist
```

Numeric Options

You can perform the following operations on a numeric option.

Command	Meaning
:set option += value	Add value to the option.
:set option -= value	Subtract value from the option.
:set option ^= value	Multiply the option by value.
:set option&	Set the option to the default value.

For example:

```
:set shiftwidth=4
:set shiftwidth += 2
:set shiftwidth?
shiftwidth=6
:set shiftwidth-=3
:set shiftwidth
shiftwidth=3
:set shiftwidth ^= 2
:set shiftwidth
shiftwidth=6
:set shiftwidth&
:set shiftwidth
shiftwidth=8
```

String-Related Commands

You can perform the following operations on string options:

Command	Meaning
:set *option* += *value*	Add *value* to the end of the option.
:set *option* -= *value*	Remove *value* (or characters) from the option.
:set *option* ^= *value*	Add *value* to the beginning of the option.

For example:

```
:set cinwords=test
:set cinwords?
cinwords=test
:set cinwords+=end
:set cinwords?
cinwords=test,end
:set cinwords-=test
:set cinwords?
cinwords=end
:set cinwords^=start
:set cinwords?
cinwords=start,end
```

Another Set Command

The following command sets a Boolean option (such as **list** and **nolist**), but it displays the value of other types of options:

```
:set option
```

However, it is not a good idea to use this form of the command to display an option value because it can lead to errors if you are not careful. It is much better to use the following command to display the value of an option:

```
:set option?
```

An alternative form of the

```
:set option = value
```

command is this command:

```
:set option:value
```

Other :set Arguments

The following command prints out all the options that differ from their default values:

```
:set
```

The following command prints all options:

```
:set all
```

This command prints out all the terminal control codes:

```
:set termcap
```

Finally, to reset everything to the default values, use this command:

```
:set all&
```

Chaining Commands

You can put several :set operations on one line. To set three different options, for example, use the following command:

```
:set list shiftwidth=4 incsearch
```

Automatically Setting Options in a File

You can put *Vim* settings in your files. When *Vim* starts editing a file, it reads the first few lines of the file, looking for a line like this:

```
vim: set option-command option-command option-command ....
```

This type of line is called a *modeline*.

In a program, for instance, a typical modeline might look like this:

```
/* vim: set shiftwidth=4 autoindent : */
```

An alternate format is:

```
Vim: option-command:.option-command: ...:
```

The option `'modeline'` turns on and off this behavior. The option `'modeline'` controls how many lines are read at the start and end of the file when *Vim* looks for setting commands.

If you set the following option, for instance, *Vim* does not look for modelines:

```
:set nomodeline
```

If the following option is set, *Vim* does look at the top and bottom of each file for the number of lines specified by the `modeline` option:

```
:set modeline
```

For example, you may see lines like the following at the end of many of the *Vim* help files:

```
vim:tw=78:ts=8:sw=8:
```

This sets the `'tw'` (`'textwidth'`) option to **78**, the `'ts'` (`'tabstop'`) to **8**, and the `'sw'` (`'shiftwidth'`) to **8**. These settings make the text in the help files look nice. By using modelines, the creators of the help file make sure that the text is formatted correctly no matter what local settings you use for your other files.

Another example: For this book, I have had to create a number of C programming examples. When I copy these programs into the word processor, the tabs get really screwed up. The solution to this problem is to make sure that there are no tabs in the program. One way to do this is to put a line like this at the end of the file:

```
/* vim: set expandtabs : */
```

This turns on `'expandtabs'` and causes *Vim* to never insert a real tab—well, almost never; you can force the issue by using **CTRL-V <Tab>**.

If you have some custom settings for your own C programs, you can put a line near the top of bottom of your program like this:

```
/* vim: set cindent:shiftwidth=4:smarttabs : */
```

Local *.vimrc* Files

Suppose you want to have different settings for each directory. One way to do this is to put a `.vimrc` or `.gvimrc` file in each directory. That is not enough, however, because by default *Vim* ignores these files.

To make *Vim* read these files, you must execute the following command:

```
:set exrc
```

Note

The `.vimrc` and `.gvimrc` files are read from the current directory, even if the file being edited is located in a different directory.

Setting this option is considered a security problem. After all, bad things can easily be dumped into these files, especially if you are editing files in someone else's directory.

To avoid security problems, you can set the security option using this command:

```
:set secure
```

This option prevents the execution of the `:autocommand`, `:write`, and `:shell` commands from inside an initialization file.

Customizing Keyboard Usage

The *Vim* editor is highly customizable. This section shows you how to fine-tune the keyboard usage so that you can get the most out of your editor.

Microsoft Windows

Most programs that run under Microsoft Windows use the Alt keys to select menu items. However, *Vim* wants to make all keys available for commands. The `'winaltkeys'` option controls how the Alt keys are used.

If you use the following command, for example, all the Alt keys are available for command mapping with the `:map` command:

```
:set winaltkeys=no
```

Typing **ALT-F** will not select the file menu, but will instead execute the command mapped to **ALT-F**. A typical mapping might be this:

```
:map <M-f> :write
```

(Remember: *Vim* "spells" ALT as **M-**, which stands for *Meta*.)

If you use the following command, all the Alt keys will select menu items and none of them can be used for mapping:

```
:set winaltkeys=yes
```

The third option is a combination of yes and no:

```
:set winaltkeys=menu
```

In this mode, if an Alt key can be used for a menu, it is; otherwise, it is used for `:map` commands. So **ALT-F** selects the File menu, whereas you can use **ALT-X** (which is not a menu shortcut) for `:map` commands.

Two options control how *Vim* reads the keyboard when you are using the console version of *Vim* from an MS-DOS window. The following option tells *Vim* to read characters directly from the console:

```
:set conskey
```

Do not set this option if you plan to use your *Vim* editor to read a script file from the standard input.

The next option tells Vim to use the BIOS for reading the keyboard:

```
:set bioskey
```

Again, do not use this if you plan using a script file for a redirected standard in. By pointing *Vim* at the BIOS, you get faster response to **CTRL-C** and **Break** interrupts.

Customizing Keyboard Mappings

Most UNIX function keys send out a string of characters beginning with **<Esc>** when they are pressed. But a problem exists: the **<Esc>** key is used to end insert mode. So how do you handle function keys in insert mode?

The solution is for *Vim* to wait a little after an **<Esc>** key is pressed to see whether anymore characters come in. If they do, *Vim* knows that a function key has been pressed and acts accordingly. To turn on this feature, execute the following command:

```
:set esckeys
```

But what about other key sequences? These are controlled by the following options:

```
:set timeout
:set ttimeout
```

The following table shows the effects of these settings.

timeout	ttimeout	Result
notimeout	nottimeout	Nothing times out.
timeout	N/A	All key codes (**<F1>**, **<F2>**, and so on) and **:map** macros time out.
notimeout	ttimeout	Key codes (**<F1>**, **<F2>**, and so on) only time out.

The option '**timeoutlen**' determines how long to wait after Esc has been pressed to see whether something follows. The default is as follows, which equals one second (1000 milliseconds):

```
:set timeoutlen=1000
```

Generally, '**timeoutlen**' controls how long to wait for both function keys and keyboard mapping strings. If you want to have a different timeout for keyboard mapping strings, use the '**timeoutlen**' options:

```
:set ttimeoutlen=500
```

These two timeouts tell *Vim* to wait 1/2 second after an **<Esc>** key has been pressed to see whether you have a function key or one second to see whether it is a keyboard mapping. (In other words, if *Vim* reads enough to determine that what comes after the Esc press cannot possibly be a keyboard mapping sequence, it will wait only one second between characters trying to figure out what function key has been typed.)

Confirmation

Generally, when you do something that *Vim* considers questionable, such as quitting from a modified buffer, the command fails. If you set the `'confirm'` option, however, and use the following command, *Vim* displays a confirmation dialog box instead of failing:

    :set confirm

When you try to `:quit` a buffer containing a modified file, for example, the *Vim* editor displays a confirmation dialog box (see Figure 28.1).

Figure 28.1   Confirmation dialog box.

Customizing Messages

Vim generally uses the bottom line of the screen for messages. Sometimes these messages exceed one line and you get a prompt that states something like `Press Return to Continue`. To avoid these prompts, you can increase the number of message lines by setting the `'cmdheight'` options. To change the height of the message space to 3, for instance, use this command:

    :set cmdheight=3

Showing the Mode

When you set the `'showmode'` option, the *Vim* editor displays the current mode in the lower-left corner of the screen. To set this mode, use the following command:

    :set showmode

Showing Partial Commands

If you set the `'showcmd'` option, any partial command is displayed at the lower-right of the screen while you type it. Suppose you execute the following command:

    :set showcmd

Now you enter an **fx** command to search for *x*. When you type the **f**, an *f* appears in the lower-right corner.

This is nice for more complex commands because you can see the command as it is assembled. For example, the command displays the entire command (incomplete as it is) in the lower-right corner:

`"y2f`

Figure 28.2 shows how `'cmdheight'`, `'showmode'`, and `'showcmd'` affect the screen.

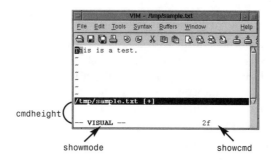

Figure 28.2   `'showmode'` and `'showcmd'`.

Short Messages

Another way to limit the "Press Return" prompts is to set the "short message" option. This shortens many common messages. The flags in the `'shortmess'` option determine which messages are shortened. The general form of this command is as follows:

`:set shortmess=`*flags*

The following table lists the flags.

Flag	Short Value	Long Value	Default
f	(3 of 5)	(file 3 of 5)	On
i	[noeol]	[Incomplete last line]	On
l	999L, 888C	999 lines, 888 characters	On
m	[+]	[Modified]	Off
n	[New]	[New File]	On
r	[RO]	[readonly]	Off
w	[w]	written	Off
x	[dos]	[dos format]	On

continues

Flag	Short Value	Long Value	Default
x	[unix]	[unix format]	On
x	[mac]	[mac format]	On
a	All the abbreviations: `filmnrwx`.		
A	Eliminate the "attention" messages issued when *Vim* finds an existing swap file. (Default = off.)		
I	Eliminate the introduction screen. (Default = off.)		
o	Sometimes you will perform an operation that writes a file and then does something else that writes a message, such as executing a `:wnext` command. If this option is not set, you will get two messages and will probably have to go through a "Press Return" prompt to see the second one. If this option is set (the default), the first message is overwritten by the second. (Default = on.)		
O	If you get a message stating that you are reading a file, it will overwrite any previous message. (Default = on.)		
s	If set, do not issue a "Search Hit Bottom, Continuing at Top" or "Search Hit Top, Continuing at Bottom" message. (Default = off.)		
t	If set, truncate the filename at the beginning of the message if it is too long to fit on one line. Thus, a long filename, such as `/home/oualline/writing/books/vim-book/editor-messages/my-replies/tuesday.txt`, appears as `<itor-messages/my-replies/tuesday.txt` (or something similar). (Default = off.) (Does not change the message in ex mode.)		
T	Truncate messages in the middle if they are too long. The deleted portion will appear as an ellipsis (...). (Default = on.) (Does not apply to ex mode.)		
W	Drop "written" or "[w]" when writing a file. Default = off.)		

The *'terse'* Option

To set the `'terse'` option, issue the following command:

```
:set terse
```

This command adds the **s** flag to the `'shortmess'` option. Setting `'noterse'` removes this flag.

The "File Modified" Warning

Generally, *Vim* warns when you do a `:shell` command and the file is modified before you return to *Vim*. If you want to turn off this option, execute the following command:

```
:set nowarn
```

Error Bells

When *Vim* gets an error, it just displays an error message. It is silent. If you are more audio-oriented than visually proficient, you might want to turn on error bells. This following command causes *Vim* to beep when there is an error:

```
:set errorbells
```

Beeping can sometimes disturb others in an office or classroom environment. An alternative to audio bells is a "visual" bell. When this option is set, the screen flashes (everything will go into reverse video and back to normal quickly). To set this option, use the following command:

```
:set visualbell
```

Status Line Format

You can customize the status line. You can use the following option to define your status line:

```
:set statusline=format
```

The *format* string is a *printf* line format string.

A **%** is used to indicate a special field. For example, **%f** tells *Vim* to include the filename in the status line. The following command

```
:set statusline=The\ file\ is\ \"%f\"
```

gives you the following status line:

```
The file is "sample.txt"
```

You can specify a minimum and maximum width for an item. For example, the command tells *Vim* that the filename must take up 8 characters, but is limited to only 19:

```
:set statusline=%8.19f
```

Items are right-justified. If you want them left-justified, put a **-** just after the **%**. For example:

```
->%10.10f<·            ->%-10.10f<·
->   foo.txt<·         ->foo.txt   <-
```

Numeric items are displayed with leading zeros omitted. If you want them, put a zero after the **%**. To display the column number, for instance, with leading zeros, use the following command:

```
:set statusline=%05.10c
```

Format	Type	Description
%(... %)		Define an item group. If all the items in this group are empty, the entire item group (and any text inside it) disappears.
%{n}*		Uses the highlight group **User**n for the rest of the line (or until another %n* is seen). The format **%0*** returns the line to normal highlighting.
		If the highlight group **User1** is underlined, for example, the status line
		`:set statusline=File:\ %1*%f%0*`
		gives you the following status line:
		`File: sample.txt`
%<		Define a location where the status line can be chopped off if it is too long.
%=		Defines a location in the "middle" of the line. All the text to the left of this will be placed on the left side of the line, and the text to the right will be put against the right margin.
		For example:
		`:set statusline=<-Left%=Right->`
		results in
		`<-Left    Right->`
%		The character %.
%B	Number	The number of the character under the cursor in hexadecimal.
%F	String	Filename including the full path.
%H	Flag	"HLP" if this is a help buffer.
%L	Number	Number of lines in buffer.
%M	Flag	"+" if the buffer is modified.
%O	Number	Byte offset in the file in hexadecimal form.
%P	String	The % of the file in front of the cursor.
%R	Flag	"RO" if the buffer is read-only.
%V	Number	Virtual column number. This is the empty string if equal to %c.
%W	Flag	"PRV" if this is the preview window.
%Y	Flag	File type.

Format	Type	Description
a%	String	If you are editing multiple files, this string is `"({current} of {arguments})"`. For example: (5 of 18) If there is only one argument in the command line, this string is empty.
%b	Number	The number of the character under the cursor in decimal.
%c	Number	Column number.
%f	String	The filename as specified on the command line.
%h	Flag	[Help] if this is a help buffer.
%l	Number	Line number.
%m	Flag	[+] if the buffer is modified.
%n	Number	Buffer number.
%o	Number	Number of characters before the cursor including the character under the cursor.
%p	Number	Percentage through file in lines.
%r	Flag	[RO] if the buffer is read-only.
%t	String	The filename (without any leading path information).
%v	Number	Virtual column number.
%w	Flag	[Preview] if this is a preview window.
%y	Flag	Type of the file as [*type*].
%{*expr*%}		The result of evaluating the expression expr.

The flag items get special treatment. Multiple flags, such as **RO** and **PRV**, are automatically separated from each other by a comma. Flags such as **+** and **help** are automatically separated by spaces. For example:

```
:set statusline=%h%m%r
```

can look like this:

```
[help] [+] [RO]
```

> **Note**
> For the purpose of this example, we are ignoring the fact that we have done the improbable and modified a read-only buffer.

Rulers

If you do not like the default status line, you can turn on the ruler option:

```
:set ruler
```

This causes *Vim* to display a status line that looks like this:

```
help.txt [help][RO]                    1,1              Top
```

After the file name and flags, this displays the current column, the virtual column, and an indicator showing you how far you are through the file.

If you want to define your own ruler format, use this command:

```
:set rulerformat=string
```

String is the same string used for the `'statusline'` option.

Reporting Changes

When you delete or change a number of lines, *Vim* tells you about it if the number of lines is greater than the value of the `'report'` option. Therefore, to report information on all changes, use the following command:

```
:set report=0
```

On the other hand, if you do not want to be told about what you have changed, you can set this to a higher value.

Help Window Height

You can set the minimum size of the help window by using the following command:

```
:set helpheight={height}
```

This minimum is used when opening the help window. The height can get smaller afterwards.

Preview Window Height

You can also specify the height of the preview window by using the following command:

```
:set previewheight={height}
```

Defining How 'list' Mode Works

Generally, `'list'` uses `^I` for `<Tab>` and `$` for the end of the line. You can customize this behavior. The `'listchars'` option defines how list mode works.

The format for this command is as follows:

```
:set listchars=key:string,key:string
```

The possible values for the *key:string* pairs are as follows:

eol:{*char*}   Define the character to be put after the end of the line.

tab:{*char1*}{*char2*}   A tab is displayed as {*char1*} followed by enough {*char2*} to fill the width.

trail:{*char*}   Character for showing trailing spaces

extends:{*char*}   Character used at the end of a line that wraps to the next line in screen space.

For example:

```
:set listchars=tab:>-
```

shows up with tabs like this:

```
>-------Tabbing
can>----be
fun if you >----know how
to set the list >------->-------command.
```

Another example:

```
:set listchars=tab:>-,trail:=
```

Gives us:

```
This line>------====
has spaces and tabs>----===
at the end=====
of the line====
```

Suppose that you have set the following options:

```
:set nowrap
:set listchars=extends:+
```

Figure 28.3 displays the results.

```
The student technicians were used to t+
technician took the back off a termina+
loose chip and instead found a large h+
board.  He decided to talk to the prof+

Technician:     Did you pile papers on+

Professor:      Yes.
```

Figure 28.3   `listchars=extends:+`.

Changing the Highlighting

You can change the highlighting of various objects by using the `'highlight'` option. The format for this option is as follows:

`:set highlight=`*key:group*`, [`*key:group*`]....`

Key is a key letter listed in the following table, and *group* is the name of a highlight group.

The keys are as follows:

Key	Default	Meaning
8	SpecialKey	This highlighting is applied when `:map` lists out a special key.
@	NonText	Applied to the ~ and @ character that *Vim* uses to display stuff that is not in the buffer.
M	ModeMsg	The mode information in the lower left of the screen. (See the `'showmode'` option.)
S	StatusLineNC	Status line for every window except the current one.
V	VisualNOS	Text selected in visual mode when *Vim* does not own the selection.
W	WildMenu	Items displayed as part of a wildcard completion set.
d	Directory	Directories listed when you press **CTRL-D**.
e	ErrorMsg	Error messages.
i	IncSearch	Text highlighted as part of an incremental search.
l	Search	Text highlighted as part of a search.
m	MoreMsg	The `-- More --` prompt.
n	LineNr	The line number printed by the `:number` command.
r	Question	The "Press Return" prompt and other questions.
s	StatusLine	The status line of the current windows.
t	Title	Titles for commands that output information in sections, such as `:syntax`, `:set all`, and others.
v	Visual	Text selected in visual mode.
w	WarningMsg	Warning messages.

You can use a number of shorthand characters for highlighting, including the following:

r   Reverse

i   Italic

b   Bold

s   Standout

u   Underline

n   None

-     None

Therefore, you can specify that the error message use the highlight group `ErrorMsg` by executing the following command:

```
:set highlight=e:ErrorMsg
```

Or, you can use the shorthand to tell *Vim* to display error message in reverse, bold, italic, by issuing this command:

```
:set highlight=evrb
```

In actual practice, you would not define just one mode with a `:set highlight` command. In practice, this command can get quite complex.

If a key is not specified, the default highlighting is used.

The *'more'* Option

When the `'more'` option is set, any command that displays more than a screen full of data pauses with a "More" prompt. If not set, the listing just scrolls off the top of the screen. The default is as follows:

```
:set more
```

Number Format

The following command defines which types of numbers can be recognized by the `CTRL-A` and `CTRL-X` commands:

```
:set nrformats=octal,hex
```

(Decimal format is always recognized.)

Restoring the Screen

When the following option is set, *Vim* attempts to restore the contents of the terminal screen to its previous value:

```
:set restorescreen
```

In other words, it tries to make the screen after you run *Vim* look just like it did before your ran the program.

Pasting Text

The X Windows *xterm* program enables you to select text by drawing the mouse over it while the left button is held down. This text can then be "pasted" into another window. However, some of *Vim's* capabilities can easily get in the way when pasting text into the window.

To avoid problems, you can set paste mode using the following command:

```
:set paste
```

This is shorthand for setting a number of options:

```
:set textwidth=0
:set wrapmargin=0
:set noautoindent
:set nosmartindent
:set nocindent
:set softtabstop=0
:set nolisp
:set norevins
:set noruler
:set noshowmatch
:set formatoptions=""
```

At times, you might want paste mode and you might not. The **'pastetoggle'** option enables you to define a key that toggles you between paste mode and nopaste mode. To use the F12 key to toggle between these two modes, for instance, use the following command:

```
:set pastetoggle=<F12>
```

When paste mode is turned off, all the options are restored to the values they had when you set paste mode.

Wildcards

When you are entering a command in ex mode, you can perform filename completion. If you want to read in the file input.txt, for example, you can enter the following command:

```
:read input<Tab>
```

Vim will try to figure out which file you want. If the only file in your current directory is input.txt, it will appear as this:

```
:read input.txt
```

If several files that with the word *input*, the first will display. By pressing Tab again, you get the second file that matches; press Tab again, and you get the third, and so on.

To define which key accomplishes the wildcard completion, use the following command:

`:set wildchar=`*character*

If you are using filename completion inside a macro, you need to set the `'wildcharm'` (which stand for *wild-char-macro*). It is the character that accomplishes filename completion from inside a macro. For example:

```
:set wildcharm=<F12>
:map <F11> :read in<F12>
```

Now when you press F11, it will start a read command for the file in-whatever.

You probably do not want to match backup file or other junk files. To tell *Vim* what is junk, use this command:

`:set wildignore=`*pattern,pattern*

Every file that matches the given pattern will be ignored. To ignore object and backup files, for example, use the following command:

`:set wildignore=*.o,*.bak`

The `'suffixes'` option lists a set of file name suffixes that will be given a lower priority when it comes to matching wildcards. In other words if a file has one of these suffixes it will be placed at the end of any wildcard list.

Generally, the filename completion code does not display a list of possible matches. If you set the option

`:set wildmenu`

when you attempt to complete a filename, a menu of possible files displays on the status line of the window (see Figure 28.4).

```
This is a test
~
~
~
~
~
in.txt  index.txt  indoors.txt  input.txt
:read /tmp/in.txt
```

Figure 28.4 Filename completion.

The arrow keys cause the selection to move left and right. The **>** at the end of the line indicates that there are more choices to the right. The **<Down>** key causes the editor to go into a directory. The **<Up>** key goes to the parent directory. Finally, **<Enter>** selects the item.

You can customize the behavior of the file completion logic by using the '**wildmode**' option. The following command causes *Vim* to complete only the first match:

`:set wildmode=`

If you keep pressing the '**wildchar**' key, only the first match displays. Figure 28.5 shows how this option works.

Figure 28.5 `wildmode=`.

The following command causes *Vim* to complete the name with the first file it can find:

`:set wildmode=full`

After that, if you keep pressing the '**wildchar**' key, the other files that match are gone through in order. Figure 28.6 shows what happens when this option is enabled.

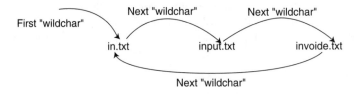

Figure 28.6 `wildmode = full`.

The following command causes the pressing of '**wildchar**' to match the longest common substring and then stop:

`:set wildmode=longest`

If you use the following command, you accomplish the same thing; but the display is just the list of files on the '**wildmenu**' line:

`:set wildmode=longest:full`

The following command displays a list of possible matches when the '**wildchar**' is pressed (see Figure 28.7):

`:set wildmode=list`

This mode does not complete the match. If you want that to happen as well, use this option:

`:set wildmode=list:full`

```
~
~
~
:read /tmp/in.txt
/tmp/in.txt         /tmp/inside.txt
/tmp/index.txt      /tmp/invoices.txt
/tmp/indoors.txt    /tmp/inward.txt
:read /tmp/in█
```

Figure 28.7 `wildmode=list`.

Finally, to complete the longest common substring and list the files, use the following option:

`:set wildmode=list:longest`

You can use these options in a set. The first option is used the first time the `'wildchar'` is pressed, the second option is used the second time you press `'wildchar'`, and so on, for up to four presses. Therefore, if you want to complete the longest substring (longest) and then go through the list (full), use the following option:

`:set wildmode=longest,full`

Customizing Behavior of the Screen Movement Commands

When the `'startofline'` option is set, the screen movement commands as well as several cursor movement commands such as **H**, **M**, **L**, and **G** move the cursor to the start of a line. If it is not set, the cursor remains in the same column (or as close as possible).

File Writing Options

If set, the `'write'` option lets *Vim* write files. If this option is not set, you can view the file only. This is useful if you want to use *Vim* as a secure viewer.

Generally, when you try to write a file that you should not, *Vim* makes you use the override option (!). If you want to live dangerously, you can tell *Vim* to always assume that this option is present for writing type commands by executing the following command:

`:set writeany`

Memory Options

To set the maximum memory for one buffer, use this command:

`:set maxmem={size}`

{*size*} is the memory limit in kilobytes.

To define total amount of memory for all buffers, use the following command:

`:set maxmemtot={size}`

Function Execution Options

The `'maxfuncdepth'` option defines the maximum number of nested functions. Similarly, the `'maxmapdepth'` parameter defines the maximum number of nested mappings.

Terminal Options

The following sections describe the terminal options.

Terminal Name

The name of your terminal is stored in the `'term'` option. Generally, you do not need to set this option because it is set by your shell or operating environment. However, you might need to read it to enable terminal-specific macros.

Lazy Redraw

The `'lazyredraw'` option is useful for a slow terminal. It prevents *Vim* from redrawing the screen in the middle of a macro. The default is as follows:

`:set nolazyredraw`

This option is has been made obsolete by current terminal technology. If you do set this option, you do not see macros being executed.

Internal Termcap

The UNIX system has a database of terminal control codes called *termcap*. The *Vim* editor has its own built-in database as well. If the `'ttybuiltin'` option is enabled, this internal database is searched first.

Fast Terminals

If the `'ttyfast'` option is set, *Vim* assumes you have a fast terminal connection and changes the output to produce a smoother update, but one with more characters. If you have a slow connection, you should reset this option.

Mouse Usage Inside a Terminal

The `'ttymouse'` option controls the terminal mouse codes. This option is of interest to those trying to do fancy things with terminal control codes. For example, if you want to use the mouse buttons **<LeftMouse>** and **<RightMouse>** in console editing, you should enable this option.

How Much to Scroll

The `'ttyscroll'` option controls how many lines to scroll the screen when an update is required. You can adjust this to a small number if you are on a slow terminal.

Some More Obscure Options

This section discusses some of the more obscure options in *Vim*. These were kept around for compatibility with *Vi* and to support equipment that was long ago rendered obsolete.

Compatibility

The following option makes *Vim* act as much like *Vi* as possible:

```
:set compatible
```

If you enable this option, many of the examples in this book will not work properly. This option is generally set unless there is a `$HOME/.vimrc` file present.

Similarly, the following command enables you to fine-tune *Vi* compatibility:

```
:set cpoptions={characters}
```

This next command makes the **g** and **c** options on the `:substitute` command to act like they do for the UNIX editor *Ed*:

```
:set edcompatible
```

The following option sets lisp mode. This sets a number of options to make Lisp programming easier:

```
:set lisp
```

The `'tildeop'` option makes ~ behave like an operator. This is for *Vi* compatibility. If this option is turned off, the ~ command will switch the case of a single character. With the following, the ~ command takes the form of *~motion*:

```
:set tildeop
```

> **Note**
> The **g~** command always behaves as an operator regardless of this option.

The `'helpfile'` option defines the location of the main help file. This option proves useful if you want to redirect where the `:help` command gets its information. For example:

```
:set helpfile=/usr/sdo/vim/my_help.txt
```

Weirdinvert

The following command has been provided for backward compatibility with version 4.0 of *Vim*:

```
:set weirdinvert
```

It has been made obsolete by the **t_xs** string. (See the *Vim* terminal help documentation for more information.) Some terminals, such as **hpterm**, need to have **t_xs** set to work. If you have one of these, you might want to look at the help text:

```
:help hpterm
```

Debugging

The following option causes a delay of *time* (in milliseconds) between each character output:

```
:set writedelay={time}
```

The **'verbose'** option controls how much Vim chatters while performing its job (the higher the number, the more output). The current numbers are as follows:

>= 1	When a file is read during a **:source** command.
>= 1	When the **.viminfo** file is read or written.
>= 8	Files for which a group of autocommands is executed.
>= 9	Every executed autocommand.
>=15	Every executed function line.

Obsolete Options

The **'textauto'** and **'textmode'** options are obsolete. Use the options **'fileformats'** and **'fileformat'** instead.

Legacy Options

Vim tries to be as compatible with the old *Vi* editor as possible. *Vi* has a number of options that mean something to *Vi*, but are not relivant to Vim. In order to be fully compatible with *Vi*, the Vim editor won't generate an error message if you set any of these options. But the options themselves have no effect on the editor.

The options are:

autoprint	beautify	flash	graphic	hardtabs
mesg	novice	open	optimize	prompt
redraw	slowopen	sourceany	window	w300
w1200	w9600			

29

Language-Dependent Syntax Options

SYNTAX COLORING IS CONTROLLED BY language-dependent syntax files that reside in $VIMRUNTIME/syntax/language.vim.

You can make your own copy of these syntax files and modify and update them if their syntax coloring is not what you desire.

You can also set a number of language-specific options. (This chapter covers the language-dependent syntax option for each language *Vim* knows about.) These options must be turned on before you edit the file. You can fake this by setting the option and then turning the syntax coloring off and back on.

Assembly Language

There are a number of different assembly languages out there. By default, *Vim* assumes that you are using a GNU-style assembly language. The other assemblers supported are as follows:

asm	GNU assembly (the default)
asmh8300	Hitachi H-8300
masm	Microsoft MASM
nasm	Netwide assembly

To let *Vim* know you are using another assembly language, execute the following command:

```
:let asmsyntax=language
```

In the preceding command, *language* is one of the assembly language keywords listed earlier.

Basic

Both Visual Basic and Standard Basic both use files that end in .BAS. To tell the difference between the two, the *Vim* editor reads the first five lines of the file and checks for the string VB_Name. (Files with the extension .FRM are always Visual Basic.)

C and C++

You can perform a number of customizations for the C and C++ syntax colors, including the following:

c_comment_strings   Highlight strings and numbers inside comments.

```
/* Example a: "Highlighted String"
```

c_space_errors   Flag trailing whitespace and spaces in front of a <Tab>.

```
/* In the following we use "." for blank and */
/* —> for tab. */
int..——>foo;......
```

c_no_trail_space_error   Do not flag trailing whitespace.

```
int..——>foo;......
```

c_no_tab_space_error   Do not flag spaces before a <Tab>.

```
int..——>foo;......
```

c_no_ansi   Do not highlight ANSI types and constants.

```
size_t foo; /* :unlet c_no_ansi */
int i = INT_MIN; /* :unlet c_no_ansi */
size_t foo; /* :let c_no_ansi = 1 */
int i = INT_MIN; /* :let c_no_ansi = 1 */
```

c_ansi_typedefs   Highlight ANSI typedefs.

```
size_t foo; /* :unlet c_ansi_typedefs */
int i = INT_MIN; /* :unlet c_ansi_typedefs */
size_t foo; /* :let c_ansi_typedefs = 1 */
```

```
                           int i = INT_MIN; /* :let c_ansi_typedefs = 1 */
```

c_ansi_constants   Highlight ANSI types.

```
                           size_t foo; /* :unlet c_ansi_constants */
                           int i = INT_MIN; /* :unlet c_ansi_constants */
                           size_t foo; /* :set c_no_ansi_constants = 1 */
                           int i = INT_MIN; /* :let c_ansi_constants = 1 */
```

c_no_utf   Highlight \u or \U in strings.

```
                           char *f = "\uFF + \Uffff"; /* :let c_no_utf = 1*/
                           char *f = "\uFF + \Uffff"; /* :unlet c_no_utf */
```

c_no_if0   Do not highlight #if 0 / #endif blocks as comments.

c_no_cformat   Do not highlight %-formats in strings.

```
                           printf("%3f\n", f); /* :let c_no_cformat = 1 */
                           printf("%3f\n", f); /* :unlet c_no_cformat */
```

Sometimes you will notice some highlighting errors in comments or #if 0 / #endif blocks. You can fix these by redrawing the screen using the CTRL-L command. To fix them permanently, you need to increase the number of lines searched for syntax matches by using the following command:

```
:let c_minlines = number
```

In the preceding command, *number* is the minimum number of lines to search. Setting this to a large number helps to eliminate syntax coloration errors.

COBOL

There are two versions of COBOL highlighting: fresh development and legacy. To enable legacy highlighting, use the following command:

```
:let cobol_legacy_code = 1
```

DTD

DTD is usually case sensitive. To make it not case sensitive, use this command:

```
:let dtd_ignore_case = 1
```

The syntax highlighting flags unknown tags as errors. To turn off this feature, use the following command:

```
:let dtd_no_tag_errors = 1
```

The parameter entity names are highlighted using the Type highlight group with the Comment group. You can turn this off by using the following command:

```
:let dtd_no_parameter_entities=1
```

Eiffel

Eiffel is not case sensitive, but the standard style guidelines require the use of upper-/lowercase. The syntax highlighting rules are designed to encourage you to follow the standard guidelines. To disable case checking, use the following command:

```
:let eiffel_ignore_case = 1
```

You cause the syntax coloring to check for the proper capitalization for Current, Void, Result, Precursor, and NONE, by using this command:

```
:let eiffel_strict = 1
```

If you want to really check the syntax against the style guide, use the following command:

```
:let eiffel_pedantic = 1
```

You can use the lowercase versions of current, void, result, precursor, and none by setting **eiffel_lower_case_predef**, as follows:

```
:let eiffel_lower_case_predef = 1
```

To handle ISE's proposed new syntax, use the following command:

```
:let eiffel_ise = 1
```

For support of hexadecimal constants, use this:

```
:let eiffel_hex_constsnts = 1
```

ERLANG

ERLANG stands for ERicsson LANGuage. The syntax coloring has two options:

erlang_keywords   Disable the highlighting of keywords.

erlang_characters   Disable the highlighting of special characters.

FVWM

FVWM is a window manager. If you are editing configuration files for this program, you need to tell *Vim* the location of the color file using the following command:

```
:let rgb_file="/usr/X11/lib/X11/rgb.txt"
```

This example shows the location of the rgb.txt file that comes with Linux. Other systems may put it in /usr/lib or other locations.

HTML

The HTML syntax file uses the following highlight tags:

htmlTitle

htmlH1

htmlH2

htmlH3

htmlH4

htmlH5

htmlH6

htmlBold

htmlBoldUnderline

htmlBoldUnderlineItalic

htmlUnderline

htmlUnderlineItalic

htmlItalic

htmlLink

If you want to turn off some of syntax coloring, use the following command:

```
:let html_no_rendering = 1
```

If you want to define your own colors for these items, put the color-setting commands in your VIMRC and use the following command:

```
:let html_my_rendering = 1
```

Some files contain `<!--` and `-->` or `<!` and `!>` for comments. If you want these comments highlighted, use the following command:

```
:let html_wrong_comments = 1
```

Java

The Java syntax has the following options:

`java_mark_braces_in_parens_as_errors`	If set, braces inside parentheses are flagged as errors (Java 1.0.2). This is legal in Java 1.1.
`java_highlight_java_lang_ids`	Highlight all the identifiers in `java.lang.*`.
`java_highlight_functions = "indent"`	Set if function declarations are always indented.

`java_highlight_function = "style"`	Function declarations are not indented.
`java_highlight_debug`	Highlight debug statement (System.out.println and System.err.println).
`java_allow_cpp_keywords`	Mark all C and C++ keywords as an error. This helps prevent you from using them, so your code is more portable to C or C++.
`java_ignore_javadoc`	Turn off highlighting for Javadoc.
`java_javascript`	Turn on highlighting for JavaScript inside Javadoc.
`java_css`	Turn on highlighting for CSS style sheets inside of Javadoc
`java_vb`	Turn on highlighting for VB scripts.

Lace

The specification of the language states that it is not case sensitive. Good style is case sensitive. If you want to turn off the "good style" case-sensitive feature, use the following command:

```
:let lace_case_insensitive=1
```

Lex

Lex files are divided up into major sections separated by lines consisting of `%%`. If you write long Lex files, the syntax highlighting may not be able to find the `%%`. To fix this problem you might need to increase the **minlines** syntax option by using a command such as this:

```
:syntax sync minlines = 300
```

Lite

Lite uses a SQL-like query language. You can enable highlighting of SQL inside strings with the following command:

```
:let lite_sql_query = 1
```

If you have large commands, you might want to increase the number of lines used for synchronizing the syntax coloring:

```
:let lite_minlines = 500
```

Maple

Maple V, by Waterloo Maple Inc., is a symbolic algebra language. It has many different packages that the user can selectively load. If you want to highlight the syntax for all packages, use the following command:

```
:let mvpkg_all = 1
```

If you want to enable specific packages, use one or more of the following options:

mv_DEtools	mv_genfunc	mv_networks	mv_process
mv_Galois	mv_geometry	mv_numapprox	mv_simplex
mv_GaussInt	mv_grobner	mv_numtheory	mv_stats
mv_LREtools	mv_group	mv_orthopoly	mv_student
mv_combinat	mv_inttrans	mv_padic	mv_sumtools
mv_combstruct	mv_liesymm	mv_plots	mv_tensor
mv_difforms	mv_linalg	mv_plottools	mv_totorder
mv_finance	mv_logic	mv_powseries	

Perl

If you include POD documentation in your files, you can enable POD syntax highlighting using the following command:

```
:let perl_include_POD = 1
```

If you do not include POD documents, you should. Perl is bad enough when it is documented.

The following option changes how Perl displays package names in references (such as $PkgName::VarName):

```
:let perl_want_scope_in_variables = 1
```

If you use complex variable declarations such as "@{${"var"}}", you need the following:

```
:let perl_extended_vars = 1
```

The following option tells the syntax coloring to treat strings as a statement:

```
:let perl_string_as_statement = 1
```

If you have trouble with synchronization, you might want to change some of the following options:

```
:let perl_no_sync_on_sub = 1
:let perl_no_sync_on_global = 1
:let perl_sync_dist = lines
```

Php3

The following options control the highlighting for Php3:

`php3_sql_query`	Highlight SQL queries inside string.
`php3_baselib`	Highlight baselib methods.
`php3_minlines`	Number of lines to synchronize the syntax coloring.

Phtml

To highlight SQL syntax in a string, use the following:

```
:let phtml_sql_query = 1
```

To change the synchronization window, use this command:

```
:let phtml_minlines = lines
```

PostScript

The options for PostScript highlighting are as follows:

`postscr_level`	Set the PostScript language level (default = 2).
`postscr_display`	Highlight display postscript features.
`postscr_ghostscript`	Hightlight GhostScript-specific syntax.
`postscr_fonts`	For font highlighting (off by default for speed).
`postscr_encodings`	Encoding tables (off by default for speed).
`postscr_andornot_binary`	Color logical operators differently.

Printcap and Termcap

If you are doing complex work, I feel for you. These files are cryptic enough as is and dealing with long and complex ones is especially difficult. As far as *Vim* is concerned, you might want to increase the number of lines used for synchronization:

```
:let ptcap_minlines = 100
```

Rexx

You can adjust the number of lines used for synchronization with the following option:

```
:let rexx_minlines = lines
```

Sed

To make tabs stand out, you can use the **:set list** option. You can highlight them differently by using the following command:

```
:let highlight_sedtabs = 1
```

Hint: If you execute a

```
:set tabstop = 1
```

as well, it makes it easy to count the number of tabs in a string.

Shell

The following options change the highlighting for shell scripts:

bash_is_sh	Highlight bash syntax.
highlight_balanced_quotes	Highlight single quotes inside double quotes (that is, "x 'x' x")
highlight_function_name	Highlight the function name in a declaration
sh_minlines	Set the number of lines for synchronization
sh_maxlines	Limit the number of lines for synchronization (speeds things up).

Speedup

The options for Speedup are as follows:

strict_subsections	Only highlight the keywords that belong in each subsection.
highlight_types	Highlight stream types as a type.
oneline_comments = 1	Allow code after any number of # comments.
oneline_comments = 2	Show code starting with the second # as an error (default).
oneline_comments = 3	If the line contains two or more # characters in it, highlight the entire line as an error.

TeX

TeX is a complex language that can fool the syntax highlighting. If the editor fails to find the end of a **texZone**, put the following comment in your file:

```
%stopzone
```

TinyFugue

To adjust the synchronization limit for TinyFugue files, use this option:

```
:let tf_minlines = lines
```

30

How to Write a Syntax File

Suppose you want to define your own syntax file. You can start by taking a look at the existing syntax files in the `$VIMRUNTIME/syntax` directory. After that, you can either adapt one of the existing syntax files or write your own.

Basic Syntax Commands

Let's start with the basic options. Before we start defining any new syntax, we need to clear out any old definitions:

```
:syntax clear
```

Some languages are not case sensitive, such as Pascal. Others, such as C, are case sensitive. You need to tell which type you have with the following commands:

```
:syntax case match
:syntax case ignore
```

The `'match'` option means that *Vim* will match the case of syntax elements. Therefore, **int** differs from **Int** and **INT**. If the `'ignore'` option is used, the following are equivalent: **Procedure**, **PROCEDURE**, and **procedure**.

The `:syntax case` commands can appear anywhere in a syntax file and affect all the syntax definitions that follow. In most cases, you have only one `:syntax case` command in your syntax file; if you work with an unusual language that contains both case-sensitive and non-case-sensitive elements, however, you can scatter the `:syntax case` command throughout the file.

The most basic syntax elements are keywords. To define a keyword, use the following form:

```
:syntax keyword group keyword .......
```

The *group* name is the name of a highlight group, which is used by the **:highlight** command for assigning colors. The *keyword* parameter is an actual keyword. Here are a few examples:

```
:syntax keyword xType int long char
:syntax keyword xStatement if then else endif
```

This example uses the group names **xType** and **xStatement**. By convention, each group name is prefixed by a short abbreviation for the language being defined. This example defines syntax for the **x** language (eXample language without an interesting name).

These statements cause the words **int**, **long**, and **char** to be highlighted one way and the words **if** and **endif** to be highlighted another way.

Now you need to connect the **x** *group* names to standard *Vim* names. You do this with the following commands:

```
:highlight link xType Type
:highlight link xStatement Statement
```

This tells *Vim* to treat **xType** like **Type** and **xStatement** like **Statement**.

The **x** command allows for abbreviations. For example, **n** and **next** are both valid keywords. You can define them by using this command:

```
:syntax keyword xStatement n[ext]
```

Defining Matches

Consider defining something a bit more complex. You want to match ordinary identifiers. To do this, you define a **match** syntax group. This one matches any word consisting of only lowercase letters:

```
:syntax match xIdentifier /[a-z]\+/
```

Now define a match for a comment. It is anything from **#** to the end of a line:

```
:syntax match xComment /#.*$/
```

Note

The match automatically ends at the end of a line by default, so the actual command is as follows:

```
:syntax match xComment /#.*/
```

Defining Regions

In the example **x** language, you enclose strings in double quotation marks (").You want to highlight strings differently, so you tell *Vim* by defining a region. For that, you need a region start (double quote) and a region end (double quote). The definition is as follows:

```
:syntax region xString start=/"/ end=/"/
```

The **start** and **end** directives define the patterns used to define the start and end of the region. But what about strings that look like this?

```
"A string with a double quote (\") in it"
```

This creates a problem: The double quotation marks in the middle of the string will end the string.You need to tell *Vim* to skip over any escaped double quotes in the string.You do this with the **skip** keyword:

```
:syntax region xString start=/"/ skip=/\\"/ end=/"/
```

> **Note**
>
> The double backslash is needed because the string you are looking for is \ ", so the backslash must be escaped (giving us \ \ ").

Nested Regions

Take a look at this comment:

```
# Do it      TODO: Make it real
```

You want to highlight **TODO** in big red letters even though it is in a comment.To let *Vim* know about this, you define the following syntax groups:

```
:syntax keyword xTodo contained
:syntax match xComment /#.*$/ contains=xTodo
```

In the first line, the **'contained'** option tells *Vim* that this keyword can exist only inside another syntax element.The next line has a **contains=xTodo** option.This indi-cates that the **xTodo** syntax element is inside it.

The results (**xTodo=underline**, **xComment=italic**) are as follows:

```
# Do it      TODO: Make it real
```

Consider the following two syntax elements:

```
:syntax region xComment start=/%.*/ end=/$/
               \ contained
:syntax region xPreProc start=/#.*/ end=/$/
               \ contains=xComment
```

You define a comment as anything from **%** to the end of the line. A preprocess directive is anything from **#** to the end of the line. Because you can have a comment on a preprocessor line, the preprocessor definition includes a **'contains=xComment'** option.

The result (**xComment=italic, xPreProc=underline**) is as follows:

```
#define X = Y % Comment
int foo = 1;
```

But there is a problem with this. The preprocessor directive should end at the end of the line. That is why you put the **end=/$/** directive on the line. So what is going wrong?

The problem is the contained comment. The comment **start** starts with **%** and ends at the end of the line. *After* the comment is processed, the processing of the preprocessor syntax contains. This is *after* the end of the line has been seen, so the next line is processed as well. To avoid this problem and to force contained syntax from eating a needed end of line, use the **'keepend'** option. This takes care of the double end-of-line matching:

```
:syntax region xComment start=/%.*/ end=/$/
            \ contained
:syntax region xPreProc start=/#.*/ end=/$/
            \ contains=xComment keepend
```

You can use the **contains** option to specify that everything can be contained. For example:

```
:syntax region xList start="\[" end="\]" contains=ALL
```

You can also use it to include a group of elements except for the ones listed:

```
:syntax region xList start="\[" end="\]"
                    \ contains=ALLBUT,xString
```

Multiple Group Options

Some syntax is context-dependent. You expect **if** to be followed by **then**, for example. Therefore, a **then/if** statement would be an error. The *Vim* syntax parser has options that let it know about your syntax order.

For example, you define a syntax element consisting of **>** at the beginning of a line. You also define a element for the **KEY** string. In this case, the **KEY** is important only if it is part of a **>** line. The definition for this is as follows:

```
:syntax match xSpecial    "^>" nextgroup=xKey
:syntax match xKey "KEY" contained
```

The **'nextgroup'** option tells *Vim* to highlight **KEY**, but only if it follows **xSpecial**. The result (**xKey=italic, xSpecial=underline**) is as follows:

```
KEY (Normal key, nothing special, no >)
>KEY Key follows the > so highlighted
```

However, the **KEY** must immediately follow the **>**. If there is a space present, the **KEY** will not be highlighted:

```
>    KEY
```

If you want to allow whitespace between the two groups, you can use the **'skipwhite'** option:

```
:syntax match xSpecial    "^>" skipwhite nextgroup=xKey
:syntax match xKey "KEY" contained
```

This gives you the following:

```
>    KEY
```

The **skipwhite** directive tells *Vim* to skip whitespace between the groups. There are two other related options. The **'skipnl'** option skips newline in the pattern. If it were present, you would get the following:

```
>
KEY
```

The **'skipempty'** option causes empty lines to be skipped as well:

```
>

KEY
```

Transparent Matches

The **'transparent'** option causes the syntax element to become transparent, so the highlighting of the containing syntax element will show through. For example, the following defines a string with all the numbers inside highlighted:

```
:syntax region xString start=/"/ skip=/\\"/ end=/"/
             \ contains=xNumbers,xSpecial
:syntax match xNumbers /[0-9]\+/ contained
```

Now add a special group that does not take on any special highlighting:

```
:syntax match xSpecial /12345/ transparent contained contains=xNothing
```

This also has a **contains** argument to spcify that xNothing can be contained. Otherwise, the **contains** argument xString would be used, and xNumbers would be included in xSpecial.

The results (**xString=italic, xNumbers=underline, xSpecial=N.A.**) look like this: *"String 12 with number 45 in it 12345 "*

Other Matches

The **'oneline'** option indicates that the region does not cross a line boundary. For example:

```
:syntax region xPrePoc start=/^#/ end=/$/ oneline
```

Things now become a little more complex. Let's allow continuation lines. In other words, any line that ends with \ is a continuation line. The way you handle this is to allow the **xPreProc** syntax element to contain a continuation pattern:

```
:syntax region xPreProc start=/^#/ end=/$/ oneline
               \ contains=xLineContinue
:syntax match xLineContinue ""\\$"" contained
```

In this case, although **xPreProc** is on a single line, the groups contained in it (namely **xLineContinue**) let it go on for more than one line.

   In this case, this is what you want. If it is not what you want, you can call for the region to be on a single line by adding **excludenl** to the contained pattern. For example, you want to highlight "end" in **xPreProc**, but only at the end of the line. To avoid making the **xPreProc** continue on the next line, use **excludenl** like this:

```
:syntax region xPreProc start=/^#/ end=/$/
               \ contains=xLineContinue,xPreProcEnd
:syntax match xPreProcEnd excludenl /end$/ contained
```

Note that **excludenl** is placed before the pattern. Now you can still use **xLineContinue** as previously. Because it doesn't have **excludenl**, a match with it will extend **xPreProc** to the next line.

Match Groups

When you define a region, the entire region is highlighted according to the group name specified. To highlight the text enclosed in parentheses () with the highlight group **xInside,** for example, use the following command:

```
:syntax region xInside start=/(/ end=/)/
```

Suppose, however, that you want to highlight the parentheses separately. You can do this with a lot of convoluted region statements, or you can use the `'matchgroup'` option. This option tells *Vim* to highlight the start and end of a region with a different highlight group (in this case, the **Xparen** group).

```
:syntax region xInside matchgroup=Xparen start=/(/ end=/)/
```

Match Offsets

Several options enable you to adjust the start and end of a pattern used in matching for the `:syntax match` and `:syntax region` directives.

   For example, the offset `'ms=s+2'` indicates that the match starts two characters from the start of the match. For example:

```
:syntax match xHex /0x[a-fA-F0-9]*/ms=s+2
```

The general form of a match offset is as follows:

```
location=offset
```

PACKING SLIP

1/12/2006
Angus Macnab
5911 35th Ave SW
Seattle, WA 98126-2819

SHIPPING METHOD SELECTED: Media Mail

ORDER#: 058-2461468-3122131
LISTING ID: 0110B257573
ISBN: 0735710015
CONDITION: Used - Like New

QUANTITY PURCHASED: 1

SELLER COMMENTS: not available
TIME OF SALE: 11-Jan-2006 10:25:08
BUYER PRICE: $19.75
TITLE: Vi iMproved (VIM) [Paperback] by Oualline, Steve
SKU: 22A-20

Thanks for your order. If you have any questions or comments, or if there is a problem,
just let me know at best_bargain_books@yahoo.com and I will respond promptly.

Location is one of the following:

ms Start of the element

me End of the element

hs Start highlighting here

he End highlighting here

rs Marks the start of a region

re Marks the end of region

lc Leading context

The offset can be as follows:

s Start of match

e End of the match

Clusters

One of the things you will notice as you start to write a syntax file is that you wind up generating a lot of syntax groups. The *Vim* editor enables you to define a collection of syntax groups called a cluster.

Suppose you have a language that contains for loops, if statements, while loops, and functions. Each of them contains the same syntax elements: numbers and identifiers. You define them like this:

```
:syntax match xFor /^for.*/ contains+xNumber,xIdent
:syntax match xIf /^if.*/ contains=xNumber,xIdent
:syntax match xWhile /^while.*/ contains=xNumber,xIdent
```

You have to repeat the same **contains=** every time. If you want to add another contained item, you have to add it three times. Syntax clusters simplify these definitions by enabling you to group elements. To define a cluster for the two items that the three groups contain, use the following command:

```
:syntax cluster xState contains=xNumber,xIdent
```

Clusters are used inside other **:syntax** elements just like any syntax group. Their names start with @. Thus, you can define the three groups like this:

```
:syntax match xFor /^for.*/ contains=@xState
:syntax match xIf /^if.*/ contains=@xState
:syntax match xWhile /^while.*/ contains=@xState
```

You can add new elements to this cluster with the add argument:

```
:syntax cluster xState add=xString
```

You can remove syntax groups from this list as well:

```
:syntax cluster xState remove=xNumber
```

Including Other Syntax Files

The C++ language syntax is a superset of the C language. Because you do not want to write two syntax files, you can have the C++ syntax file read in the one for C by using the following command:

```
:source <sfile>:p:h/c.vim
```

The word **<sfile>** is the name of the syntax file that is currently being processed. The **:p:h** modifiers remove the name of the file from the **<sfile>** word. Therefore, **<sfile>:p:h/c.vim** is used to specify the file c.vim in the same directory as the current syntax file.

Now consider the Perl language. The Perl language consists of two distinct parts: a documentation section in POD format, and a program written in Perl itself. The POD section starts with **"=head"** and the end starts with **"=cut"**.

You want to construct the Perl syntax file to reflect this. The **:syntax include** reads in a syntax file and stores the elements it defined in a syntax cluster. For Perl, the statements are as follows:

```
:syntax include @Pod <sfile>:p:h/pod.vim
:syntax region perlPOD start="^=head" end="^=cut"
              \ contains=@POD
```

In this example, the top-level language is Perl. All the syntax elements of the POD language are contained in the Perl syntax cluster **@Pod**.

Listing Syntax Groups

The following command lists all the syntax items:

```
:syntax
```

To list a specific group, use this command:

```
:syntax list group-name
```

This also works for clusters as well:

```
:syntax list @cluster-name
```

Synchronization

Compilers have it easy. They start at the beginning of a file and parse it straight through. The *Vim* editor does not have it so easy. It must start at the middle, where the editing is being done. So how does it tell where it is?

The secret is the **:syntax sync** command. This tells *Vim* how to figure out where it is. For example, the following command tells *Vim* to scan backward for the beginning or end of a C-style comment and begin syntax coloring from there:

```
:syntax sync ccomment
```

You can tune this processing with some options. The `'minlines'` option tells *Vim* the minimum number of lines to look backward, and `'maxlines'` tells the editor the maximum number of lines to scan.

For example, the following command tells *Vim* to look at 10 lines before the top of the screen:

```
:syntax sync ccomment minlines=10 maxlines=500
```

If it cannot figure out where it is in that space, it starts looking farther and farther back until it figures out what to do. But it looks no farther back than 500 lines. (A large `'maxlines'` slows down processing. A small one might cause synchronization to fail.)

By default, the comment to be found will be colored as part of the **Comment** syntax group. If you want to color things another way, you can specify a different syntax group:

```
:syntax sync ccomment xAltComment
```

If your programming language does not have C-style comments in it, you can try another method of synchronization. The simplest way is to tell *Vim* to space back a number of lines and try to figure out things from there. The following command tells *Vim* to go back 150 lines and start parsing from there:

```
:syntax sync minline=150
```

A large `'minlines'` option can make *Vim* slower.

Finally, you can specify a syntax group to look for by using this command:

```
:syntax sync match sync-group-name
            \ grouphere group-name pattern
```

This tells *Vim* that when it sees *pattern* the syntax group named *group-name* begins just after the pattern given. The *sync-group-name* is used to give a name to this synchronization specification. For example, the sh scripting language begins an **if** statement with **if** and ends it with **fi**:

```
if [ -f file.txt ] ; then
      echo "File exists"
fi
```

To define a `'grouphere'` directive for this syntax, you use the following command:

```
:syntax sync match shIfSync   grouphere  shIf   "\<if\>"
```

The `'groupthere'` option tells *Vim* that the pattern ends a group. For example, the end of the **if**/**fi** group is as follows:

```
:syntax sync match shIfSync   groupthere NONE   "\<fi\>"
```

In this example, the **NONE** tells *Vim* that you are not in any special syntax region. In particular, you are not inside an **if** block.

You also can define matches and regions that are with no **'grouphere'** or **'groupthere'** options. These groups are for syntax groups skipped during synchronization. For example, the following skips over anything inside **{}**, even if would normally match another synchronization method:

```
:syntax sync match xSpecial /{.*}/
```

To clear out the synchronization commands, use the following command:

```
:syntax sync clear
```

To remove just the named groups, use this command:

```
:syntax sync clear sync-group-name sync-group-name ...
```

Adding Your Syntax File to the System

Suppose that you have defined your own language and want to add it to the system. If you want it to be a part of *Vim*, you need to perform the following steps:

1. Create your syntax file and put it in the $VIMRUNTIME/syntax/{language}.vim file.

2. Edit the file $VIMRUNTIME/syntax/synload.vim and add a line to this file for your language. The line should look like this:

   ```
   SynAu language
   ```

3. Edit the file $VIMRUNTIME/filetype.vim and insert an **:autocmd** that recognizes your files and sets the **ft** to your language. For example, for the foo language, execute the following command:

   ```
   :autocmd BufRead,BufNewFile *.foo set ft=foo
   ```

Now *Vim* should automatically recognize your new language.

If the file works well, you might want to send your changes to the *Vim* people so that they can put it in the next version of *Vim*.

Option Summary

contained	Syntax group is contained in another group. Items that are contained cannot appear at the top level, but must be contained in another group.
contains=*group-list*	Define a list of syntax groups that can be included inside this one. The group name can be **ALL** for all groups or **ALLBUT,** *group-name* for all groups except the names specified.
nextgroup=*group*	Define a group that may follow this one.
skipwhite	Skip whitespace between this group and the next one specified by **nextgroup**.
skipnl	Skip over the end of a line between this group and the next one specified by **nextgroup**.

skipempty	Skip over empty lines between this group and the next one specified by **nextgroup**.
transparent	This group takes on the attributes of the one in which it is contained.
oneline	Do not extend the match over more than one line.
keepend	Do not let a pattern with an end-of-line (**$**) match in it extend past the end of a line. This avoids the inner pattern inside a nested pattern eating an end of line. If this is a contained match, the match will not match the end-of-line character.
excludenl	Do not let a contained pattern extend the item in which it is contained past the end of a line.

III

Appendixes

Installing *Vim*

Y OU CAN OBTAIN *VIM* FROM THE WEB site at www.vim.org. This site contains the source to *Vim* as well as precompiled binaries for many different systems.

UNIX

You can get precompiled binaries for many different UNIX systems from www.vim.org. Go to www.vim.org, click the "Download Vim" link, and then follow the "Binaries Page" link.

This takes you to the "Binaries" page, which lists the various precompiled binaries for many different systems along with the links to download them.

Volunteers maintain the binaries, so they are frequently out of date. It is a good idea to compile your own UNIX version from the source. Also, creating the editor from the source allows you to control which features are compiled.

To compile and install the program, you'll need the following:

- A C compiler (GCC preferred)
- The GNU GZIP program (you can get it from www.gnu.org)

To obtain *Vim*, go to www.vim.org and click the "Download Vim" link. This page displays a list of sites that contain the software. Click a link to one that's near you. This takes you to a directory listing. Go into the "UNIX" directory and you'll find the sources for *Vim*. You'll need to download two files:

- vim-5.7-src.tar.gz
- vim-5.7-rt.tar.gz

Now unpack the sources using these commands:

```
$ gzip -u -d vim-5.7-src.tar.gz ¦ tar xvf -

$ gzip -u -d vim-5.7-rt.tar.gz ¦ tar xvf -
```

Build the Program

Go to the newly created *Vim* source directory:

```
$ cd vim-5.7/src
```

Now is a good time to read the files README.TXT and README_SRC.TXT. The instructions for compiling are in the file INSTALL. Configure the system with the following command:

```
$ ./configure
```

This configuration command assumes that you are going to install the system with a default set of features in the directory /usr/local. If you want to install in another directory, you need to use the **--prefix**=*directory*, where *directory* is the directory in which you want to install the editor. To install it in /apps/vim, for example, use this command:

```
$ ./configure --prefix=/apps/vim
```

The *Vim* editor has a lot of features that you can turn on and off at compile time. If this is the first time you are compiling *Vim*, you probably want to use the default set of features. After you have become familiar with the editor, you can enable the more exotic ones.

To get more information on *configure*, execute the following command:

```
$ ./configure --help
```

To find out about which features are available, see the file runtime/doc/various.txt or src/features.h.

Next compile the program with this command:

```
$ make
```

Finally, if all goes well, you can install it with the following command:

```
$ make install
```

Installation for Each UNIX User

Each UNIX user should make sure that *Vim* is in his path. If you have an EXRC file, copy it to VIMRC:

```
$ cp ~/.exrc ~/.vimrc
```

If you do not have an EXRC file, create an empty VIMRC file by executing the following command:

```
$ touch ~/.vimrc
```

> **Note**
>
> The presence of the VIMRC file turns on all the fancy features of *Vim*. If this file is not present, *Vim* tries very hard to look like *Vi*, even disabling some of its features to do so.

Installing on Microsoft Windows

To install the *Vim* program for Microsoft Windows, you'll need:

- The Windows binaries for Vim (gvim57.zip)
- The *Vim* runtime package (vim57rt.zip)
- A program to unpack the zip files

To download the *Vim* binaries, go to the *Vim* Web site, www.vim.org. Click "Download Vim." Do not click the "Binaries Page" link. Instead, select a mirror site and click the link provided. This takes you to a directory listing. Click the "pc" directory and download these files:

- gvim57.zip
- vim57rt.zip

If you already have a zip program, such as WinZip, installed, you can use it to unpack the sources. If not, go to the *Vim* home page (www.vim.org), scroll to the bottom of the page, and click the "Utilities" link. Click the "zip" link, which takes you to a link on an FTP site (ftp://ftp.uu.net/pub/archiving/zip). Follow this link to a directory listing. Select "WIN32" and then download the unz540xN.exe file.

Run this program to install the program InfoZip.

To install *Vim* itself, create a directory to be the root of your installation (for example: C:\VIM). Unzip the following archives into this directory:

```
vim\pc\gvim57.zip
vim\pc\vim57rt.zip
```

Open a MS-DOS command window, go the directory in which you installed *Vim* and execute the following command:

```
C:> install
```

The installer starts:

```
This program sets up the installation of Vim 5.7
It prepares the _VIMRC file, $VIM and the EXECUTAB.S
Do you want to continue? (Y/N)
```

Answer Y to continue. Installation continues:

```
Choose the default way to run Vim:
[1] Conventional Vim setup
[2] With syntax highlighting and other features switched on
[3] Vi compatible
Choice:
```

Because we want all the goodies, choose 2. (If you want to, choose 1. Do not choose 3, however; otherwise you turn off all the distinct features of this editor.)

```
Choose the way text is selected:
[1] With Visual mode (the UNIX way)
[2] With Select mode (the Windows way)
[3] Mouse with Select mode, keys with Visual mode
Choice:
```

To be compatible with the examples in this book, choose 1. (You can later change it if you want to customize your editor.)

```
You have chosen:
[2] With syntax highlighting and other features switched on
[1] With Visual mode (the UNIX way)
(You can adjust your _VIMRC file afterwards)

Do you want to write the file C:\VIM\VIM\_VIMRC? (Y/N)
```

Answer Y to continue. The editor creates the file and then asks the following:

```
I can append a command to C:\AUTOEXEC.BAT to set $VIM.
(This will not work if C:\AUTOEXEC.BAT contains sections)
Do you want me to append to your C:\AUTOEXEC.BAT (Y/N)
```

Answer Y if you want to be able to run *Vim* from within an MS-DOS window.

```
I can install an entry in the popup menu for the right
mouse button, so that you can edit any file with Vim.
Do you want me to do this? (Y/N)
```

> **Note**
>
> These installation instructions install only the GUI version of *Vim* named *gvim*. If you are doing a lot of editing inside the MS-DOS command-prompt windows, you might want to install the package:
>
> vim.org\pc\vim56w32.zip
>
> The console-mode *Vim* (for example, the non-BUI version on Windows) is not as good as the GUI version on Windows, for the simple reason that Windows does not support console mode very well or consistently among Windows versions.

This one is up to you. You can always choose N and reinstall later if you want this feature.

```
That finishes the installation. Happy Vimming!
```

Common Installation Problems and Questions

This section describes some of the common problems that occur when installing *Vim* and suggests some solutions. It also contains answers to many installation questions.

I Do Not Have Root Privileges. How Do I Install *Vim*? (UNIX)

Use the following configuration command to install *Vim* in a directory called $HOME/vim:

```
$ configure --prefix=$HOME/vim
```

This gives you a personal copy of *Vim*. You need to put $HOME/vim/bin in your path to access the editor.

The Colors Are Not Right on My Screen. (UNIX)

Check your terminal settings by using the following command:

```
$ echo $TERM
```

If the terminal type listed is not correct, fix it. UNIX has a database called termcap, which describes the capabilities of your terminal. Almost all xterm programs support color. Frequently, however, the termcap entry for xterm defines a terminal without color. To get color to work, you might have to tell the system that you have an xtermc or cxterm terminal. (Another solution is to always use the GUI version of *Vim* called *gvim*.)

I Am Using RedHat Linux. Can I Use the *Vim* That Comes with the System?

By default RedHat installs a minimal version of *Vim*. Check your RPM packages for something named *Vim-enchanced-version*.rpm and install that.

How Do I Turn Syntax Coloring On? (All)

Use the following command:

```
:syntax on
```

What Is a Good *vimrc* File to Use? (All)

See the www.vim.org Web site for several good examples.

UNIX Source Checklist

1. Start at www.vim.org.

2. Click "Download *Vim*".

3. Select the mirror site closest to you.

4. Click "UNIX".

5. Click "vim-5.7-src.tar.gz" to download this file.

6. Click "vim-5.7-rt.tar.gz" to download this file.

7. On your local system, execute these commands:

   ```
   $ gzip -u -d vim-5.7-src.tar.gz ¦ tar xvf -
   $ gzip -u -d vim-5.7-rt.tar.gz ¦ tar xvf -
   ```

8. Configure and build the program with these commands:

   ```
   $ cd vim-5.7/src
   $ ./configure -prefix=<directory>
   $ make
   $ make install
   ```

   <directory> is the directory where *Vim* is to be installed.

Microsoft Windows Checklist

1. Start at www.vim.org.

2. Click "Download *Vim*".

3. Select the mirror nearest you and click it.

4. Click "pc".

5. Click "gvim56.zip" to download this file.

6. Click "vim57rt.zip: to download this file.

7. Unzip these files into the installation directory on your machine. (If you do not have an UNZIP program, see the instructions in the following section.)

8. Execute the installation script with this command:

   ```
   C:> install
   ```

Installing the InfoZip Program

1. Start at the Web site www.vim.org.

2. Near the end of the page, you'll find the "Utilities" link. Click it.

3. Click "zip".

4. Click ftp://ftp.uu.net/pub/archiving/zip.

5. Click "WIN32".

6. Click "unz540xN.exe" to download this file.

7. Run the program "unz540xN.exe" to install InfoZip.

B

The <> Key Names

THIS APPENDIX PROVIDES A QUICK reference for the <> key names in *Vim*.

The Function Keys

<F1>	<F2>	<F3>	<F4>	<F5>	<F6>
<F7>	<F8>	<F9>	<F10>	<F11>	<F12>
<F13>	<F14>	<F15>	<F16>	<F17>	<F18>
<F19>	<F20>	<F21>	<F22>	<F23>	<F24>
<F25>	<F26>	<F27>	<F28>	<F29>	<F30>
<F31>	<F32>	<F33>	<F34>	<F35>	

Line Endings

<CR>	<Return>	<Enter>
<LF>	<LineFeed>	
<NL>	<NewLine>	

Other Special Characters

    \<BS>   \<BackSpace>

    \<Ins>   \<Insert>

    \<Del>   \<Delete>

Editing Keys

    \<End>   \<Home>   \<PageDown>   \<PageUp>

Arrow Keys

    \<Left>   \<Right>   \<Up>   \<Down>

Keypad Keys

    \<kDivide>   \<kEnd>   \<kEnter>   \<kHome>   \<kMinus>   \<kMultiply>

    \<kPlus>   \<kPageDown>   \<kPageUp>

VT100 Special Keys

The VT100 terminal has an extra set of function keys, as follows:

    \<xF1>   \<xF2>   \<xF3> ·   \<xF4>   \<xEnd>   \<xHome>

Printable Characters

    \<Bar> |

    \<Bslash>   \

    \<Space>

    \<Tab>

    \<Lt>   \<

Other Keys

    \<Esc>   \<Help>   \<Nul>   \<Undo>

Termcap Entries

On UNIX systems, the Termcap or Terminfo database contains a description of the terminal, including function keys. The special key <t_*XX*> represents the key defined by *XX* Termcap entry.

See your UNIX documentation for a complete list of keys. One way to get a list (for most systems) is to execute the following command:

```
$ man terminfo
```

Mouse Actions

<LeftDrag>	<Mouse>
<LeftMouse>	<MouseDown>
<LeftRelease>	<MouseUp>
<MiddleDrag>	<RightDrag>
<MiddleMouse>	<RightMouse>
<MiddleRelease>	<RightRelease>

Modifiers

M	Meta (Alt)
C	Control
S	Shift
D	Macintosh command key

Mouse Modifiers

<Blank>	Mouse button one
2	Mouse button two
3	Mouse button three
4	Mouse button four

> **Note**
>
> If you want to find the name of a key on the keyboard, you can go into Insert mode and press **CTRL-K** *key*. The <> name of the key will be inserted. This works for the function keys and many other keys.

C

Normal-Mode Commands

[count] **<BS>**   Move count characters to the left. See the **'backspace'** option to change this to delete rather than backspace. (Same as: **<Left>**, **CTRL-H, CTRL-K, h**. See page 6.)

[count] **<C-End>**   Move to the end of line *count*. If no count is specified, go to the end of the file. (Same as: **G**. See pages 18, 40, 161, and 188.)

[count] **<C-Home>**   Move to the start (first non-blank character) of line *count*. Default is the beginning of the file. (Same as: **gg**. See page 156.)

[count] **<C-Left>**   Move *count* WORDS backward. (Same as: **B**. See page 186.)

<C-LeftMouse>   Jump to the location of the tag whose name is under the cursor. (Same as: **CTRL-]**, **g<LeftMouse>**. See pages 12, 79, and109.)

<C-Right>   Move *count* WORDS forward. (Same as: **W**. See page 86.)

[count] **count<C-RightMouse>**   Jump to a previous entry in the tag stack. (Same as: **CTRL-T, g<RightMouse>**. See pages 12, 80–81, and 109.)

[count] **<CR>**   Move down *count* lines. Cursor is positioned on the first nonblank character on the line. (Same as: **<ENTER>, CTRL-M**, and **+**. See page 187.)

["{register}] *[count]* **<Del>**   Delete characters. If a "{*register* } is present, the deleted text is stored in it. (Same as: **x**. See pages 7, 13, 36–37, 160, and 196–197.)

[count] **<Down>**   Move *count* lines down. (Same as: **<NL>**, **CTRL-J**, **CTRL-N**, **j**. See pages 6 and 235.)

[count] **<End>**   Move the cursor to the end of the line. If a *count* is present, move to the end of the *count* line down from the current one. (Same as: **<kEnd>**, **$**. See pages 16 and 234.)

[count] **<Enter>**   Move down *count* lines. (Default = 1.) Cursor is positioned on the first nonblank character on the line. (Same as: **<CR>**, **CTRL-M**, **+**. See pages 7 and 187.)

<F1>   Go to the initial help screen. (Same as: **<Help>**, **:h**, **:help**. See pages 11, 13, and 157.)

<F8>   Toggle between left-to-right and right-to-left modes. (See page 174.)

<F9>   Toggles the encoding between ISIR-3342 standard and *Vim* extended ISIR-3342 (supported only in right-to-left mode when **'fkmap'** [Farsi] is enabled). (See page 176.)

<Help>   Go to the initial help screen. (Same as: **<F1>**, **:h**, **:help**. See pages 11 and 157.)

<Home>   Move to the first character of the line. (Same as: **<kHome>**. See page 16.)

[count] **<Insert>text<Esc>**   Insert text. If *count* is present, the text will be inserted *count* times. (Same as: **i**. See pages 5 and 9.)

[count] **<kEnd>**   Move the cursor to the end of the line. If a *count* is present, move to the end of the *count* line down from the current one. (Same as: **<End>**, **$**. See page 16.)

<kHome>   Move to the first character of the line. (Same as: **<Home>**. See page 16.)

[count] **<Left>**   Move left *count* characters. (Same as: **<BS>**, **CTRL-H**, **CTRL-K**, **h**. See page 6.)

<LeftMouse>   Move the text cursor to the location of the mouse cursor. (See pages 109 and 332.)

["register] **<MiddleMouse>**   Insert the text in register at the location of the mouse cursor. (Same as: **P**. See pages 109 and 332.)

<MouseDown>   Scroll three lines down. (See page 332.)

<MouseUp>   Scroll three lines up. (See page 332.)

[count] **<M>**   Move *count* lines down. (See page 192.)

[count] **<PageDown>**   Scroll *count* pages forward. (Same as: **<S-Down>**, **CTRL-F**. See page 192.)

[count] **<PageUp>**   Scroll the window *count* pages backward. (Same as: **<S-Up>**, **CTRL-B**. See page 192.)

£   Same as £. (See page 206.)

[count] **<Right>**   Move right *count* characters. (Same as: **<Space>**, **1**. See page 6.)

<RightMouse>   Start select mode with the text from the text cursor to the mouse cursor highlighted. (See pages 109 and 332.)

[count] **<S-Down>**   Scroll *count* pages forward. If you are running Windows GUI version, **<S-Down>** enters visual mode and selects down. (Same as: **<PageDown>**, **CTRL-F**. See page 192.)

[count] **<S-Left>**   Move left *count* words. (Same as: **b**. See page 16.)

[count] **<S-LeftMouse>**   Find the next occurrence of the word under the cursor. (See page 109.)

<S-MouseDown>   Scroll a full page up three lines down. (See page 332.)

<S-MouseUp>   Scroll a full page down three lines up. (See page 332.)

[count] **<S-Right>**   Move *count* words forward. (Same as: **w**. See pages 16, 20, and 184.)

[count] **<S-RightMouse>**   Search backward for the word under the cursor. (See page 109.)

[count] **<S-Up>**   Scroll *count* pages up. (Same as: **<PageUp>**, **CTRL-B**. See page 192.)

[count] **<Space>**   Move *count* spaces to the right. (Same as: **<Right>**, **1**. See page 6.)

[count] **<Tab>**   Go to the *count* position in the jump list. (Same as: **CTRL-I**. See page 189.)

[count] **<Undo>**   Undo the last *count* changes. (Same as: **u**. See page 8.)

[count] **<Up>**   Move *count* lines up. (Same as: **CTRL-P**, **k**. See pages 6 and 13.)

CTRL-\ CTRL-N   Enter normal mode from any other mode. (See page 58.)

CTRL-]   Jump to the function whose name is under the cursor. (In the help system, jump to the subject indicated by a hyperlink.) (Same as: **<C-LeftMouse>**, **g<LeftMouse>**. See pages 12 and 79.)

[count] **CTRL-^**   If a *count* is specified, edit the *count* file on the command line. If no *count* is present, edit the previously edited file. Thus repeated **CTRL-^** can be used to toggle rapidly between two files. (See pages 43 and 244.)

CTRL-_   Switch between English and a foreign language keyboard. (See pages 176-177.)

[count] **CTRL-A**   Add *count* to the number under the cursor. If no *count* is specified, increment the number. (See pages 43 and 244.)

[count] **CTRL-B**   Move back *count* screens. (Default = 1.) (Same as: **<PageUp>**, **<S-Up>**. See pages 191–192.)

CTRL-BREAK   Interrupt search (same as **CTRL-C**). (See page 206.)

CTRL-C   Interrupt search. (same as **CTRL-BREAK**). (See page 206.)

[count] **CTRL-D**   Move down the number of lines specified by the 'scroll' option. If a *count* is specified, set the 'scroll' option to *count* and then move down. (See pages 20 and 190–192.)

[count] **CTRL-E**   Move down *count* lines. (See page 192.)

[count] **CTRL-F**   Scroll the window *count* pages forward. (Same as: **<PageDown>**, **<S-Down>**. See page 192.)

CTRL-G   Display the current file and location of the cursor within that file. (Same as: **:file**. See pages 19–20 and 190.)

1 CTRL-G   Same as **CTRL-G**, but include the full path in the filename. (See pages 19–20 and 190.)

2 CTRL-G   Same as **1 CTRL-G**, but adds a buffer number. (See pages 19–20 and 190.)

[count] **CTRL-H**   Move *count* characters to the left. See the **'backspace'** option to change this to delete rather than backspace. (Same as: **<BS>**, **<Left>**, **CTRL-K**, **h**. See page 6.)

[count] **CTRL-I**   Jump to the *count* next item in the jump list. (Same as: **<Tab>**. See page 189.)

[count] **CTRL-J**   Move down *count* lines. (Same as: **<Down>**, **<NL>**, **CTRL-J**, **j**. See pages 6 and 235.)

[count] **CTRL-K**   Move *count* characters to the left. (Same as: **<BS>**, **<Left>**, **CTRL-H**, **h**. See page 25.)

CTRL-L   Redraw screen. (See page 156.)

CTRL-L   Leave insert mode if insertmode is set. (See page 179.)

CTRL-M   Copy **<CR>** entry. (Same as **<CR>**, **+**. See page 187.)

[count] **CTRL-N**   Move *count* lines down. (Same as: **<Down>**, **<NL>**, **CTRL-J**, **j**. See pages 6 and 235.)

[count] **CTRL-O**   Jump to the *count* previous item in the jump list. (See page 189.)

[count] **CTRL-P**   Move *count* lines upward. (Same as: **<Up>**, **k**. See pages 6 and 13.)

CTRL-Q   Used by some terminals to start output after it was stopped by **CTRL-S**. (See page 156.)

CTRL-R   Redo the last change that was undone. (See page 8.)

CTRL-S   Used by some terminals to stop output. (See page 156.)

[count] **CTRL-T**   Go back *count* tags. If the current buffer has been modified, this command fails unless the force (**!**) option is present. When using the help system, this command returns to the location you were at before making the last hyperlink jump. (Same as: **<C-RightMouse>**, **g<RightMouse>**. See pages 12 and 80-81.)

[count] **CTRL-U**   Move up the number of lines specified by the **'scroll'** option. If a *count* is specified, set the **'scroll'** option to *count* and then scroll up. (See pages 20 and 190-192.)

CTRL-V   Start visual block mode. (See pages 57 and 60.)

[count] **CTRL-W<Down>**   Move down a window. If a *count* is specified, move to window number *count*. (Same as: **CTRL-W CTRL-J**, **CTRL-Wj**. See page 46.)

[count] **CTRL-W<Up>**   Move up a window. If a *count* is specified, move to window number *count*. (Same as: **CTRL-W CTRL-K**, **CTRL-Wk**. See page 46.)

[count] **CTRL-W CTRL-]**   Split the current window and jump to the function whose name is under the cursor. If a *count* is specified, it is the height of the new window. (Same as: **CTRL-W]**. See page 82.)

CTRL-W CTRL-^   Split the window and edit the alternate file. If a *count* is specified, split the window and edit the *count* file on the command line. (Same as: **CTRL-W^**. See page 244.)

[count] **CTRL-W CTRL-_**   Set the height of the current window to *count*. (Same as: **CTRL-W+, CTRL-W-, CTRL-W_,** :resize. See page 49.)

CTRL-W CTRL-B   Move to the bottom window. (Same as: **CTRL-Wb**. See page 240.)

CTRL-W CTRL-C   Cancel any pending window command. (See page 46.)

CTRL-W CTRL-D   Split the window and find the definition of the word under the cursor. If the definition cannot be found, do not split the window. (Same as: **CTRL-Wd**. See page 245.)

CTRL-W CTRL-F   Split the window and edit the file whose name is under the cursor. Looks for the file in the current directory, and then all the directories specified by the **'path'** option. (Same as: **CTRL-Wf**. See page 245.)

[count] **CTRL-W CTRL-G CTRL-]**   :split followed a **CTRL-]**. If a *count* is specified, make the new window *count* lines high. (Same as: **CTRL-Wg CTRL-]**, **CTRL-Wg**. See page 245.)

[count] **CTRL-W CTRL-G }**   Do a :ptjump on the word under the cursor. If a *count* is specified, make the new window *count* lines high. (Same as: **CTRL-W CTRL-G}**. See page 277.)

[count] **CTRL-W CTRL-I**   Split the window and search for the *count* occurrence of the word under the cursor. Start the search at the beginning of the file. (Same as: **CTRL-Wi**. See page 244.)

[count] **CTRL-W CTRL-J**   Move down a window. If a *count* is specified, move to window number *count*. (Same as: **CTRL-W<Down>**, **CTRL-Wj**. See page 46.)

[count] **CTRL-W CTRL-K**   Move *count* windows up. (Same as: **CTRL-W<Up>**, **CTRL-Wk**. See page 46.)

CTRL-W CTRL-N   Split the window like **:split**. The only difference is that if no filename is specified, a new window is started on a blank file. (Same as: **CTRL-Wn**, **:new**. See page 48.)

CTRL-W CTRL-O   Make the current window the only one. (Same as: **CTRL-Wo**, **:on**, **:only**. See page 243.)

CTRL-W CTRL-P   Move to the previous window. (Same as: **CTRL-Wp**. See pages 162–163 and 240.)

CTRL-W CTRL-Q   Close a window. If this is the last window, exit *Vim*. The command fails if this is the last window for a modified file, unless the force (**!**) option is present. (Same as: **CTRL-W q**, **:q**, **:quit**. See pages 9, 46, 144, 202, and 242–243.)

[count] **CTRL-W CTRL-R**   Rotate windows downward. (Same as: **CTRL-Wr**. See page 241.)

[count] **CTRL-W CTRL-S**   Split the current window. (Make the new window *count* lines high.) (Same as: **CTRL-Ws**, **CTRL-WS**, **:sp**, **:split**. See pages 45, 47–48, 162, and 247.)

CTRL-W CTRL-T   Move the top window. (Same as: **CTRL-Wt**. See page 240.)

CTRL-W CTRL-W   Move to the next window. If there is no next window, move to the first one. If a *count* is specified, move to window number *count*. (Same as: **CTRL-Ww**. See pages 46 and 240.)

[count] **CTRL-W CTRL-X**   Exchange the current window with the next one. If there is no next one, exchange the last window with the first. If a *count* is specified, exchange the current window with window number *count*. (Same as: **CTRL-Wx**. See page 242.)

CTRL-W CTRL-Z   Close the preview window. Discard any changes if the force (**!**) option is present. (Same as: **CTRL-Wz**, **:pc**, **:pclose**. See page 276.)

[count] **CTRL-W +**   Increase the size of the current window by *count*. (Default = 1.) (Same as: **:res +, :resize +**. See page 48.)

[count] **CTRL-W - (CTRL-W <dash>)**   Decrease the size of the current window by *count*. (Default = 1.) (Same as: **res -, :resize -**. See page 48.)

CTRL-W=   Make all windows the same size (or as close as possible). (See page 48.)

[count] **CTRL-W]**   Split the current window and jump to the function whose name is under the cursor. If a *count* is specified, it is the height of the new window. (Same as: **CTRL-W CTRL-]**. See page 82.)

CTRL-W ^   Split the window and edit the alternate file. If a *count* is specified, split the window and edit the *count* file on the command line. (Same as: **CTRL-W CTRL-^**. See page 244.)

[count] **CTRL-W _**   Set the current window to be *count* lines high. If no *count* is specified, make the window as big as possible. (Same as: **CTRL-W CTRL-_, :res, :resize**. See page 49.)

CTRL-W }   Do a **:ptag** on the word under the cursor. (See page 277.)

CTRL-W b   Move to the bottom window. (Same as: **CTRL-W CTRL-B**. See page 240.)

CTRL-W c   Close the current window. (Same as: **:clo, :close**. See page 46.)

CTRL-W d   Split the window and find the definition of the word under the cursor. If the definition cannot be found, do not split the window. (Same as: **CTRL-W CTRL-D**. See page 245.)

CTRL-W f   Split the window and edit the file whose name is under the cursor. Looks for the file in the current directory, then all the directories specified by the path option. (Same as: **CTRL-W CTRL-F**. See page 245.)

CTRL-W g CTRL-]   **:split** followed a **CTRL-]**. (Same as: **CTRL-W CTRL-G], CTRL-Wg]**. See page 245.

CTRL-W g]   **:split** followed a **CTRL-]**. (Same as: **CTRL-Wg CTRL], CTRL-W CTRL-G]**. See page 245.)

CTRL-W g }   Do a **:ptjump** on the word under the cursor. (Same as: **CTRL-W CTRL-G}**. See page 277.)

[count] **CTRL-W i**   Split the window and search for the *count* occurrence of the word under the cursor. Start the search at the beginning of the file. (Same as: **CTRL-W CTRL-I**. See page 244.)

[count] **CTRL-W j**   Move down a window. If a *count* is specified, move to window number *count*. (Same as: **CTRL-W CTRL-J, CTRL-W<Down>**. See page 46.)

[count] **CTRL-W k**   Go up *count* windows. (Same as: **CTRL-W CTRL-K**, **CTRL-W<Up>**. See page 46.)

CTRL-W n   Split the window like **:split**. The only difference is that if no filename is specified, a new window is started on a blank file. (Same as: **CTRL-W CTRL-N**, :new. See page 48.)

CTRL-W o   Make the current window the only one. If ! is specified, modified files whose windows are closed will have their contents discarded. (Same as: **CTRL-W CTRL-O**, :on, :only. See page 243.)

CTRL-W p   Move to the previous window. (Same as: **CTRL-W CTRL-P**. See pages 162–163 and 240.)

CTRL-W q   Close a window. If this is the last window, exit *Vim*. The command fails if this is the last window for a modified file, unless the force (!) option is present. (Same as: **CTRL-W CTRL-Q**, :q, :quit. See pages 9, 46, 144, 202 and 242–243.)

[count] **CTRL-W r**   Rotate windows downward. (Same as: **CTRL-W CTRL-R**, **CTRL-WR**. See page 241.)

[count] **CTRL-W R**   Rotate windows upward. (Same as: **CTRL-W CTRL-R**, **CTRL-Wr**. See page 241.)

[count] **CTRL-W s**   Split the current window. Make the new window *count* lines high (same as *[count]* **CTRL-W S**). (Same as: **CTRL-W CTRL-S**, **CTRL-WS**, :sp, :split. See pages 45–48, 162, 247.)

[count] **CTRL-W S**   Split the current window. Make the new window *count* lines high (same as *[count]* **CTRL-W s**). (Same as: **CTRL-W CTRL-S**, **CTRL-Ws**, :sp, :split. See page 162.)

CTRL-W t   Move the top window. (Same as: **CTRL-W CTRL-T**. See page 240.)

[count] **CTRL-W w**   Move to the next window. If there is no next window, move to the first one. If a *count* is specified, move to window number *count*. (Same as: **CTRL-W CTRL-W**. See pages 46 and 240.)

[count] **CTRL-W W**   Move to the previous window. If at the top window, go to the bottom one. If a *count* is specified, move to window number *count*. (See page 240.)

[count] **CTRL-W x**   Exchange the current window with the next one. If there is no next one, exchange the last window with the first. If a *count* is specified, exchange the current window with window number *count*. (Same as: **CTRL-W CTRL-X**. See page 242.)

CTRL-W z   Close the preview window. (Same as: **CTRL-W CTRL-Z**, :pc, :pclose. See page 276.)

[count] **CTRL-X**   Subtract *count* to the number under the cursor. If no *count* is specified, decrement the number. (See pages 197–198 and 395.)

[count] **CTRL-Y**   Move up *count* lines. (See pages 191–192.)

CTRL-Z   Suspend the editor (Unix only). (See page 156.)

!{motion}{command}   Filter the block of text represented by {motion} through the an external {*command*}command. (See pages 40, 85, 120, 164, and 166–167.)

[count] !!{command}   Filter the current line (or *count* lines} through the an external command. (See page 40.)

[count] £   Search for the word under the cursor, backward. (Same as: **£**. See page 206.)

[count] $ Move the cursor to the end of the line. If a *count* is present, move to the end of the *count* line down from the current one. (Same as: **<End>**, **<kEnd>**. See pages 16 and 234.)

[count] %   Jump to the line whose *count* percent of the way through the file. (See pages 73, 76–77, and 278.)

&   Synonym for ":s//~/" – repeat last substitution. (See page 311.)

'{letter}   Go to the line containing mark named {letter}. (See pages 37, 85, 161–162, 164, and 228.)

[count] (Move backward *count* sentences. (See page 121.)

[count])   Move forward *count* sentences. (See page 121.)

[count] *   Search for the word under the cursor, forward. (See page 206.)

[count] +   Move down *count* lines. (Default = 1.)Cursor is positioned on the first nonblank character on the line. (Same as: **<CR>**, **CTRL-M**. See page 187.)

[count] ,   Reverse the direction of the last single character and perform the search *count* times. (See page 187.)

[count] -   Move up *count* lines. (Default = 1.) Cursor is positioned on the first nonblank character on the line. (See page 187.)

[count] /   Repeat last search in the forward direction. (See pages 27–30, 32, 161, 203, and 227.)

[count] /{pattern}   Search forward. (See pages 27–30, 32, 161, 203, and 227.)

[count] /{pattern}/{offset}   Search forward, position the cursor at **{offset}** from the search pattern. (See page 208.)

[count] //{offset}   Repeat last search in the forward direction with a new offset. (See page 208.)

[count] ;   Repeat the last single character search *count* times. (Default = 1.) (See page 187.)

[count] <<   Shift *count* lines to the left. (See pages 69–70.)

<*{motion}*   Shift lines from cursor to *{motion}* to the left. (See pages 69–70.)

[count] >>   Shift *count* lines to the right. (See page 67.)

>*{motion}*   Shift lines from cursor to *{motion}* to the right. (See pages 69–70.)

=*{motion}*   Filter *{motion}* lines through the external program given with the '**equalprg**' option. (See page 73.)

[count] ?   Repeat last search in the backward direction. (See pages 31–32.)

[count] ?*{pattern}*   Search backward. (See page 29.)

[count] ?*{pattern}*?*{offset}*   Search backward, position the cursor at *{offset}* from the search pattern. (See page 208.)

[count] ??*{offset}*   Repeat last search in the backward direction with a new *{offset}*. (See page 208.)

[count] @*{character}*   Execute the macro in register *{character}*. (See page 24.)

["{register}] **[<MiddleMouse>**   Put the **{register}** in the buffer like the p command, but adjust the text to fit the indent of the current line. (Same as: **[p, [P,]P**. See page 265.)

[count] **[CTRL-D**   Find definition of the macro currently sitting under the cursor. Start the search from the beginning of the file. (See page 75.)

[count] **[CTRL-I**   Search for the word under the cursor starting at the beginning of the file. (See pages 73–74 and 284.)

[count] *["{register}*<**MiddleMouse>**   Put the {register} in the buffer like the p command, but adjust the text to fit the indent of the current line. (See page 265.)

[£   Finds the previous unmatched **£if/£else/£endif**. (See page 279.)

[count] **[***   Move backward to the beginning of the *count* comment from the cursor. (Same as: **[/**. See page 280.)

[count] **[/**   Same as: **[***. (See page 280.)

[count] **[(**   Move backward to the *count* previous unmatched '(' in column 1. (See page 279.)

[count] **[)**   Move backward to the *count* previous unmatched ')'. (See page 279.)

[count] **[[**   Move backward *count* sections or to the previous **{** in column 1. (See pages 122 and 279.)

[count] **[]**   Move *count* sections backwards or to the previous **}** in column 1. (See pages 122 amd 279.)

[count] **[}**   Finds the *count* previous unmatched **}**. (See page 278.)

[count] **[d**   List the definition of the macro. Start search at the current cursor locationbeginning of the file. (See pages 73, 75, and 284.)

[count] **[D**   List all definitions of the macro whose name is under the cursor. Start the list with the next first definition in the file. (See pages 73 and 76.)

[f   Deprecated. Use **gf** instead. (Same as: **gf**, **]f**. See page 281.)

[count] **[i**   Display the *count* line that contains the keyword under the cursor. The search starts from the beginning of the file. (See page 284.)

[I   List all lines in the current and included files that contain the word under the cursor. (See page 284.)

[m   Search backward for the start of a method. (See page 279.)

[M   Search backward for the end of a method. (See page 279.)

["{register}] **[p**   Put the *{register}* in the buffer like the **P** command, but adjust the text to fit the indent of the current line. (Same as: **[<MiddleMouse>**, **[P**, **]P**. See page 265.)

["{register}] **[P**   Put the {register} in the buffer like the P command, but adjust the text to fit the indent of the current line. (Same as: **[<MiddleMouse>**, **[p**, **[P**. See page 265.)

["{register}] **]<MiddleMouse>**   Put the *{register}* in the buffer like the **p** command, but adjust the text to fit the indent of the current line. (Same as: **]p**. See page 265.)

[count] **]CTRL-D**   Find definition of the macro currently sitting under the cursor. Start the search from the beginning current location.of the file. (See page 73.)

[count] **]CTRL-I**   Search for the word under the cursor starting at the beginning of the filecurrent cursor location. (See pages 73-74 and 284.)

[count] **]#**   Finds the next unmatched **#if**/**#else**/**#endif**. (See page 279.)

[count] **])**   Move forward to the *count* next unmatched **)**. (See page 280.)

[count] **]/**   -or-

[count] **]***   Move forward to the end of the *count* comment from the cursor. (See page 280.)

[count] **](**   Move forward to the *count* next unmatched **(**. (See page 279.)

[count] **][**   Move *count* sections forward or to the next **}** in column 1. (See pages 122 and 279.)

[count] **]]** Move *count* sections forward or to the next **{** in column 1. (See pages 122 and 279.)

[count] **]{** Finds the *count* previous unmatched **{**.(See page 278.)

[count] **]}** Finds the *count* previous unmatched **}**. (See page 278.)

[count] **]d** List the definition of the macro. Start search at the beginning of the current cursor position. (See pages 73, 75, and 284.)

[count] **]D** List all definitions of the macro whose name is under the cursor. Start the list with the first next definition. (See pages 73 and 76.)

]f Deprecated. Use **gf** instead. (Same as: **gf**, **[f**. See page 281.)

[count] **]i** Display the *count* line that contains the keyword under the cursor. The search starts from the beginning of the filecurrent cursor position. (See page 284.)

]I List all lines in the current and included files that contain the word under the cursor starting at the current location. (See page 284.)

]m Search forward for the start of a method. (See page 279.)

]M Search forward for the end of a method. (See page 279.)

["{register}] **]p** Put the *{register}* in the buffer like the P command, but adjust the text to fit the indent of the current line. (Same as: **]<MiddleMouse>**. See page 265.)

["{register}] **]P** Put the *{register}* in the buffer like the **P** command, but adjust the text to fit the indent of the current line. (Same as **]<MiddleMouse>**, **[p**, **[P**. See page 265.)

^ Move to the first nonblank character of the line. (See pages 16, 187, and 234.)

[count] **_** Move to the first printing character of the *count*-1 line below the cursor. (See page 188.)

`{mark} Go to the mark named mark. Cursor is positioned exactly on the mark. (See page 37.)

'{mark} Go to the line containing mark. Position the cursor at the first non-blank character on the line. (See page 37.)

[count] **{** Move backward *count* paragraphs. (See page 121.)

[count] **¦** Move to the column *count* on the current line. (See page 235.)

[count] **}** Move forward *count* paragraphs. (See page 121.)

~{motion} Change the case of the indicated characters. (This version of the command depends on the **'tildeop'** option being on. (The default is off.) To turn on the option, use the **:set tildeop** command. (See pages 24, 200-201, and 401.)

[count] ~   Change the case of *count* characters. (This version of the command depends on the **'tildeop'** option being off (the default). To turn off the option, use the :set notildeop command. (See pages 24, 200-201, and 401.)

[count] £   Search for the word under the cursor, backward. (See page 202.)

0 *(Zero)*   Move to the first character on the line. (See pages 16, 187, and 234.)

[count] **a**{*text*}**<Esc>**   Insert text starting after the character under the cursor. If a *count* is specified, the text is inserted *count* times. (See page 9.)

[count] **A**{*text*}**<Esc>**   Append the text on to the end of the line. (See page 197.)

[count] **b**   Move backward *count* words. (Same as: **<S-Left>**. See page 16.)

[count] **B**   Move *count* WORDS backward. (Same as: **<C-Left>**. See page 186.)

c{*motion*}   Delete from the cursor to the location specified by the {*motion*} to enter insert mode. (See pages 21 and 161.)

[count] **C**   Delete from the cursor to the end of the current line and *count*-1 more lines, and then enter insert mode. (See page 195.)

[count] **cc**   Delete *count* entire lines (default = 1) and enter insert mode. (See page 22.)

["{register}] **d**{*motion*}   Delete from the cursor location to where {*motion*} goes. (See pages 36, 161, and 195.)

[count] **D**   Delete from the cursor to the end of the line. If a *count* is specified, delete an additional *count*-1 lines. (See pages 21 and 195.)

["{register}]count[count] **dd**   Delete *count* lines. (See pages 10, 20, 36, and 224.)

[count] **e**   Move *count* words forward, stop at the end of the word. (See page 184.)

[count] **E**   Move *count* WORDS forward to the end of the WORD. (See page 186.)

[count] **f**{*char*}   Search forward for character {*char*} on the current line. Stop on the character. (See pages 17 and 187.)

[count] **F**{*char*}   Search backward for character {*char*} on the current line. Stop on the character. (See page 17.)

[count] **G**   Go to the line *count*. If no line is specified, go to the last line in the file. (Same as: <C-End>. See pages 18, 40, 161, and 188.)

[count] **g<Down>**   Move down one line on the screen. (Same as: **gj**. See page 235.)

g<End>   Move to the rightmost character on the screen. (Same as: **g$**. See page 234.)

g<Home>   Move to the leftmost character on the screen. (In other words, move to column 1.) (Same as: **g0**. See page 234.)

g\<LeftMouse> Jump to the location of the tag whose name is under the cursor. (Same as: **\<C-LeftMouse>**, **CTRL-]**. See page 12.)

[count] **g** **\<RightMouse>** Jump to a previous entry in the tag stack. (Same as: **\<C-RightMouse>**, **CTRL-T**. See page 12.)

[count] **]g\<Up>** Move up lines in one the screen space. (Same as: **gk**. See page 235.)

g **CTRL-]** Do a **:tjump** on the word under the cursor. (See page 83.)

g **CTRL-G** Display detailed information about where you are in the file. (See page 156.)

g **CTRL-H** Start select block mode. (See page 258.)

[count] **g£** Search for the word under the cursor, backward. Unlike **£**, this finds partial words. (Same as: **g£**. See page 206.)

g$ Move to the rightmost character on the screen. (Same as: **g\<End>**. See page 234.)

[count] **g*** Search for the word under the cursor, forward. Unlike *****, this finds partial words. (See page 206.)

[count] **g??** Encrypt the lines using the rot13 encryption. (Same as: **g?g?**. See page 123.)

[count] **g?g?** Encrypt the lines using the rot13 encryption. (Same as: **g??**. See page 123.)

g£ Search for the word under the cursor, backwards. Unlike **£**, this finds partial words. (Same as: **g£**. See page 206.)

g?{*motion*} Encrypt the text from the current cursor location to where {*motion*} takes you using rot13 encryption. (See page 123.)

g] Do a :tselect on the word under the cursor. (See page 83.)

g^ Move to the leftmost printing character visible on the current line. (See page 234.)

g~{*motion*} Reverse the case of the text from the cursor to {**motion**}(same as *[count]***g~g~**). (See pages 201 and 401.)

[count] **g~g~** –or–

[count] **g~~** Reverse the case of the entire line. If a *count* is specified, change the case of *count* lines. (Same as: **g~g~**. See page 201.)

g0 (zero) Move to the leftmost character on the screen. (In other words, move to column 1.) (Same as: **g\<Home>**. See page 234.)

ga Print the ASCII value of the character under the cursor. (Same as: **gs**, **:as**, **:ascii**, **:sleep**. See page 155.)

gd Find the local definition of the variable under the cursor. (See pages 73-74.)

gD Find the global definition of the variable under the cursor. (See pages 73-74.)

[count] **ge** Move *count* words backward stopping on the end of the word. (See page 184.)

[count] **gE** Move *count* WORDS backward to the end of the WORD. (See page 186.)

gf Edit the file whose name is under the cursor. If the file is not in the current directory, search the directory list specified by the 'path' option. (Same as: **[f,]f**. See page 281.)

[count] **gg** Move to line *count*. Default is the first line. (Same as: **<C-Home>**. See page 156.)

gh Start select mode characterwise. (See page 258.)

gH Start select mode linewise. (See page 258.)

[count] **gI**{*text*}**<Esc>** Insert text in column 1, *count* times. (See page 197.)

[count] **gj** Move down one line on the screen. (Same as: **g<Down>**. See page 231.)

[count] **gJ** Join lines. No spaces are put between the assembled parts. If a *count* is specified, *count* lines are joined (minimum of two lines). (See page 198.)

[count] **] gk** Move up lines in inone the screen space. (Same as: **g<Up>**. See page 235.)

gm Move to the middle of the screen. (See page 234.)

[count] **go** Go to *count* byte of the file. (Same as: **:go**, **:goto**. See page 156.)

[""*{register}]* **gp** Paste the text before the cursor, but do not move the cursor. (See page 220.)

[""*{register}]* **gP** Paste the text after the cursor, but do not move the cursor. (See page 220.)

gq{*motion*} Format the text from the line the cursor is on to the line where {*motion*} takes you. (See pages 115, 117, 119, 269, and 271.)

gqq Format the current line. (Same as: **gqgq**. See page 115.)

gqgq Format the current line. (Same as: **gqq**. See page 115.)

[count] **gr**{*character*} Replace the virtual character under the cursor with {*character*}. (See pages 199-200.)

[count] **gR**{*string*}**<Esc>**   Enter virtual replace mode until **<Esc>** is pressed. (See page 200.)

seconds gs   Sleep for the specified number of seconds. (Same as: **:sl**, **:sleep**. See page 156.)

gu{*motion*}   Uppercase of the text from the cursor to {*motion*}. (See page 201.)

gU{*motion*}   Uppercase of the text from the cursor to {*motion*}. (See page 201.)

[count] **gugu**   -or-

[count] **guu**   Uppercase of the entire line. If a *count* is specified change the case of *count* lines. (See page 201.)

[count] **gUgU**   -or-

[count] **gUU**   Uppercase of the entire line. If a *count* is specified change the case of *count* lines. (See page 201.)

gv   Repeat the last visual-mode selection. (See pages 252-253.)

gV   Do not automatically reselect the selected text. (See page 260.)

[count] **h**   Left. (Same as: **<BS>**, **<Left>**, **CTRL-H**, **CTRL-K**. See page 6.)

[count] **H**   Move to the cursor to the top of the screen. If a *count* is specified, move to the *count* line from the top. (See page 188.)

[count] **i**{*text*}**<Esc>**   Insert text starting before the character under the cursor. If a *count* is specified, the text is inserted *count* times. (Same as: **<Insert>**. See pages 5, 7, and 9.)

[count] **I**{text}**<Esc>**   Insert the text at the beginning of the line. (See page 197.)

[count] **j**   Down. (Same as: **<Down>**, **<NL>**, **CTRL-J**, **CTRL-N**. See pages 6 and 235.)

[count] **J**   Join lines. Spaces are put between the assembled parts. If a *count* is specified, *count* lines are joined (minimum of 2 lines). (See pages 23, 116, and 198.)

[count] **k**   Up. (Same as: **<Up>**, **CTRL-P**. See pages 6 and 13.)

[count] **K**   Run the "man" command on the word under the cursor. If a *count* is specified, use *count* as the section number. On Microsoft Windows, by default, this command performs a :help on the word under the cursor. (See page 78.)

[count] **l**   Right. (Same as: **<Right>**, **<Space>**. See page 6.)

[count] **L**   Move the cursor to the bottom of the screen. If a *count* is specified, move to the *count* line from the bottom. (See page 188.)

m{*letter*}   Mark the current text with the name {*letter*}. If {*letter*} is lowercase, the mark is local to the buffer being edited. In other words, just the location in the file is marked, and you have a different set of marks for each file. If an uppercase letter is specified, the mark is global. Both the file and the location within are marked. If you execute a **"go to mark(')"** command to jump to a global mark, you may switch files. (See pages 85, 161-162, 164, and 227.)

M   Move to the cursor to the middle of the screen. (See page 188.)

[count] **n**   Repeat last search. Search in the same direction. (See pages 31-32 and 161.)

[count] **N**   Repeat last search. Search in the reverse direction. (See pages 31-32.)

[count] **o**   Open a new line below the cursor and put the editor into insert mode. (See page 10.)

[count] **O**   Open a new line above the cursor and put the editor into insert mode. (See page 11.)

["{*register*}**]** **p**   Paste the test in the unnamed register **(")** after the cursor. (If the register contains complete lines, the text will be placed after the current line.) (See pages 36-37, 39, 160-161, 220, and 224.)

[""{*register*}**]** **P**   Paste the text in the {*register*} before the cursor. If no {register} is specified, the unnamed register is used. (Same as: **<MiddleMouse>**. See pages 37, 162-163, and 220.)

q{*character*}   Begin recording keys in register {*character*} (character is a–z). Stop recording with a **q** command. (See page 24.)

Q   Enter ex mode. (See page 100.)

[count] **r**{*char*}   Replace *count* characters with the given character. (See pages 23 and 199.)

[count] **R**{*text*}**<Esc>**   Enter replace mode and replace each character in the file with a character from {*text*}. If a *count* is specified, repeat the command *count* times. (See page 199.)

[count] **s**   Delete *count* characters and enter insert mode. (See page 196.)

[count] **S**   Delete *count* lines and enter insert mode. (See page 196.)

[count] **t**{*char*}   Search forward for character {*char*} on the current line. Stop one before the character. (See page 17.)

[count] **T**{*char*}   Search backward for character {*char*} on the current line. Stop one after the character. (See page 17.)

u   Undo the last change. (Same as: **<Undo>**. See page 8.)

U   Undo all the changes on the last line edited. (A second **U** redoes the edits.) (See page 8.)

v   Start visual character mode. (See pages 56 and 164.)

V   Start visual line mode. (See pages 56, 86, 162, and 163.)

[count] **w**   Move *count* words forward. (Same as: **<S-Right>**. See pages 16, 20, and 184.)

[count] **W**   Move *count* WORDS forward. (Same as: **<C-Right>**. See page 186.)

["{register}] count[count] **x**   Delete *count* characters. (Default = 1.) Deleted text goes into {register} or the unnamed register if no register specification is present. (Same as: **<Del>**. See pages 7, 13, 36-37, 160, and 196-197.)

["{register}]count[count] **X**   Delete the characters before the cursor. (See pages 196-197.)

xp   Exchange the character under the cursor with the next one. Useful for turning "teh" into "the". (See pages 37 and 160.)

["{register}] **y{motion}**   Yank the text from the current location to {*motion*} into the register named {*register*}. Lowercase register specifications cause the register to be overwritten by the yanked text. Uppercase register specifications append to the contents of the register. (See pages 39 and 162.)

["{register}]count[count] **Y**   -or-

["{register}] count[count] **yy**   -or-

[count] ["{register}] **yy**   Yank *count* lines into the register named {register}. Lowercase register specifications cause the register to be overwritten by the yanked text. Uppercase register specifications append to the contents of the register. (See pages 39 and 221-222.)

[count] **z<CR>**   (Same as: **z<Enter>**. See page 193.)

[count] **z<Enter>**   Position the line *count* at the top of the screen. If no *count* is specified, the current line is used. Cursor is positioned on the first nonblank character after this command. (Same as: **z:<CR>**. See page 193.)

[count] **z<Left>**   Scroll the screen *count* characters to the right. (Same as: **zh**. See page 235.)

[count] **z<Right>**   Scroll the screen *count* characters to the left. (Same as: **zl**. See page 235.)

[count] **z-**   Position the line *count* at the bottom of the screen. If no *count* is specified, the current line is used. Cursor is positioned on the first nonblank character after this command. (See page 194.)

[count] **z.**   Position the line *count* at the middle of the screen. If no *count* is specified, the current line is used. Cursor is positioned on the first nonblank character after this command. (See pages 194–195.)

[count] **zb**   Position the line *count* at the bottom of the screen. If no *count* is specified, the current line is used. Cursor is positioned on the same column after this command. (See page 194.)

[count] **zh**   Scroll the screen *count* character to the right. (Same as z<Left>. See page 235.)

[count] **zl**   Scroll the screen *count* character to the left. (Same as z<Right>. See page 235.)

ZQ   Do a **:quit!** command. (See page 202.)

[count] **zt**   Position the line *count* at the top of the screen. If no *count* is specified, the current line is used. Cursor is positioned on the same column after this command. (See pages 193–194.)

[count] **zz**   Position the line *count* at the middle of the screen. If no *count* is specified, the current line is used. Cursor is positioned on the same column after this command. (See pages 194–195.)

ZZ   Write file and exit. (See pages 151 and 168.)

Motion Commands

[count] **a(**   From with text enclosed in (), select the text up to and including the ().

[count] **a)**   From with text enclosed in (), select the text up to and including the ().

[count] **ab**   From with text enclosed in (), select the text up to and including the ().

[count] **a<**   Select matching <> pair, include the "<>".

[count] **a>**   Select matching <> pair, include the "<>".

[count] **a**   Select matching pair, including the "".

[count] **a{**   Select matching {} pair, including the "{}".

[count] **a}**   Select matching {} pair, including the "{}".

[count] **aB**   Select matching {} pair, including the "{}".

[count] **ap**   Select a paragraph and the following space.

[count] **as**   Select a sentence (and spaces after it).

[count] **aw**   Select a word and the space after it. (Word is defined by the **'iskeyword'** option.)

[count] **aW**   Select a word and the space after it. (Word is defined to be any series of printable characters.)

[count] **i(**   Like **ab**, but the () characters are not selected.

[count] **i)**   Like **ab**, but the () characters are not selected.

[count] **ib**   Like **ab**, but the () characters are not selected.

[count] **i<**   Select matching <> pair, excluding the "<>".

[count] **a>**   Select matching <> pair, excluding the "<>".

[count] **i**   Select matching pair, excluding the "".

[count] **i{**   Select matching {} pair, excluding the "{}".

[count] **iB**   Select matching {} pair, excluding the "{}".

[count] **ip**   Select a paragraph only.

[count] **is**   Select the sentence only. Do no select whitespace after a sentence.

[count] **iw**   Select inner word (the word only). (Word is defined by the 'iskeyword' option.)

[count] **iW**   Select inner word (the word only). (Word is defined to be any series of printable characters.)

D

Command-Mode Commands

`:!{cmd}`   Execute shell command. (See page 319.)

`:!!`   Repeat last `:!{cmd}`. (See page 319.)

`:[range] £`   Print the lines with line numbers. (See pages 293 and 308.)

`:[count] &`   Repeat the last `:substitute` command on the next count lines. (Default = 1.) (See page 311.)

`:[range] &` flags count   Repeat the last substitution with a different range and flags. (See page 304.)

`:[line] *{register}`   Execute the contents of the register as an ex-mode command. (Same as: `:@`. See page 317.)

`:[line] < {count}`   Shift lines left. (See page 317.)

`:=`   Print line number. (See page 316.)

`:[line] > {count}`   Shift lines right. (See page 317.)

`:[line] @{register}`   Go to line and execute {register} as a command. (Same as: `:*`. See page 317.)

`:[line] @:`   Repeat the last command-mode command. (See page 317.)

`:[line] @@`   Repeat the last `:@{register}` command. (See page 317.)

: *[range]~ flags count*   Repeat the last substitution, but the last search string as the {*from*} pattern instead of the {*from*} from the last substitution. (See page 311.)

:*[line]* **a**   Insert text after the specified line. (Default = current.) (Same as: **:append**. See page 307.)

:**ab**   List all abbreviations. (Same as: **:abbreviate**. See pages 91–92, 95, 97, 166 and 296.)

:**ab** {*lhs*} {*rhs*}   Define an abbreviation. When {*lhs*} is entered, put {*rhs*} in the text.

:**abbreviate**   List all abbreviations. (Same as: **:ab**. See pages 91–92, 95, 97, 166, and 296.)

:**abbreviate** {*lhs*} {*rhs*}   Define an abbreviation. When {*lhs*} is entered, put {*rhs*} in the text.

:**abc**   -or-

:**abclear**   Remove all abbreviations. (See page 296.)

:*[count]* **al**   -or-

:*[count]* **all**   Open a window for all the files being edited. When a [count] is specified, open up to [count] windows. (Note that the count can be specified after the command, such as "**:all** *[count]*.) (Same as: **:al**, **:sal**, **:sall**. See page 243.)

:{*[priority]* **ame** {*menu-item*} {*command-string*}   -or-

:{*[priority]* **amenu** {*menu-item*} {*command-string*}   Define a menu item that's that is valid for all modes . (Same as: **:am**, **:ame**. See page 334.) The following characters are automatically inserted for some modes:

Mode	Prefix Character Inserted	Meaning
Normal	(Nothing)	—N/A–
Visual	**<Esc>**	Exit visual mode
Insert	**CTRL-O**	Execute one normal command.
Command Line	**CTRL-C**	Exit command-line mode
Operator pending	**<ESC>**	End operator–Pending mode

:{*[priority]* **an** {*menu-item*} {*command-string*}   -or-

:{*[priority]* **anoremenu** {*menu-item*} {*command-string*}   Perform a **:amenu** command in which the {*command-string*} is not remapped. (Same as: **:an**. See page 338.)

:*[line]* **append**   Insert text after the specified line. (Default = current). (Same as: **:a**. See page 307.)

:ar   List the files being edited. The name of the current file is enclosed in square brackets ([]). (See page 222.)

:ar *{file-list}*   Change the list of files to *{file-list}* and start editing the first one. (Same as: **:args**, **:n**, **:next**. See pages 43, 170, and 226.)

:args   List the files being edited. The name of the current file is enclosed in square brackets ([]). (Same as: **:ar**, **:n**, **:next**. See pages 43, 170, and 226.)

:args *{file-list}*   Change the list of files to *{file-list}* and start editing the first one. (See page 226.)

:argu *{number}*   –or–

:argument *{number}*   Edit the *{number}* file in the file list. (Same as: **:argu**. See pages 225 and 243.)

:as   –or–

:ascii   Print the number of the character under the cursor. (Same as: **ga**, **:as**. See page 155.)

:au   List all the autocommands. (Same as: **:autocmd**. See pages 71, 97, 134, 135, 293, and 422.)

:au *{group}* *{event}* *{pattern}*   Lists the autocommands that match the given specification. If "*★*" is used for the event, all events will match. (See pages 134–135.)

:au *{group}* *{events}* *{file_pattern}* **nested** *{command}*   Define an autocommand to be executed when one of the *{events}* happens on any files that match *{pattern}*. The group parameters enables you to put this command in a named group for easier management. The nested flag allows for nested events. (See page 134–135.)

:au! *{group}* *{event}* *{pattern}* **nested** *{command}*   Remove any matching autocommands and replace them with a new version. (See page 135.)

:aug *{name}*   –or–

:augroup *{name}*   Start an autocommand group. The group ends with a **:augroup** END statement. (Same as: **:aug**. See page 134.)

:aun *{menu-item}*   –or–

:aunmenu *{menu-item}*   Remove the menu item named *{menu-item}* that was defined with an **:amenu** command. The wildcard "*★*" will match all menu items. (Same as: **:aun**. See page 339.)

:autocmd   List all the autocommands. (Same as: **:au**. See pages 71, 97, 134, 135, 293, and 422.)

:autocmd {*group*} {*event*} {*pattern*}   Lists the autocommands that match the given specification. If "**★**" is used for the event, all events will match. (See pages 134–135.)

:autocmd {*group*} {*events*} {*file_pattern*} [**nested**] {*command*}   Define an autocommand to be executed when one of the {*events*} happens on any files that match {*pattern*}. The group parameters enables you to put this command in a named group for easier management. The nested flag allows for nested events. (See pages 134–135.)

:autocmd!   Delete all the autocommands. (See page 136.)

:autocmd! {*group*} {*event*} {*pattern*}   Remove the specified autocommands. (See page 136.)

:autocmd! {*group*} {*event*} {*pattern*} [**nested**] {*command*}   Remove any matching autocommands and replace them with a new version. (See page 136.)

:*[count]* **b[!]**   Switch the current window to buffer number count. (If a count is not specified, the current buffer is used.) If **!** is specified, if the switch abandons a file, any changes might be discarded. (An alternative version of this command has count at the end—for example, **:buffer 5**.) (Same as: **:buffer**. See page 50.)

:b[!] {*file-name*}   Switch the current window to the buffer containing {*file-name*}. If **!** is specified, if the switch abandons a file, any changes might be discarded. (See page 50.)

:*[count]* **ba**   Open a window for each buffer. If a count is specified, open at most count windows. (Same as: **:ball**, **:sba**, **:sball**. See page 246.)

:bad *[+line]* {*file*}   -or-

:badd *[+line]* {*file*}   Add the file to the buffer list. If a *+line* is specified, the cursor will be positioned on that line when editing starts. (Same as: **:bad**. See page 246.)

:*[count]* **ball**   Open a window for each buffer. If a count is specified, open at most count windows. (Same as: **:ba**, **:sba**, **:sball**. See page 246.)

:bd[[!]] {*file*}   -or-

:bdelete[[!]] {*file*}   -or-

:*[[n]* **]bd[[!]]**   -or-

:*[[n]* **]bdelete[!]**   -or-

:*[[n,m]* **]bd[[!]]**   -or-

:*[[n,m]* **]bdelete[!]**   -or-

:bd[[!]] *[n]*   -or-

:**bdelete[!]** *n*   Delete the specified buffer, but leave it on the buffer list. (Reclaims all the memory allocated to the buffer and closes all windows associated with.) If the override option (**!**) is specified, any changes made are discarded. If {*file*} is specified, the buffer for that file is deleted. A buffer number [n] or a range of buffer numbers [n,m] can be specified as well. (Same as: :**bd**. See page 246.)

:**be** {*mode*}   -or-

:**behave** {*mode*}   Sets the behavior of the mouse. The {*mode*} is either "xterm" for X Windows System–style mouse usage or "mswin" for Microsoft Windows–style usage. (Same as: :**be**. See page 108.)

:**bl[!]**   -or-

:**blast[!]**   Go to the last buffer in the list. (Same as: :**bl**. See page 52.)

:**bm** *[count]*   -or-

:**bmodified** *[count]*   Go to count-modified buffer. (Same as: :**bm**. See page 52.)

:*[count]* **bn[!]**   -or-

:*[count]* **bnext[!]**   -or-

:*[count]* **bNext**   Go to the next buffer. If **!** is specified, if the switch abandons a file, any changes might be discarded. If a count is specified, go to the count next buffer. (Same as: :**bN**, :**bp**, :**bprevious**. See page 51.)

:*[count]* **bp**   -or-

:*[count]* **bprevious**   Go to previous buffer. If a count is specified, go to the count previous buffer. (Same as: :**bN**, :**bNext**, :**bp**. See page 51.)

:**br[!]**   Go to the first buffer in the list. (Same as: :**brewind**. See page 52.)

:**brea**   -or-

:**break**   Break out of a loop. (Same as: :**brea**. See page 356.)

:**brewind[!]**   Go to the first buffer in the list. (Same as: :**br**. See page 52.)

:**bro** {command}   Open a file browser window and then run {*command*} on the chosen file. (Same as: :**browse**. See page 339.)

:**bro set**   Enter an option browsing window that enables you to view and set all the options. (Same as: :**browse set**, :**options**. See page 342.)

:**browse** {*command*}   Open a file browser window and then run {*command*} on the chosen file. (Same as: :**bro**. See page 339.)

:**browse set**   Enter an option browsing window that enables you to view and set all the options. (Same as: :**bro set**, :**options**. See page 342.)

:*[count]* **buffer[!]**   Switch the current window to buffer number count. (If a count is not specified, the current buffer is used.) If **!** is specified, if the switch abandons a file, any changes might be discarded. (An alternative version of this command has count at the end—for example, **:buffer 5**.) (Same as: **:b**. See page 50.)

:**buffer[!]** *{file-name}*   Switch the current window to the buffer containing *{file-name}*. If **!** is specified, if the switch abandons a file, any changes might be discarded. (See page 50.)

:**buffers**   List all the specified buffers. (Same as: **:bu**, **:files**, **:ls**. See pages 49–50.)

:**bun[[!]]** *{file}*   –or–

:**bunload[[!]]** *{file}*   –or–

:*[n]***bun[[!]]**   –or–

:*[n]***bunload[[!]]**   –or–

:*[n,m]***bun[[!]]**   –or

:*[n,m]***bunload[[!]]**   –or–

:**bun[[!]]** *[n]*   –or–

:**bunload[!]** *n*   Unload the specified buffer. If the override option is specified, if there are any changes, discard them. (Same as: **:bun**. See page 246.)

:*[range]* **c**   Delete the specified lines, and then do a **:insert**. (Same as: **:change**. See page 317.)

:**ca** *{lhs}* *{rhs}*   –or–

:**cabbrrev** *{lhs}* *{rhs}*   Define an abbreviation for command-mode only. (Same as: **:ca**. See page 296.)

:**cabc**   –or–

:**cabclear**   Remove all for command mode. (Same as: **:cabc**. See page 296.)

:*[range]* **cal** *{name}(argument list)*   –or–

:*[range]* **call** *{name}(argument list)*   Call a function. (Same as: **:cal**. See page 134, 358, and 361.)

:**cc[!]** *number*   Display error number. If the number is omitted, display the current error. Position the cursor on the line that caused it. (See page 88.)

:**cd** *{path}*   Change the directory to the specified path. If path is **"-"**, change the previous path. If no path is specified, on UNIX go to the home directory. On Microsoft Windows, print the current directory. (See page 314.)

`:[range]` **ce** `[width]`   –or–

`:[range]` **center** `[width]`   Center the specified lines. If the width of a line is not specified, use the value of the `'textwidth'`. (If `'textwidth'` is 0, 80 is used.) (Same as: `:ce`. See page 115.)

`:cf[!]` `[errorfile]`   –or–

`:cfile[!]` `[errorfile]`   Read an error list from file. (Default = the file specified by the errorfile option.) Go to the first error. If the override option is specified and a file switch is made, any unsaved changes might be lost. (Same as: `:cf`. See page 89.)

`:[range]` **ch** (Same as: `:chdir`. See page 314.)

`:[range]` **change**   Delete the specified lines, and then do an `:insert`. (Same as: `:c`. See page 317.)

`:chd` `[path]`   –or–

`:chdir` `[path]`   Change the directory to the specified path. If path is `"-"`, change the previous path. If no path specified, on UNIX go to the home directory. On Microsoft Windows, print the current directory. (Same as: `:chd`, `:chdir`. See page 314.)

`:che[!]`   –or–

`:checkpath[!]`   Check all the **£include** directives and make sure that all the files listed can be found. If the override option (**!**) is present, list all the files. If this option is not present, only the missing files are listed. (Same as: `:che`. See page 282.)

`:cl[!]` `[from]`, `[to]`   List out the specified error messages. If the override option is present, list out all the errors. (Same as: `:clist`. See page 88.)

`:cla` `[number]`   –or–

`:clast` `[number]`   Go the last error in the list. If a number is specified, display that error. (Same as: `:cla`. See page 88.)

`:clist[!]` `[from]`, `[to]`   List out the specified error messages. If the override option is present, list out all the errors. (Same as: `:cl`. See page 88.)

`:clo[!]`   –or–

`:close[!]`   Close a window. If this is the last window, exit *Vim*. The command fails if this is the last window for a modified file, unless the force (**!**) option is present. (Same as: **CTRL-Wc**, `:clo`. See page 46.)

`:cm`   Listing all the mappings for command-line mode maps. (Same as: `:cmap`. See page 298.)

`:cm` `{lhs}`   List the command-line mapping of {*lhs*}. (See page 298.)

:cm *{lhs} {rhs}*   Define a keyboard mapping for command-line mode. (See page 298.)

:cmap   Listing all the command-line mode mappings. (Same as: **:cm**. See page 298.)

:cmap *{lhs}*   List the command-line mode mapping of *{lsh}*. (See page 298.)

:cmap *{lhs} {rhs}*   Define a keyboard mapping for command-line mode. (See page 298.)

:cmapc   -or-

:cmapclear   Clear all the command-mode mappings. (Same as: **:cmapc**. See page 301.)

:*[priority]* **cme** *{menu-item} {command-string}*   -or-

:*[priority]* **cmenu** *{menu-item} {command-string}*   Define a menu item that is available for command-line mode only. The priority determines its placement in a menu. Higher numbers come first. The name of the menu item is *{menu-item}*, and when the command is selected, the command *{command-string}* is executed. (Same as: **:cme**. See page 334.)

:*[count]* **cn[!]**   Go to the count next error. (Same as: **:cnext**. See pages 87–88 and 170.)

:*[count]* **cN[!]**   Go the previous error in the error list. (Same as: **:cN**. See page 88.)

:cnew *[count]*   -or-

:cnewer *[count]*   Go to the count newer error list. (Same as: **:cnew**. See page 285.)

:*[count]* **cnext[!]**   Go to the count next error. (Same as: **:cn**. See pages 87–88 and 170.)

:*[count]* **cNext[!]**   Go the previous error in the error list. (Same as: **:cN**. See page 88.)

:*[count]* **cnf[!]**   -or-

:*[count]* **cnfile[!]**   Go the first error in the next file. If the override option (**!**) is present, if there are any unsaved changes, they will be lost. (Same as: **:cnf**. See pages 88 and 90.)

:cno *{lhs} {rhs}*   Same as **:cmap**, but does not allow remapping of the *{rhs}*. (Same as: **:cnoremap**. See page 301.)

:cnorea *{lhs} {rhs}*   -or-

:cnoreabbr *{lhs} {rhs}*   Do a **:noreabbrev** that works in command-mode only. (Same as: **:cnorea**. See page 301.)

:[priority] **cnorem** *{menu-item} {command-string}*   Like **:cmenu**, except the *{command-string}* is not remapped. (Same as: **:cnoremenu**. See page 338.)

:cnoremap *{lhs} {rhs}*   Same as **:cmap**, but does not allow remapping of the *{rhs}*. (Same as: **:cno**. See page 301.)

:[priority] **cnoremenu** *{menu-item} {command-string}*   Like **:cmenu**, except the *{command-string}* is not remapped. (Same as: **:cnorem**. See page 338.)

:[range] **co** *{address}*   Copy the range of lines below *{address}*. (Same as: **:copy**, **:t**. See page 306.)

:col *[count]*   –or–

:colder *[count]*   Go to the count older error list. (Same as: **:col**. See page 284.)

:com   List the user-defined commands. (Same as: **:command**. See pages 360–361.)

:com *{definition}*   Define a user-defined command. (See pages 360–361.)

:comc   –or–

:comclear   Clear all user-defined commands. (Same as: **:comc**. See page 360.)

:command   List the user-defined commands. (See page 354.)

:command *{definition}*   Define a user-defined command. (Same as: **:com**. See pages 360–361.)

:con *{command}*   (Same as: **:continue**. See page 356.)

:conf *{command}*   Execute the *{command}*. If this command would result in the loss of data, display a dialog box to confirm the command. (Same as: **:confirm**. See page 341.)

:confirm *{command}*   Execute the *{command}*. If this command would result in the loss of data, display a dialog box to confirm the command. (Same as: **:conf**. See page 341.)

:con   –or–

:continue   Start a loop over. (Same as: **:con**. See page 356.)

:[range] **copy** *{address}*   Copy the range of lines below *{address}*. (Same as: **:co**, **:t**. See page 306.)

:[count] **cp[!]**   –or–

:[count] **cprevious[!]**   Go to the count previous error. (Same as: **:cp**, **:cN**, **:cNext**. See pages 88 and 170.)

:cq   -or-

:cquit   Exit *Vim* with an error code. (This is useful in integrating *Vim* into an IDE.) (Same as: **:cq**. See page 89.)

:cr[!] *number*   -or-

:crewind[!] *number*   Go the first error in the list. If a number is specified, display that error. (Same as: **:cr**. See page 88.)

:cs {*arguments*}   -or-

:cscope {*argument*}   Handle various activities associated with the CScope program. (Same as: **:cs**. See page 172.)

:cst {*procedure*}   -or-

:cstag {*procedure*}   Go to the tag in the CScope database named {*procedure*}. (Same as: **:cst**. See page 172.)

:cu {*lhs*}   (Same as: **:cunmap**. See page 301.)

:cuna {*lhs*}   -or-

:cunabbreviate {*lhs*}   Remove the command-line mode abbreviation. (Same as: **:cuna**. See page 296.)

:cunm   Same as: **:cunmenu**. (See page 339.)

:cunmap {*lhs*}   Remove a command-mode mapping. (Same as: **:cu**. See page 301.)

:cunmenu {*menu-item*}   Remove the command-mode menu item named {*menu-item*}. The wildcard "*****" will match all menu items. (Same as: **:cunm**. See page 339.)

:[*range*] **d** *register* [*count*]   Delete text. (Same as: **:delete**. See page 303.)

:delc {*command*}   -or-

:delcommand {*command*}   Delete a user-defined command. (Same as: **:delc**. See page 360.)

:[*range*] delete *register* [*count*]   Delete text. (Same as: **:d**. See page 303.)

:delf {*name*}   -or-

:delfunction {*name*}   Delete the function named {*name*}. (Same as: **:delf**. See page 360.)

:di list   Edit the last file in the list. (Same as: **:display**. See page 222.)

:dig   List all the digraph definitions. (Same as: **:digraphs**. See page 25.)

:dig {*character1*}{*character2*} {*number*}   Define a digraph. When **CTRL-K**{*character1*}{*character2*} is pressed, inset character whose number is {*number*}. (See page 200.)

:digraphs   List all the digraph definitions. (Same as: **:dig**. See page 25.)

:digraphs *{character1}{character2} {number}*   Define a digraph. When **CTRL-K***{character1}{character2}* is pressed, insert character whose number is *{number}*. (See page 200.)

:display *[arg]*   Same as **:registers**, **:di**. (See page 222.)

:[range] **dj** count*[count]* /*{pattern}*/   -or-

:[range] **djump** count*[count]* /*{pattern}*/   Search the range (default = whole file) for the definition of the macro named *{pattern}* and jump to it. If a count is specified, jump to the count definition. If the pattern is enclosed in slashes (/), it is a regular expression; otherwise, it is the full name of the macro. (Same as: **:dj**. See page 314.)

:[range] **dl** /*{pattern}*/   -or-

:[range] **dlist** /*{pattern}*/   List the all the definitions of the macro named *{pattern}* in the range. (Default = the whole file.) If the pattern is enclosed in slashes (/),it is a regular expression; otherwise, it is the full name of the macro. (Same as: **:dl**. See page 314.)

:do *{group} {event} [file_name]*   Execute a set of autocommands pretending that *{event}* has just happened. If a group is specified, execute only the commands for that group. If a filename is given, pretend that the filename is file_name rather than the current file during the execution of this command. (Same as: **:doautocmd**. See pages 135 and 137.)

:doautoa *{group} {event} [file_name]*   -or-

:doautoall *{group} {event} [file_name]*   Like **:doautocmd**, but repeated for every buffer. (Same as: **:doautoa**. See page 135.)

:doautocmd *{group} {event} [file_name]*   Execute a set of autocommands, pretending that *{event}* has just happened. If a group is specified, execute only the commands for that group. If a filename is given, pretend that the filename is file_name rather than the current file during the execution of this command. (Same as: **:do**. See pages 135 and 137.)

:[range] **ds** /*{pattern}*/   -or-

:[range] **dsearch** /*{pattern}*/   List the first definition of the macro named *{pattern}* in the *range*. (Default = the whole file.) If the pattern is enclosed in slashes (/), it is a regular expression; otherwise, it is the full name of the macro. (Same as: **:ds**. See page 314.)

:[range] **dsp** count*[count]* */{pattern}/* –or–

:[range] **dsplit** count*[count]* */{pattern}/* Do a **:split** and a **:djump**. (Same as: **:dsp**. See page 314.)

:e *[+cmd] [file]* Close the current file and start editing the named file. If no file is specified, re-edit the current file. If *+cmd* is specified, execute it as the first editing command. (Same as: **:edit**. See page 41.)

:ec *{arguments}* –or–

:echo *{arguments}* Print the arguments. (Same as: **:ec**. See pages 354–355.)

:echoh *{name}* –or–

:echohl *{name}* Change the color of future echoes to be in the color of highlight group *{name}*. (Same as: **:echoh**. See page 355.)

:echon *{arguments}* Echo the arguments without a newline. (See page 355.)

:edit *[+cmd] [file]* Close the current file and start editing the named file. If no file is specified, re-edit the current file. If *+cmd* is specified, execute it as the first editing command. (Same as: **:e**. See page 41.)

:el –or–

:else Reverse the condition of an **:if**. (Same as: **:el**. See page 356.)

:elsei –or–

:elseif A combination of **:else** and **:if**. (Same as: **:elsei**. See page 356.)

:em (Same as: **:emenu**. See page 338.)

:emenu *{menu-item}* Execute the given *{menu-item}* as if the user had selected it. (Same as: **:em**. See page 338.)

:en End an **:if** statement. (Same as: **:endif**. See page 356.)

:endf End a function. (Same as: **:endfunction**. See pages 134 and 357.)

:endfunction End a function. (Same as: **:endf**. See pages 134 and 357.)

:endif End an :if statement. (Same as: **:en**. See page 356.)

:endw –or–

:endwhile End a loop. (Same as: **:endw**. See page 356.)

:ex[!] *+command filename* Enter ex mode. If a filename is specified, edit that file; otherwise, use the current file. The *+command* argument is a single command that will be executed before any editing begins. If the override option (**!**) is specified, switching files will discard any changes that have been made. (See page 100.)

:*[range]* **ex[!]** *file* If the buffer has been modified, write the file and exit. If a range is specified, write only the specified lines. If a file is specified, write the data to that file. When the override option (!) is present, attempt to overwrite existing files or read-only files. (See page 322.)

:exe *{string}* –or–

:execute *{string}* Execute a string as a command. (Same as: **:exe**. See page 357.)

:exi –or–

:exit –or–

:*[range]* **exit[!]** *[file]* If the buffer has been modified, write the file and exit. If a range is specified, write only the specified lines. If a file is specified, write the data to that file. When the override option (!) is present, attempt to overwrite existing files or read-only files. (Same as: **:exi**. See page 322.)

:f Print the current filename. If a file is specified, set the name of the current file to file. (Same as: **:file**, **CTRL-G**. See pages 135 and 315.)

:file *[file]* Print the current filename. If a file is specified, set the name of the current file to file. (Same as: **:f**, **CTRL-G**. See pages 135 and 315.)

:files List all the specified buffers. (Same as: **:buffers**, **:ls**. See pages 49–50.)

:filet *{on¦off}* –or–

:filetype *{on¦off}* Tell *Vim* to turn on or off the file type detection logic. (Same as: **:filet**. See page 71.)

:fin[!] *{+command}* *{file}* –or–

:find[!] *{+command}* *{file}* Like :**vi**, but searches for the file in the directories specified by the path option. (Same as: **:fin**. See page 281.)

:fix –or–

:fixdel Make the Delete key do the right thing on UNIX systems. (Same as: **:fix**. See page 94.)

:fu List all functions. (Same as: **:function**. See pages 134, 357, and 359.)

:fu *{name}* List the contents of function *{name}*. (See page 359.)

:fu *{function definition}* Start a function definition. (See page 359.)

:function List all functions. (Same as: **:fu**. See pages 134, 357, and 359.)

:function *{name}* List the contents of function *{name}*. (See page 359.)

:function *{function definition}* Start a function definition. (See page 359.)

: *[range]* **g** */{pattern}/ {command}*   Perform *{command}* on all lines that have *{pattern}* in them in the given range. (Same as: **:global**. See page 311.)

: *[range]* **g!** */{pattern}/ {command}*   Perform *{command}* on all lines that do not have *{pattern}* in them in the given range. (See page 311.)

: *[range]* **global** */{pattern}/ {command}*   Perform *{command}* on all lines that have *{pattern}* in them in the given range. (Same as: **:g**. See page 311.)

: *[range]* **global!** */{pattern}/ {command}*   Perform *{command}* on all lines that do not have *{pattern}* in them in the given range. (See page 311.)

:go *{[count]}*   –or–

:goto *{[count]}*   Go to count byte of the file. (Same as: **:go**, **go**. See page 156.)

:gr *{arguments}*   –or–

:grep *{arguments}*   Run the gGrep program with the given *{arguments}* and capture the output so that the **:cc**, **:cnext**, and other commands will work on it. (Like **:make**, but with gGrep rather than mMake.) (Same as: **:gr**. See pages 89, 170, 225, 284, and 289.)

:gu *[+command] [-f¦-b] [files...]*   –or–

:gui *[+command] [-f¦-b] [files...]*   (Same as: **:gu**. See page 323.)

:gv *[+command] [-f¦-b] [files...]*   –or–

:gvim *[+command] [-f¦-b] [files...]*   Start GUI mode. If a +command is specified, execute that after loading the files. If the –b flag is specified, execute the command in the background (the default). The –f flag tells *Vim* to run in the foreground. If a list of files is specified, they will be edited; otherwise, the current file is edited. (Same as: **:gv**. See page 323.)

:h *[topic]*   –or–

:help *[topic]*   Display help on the given topic. If no topic is specified, display general help. (Same as: **<F1>**, **<Help>**, **:h**. See pages 11, 13, 50, 157, and 401.)

:helpf   –or–

:helpfind   Open a dialog box that enables you to type in a help subject. (Same as: **:helpf**. See page 341.)

:hi   List all highlight groups. (Same as: **:highlight**. See pages 290 and 355.)

:hi *{options}*   Customize the syntax coloration. (See page 290.)

:hi link *{new-group} {old-group}*   Highlight the *{new-group}* the same as *{old-group}*. (See page 414.)

:hid   –or–

:hide   Hide the current buffer. (Same as: **:hid**. See page 49.)

:highlight   List all highlight groups.

:highlight link {*new-group*} {*old-group*}   Highlight the {*new-group*} the same as {*old-group*}. (See page 408.)

:highlight {*options*}   Customize the syntax coloration. (Same as: **:hi**. See pages 290 and 355.)

:his {*code*} *[first]* ,*[last]*   –or–

:history {*code*} *[first]* ,*[last]*   Print the last few commands or search strings (depending on the code). The code parameter defaults to **"cmd"** for command-mode command history. The first parameter defaults to the first entry in the list and last defaults to the last. (Same as: **:his**. See page 320.)

:[line] **i**   Start inserting text before line. Insert ends with a line consisting of just "**.**". (Same as: **:insert**. See page 308.)

:ia {*lhs*} {*rhs*}   –or–

:iabbrev {*lhs*} {*rhs*}   Define an abbreviation for insert mode only. (Same as: **:ia**. See page 296.)

:iabc   –or–

:iabclear   Remove all for insert mode. (Same as: **:iabc**. See page 296.)

:if {*expression*}   Start a conditional statement. (See page 356.)

:[range] **ij** [count] /{*pattern*}/   –or–

:[range] **ijump** [count] /{*pattern*}/   Search the range (default = whole file) for the {*pattern*} and jump to it. If a count is specified, jump to the count occurrence. If the pattern is enclosed in slashes (/), it is a regular expression; otherwise, it is just a string. (Same as: **:ij**. See page 312.)

:[range] **il** /{*pattern*}/   –or–

:[range] **ilist** /{*pattern*}/   List all the occurrences {*pattern*} in the range. (Default = the whole file.) If the pattern is enclosed in slashes (/), it is a regular expression; otherwise, it is a string. (Same as: **:il**. See page 312.)

:im   List all the insert-mode mappings. (Same as: **:imap**. See page 298.)

:im {*lhs*}   List the insert-mode mapping of {*lhs*}. (See page 298.)

:im {*lhs*} {*rhs*}   Define a keyboard mapping for insert mode. (See page 298.)

:imap   List all the insert-mode mappings. (Same as: **:im**. See page 298.)

:imap {*lhs*}   List the insert-mode mapping of {*lhs*}. (See page 298.)

:imap {*lhs*} {*rhs*}   Define a keyboard mapping for insert mode. (See page 298.)

:imapc   -or-

:imapclear   Clear all the insert-mode mappings. (Same as: **:imapc**. See page 301.)

:[*priority***] ime** {*menu-item*} {*command-string*}   -or-

:[*priority***] imenu** {*menu-item*} {*command-string*}   Define a menu item that is available for insert mode only. The priority determines its placement in a menu. Higher numbers come first. The name of the menu item is {*menu-item*}, and when the command is selected, the command {*command-string*} is executed. (Same as: **:ime**. See page 334.)

:[*line***] in**   Start inserting text before line. Insert ends with a line consisting of just "**.**". (Same as: **:inoremap**. See page 301.)

:inorea {*lhs*} {*rhs*}   -or-

:inoreabbrev {*lhs*} {*rhs*}   Do a **:noreabbrev** that works in insert mode only. (Same as: **:inorea**. See page 296.)

:inorem {*lhs*} {*rhs*}   Same as: **:inoremenu**. (See page 338.)

:inoremap {*lhs*} {*rhs*}   Same as **:imap**, but does not allow remapping of the {rhs}. (Same as: **:in**. See page 301.)

:[*priority***] inoremenu** {*menu-item*} {*command-string*}   Like **:imenu**, except the {*command-string*} is not remapped. (Same as: **:inorem**. See page 338.)

:[*line***] insert**   Start inserting text before line. Insert ends with a line consisting of just "**.**". (Same as: **:i**. See page 308.)

:int   -or-

:intro   Display the introductory screen. (Same as: **:int**. See page 157.)

:*range***[***range***] is** /{*pattern*}/   -or-

:*range***[***range***] isearch** /{*pattern*}/   List the first occurrence {*pattern*} in the range. (Default = the whole file.) If the pattern is enclosed in slashes (/), it is a regular expression; otherwise, it is a string. (Same as: **:is**. See page 313.)

:[*range***] isp** count[*count*] /{*pattern*}/   -or-

:[*range***] isplit** count[*count*] /{*pattern*}/   Remove an insert-mode mapping. (Same as: **:isp**. See page 313.)

:iu {*lhs*}   Remove an insert-mode mapping. (Same as: **:iunmap**. See page 301.)

:iuna {*lhs*}   -or-

:iunabbreviate {*lhs*}   Remove the insert line-mode abbreviation. (Same as: **:iuna**. See page 296.)

`:iunm {`*lhs*`}`   -or-

`:iunmap {`*lhs*`}`   Remove an insert-mode mapping. (Same as: `:iunm`. See page 301.)

`:iunm {`*menu-item*`}`   -or-

`:iunmenu {`*menu-item*`}`   Remove the insert-mode menu item named {*menu-item*}. The wildcard "`*`" will match all menu items. (Same as: `:iunm`. See page 339.)

`:[`*range*`] j[!]`   -or-

`:[`*range*`] join[!]`   Join the lines in range into one line. Spaces are used to separate the parts unless the `!` is specified. (Same as: `:j`. See page 318.)

`:ju`   -or-

`:jumps`   List out the jump list. (Same as: `:ju`. See page 188.)

`:[`*line*`] k{`*letter*`}`   Place mark {*letter*} on the indicated line. (Same as: `:mar`, `:mark`. See page 318.)

`:[`*range*`] l [`*count*`]`   Like `:print`, but assumes that the '`list`' option is on. (Same as: `:l`. See page 308.)

`:la [`*+command*`]`   -or-

`:last [`*+command*`]`   Edit the last file in the list. (Same as: `:la`. See page 44.)

`:[`*range*`] le [`*margin*`]`   -or-

`:[`*range*`] left [`*margin*`]`   Left justify the text putting each line margin characters from the left margin. (Default = 0.) (Same as: `:le`. See page 116.)

`:let {`*variable*`} = {`*expression*`}`   Assign a {*variable*} a value. (See page 349.)

`:[`*range*`] list [`*count*`]`   Like `:print`, but assumes that the '`list`' option is on. (Same as: `:l`. See page 308.)

`:ls`   List all the buffers. (Same as: `:buffers`, `:files`. See pages 49-50.)

`:[`*range*`] m {`*address*`}`   Move the range of lines from their current location to below {*address*}. (Same as: `:move`. See pages 161 and 306.)

`:[`*line*`] ma{`*letter*`}`   Mark the current line with mark {*letter*}. (Same as: `:k`, `:mar`, `:mark`. See page 318.)

`:mak {`*arguments*`}`   -or-

`:make {`*arguments*`}`   Run the external Mmake program, giving it the arguments indicated. Capture the output in a file so that error-finding commands such as `:cc` and `:cnext` can be used. (Same as: `:mak`. See pages 87, 284, and 288.)

:map   List all the mappings. Note: Only **:map** and **:map!** list the mappings for all modes. The other mode-dependent versions of these commands list the mapping for their modes only. (See pages 93, 95, 134, 156, 293, 297, and 394.)

:map {*lhs*}   List the mapping of {*lhs*}. (See page 297.)

:map {*lhs*} {*rhs*}   Define a keyboard mapping. When the {*lhs*} is typed in normal mode, pretend that {*rhs*} was typed. (See page 297.)

:map[!]   List all mappings for insert and command line notes. (See page 298.)

:{*mode*}**mapc**   Clear all the mappings. (Same as: **:mapclear**. See page 299.)

:{*mode*}**mapclear**   Clear all the mappings. (Same as: **:mapc**. See page 299.)

:mapclear[!]   See page 301.

:mar –or–

:[*line*] **mark**{*letter*}   Mark the given line with mark {*letter*}. (Same as: **:k**, **:mar**. See page 38.)

:marks   List all the marks. (See page 38.)

:marks {*chars*}   List the marks specified by the character list: {*chars*}. (See page 36.)

:[*priority*][*mode*] **me** {*menu-item*} {*command-string*}   –or–

:[*priority*][*mode*] **menu** {*menu-item*} {*command-string*}   Define a menu item. The priority determines its placement in a menu. Higher numbers come first. The mode parameter defines which *Vim* mode the item works in. The name of the menu item is {*menu-item*}, and when the command is selected, the command {*command-string*} is executed. (Same as: **:me**. See pages 333 and 338.)

:mes –or–

:messages   View previous messages. (Same as: **:mes**. See page 321.)

:mk[!] {[*file*]}   –or–

:mkexrc[!] {[*file*]}   Like **:mkvimrc**, except the file defaults to .exrc. This command has been superseded by the **:mkvimrc** command. (Same as: **:mk**. See page 96.)

:mks[!] [*file*]}   –or–

:mksession[!] [*file*] }   Create a session file and save the current settings. If **!** is specified, overwrite any existing session file. (Same as: **:mks**. See page 350.)

:mkv[!] {*file*}   –or–

:mkvimrc[!] {*file*}   Write out setting to {*file*} in a manner suitable for including in a *vim*rc file. In fact, if you do not specify {*file*}, it defaults to *vim*rc. If the file exists, it will be overwritten if the override option (**!**) is used. (Same as: **:mkv**. See page 95.)

`:[range]` **mo** `{address}`   Move the range of lines from their current location to below {*address*}. (See page 307.)

:mod `{mode}`   –or–

:mode `{mode}`   Set the screen mode for an MS-DOS editing session. (Same as: **:mod**. See page 347.)

`:[range]` **move** `{address}`   Move the range of lines from their current location to below {*address*}. (Same as: **:m**. See pages 161 and 306.)

`:[count]` **n** `{+cmd}` `{file-list}`   When editing multiple files, go to the next one. If count is specified, go to the count next file. (Same as: **:args**, **:next**. See pages 42, 170, 226–228.)

`:[count]` **N** `{+cmd}` `{file-list}`   When editing multiple files, go to the previous one. If a count is specified, go to the count previous file. (Same as: **:Next**. See page 43.)

:new[!] `[+command]` `[file-name]`   Split the window like **:split**. The only difference is that if no filename is specified, a new window is started on a blank file. (Same as: **CTRL-W CTRL-N**, **CTRL-Wn**. See page 48.)

`:[count]` **next** `{[+cmd]}` `[{file-list}]`   When editing multiple files, go to the next one. If count is specified, go to the count next file. (Same as: **:args**, **:n**. See pages 42, 170, and 226–228.)

`:[count]` **Next** `[{+cmd}]` `{[file-list]}`   When editing multiple files, go to the previous one. If count is specified, go to the count previous file. (Same as: **:N**. See page 43.)

:nm   Listing all the mappings for normal-mode maps. (Same as: **:nmap**. See page 298.)

:nm `{lhs}`   List the normal mapping of {*lhs*}.

:nm `{lhs}` `{rhs}`   Define a keyboard mapping for normal mode.

:nmap   Listing all the normal-mode mappings. (Same as: **:nm**. See page 298.)

:nmap `{lhs}`   List the normal-mode mapping of {*lhs*}. (See page 298.)

:nmap `{lhs}` `{rhs}`   Define a keyboard mapping for normal mode. (See page 298.)

:nmapc   –or–

:nmapclear   Clear all the normal mappings. (Same as: **:nmapc**. See page 301.)

`:[priority]`**nme** `{menu-item}` `{command-string}`   –or–

`:[priority]`**nmenu** `{menu-item}` `{command-string}`   Define a menu item that is available for normal mode only. The priority determines its placement in a menu. Higher numbers come first. The name of the menu item is {*menu-item*}, and when the command is selected, the command {*command-string*} is executed. (Same as: **:nme**. See page 334.)

:nn *{lhs} {rhs}*   -or-

:nnoremap *{lhs} {rhs}*   Same as **:nmap**, but does not allow remapping of the *{rhs}*. (Same as: **:nn**. See page 301.)

:[priority] **nnoreme** *{menu-item} {command-string}*   -or-

:[priority] **nnoremenu** *{menu-item} {command-string}*   Like **:nmenu**, but the *{command-string}* is not remapped. (Same as: **:nnorem**. See page 301.)

:no *{lhs} {rhs}*   Same as **:map**, but does not allow remapping of the *{rhs}*. (Same as: **:noremap**. See pages 298 and 301.)

:noh   -or-

:nohlsearch   Turn off the search highlighting. (It will be turned on by the next search. To turn it off permanently, use the **:set nohisearch** command.) (Same as: **:noh**. See page 29.)

:nor *{lhs} {rhs}*   -or-

:noreabbrev *{lhs} {rhs}*   Define an abbreviation, but do not allow remapping of the right side. (Same as: **:nor**. See page 301.)

:norem *{lhs} {rhs}*   Same as: **:noremenu**. (See page 338.)

:noremap *{lhs} {rhs}*   Same as **:map**, but does not allow remapping of the *{rhs}*. (Same as: **no**. See pages 298 and 301.)

:nremap[!]   See page 301.

:[priority][mode] **norem** *{menu-item} {command-string}*   -or-

:[priority][mode] **noremenu** *{menu-item} {command-string}*   Define a menu item like defined with **:menu**, but do not allow remapping of the *{command-string}*. (Same as: **:norem**. See page 338.)

:norm[!] *{commands}*   -or-

:normal[!] *{commands}*   Execute the commands in normal mode. (Same as: **:norm**. See page 322.)

:[range] **nu**   -or-

:[range] **number**   Print the lines with line numbers. (Same as: **:nu**. See pages 293–294.)

:nun *{lhs}*   -or-

:nunmap *{lhs}*   Remove a normal mapping. (Same as: **:nun**. See page 301.)

:nunme *{menu-item}*   -or-

:nunmenu *{menu-item}*   Remove the normal menu item named *{menu-item}*. The wildcard "*****" will match all menu items. (Same as: **:nunme**. See page 339.)

:o   The one command that Vi has that *Vim* does not. (In *Vi*, this command puts the editor into "open" mode, a mode that no sane persons ever use if they can avoid it.) (Same as: **:open**. See page 157.)

:om   List all the mappings for operator-pending-mode maps. (Same as: **:omap**. See page 298.)

:om *{lhs}*   List the operator-pending mapping of *{lhs}*. (See page 298.)

:om *{lhs}* *{rhs}*   Define a keyboard mapping for operator-pending mode. (See page 298.)

:omap   List all the operator-pending-mode mappings. (Same as: **:om**. See page 298.)

:omap *{lhs}*   List the operator-pending-mode mapping of *{lhs}*. (See page 292.)

:omap *{lhs}* *{rhs}*   Define a keyboard mapping for operator-pending mode. (See page 298.)

:omapc   –or–

:omapclear   Clear all the operator-pending-mode mappings. (Same as: **:omapclear**. See page 301.)

:[priority] **ome** *{menu-item}* *{command-string}*   –or–

:[priority] **omenu** *{menu-item}* *{command-string}*   Define a menu item that is available for operator-pending mode only. The priority determines its placement in a menu. Higher numbers come first. The name of the menu item is *{menu-item}*, and when the command is selected, the command *{command-string}* is executed. (Same as: **:ome**. See page 334.)

:on[!]   –or–

:only[!]   Make the current window the only one. If **!** is specified, modified files whose windows are closed will have their contents discarded. (Same as: **:CTRL-W CTRL-O**, **CTRL-Wo**, **:on**. See page 243.)

:ono *{lhs}* *{rhs}*   –or–

:onoremap *{lhs}* *{rhs}*   Same as **:omap**, but does not allow remapping of the *{rhs}*. (Same as: **:ono**. See page 301.)

:[priority] **onoreme** *{menu-item}* *{command-string}*   –or–

:priorityonoremenu *{menu-item}* *{command-string}*   Like **:omenu**, but the the *{command-string}* is not remapped. (Same as: **:onoreme**. See page 338.)

:op   Enter an option-browsing window that enables you to view and set all the options. (Same as: **:bro set**, **:browse set**, **:options**. See page 342.)

:open   The one command that *Vi* has that *Vim* does not. (In *Vi*, this command puts the editor into "open" mode, a mode that no sane persons ever use if they can avoid it.) (Same as: **:o**. See page 157.)

:options   Enter an option-browsing window that enables you to view and set all the options. (Same as: **:bro set**, **:browse set**, **:op**. See page 342.)

:ou {*lhs*}   –or–

:ounmap {*lhs*}   Remove an operator-pending-mode mapping. (Same as: **:ounmap**. See page 301.)

:ounme {*menu-item*}   –or–

:ounmenu {*menu-item*}   Remove the command-mode menu item named {*menu-item*}. The wildcard "*****" will match all menu items. (Same as: **:ounme**. See page 339.)

:range[*range*] **p**   –or–

:range[*range*] **P**   Print the specified lines. (Same as: **:Print**. See pages 100 and 308.)

:pc[!]   –or–

:pclose[!]   Close the preview window. Discard any changes if the force (**!**) option is present. (Same as: **CTRL-W CTRL-Z**, **CTRL-Wz**, **:pc**. See page 276.)

:pe {*command*}   –or–

:perl {*command*}   Execute a single Perl command. Requires *Vim* be compiled with Perl support (not on by default). (Same as: **:pe**. See page 173.)

:[*range*] **perld** {*command*}   –or–

:[*range*] **perldo** {*command*}   Execute a Perl command on a range of lines. The Perl variable $_ is set to each line in range. (Same as: **:perld**. See page 173.)

:[*count*]**po[!]**   –or–

:[*count*]**pop[!]**   Go back count tags. If the current buffer has been modified, this command will fail unless the force (**!**) option is present. (Same as: **:po**. See page 81.)

:[*count*]**pp[!]**   –or–

:[*count*] **ppop[!]**   Do a **:pop** command in the preview window. If the force option (**!**) is specified, discard any changes made on the file in the preview window. If a count is specified, pop that many tags. (Same as: **:pp**. See page 276.)

:pr   –or–

:preserve   Write out entire file to the swap file. This means that you can recover the edit session from just the swap file alone. (Same as: **:pr**. See pages 151 and 319.)

:[count] **prev** *{[+cmd]} {[file – list]}* –or–

:[count] **previous** *{[+cmd]} [{file – list}]* Edit the previous file in the file list. (Same as: **:prev**. See page 43.)

:[range] **print** –or–

:[range] **Print** Print the specified lines. (Same as: **:P**. See pages 100 and 308.)

:pro –or–

:promptfind Open a Find dialog box. (Same as: **:pro**. See page 340.)

:promptr –or–

:promptrepl Open a Replace dialog box. (Same as: **:promptr**. See page 340.)

:pt[!] *{identifier}* –or–

:ptag[!] *{identifier}* Open a preview window and do a **:tag**. Discard any changes in the preview window if the override (**!**) option is present. (Same as: **:pt**. See page 276.)

:ptj[!] *{identifier}* –or–

:ptjump[!] *{identifier}* Open a preview window and do a **:tjump**. Discard any changes in the preview window if the override (**!**) option is present. (Same as: **:ptj**. See page 276.)

:ptl[!] –or–

:ptlast[!] Do a **:tlast** in the preview window. Discard any changes in the preview window if the override (**!**) option is present. (Same as: **:ptlast**. See page 277.)

:[count] **ptn[!]** Open a preview window and do a *:[count]* **tnext**. Discard any changes in the preview window if the override (**!**) option is present. (Same as: **:ptn**. See page 276.)

:[count] **ptN[!]** Same as *:[count]* **ptnext!**. (Same as: **:ptNext**, **:ptprevious**. See page 277.)

:[count] **ptnext[!]** Open a preview window and do a *:[count]* **tnext**. Discard any changes in the preview window if the override (**!**) option is present. (Same as: **:ptn**. See page 276.)

:[count] **ptNext[!]** Same as *:[count]* **ptnext!**. (Same as: **:ptNext**, **:ptprevious**. See page 277.)

:[count] **ptp[!]** –or–

:[count] **ptprevious[!]** Do a **:tprevious** in the preview window. Discard any changes in the preview window if the override (**!**) option is present. (Same as: **:ptN**, **:ptNext**, **:ptp**. See page 277.)

:[count] **ptr[!]**   –or–

:[count] **ptrewind[!]**   Do a **:trewind** in the preview window. Discard any changes in the preview window if the override (**!**) option is present. (Same as: **:ptr**. See page 277.)

:pts[!] *{identifier}*   –or–

:ptselect[!] *{identifier}*   Open a preview window and do a **:tselect**. Discard any changes in the preview window if the override (**!**) option is present. (Same as: **:pts**. See page 276.)

:[line] **pu[!]! register**   –or–

:[line] **put[!]! register**   Put the text in the register after (before **!** is specified) the specified line. If a register is not specified, it defaults to the unnamed register. (Same as: **:pu**. See page 318.)

:pw   –or–

:pwd   Print current working directory. (Same as: **:pw**. See page 314.)

:[range] **py** *{statement}*   Execute a single Python *{statement}*. (Same as: **:python**. See page 173.)

:[range] **pyf** *{file}*   Executes the Python program contained in *{file}*. (Same as: **:pyfile**. See page 173.)

:[range] **pyfile** *{file}*   Executes the Python program contained in *{file}*. (Same as: **:pyf**. See page 173.)

:[range] **python** *{statement}*   Execute a single Python *{statement}*. This works only if Python support was compiled into *Vim*; it is does not work by default. (Same as: **:py**. See page 173.)

:q[!]   Close a window. If this is the last window, exit *Vim*. The command fails if this is the last window for a modified file, unless the force (**!**) option is present. (Same as: **:CTRL-W CTRL-Q, CTRL-Wq, :quit**. See pages 9, 46, 144, 202, and 242–243.)

:qa[!]   –or–

:qall[!]   Close all windows. If the force option is present, any modifications that have not been saved will be discarded. (Same as: **:qa**. See page 242.)

:quit[!]   Close a window. If this is the last window, exit *Vim*. The command fails if this is the last window for a modified file, unless the force (**!**) option is present. (Same as: **CTRL-W CTRL-Q, CTRL-Wq, :q**. See pages 9, 46, 144, 202, and 242–243.)

:r *{filename}*   Read in the specified file and insert it after the current line. (Same as: **:read**. See pages 104, 135, 317, and 396.)

:[line] **r** *{file}*   Read the specified file (default = current file) and insert it after the given line (default = current line). (See page 317.)

:[line] **r** !*{command}*   Run the given command, capture the output, and insert it after the given line (default = current line). (See page 317.)

:read *{filename}*   Read in the specified file and insert it after the current line. (Same as: **:r**. See pages 104, 135, 317, and 396.)

:[line] **read file**   Read the specified file (default = current file) and insert it after the given line (default = current line). (See page 317.)

:[line] **read** !*{command}*   Run the given command, capture the output, and insert it after the given line. (Default = current line.) (See page 104.)

:rec[!] *{file}*   –or–

:recover[!] *{file}*   Recover the editing session from the specified file. If no file is specified, the current file is used. If changes have been made to the file, this command will result in an error. If the force **(!)** option is present, attempting to recover a file changed in the current session will discard the changes and start recovery. (Same as: **:rec**. See page 152.)

:red   Redo the last edit. (Same as: **:redo**. See page 318.)

:redi[!] *{>|>>}* *{file}*   –or–

:redir[!] *{>|>>}* *{file}*   Copy messages to the file as they appear on the screen. If the override option **(!)** is present, the command will overwrite an existing file. The flag "**>**" tells the command to write the file; the "**>>**" indicates append mode. To close the output file, use the command **:redir END**. (Same as: **:redi**. See page 321.)

:redo   Redo the last edit. (Same as: **:red**. See page 318.)

:reg *{list}*   –or–

:registers *{list}*   Show the registers in list. If no list is specified, list all registers. (Same as: **:reg**. See page 222.)

:res count   Change the size of the current window to count. If no count is specified, make the window as large as possible. (Same as: **CTRL-W CTRL-_**, **CTRL-W+**, **CTRL-W-**, **CTRL-W_**, **:resize**. See page 49.)

:res +count   Increase the size of the current window by count. (Default = 1.) (Same as: **CTRL-W CTRL-_**, **CTRL-W+**, **CTRL-W-**, **CTRL-W_**, **:resize-**. See page 48.)

:res -count   Decrease the size of the current window by count. (Default = 1.) Same as: **CTRL-W CTRL-_**, **CTRL-W+**, **CTRL-W-**, **CTRL-W_**, **:resize-**. See page 48.)

:resize count   Change the size of the current window to count. If no count is specified, make the window as large as possible. (Same as **CTRL-W CTRL-_**, **CTRL-W+**, **CTRL-W-**, **CTRL-W_**, **:res**. See page 49.)

`:resize +count`   Increase the size of the current window by count. (Default = 1.) (Same as: **CTRL-W+**, `:res +`. See page 48.)

`:resize -count`   Decrease the size of the current window by count. (Default = 1.) (Same as: **CTRL-W-**, `:res -`. See page 48.)

`:[range]` **ret** `[!]` **tabstop**   –or–

`:[range]` **retab** `[!]` **tabstop**   Replace tabs at the current tab stop with tabs with the tab stops set at {*tabstop*}. If the `'expandtab'` option is set, replace all tabs with space. If the force option (`!`) is present, multiple spaces will be changed into tabs where appropriate. (Same as: `:ret`. See pages 267-268.)

`:retu` {*expression*}   –or–

`:return` {*expression*}   Return a value from a function. (Same as: `:retu`. See page 358.)

`:rew` {*file-list*}   –or–

`:rewind` {*file-list*}   Edit the first file in the list. (Same as: `:rew`. See pages 44 and 170.)

`:[range]` **ri** {*width*}   –or–

`:[range]` **right** {*width*}   Right-justify the specified lines. If the width of a line is not specified, use the value of the `'textwidth'`. (If `'textwidth'` is 0, 80 is used.) (Same as: `:ri`. See page 115.)

`:rv[!]` {*file*}   –or–

`:rviminfo[!]` {*file*}   Read the *vim*info file specified. If the override option is present (`!`), settings in the file override the current settings. (Same as: `:rv`. See page 233.)

`:[range]` **s** `/`{*from*}`/`{*to*}`/`{*flags*}   Change the regular expression {*from*} to the string {*to*}. See `:substitute` for a list of flags. (Same as: `:substitute`. See pages 102, 144, 160-161, 167-168, 309, and 401.)

`:[count]` **sa**`[!]` {*number*}   Do a `:[count]split` followed by `:argument[!]` number. (Same as: `:sargument`. See page 245.)

`:[count]` **sal**   –or–

`:[count]` **sall**   Open a window for all the files being edited. When a count is specified, open up to count windows. (Note that the count can be specified after the command—for example, `:all` count.) (Same as: `:all`, `:sal`. See page 243.)

`:[count]` **sargument**`[!]` {*number*}   Do a `:[count]split` followed by `:argument[!]` number. (Same as: `:sa`. See page 245.)

`:sb`   Same as: `:sbuffer`. (See page 51.)

:[count] **sba**   –or–

:[count] **sball**   Open a window for each buffer. If a count is specified, open at most count windows. (Same as: **:ba**, **:ball**, **:sba**. See page 246.)

:sb number   Shorthand for **:split** and **:buffer** number. (See page 51.)

:sbl[!]   –or–

:sblast[!]   Shorthand for **:split** and **:blast**. (Same as: **:sbl**. See page 52.)

:sbm count*[count]*   –or–

:sbmodified count*[count]*   Shorthand for **:split** and **:bmodified**. (Same as: **:sbm**. See page 52.)

:[count] **sbn**   Shorthand for **:split** followed by *:[count]* **bnext**. (Same as: **:sbnext**. See page 51.)

:[count] **sbN**   Shorthand for **:split** and *:[count]* **bprevious**. (Same as: **:sbNext**, **:sbp**, **:sbprevious**. See page 52.)

:[count] **sbnext**   Shorthand for **:split** followed by *:[count]* **bnext**. (Same as: **:sbn**. See page 51.)

:[count] **sbNext**   Shorthand for **:split** and *:[count]* **bprevious**. (Same as: **:sbN**, **:sbp**, **:sbprevious**. See page 52.)

:[count] **sbp**   –or–

:[count] **sbprevious**   Shorthand for **:split** and *:[count]* **bprevious**. (Same as: **:sbN**, **:sbNext**, **:sbprevious**. See page 51.)

:sbr[!]   –or–

:sbrewind[!]   Shorthand for **:split** and **:brewind**. (Same as: **:sbr**. See page 52.)

:sbuffer number   Shorthand for **:split** and **:buffer number**. (Same as: **:sb**. See page 51.)

:se   List all options that are not set to the default. (Same as: **:set**. See pages 95, 100, 379, 382, and 394.)

:se {*option*}   Set Boolean option. Depreciated: For all other types of options, show the value of the option. (See page 379.)

:se {*option*}:{*value*}   –or–

:se {*option*}={*value*}   Set an {*option*} to a {*value*}. (See page 379.)

:se {*option*}^={*number*}   –or–

:se {*option*}**[!]**   Invert a Boolean option. (See page 379.)

:se *{option}*& Set the option to the default value. (See page 379.)

:se *{option}*+=*{value}* Add a number to a numeric option. For a string option, append the *{value}* to the string. (See page 379.)

:se *{option}*-=*{number}* Subtract a number to a numeric option. For a string option, remove the *{value}* from the string. (See page 379.)

:se *{option}*? List the value of an option. (See page 379.)

:se *{option}*^=*{number}* Multiply a number to a numeric option. Prepend string to the beginning of the option. (See page 379.)

:se all List all options. (See page 382.)

:se all& Set all options to their default values. (See page 382.)

:se inv{*option*} Invert a Boolean option. (See page 380.)

:se no{*option*} Clear a Boolean option. (See page 380.)

:set List all options not set to the default. (Same as: **:se**. See pages 18, 95, 100, 379, 382, and 394.)

:set *{option}* Set Boolean option. Depreciated: For all other types of options, show the value of the option.Depreciated: show all others. (See page 382.)

:set *{option}*:*{value}* -or-

:set *{option}*=*{value}* Set an option. (See page 382.)

:set *{option}*[!] Invert a Boolean option. (See page 382.)

:set *{option}*& Set the option to the default value. (See page 382.)

:set *{option}*+=*{value}* Add a number to a numeric option. Append a string to a string option. (See page 382.)

:set *{option}*-=*{value}* Subtract a number from a numeric option. Remove a string from a string option. (See page 382.)

:set *{option}*? List the value of an option. (See page 382.)

:set *{option}*^=*{number}* Multiply a number to a numeric option. Prepend string to the beginning of the option. (See page 382.)

:set all List all options. (See page 382.)

:set all& Set all options to their default values. (See page 382.)

:set inv{*option*} Invert a Boolean option. (See page 380.)

:set no{*option*} Clear a Boolean option. (See page 380.)

:[count] **sf[!]** *+command {file}* -or-

:[count] **sfind[!]** **+command** *{file}*   A combination of :count*[count]* **split** and **:find**. (Same as: **:sf**. See page 281.)

:sh   –or–

:shell   Suspend the editor and enter command mode (a.k.a. run a shell). (Same as: **:sh**. See pages 104, 144, 152, 319, and 346.)

:si *{char}*   –or–

:simlat *{char}*   Simulate the pressing of Alt-*{char}*. (See page 344.)

:sl *{seconds}*   –or–

:sl *{milliseconds)* **m**   Sleep the specified number of seconds or milliseconds. (Same as: **gs**, **:sleep**. See page 156.)

:sla[!]!   –or–

:slast![!]   **:split** followed by **:last**. If **!** is specified, modified files whose windows are closed will have their contents discarded. (Same as: **:sla**. See page 245.)

:sleep *{seconds}*   –or–

:sleep *{milliseconds)* **m**   Sleep the specified number of seconds or milliseconds. (Same as: **gs**, **:sl**. See page 156.)

:sm *{char}*   Simulate the pressing of Alt-*{char}*. (Same as: **:smagic**. See page 310.)

: [range] **sm** */{from}/{to}/flags*   –or–

: [range] **smagic** */{from}/{to}/flags*   Substitute the pattern *{to}* for the pattern *{from}* for the given range assuming that the **"magic"** option is set for the duration of the command. (Same as: **:sm**. See page 310.)

:[count] **sn[!]** *[file-list]*   **:split** followed by *:[count]* next If **!** is specified, discard any changes to buffers that have been modified, but not written. If file-list is specified, change the arguments to that list. (Same as: **:snext**. See page 245.)

:[count] **sN[!]**   **:split** followed by :count[count] previous. If **!** is specified, discard any changes to buffers that have been modified, but not written. (Note: The count parameter can be specified after the command—for example, **:sN** *count[count]* .) (Same as: **:sNext**, **:spr**, **:sprevious**. See page 245.)

:[count] **snext[!]** **file-list**   **:split** followed by :[count] next If **!** is specified, discard any changes to buffers that have been modified, but not written. If file-list is specified, change the arguments to that list. (Same as: **:sn**. See page 246.)

:[count] **sNext[!]**   **:split** followed by *:[count] previous*. If **!** is specified, discard any changes to buffers that have been modified, but not written. (Note: The count parameter can be specified after the command—for example, **:sN** *[count]* .) (Same as: **:sN**, **:spr**, **:sprevious**. See page 245.)

:sni *{command}*   –or–

:sniff *{command}*   Perform a command using the interface to Sniff+. If no command is present, list out information on the current connection. Sniff+ support has to be compiled in for this to work (not on by default). (Same as: **:sni**. See page 174.)

: [range] **sno** */{from}/{to}/flags*   –or–

: [range] **snomagic** */{from}/{to}/flags*   Substitute the pattern *{to}* for the pattern *{from}* for the given range assuming that the **'nomagic'** option is set. (Same as: **:sno**. See page 310.)

:so *{file}*   –or–

:source *{file}*   Read in a session file. (Actually read in a whole set of commands.) (Same as: **:so**. See pages 95, 294, and 402.)

:[count] **sp** *[+cmd] [file-name]*   –or–

:[count] **split** *[+cmd] [file-name]*   Split the current window. If a count is specified, make the new window count lines high. If a filename is present, put that file in the new window. (Otherwise, use the current file.) (Same as: **CTRL-W CTRL-S**, **CTRL-Ws**, **CTRL-WS**, **:sp**. See pages 45, 47–48, 162, and 247.)

:[count] **spr[!]**   –or–

:[count] **sprevious[!]**   **:split** followed by *:[count]* previous. If **!** is specified, discard any changes to buffers that have been modified, but not written. (Note: The count parameter can be specified after the command—for example, **:sN** *[count]* .) (Same as: **:sN**, **:sNext**, **:spr**. See page 245.)

:sr[!]   –or–

:srewind[!]   **:split** followed by **:rewind**. If **!** is specified, modified files whose windows are closed will have their contents discarded. (Same as: **:sr**. See page 245.)

:st!   Suspend the editor (UNIX terminal only). If the **!** option is not present and **'autowrite'** is set, all changed files will be saved. (Same as: **:stop**, **:sus**, **:suspend**. See page 156.)

:[count] **sta[!]** *{function}*   –or–

:[count] **stag[!]!** *{function}*   A combination of **:split** and **:tag**. If a count is specified it is the height of the new window. (Same as: **:sta**. See page 81.)

:star[!]!   –or–

:startinsert[!] !   Begin insert mode as if a normal **i** command had been entered. If the **!** is present, the insert starts at the end of line as if an A command had been issued. (Same as: **:star**. See page 318.)

`:stj[!]! {ident}`   -or-

`:stjump[!]! {ident}`   Do a `:split` and a `:tjump`. (Same as: `:stj`. See page 84.)

`:stop[!] !`   Suspend the editor (UNIX terminal only). If the `!` option is not present and `'autowrite'` is set, all changed files will be saved. (Same as: `:st`, `:sus`, `:suspend`. See page 156.)

`:sts[!]! {ident}`   -or-

`:stselect[!]! {ident}`   Do a `:split` and a `:tselect`. (Same as: `:sts`. See page 84.)

`:[range]` **substitute** `/{[from}]/{[to}]/{[flags}]`   Change the regular expression *{from}* to the string *{to}*. (Same as: `:s`. See pages 102, 144, 160-161, 167-168, 309, and 401.) The *{flags}* include the following:

c   Confirm. Ask before making a change.

e   If the search pattern fails, do not issue an error message (useful for scripts).

g   Global. Change each occurrence on the line (not just the first one).

i   Ignore case.

p   Print each changed line.

r   When *{from}* is empty, use the last search pattern rather than the last *{from}* for a `:substitute` command. (See page 100.)

`:sun [count]`   -or-

`:sunhide [count]`   Open a new window for all hidden buffer. Limit the number of window to count, if specified. (Same as: `:sun`, `:unh`, `:unhide`. See page 244.)

`:sus[!]`   -or-

`:suspend[!]`   Suspend the editor (UNIX terminal only). Actually, works in Win32 also.). If the `!` option is not present and `'autowrite'` is set, all changed files will be saved. (Same as: `:stop`, `:sus`. See page 156.)

`:sv [+command] [filename]`   -or-

`:sview [+command] [file-name]`   Split the window like `:split`. The only difference is that the file is opened for viewing. (Same as: `:sv`. See page 48.)

`:sw`   -or-

`:swapname`   List name of the current swap file. (Same as: `:sw`. See page 150.)

`:sy`   List out all the syntax elements. (Same as: `:syntax`. See pages 96, 394, and 405-407.)

`:sy case match`   Syntax definitions are case sensitive. In other words, the case of the letters must match. (See page 407.)

:sy case ignore   Syntax definitions are case not sensitive. In other words, case differences are ignored. (See page 407.)

:sy clear   Clear out any existing syntax definitions. (See page 407.)

:sy cluster {*name*} **contains**={*groups*} **add**={*groups*} **remove**={*group*}   Define a cluster of syntax groups. (See page 413.)

:sy sync ccomment group-name minlines={*min*} **maxlines**={*max*}   Tell *Vim* to synchronize based on C-style comments. If a group name is specified, use that group for highlighting; otherwise, use the group name *Comment*. The 'minlines' and 'maxlines' options tell *Vim* how much to look backward through the file for a comment. (See page 414.)

:sy include @{*cluster*} {*file*}   Read in a syntax file and put all the defined groups in the specified cluster. (See page 413.)

:sy keyword {*group*} {*keyword*} ... {*keyword*} *options*   Define a set of keywords for syntax highlighting. They will be highlighted according to {*group-name*}. The options may appear anywhere within the {*keyword*} list. Options can include 'contained', 'nextgroup', 'skipwhite', 'skipnl', 'skipempty', and 'transparent'. Keywords for abbreviations can be defined like 'abbreviation'. This matches both 'abb' and 'abbreviation'. (See page 408.)

:sy list {*group-name*}   List out the named syntax groups. (See page 414.)

:sy list @{*cluster-name*}   List out the elements for syntax cluster. (See page 414.)

:sy match {*group*} **excludenl** {*pattern*} *options*   Define a regular expression that matches a syntax element. Options can be 'contained', 'nextgroup', 'skipwhite', 'skipnl', 'skipempty', 'transparent', and 'contains'. (See page 408.)

:sy region options matchgroup={*group*} **keepend excludenl** \   **start**={*pattern*} **skip**={*pattern*} **end**={*pattern*}   Define a syntax-matching region that starts and ends with the specified pattern. Options can be 'contained', 'nextgroup', 'skipwhite', 'skipnl', 'skipempty', 'transparent', 'contains', and 'oneline'. (See page 408.)

:sy sync clear   Remove all syntax synchronization directives. (See page 414.)

:sy sync clear {*sync-group-name*} **sync-group-name** ...   Clear all the syntax synchronization commands for the named groups. (See page 414.)

:sy sync match {*sync-group-name*} **grouphere** {*group-name*} {*pattern*}   Define a synchronization command (in the group {*sync-group-name*}) that tells *Vim* that when it sees {*pattern*} that the group {*group-name*} follows the match. (See page 414.)

:sy sync match {*sync-group-name*} groupthere {*group-name*} {*pattern*}   Define a synchronization command (in the group {*sync-group-name*}) that tells *Vim* that when it sees {*pattern*} that the group {*group-name*} precedes the match. (See page 414.)

:sy sync minlines={*min*}   Define the minimum number of lines for a brute-force synchronization match. (See page 414.)

:sy sync match {*match-specification*}   Define a match or region to be skipped during synchronization. (See page 414.)

:sync   –or–

:syncbind   Cause all scroll-bound windows to go to the same location. (Same as: **:sync**. See page 276.)

:syntax   List out all the syntax elements. (Same as: **:sy**. See pages 96, 394, and 405-407.)

:syntax case match   Syntax definitions are case sensitive. In other words, the case of the letters must match. (See page 407.)

:syntax case ignore   Syntax definitions are not case sensitive. In other word, case differences are ignored. (See page 407.)

:syntax clear   Clear out any existing syntax definitions. (See page 407.)

:syntax cluster {*name*} **contains**={*groups*} **add**={*groups*} **remove**={*group*}   Define a cluster of syntax groups. (See page 414.)

:syntax sync ccomment group-name minlines={*min*} **maxlines**={*max*}   Tell *Vim* to synchronize based on C-style comments. If a group name is specified, use that group for highlighting; otherwise, use the group name 'Comment'. The 'minlines' and 'maxlines' options tell *Vim* how much to look backward through the file for a comment. (See page 414.)

:syntax include @{*cluster*} {*file*}   Read in a syntax file and put all the defined groups in the specified cluster. (See page 414.)

:syntax keyword {*group*} {*keyword*} ... {*keyword*} *options*   Define a set of keywords for syntax highlighting. They will be highlighted according to {*group-name*}. The options may appear anywhere within the {*keyword*} list. Options can include 'contained', 'nextgroup' 'skipwhite', 'skipnl', 'skipempty', and 'transparent'. Keywords for abbreviations can be defined like 'abbreviation'. This matches both 'abb' and 'abbreviation'. (See page 408.)

:syntax list {*group-name*}   List out the named syntax groups. (See page 414.)

:syntax list @{*cluster-name*}   List out the elements for syntax cluster. (See page 414.)

:syntax match {*group*} **excludenl** {*pattern*} **options**   Define a regular expression that matches a syntax element. Options can be 'contained', 'nextgroup', 'skip-white', 'skipnl', 'skipempty', 'transparent', and 'contains'. (See page 408.)

`:syntax region options matchgroup=`{*group*} **keepend excludenl \ start**={*pattern*} **skip**={*pattern*} **end**={*pattern*}   Define a syntax-matching region that starts and ends with the specified pattern. Options can be `'contained'`, `'nextgroup'`, `'skipwhite'`, `'skipnl'`, `'skipempty'`, `'transparent'`, `'contains'`, and `'oneline'`. (See page 408.)

`:syntax sync clear`   Remove all syntax synchronization directives. (See page 414.)

`:syntax sync clear` {*sync-group-name*} **sync-group-name ...**   Clear all the syntax synchronization commands for the named groups. (See page 414.)

`:syntax sync match` {*sync-group-name*} **grouphere** {*group-name*} {*pattern*}   Define a synchronization command (in the group {*sync-group-name*}) that tells *Vim* that when it sees {*pattern*} that the group {*group-name*} follows the match. (See page 414.)

`:syntax sync match` {*sync-group-name*} **groupthere** {*group-name*} {*pattern*}   Define a synchronization command (in the group {*sync-group-name*}) that tells *Vim* that when it sees {*pattern*} that the group {*group-name*} precedes the match. (See page 414.)

`:syntax sync minlines=`{*min*}   Define the minimum number of lines for a brute-force synchronization match. (See page 414.)

`:syntax sync region` {*region-specification*}   Define a match or region to be skipped during synchronization. (See page 414.)

`:[range]` **t** {*address*}   Copy the range of lines below {*address*}. (Same as: `:copy`. See page 306.)

`:[count]` **ta!**   Go forward count tags. (Same as: `:tag`. See pages 81–82.)

`:ta!` /{*pattern*}   Search for all functions that match the regular expression defined by {*pattern*} and jump to the first one. (See pages 81–82.)

`:[count]` **tag!**   Go forward count tags. (Same as: `:ta`. See pages 81–82.)

`:tag!` /{*pattern*}   Search for all functions that match the regular expression defined by {*pattern*} and jump to the first one. (See pages 81–82.)

`:tags`   List the tags. (See page 80.)

`:tc` {*command*}   –or–

`:tcl` {*command*}   Execute a single Tcl {*command*}. (Same as: `:tc`. See page 174.)

`:[range]` **tcld** {*command*}   –or–

`:[range]` **tcldo** {*command*}   Execute a Tcl {*command*} once for each line in the range. The variable "line" is set to the contents of the line. (Same as: `:tcld`. See page 174.)

:tclf {*file*} –or–

:tclfile {*file*} Execute the Tcl script in the given {*file*}. (Same as: **:tclf**. See page 174.)

:te {*name*} –or–

:tearoff {*name*} Tear off the named menu. (Same as: **:te**. See page 339.)

:tj! **ident** –or–

:tjump! **ident** Like :tselect, but if there is only one tag, automatically pick it. (Same as: **:tj**. See page 83.)

:[count] **tl** –or–

:[count] **tlast** Go to the last tag. (Same as: **:tl**. See page 81.)

:tm {*menu-item*} {*tip*} –or–

:tmenu {*menu-item*} {*tip*} Define the "tip" text that displays when the cursor is placed over an icon in the toolbar. (Same as: **:tm**. See page 337.)

:[count] **tn** Go to the next tag. (Same as: **:tnext**. See page 83.)

:[count] **tN** Go to the previous tag. (Same as: **:tNext**, **:tp**, **:tprevious**. See page 83.)

:[count] **tnext** Go to the next tag. (Same as: **:tn**. See page 83.)

:[count] **tNext** Go to the next tag. (Same as: **:tN**, **:tp**, **:tprevious**. See page 83.)

:[count] **tp** –or–

:[count] **tprevious** Go to the previous tag. (Same as: **:tp**. See page 83.)

:[count] **tr** –or–

:[count] **trewind** Go to the first tag. (Same as: **:tr**. See page 83.)

:ts! **ident** –or–

:tselect! **ident** List all the tags that match ident. If ident is not present, use the results of the last **:tag** command. After listing the tags, give the user a chance to select one and jump to it. (Same as: **:ts**. See page 83.)

:tu {*menu-item*} –or–

:tunmenu {*menu-item*} Remove a "tip" from an menu item. (Same as: **:tu**. See page 339.)

:u Undo a change. (Same as: **:undo**. See page 318.)

:una {*lhs*} –or–

:unabbreviate {*lhs*} Remove the abbreviation. (Same as: **:una**. See page 296.)

:**undo**   Undo a change. (Same as: :**u**. See page 318.)

:**unh count**[*count*]   –or–

:**unhide count**[*count*]   Write the file in all windows. (Same as: :**su**, :**sunhide**, :**unh**. See page 244.)

:**unl**[!] {*variable*}   –or–

:**unlet**[!]! {*variable*}   Remove the definition of the variable. If the force (!) option is present, do not issue an error message if the variable is not defined. (Same as: :**unl**. See page 353.)

:**unm**[!] {*lhs*}   –or–

:**unmap** {*lhs*}   Remove a mapping. (Same as: :**unm**. See pages 299 and 301.)

:[*mode*] **unme** {*menu-item*}   –or–

:[*mode*] **unmenu** {*menu-item*}   Remove the menu item named {*menu-item*}. The wildcard "*****" will match all menu items. (Same as: :**unme**. See page 339.)

:[*range*] **up**[!] [*file*]   –or–

:[*range*] **up**[!] >> [*file*]   –or–

:[*range*] **up** !{*command*}   –or–

:[*range*] **update**[!] [*file*]   –or–

:[*range*] **update**[!] >> [*file*]   –or–

:[*range*] **update** !{*command*}   Acts just like the :write command if the buffer is modified. Does absolutely nothing if it's it is not. (Same as: :**up**. See page 316.)

: [*range*] **v** /{*pattern*}/ {*command*}   Perform {*command*} on all lines that do not have {*pattern*} in them in the given range. (Same as: :**vglobal**. See page 312.)

:**ve**   –or–

:**version**   List version and configuration information, including the list of VIMRC files read in at startup. (Same as: :**ve**. See pages 95-96.)

: [*range*] **vg** /{*pattern*}/ {*command*}   –or–

: [*range*] **vglobal** /{*pattern*}/ {*command*}   Perform {*command*} on all lines that do not have {*pattern*} in them in the given range. (Same as: :**v**. See page 312.)

:**vi** [*+cmd*] {*file*}   Close the current file and start editing the named file. If +cmd is specified, execute it as the first editing command. (Same as: :**visual**. See page 41.)

:**vie** [*+cmd*] {*file*}   –or–

:**view** [*+cmd*] {*file*}   Like :vi, but open the file read-only. (Same as: :**vie**. See page 41.)

:visual *[+cmd]* *{file}*   Close the current file and start editing the named file. If +cmd is specified, execute it as the first editing command. (Same as: **:vi**. See page 41.)

:vm   List all the mappings for visual-mode maps. (Same as: **:vmap**. See pages 297-298.)

:vm *{lhs}*   List the visual mode mapping of *{lhs}*. (See pages 297-298.)

:vm *{lhs}* *{rhs}*   Define a keyboard mapping for visual mode. (See pages 297-298.)

:vmap   List all the visual-mode mappings. (Same as: **:vm**. See pages 297-298.)

:vmap *{lhs}*   List the visual-mode mapping of *{lhs}*. (See page 297-298.)

:vmap *{lhs}* *{rhs}*   Define a keyboard mapping for visual mode. (See page 297-298.)

:vmapc   –or–

:vmapclear   Clear all the visual-mode mappings. (Same as: **:vmapc**. See page 301.)

:[priority] **vme** *{menu-item}* *{command-string}*   –or–

:[priority] **vmenu** *{menu-item}* *{command-string}*   Define a menu item that is available for visual mode only. The priority determines its placement in a menu. Higher numbers come first. The name of the menu item is *{menu-item}*, and when the command is selected, the command *{command-string}* is executed. (Same as: **:vme**. See page 334.)

:vn *{lhs}* *{rhs}*   –or–

:vnoremap *{lhs}* *{rhs}*   Same as **:vmap**, but does not allow remapping of the *{rhs}*. (Same as: **:vn**. See page 301.)

:[priority] **vnoreme** *{menu-item}* *{command-string}*   –or–

:[priority] **vnoremenu** *{menu-item}* *{command-string}*   Like :vmenu, but the *{command-string}* is not remapped. (Same as: **:vnoreme**. See page 338.)

:[range] **w[!]!** **filename**   Write out the specified file. If no filename is specified, write to the current file. The range defaults to the entire file. If the force **(!)** option is present, overwrite an existing file, or override the read-only flag. (Same as: **:write**. See pages 41-42, 104, 134, 144, 151, 168, 242, and 315-316)

:[range] **w[!]!** **>> file**   Append the specified range to the file. This will fail if the file does not exist unless the force **(!)** option is specified. (See page 310.)

:wa   –or–

:wall   Write the file in all windows. (Same as: **:wa**. See page 242.)

:wh *{expression}*   –or–

:while *{expression}*   Start a loop. (Same as: **:wh**. See page 356.)

:wi {*width*} {*height*}   Obsolete older command to set the number of rows and columns. Use :set rows and :set columns instead. (Same as: **:winsize**. See page 325.)

:winp {*X*} {*Y*}   -or-

:winpos {*X*} {*Y*}   Set the position of the window on the screen. (Same as: **:winp**. See page 325.)

:winsize {*width*} {*height*}   Obsolete older command to set the number of rows and columns. Use :set rows and :set columns instead. (Same as: **:wi**. See page 325.)

:wn   Shorthand for **:write** and **:next**. (Same as: **:wnext**. See pages 42-43.)

:[count] **wnext[!]** {*+command*}   -or-

:[count] **wNext[!]** {*+command*}   Shorthand for **:write** and **:[count] next**. (Same as: **:wN**, **:wp**, **:wprevious**. See page 43.)

:wp   -or-

:[count] **wprevious[!]**   Shorthand for :write and **:[count] previous**. (Same as: **:wN**, **:wNext**, **:wp**. See page 43.)

:[range] **wq[!] file**   Write the file and exit. If a range is specified, only write the specified lines. If a file is specified, write the data to that file. When the override option (**!**) is present, attempt to overwrite existing files or read-only files. (See pages 202 and 322.)

:wqa[!]   -or-

:wqall[!]   Shorthand for **:wall** and **:qall**. (Same as: **:wqa**, **:xa**, **:xall**. See page 242.)

:write[!]   Write out the current file. (See page 31.)

:[range] **write[!]!** {*filename*}   Write out the specified file. If no filename is specified, write to the current file. The range defaults to the entire file. If the force (**!**) option is present, overwrite an existing file, or override the read-only flag. (Same as: **:w**. See pages 41-42, 104, 134, 144, 151, 168, 242, and 315-316.)

:[range] **write[!]! >>** {*file*}   Append the specified range to the file. This will fail if the file does not exist unless the force (**!**) option is specified. (See page 310.)

:wv[!]! {*file*}   -or-

:wviminfo[!]! {*file*}   Write the *vim*info file specified. If the override option is present (**!**), any existing file will be overwritten. (Same as: **:wv**. See page 233.)

:[range] **x[!]! file**   If the file has been modified, write it. Then exit. If the override (**!**) option is present, overwrite any existing file. (Same as: **:xit**. See page 202.)

:X   Prompt for an encryption key and assign the resulting value to the "key" option. (See page 143.)

:range ~flags count   Repeat the last substitution, but the last search string as the {*from*} pattern rather than the {*from*} from the last substitution. (See page 311.)

:[range] **xit[!]** *{file}*   If the file has been modified, write it. Then exit. If the override (**!**) option is present, overwrite any existing file. (Same as: **:x**. See page 202.)

:[range] **y** *{register}*   –or–

:[range] **yank** *{register}*   Yank the range (default = current line) into the register (default = the unnamed register). (Same as: **:y**. See page 318.)

:[line] **z**{*code*} *count[count]*   List the given line (default = current) and a few lines after it. The code controls what section of the text is listed. The count defines what "a few" is. (See page 309.)

:map Mode Table

NVO	N	V	O	IC	I	C
:map	:nm	:vm	:om	:map!	:im	:cm
	:nmap	:vmap	:omap		:imap	:cmap
:no	:nn	:vn	:ono	:no!	:ino	:cno
:noreamp	:nnremap	:vnoremap	:onoremap	:noremap!	:inoremap	:cnoremap
:unm	:nun	:vu	:ou	:unm!	:iu	:cu
:unmap	:numap	:vumap	:oumap	:unmap!	:iunmap	:cunmap
:mapc	:nmapc	:vmapc	:omapc	:mapc!	:imapc	:cmapc
:mapclear	:nmapclear	:vmapclear	:omapclear	:mapclear!	:imapclear	:cmapclear

Modes

N   Normal
V   Visual
O   Operator pending
I   Insert
C   Command line

E

Visual–Mode Commands

<Esc>	Cancel visual mode. (See page 57.)
CTRL-]	Jump to highlighted tag. (See page 60.)
CTRL-\ CTRL-N	Enter normal mode. (See page 58.)
CTRL-G	Toggle between select and visual mode. (See page 259.)
CTRL-V	Switch to visual block mode or exit block visual mode. (See page 59.)
!program	Pipe the selected text through an external program. (See page 57.)
$	Move to the end of the line. (See page 63.)
<	Shift lines to the left (different in block visual mode.) (See page 60.)
=	Indent the lines. (See page 60.)
>	Shift lines to the right (different in block visual mode.)
:command	Execute a colon-mode command on the selected lines.
~	Invert the case of the selected text.
"{register}c	Delete and enter insert mode. (See page 59.)
"{register}C	Delete the selected lines and enter insert mode. (See page 59.)
"{register}d	Delete the highlighted text. (See pages 56, 251, and 252.)

`"{register}D`	Delete the highlighted lines. (See page 58.)
g?	Rot13 the text. (See page 257.)
gJ	Join the selected lines with no spaces inserted between the words. (See pages 59 and 256.)
gq	Format a block. (See page 256.)
gv	Toggle between the current and previous visual-mode selection. (See pages 252–253.)
J	Join the selected lines.(See pages 59 and 256.)
K	Look up the selected word using the **man** command. (See page 60.)
o	Jump to the other end of a visual selection. (See pages 254 and 255.)
r	Delete and enter insert mode (different in block visual mode.) (See page 59.)
R	Delete the selected lines and enter insert mode. (See page 59.)
`"{register}s`	Delete and enter insert mode. (See page 59.)
`"{register}s`	Delete the selected lines and enter insert mode. (See page 59.)
u	Make the selected case all lowercase. (See page 255.)
U	Make the selected case all uppercase. (See page 255.)
v	Enter line visual mode, or exit to normal mode. (See page 59.)
`"{register}x`	Delete the highlighted text. (See pages 56, 251, and 252.)
`"{register}X`	Delete the highlighted lines. (See page 58.)
`"{register}y`	Yank the highlighted text into a register. (See pages 59, 162, 156.)
`"{register}Y`	Yank the highlighted lines into a register. (See page 59.)

Visual Block Commands

>	Move the block to the right. (See page 64.)
<	Move the block to the left. (See page 164.)
A_string_**<Esc>**	Append _string_ to the right side of each line. (See page 63.)
c_string_**<Esc>**	Delete the selected text and then insert the _string_ on each line. (See page 62.)
C_string_**<Esc>**	Delete selected text to end of line, then insert on each line. (See page 62.)
I_string_**<Esc>**	Insert text on the left side of each line. (See page 60.)
O	Go to the other corner diagonally. (See page 255.)
r_char_	Replace all the text with a single character. (See page 64.)

Select-Mode Commands

Starting Select Mode

gCTRL-H	Start select block mode. (See page 258.)
gh	Start select character mode. (See page 258.)
gH	Start select line mode. (See page 258.)
gV	Do not automatically reselect an area after a command has been executed. (See page 260.)

Select Mode Commands

Arrow, CTRL, Function Keys (cursor motion)	Extend selection. (See page 258.)
string<**Esc**>	Delete the selected text and replace it with *string*. (See page 258.)
<**BS**>	Backspace. (See page 258.)
CTRL-H	Delete the selected text. (See page 259.)
CTRL-O	Switch from select mode to visual mode for one command. (See page 259.)

Insert–Mode Commands

<BS>	Delete character before the cursor.
char1<**BS**>*char2*	Enter digraph (only when **digraph** option set).
<C-End>	Cursor past end of file. (See page 228.)
<C-Home>	Cursor to start of file. (See page 228.)
<C-Left>	Cursor one word left. (See page 228.)
<C-Right>	Cursor one word right. (See page 228.)
<CR>	Begin new line.
<Del>	Delete character under the cursor.
<Down>	Cursor one line down. (See page 228.)
<End>	Cursor past end of line. (See page 228.)
<Esc>	End insert mode (unless '**insertmode**' set).(See page 6 and 10.)
<F1>	Same as **<Help>**.
<Help>	Stop insert mode and display help window.
<Home>	Cursor to start of line. (See page 228.)
<Insert>	Toggle insert/replace mode.
<Left>	Cursor one character left. (See page 228.)
<LeftMouse>	Cursor at mouse click. (See page 109.)

`<MouseDown>`	Scroll three lines downward.
`<MouseUp>`	Scroll three lines upward.
`<NL>`	Same as `<CR>`.
`<PageDown>`	Scroll one screen forward.
`<PageUp>`	Scroll one screen backward.
`<Right>`	Cursor one character right. (See page 228.)
`<S-Down>`	Move one screen forward.
`<S-Left>`	Cursor one word left.
`<S-MouseDown>`	Scroll a full page downward.
`<S-MouseUp>`	Scroll a full page upward.
`<S-Right>`	Cursor one word right.
`<S-Up>`	Scroll one screen backward.
`<Tab>`	Insert a `<Tab>` character.
`<Up>`	Cursor one line up. (See page 228.)
`CTRL-@`	Insert previously inserted text and stop insert.
`CTRL-[`	Same as `<Esc>`.
`CTRL-\ CTRL-N`	Go to Normal mode.
`CTRL-]`	Trigger abbreviation.
`CTRL-_`	When `'allowrevins'` is set: change language (Hebrew, Farsi) {only works when compiled with +rightleft feature}
`CTRL-A`	Insert previously inserted text. (See page 229.)
`CTRL-C`	Quit insert mode, without checking for abbreviation, unless `'insertmode'` set. (See page 297.)
`CTRL-D`	Delete one shift width of indent in the current line. (See page 72 and 262.)
`CTRL-E` `CTRL-F`	Insert the character that is below the cursor. (See page 230.)
`CTRL-H`	Same as `<BS>`.
`CTRL-I`	Same as `<Tab>`.
`CTRL-J`	Same as `<CR>`.
`CTRL-K {character1}{character2}`	Insert digraph. (See page 200.)
`CTRL-L`	When insertmode is set, this command enables you to leave insert mode. (See page 179.)

CTRL-M	Same as **<CR>**.
CTRL-N	Find next match for keyword in front of the cursor. (See page 126 and 128.)
CTRL-O	Quote next character. **CTRL-V** is perferred since some terminals intercept **CTRL-Q** and interpret it as a stop code. (See page 231.)
CTRL-P	Find previous match for keyword in front of the cursor. (See page 125, 126, and 128.)
CTRL-Q	Same as **CTRL-V** (used for terminal control flow). (See page 156.)
CTRL-R *register*	Insert the contents of a register. (See page 230, 263, and 264.)
CTRL-R CTRL-O *register*	Insert the contents of a register literally and do not auto-indent. (See pages 263-264.)
CTRL-R CTRL-P *register*	Insert the contents of a register literally and fix indent. (See pages 263-264.)
CTRL-R CTRL-R *register*	Insert the contents of a register literally. (See pages 230.)
CTRL-S	Used for terminal control flow.
CTRL-T	Insert one shift width of indent in current line. (See page 263.)
CTRL-U	Delete all entered characters in the current line. (See page 228.)
CTRL-V *char*	Insert next non-digit literally. (See pages 85, 92, 229, and, 268.)
CTRL-V *number*	Insert three-digit decimal number as a single byte. (See page 229.)
CTRL-W	Delete word before the cursor. (See page 228.)
CTRL-X *mode*	Enter **CTRL-X** sub mode, see the following entries.
CTRL-X CTRL-]	Search for the tag that completes the word under the cursor. (See pages 128-130).
CTRL-X CTRL-D	Search for a macro definition for completion. (See pages 128 and 129.)
CTRL-X CTRL-E	Scroll up. (See pages 131.)
CTRL-X CTRL-F	Search filenames for completion. (See pages 128 and 130.)
CTRL-X CTRL-I	Search the current file and **#include** files for completion. (See page 128.)

CTRL-X CTRL-K	Complete identifiers from dictionary. (See page 128.)
CTRL-X CTRL-L	Search the line completion of the line under of the cursor. (See pages 128 and 131.)
CTRL-X CTRL-N	Search for next word that matches the word under the cursor. (See page 128.)
CTRL-X CTRL-P	Search for previous word that matches the word under the cursor. (See page 128.)
CTRL-X CTRL-Y	Scroll down. (See page 131.)
CTRL-Y	Insert the character that is above the cursor. (See pages 229 and 230.)
CTRL-Z	When in insert mode, suspend *Vim*.
^ CTRL-D	Delete all indent in the current line, and restore it in the next. (See page 262.)
0 CTRL-D	Delete all indent in the current line. (See page 262.)

G

Option List

Option	Abbreviation	Type	Scope	Default
aleph	**al**	Number	Global	MS-DOS: 128 Others: 224
Define the first character of the Hebrew alphabet. (See page 177.)				
allowrevins	**ari**	Boolean	Global	Off
Allow the **CTRL-_** command toggle the **'revins'** option. (See page 175.)				
altkeymap	**akm**	Boolean	Global	Off
Define which keyboard map to use as the alternate one. (See pages 176–177.)				
autoindent	**ai**	Boolean	Buffer	Off
Automatically indent each line like the previous one. (See pages 70, 72, 97, 262, 396.)				
autoprint	**ap**	Boolean	Global	Off
Inoperative option put in for *Vi* compatibility. (See page 402.)				
autowrite	**aw**	Boolean	Global	Off
Automatically write files as needed. (See pages 42 and 97.)				
background	**bg**	String	Global	Depends on GUI background
Light or dark, depending on the background color. (See pages 68 and 343.)				
backspace	**bs**	String	Global	""
Define how **<BS>** works in insert mode. (See page 94.)				

continues

Option	Abbreviation	Type	Scope	Default
backup	**bk**	Boolean	Global	Off
Produce a backup file. (See pages 146-147.)				
backupdir	**bdir**	String	Global	Amiga: `".,t:"` MS-DOS: `".,c:/tmp,c:/temp"` UNIX: `".,~/tmp,~/"`
Specify where the backup files are to go. (See page 147.)				
backupext	**bex**	String	Global	VMS: `"_"` Others: `"~"`
Define the extension to append to a backup file. (See page 146.)				
beautify	**bf**	Boolean	Global	Off
Inoperative option put in for *Vi* compatibility. (See page 402.)				
binary	**bin**	Boolean	Buffer	Off
This option enables you to edit binary files. (See pages 121 and 178.)				
bioskey	**biosk**	Boolean	Global	On
On Microsoft Windows, use the BIOS to read keys. (See page 340.)				
breakat	**brk**	String	Global	`" ^I!@*-+_;:,./?"`
Define character at which a line can be broken. (See page 236.)				
browsedir	**bsdir**	String	Global	`"last"`
Define which directory in which to start the `:browse` command. (See page 340.)				
cindent	**cin**	Boolean	Buffer	Off
Do C-style indentation. (See pages 70, 71, and 396.)				
cinkeys	**cink**	String	Buffer	`"0{,0},:,0#,!^F,o,0,e"`
Define the keys that cause a re-indent. (See page 272.)				
cinoptions	**cino**	String	Buffer	`""`
Define how C indentation is performed. (See pages 272-274.)				
cinwords	**cinw**	String	Buffer	`"if,else,while,do,for,switch"`
Define keywords that cause an extra indent. (See pages 71, 272, and 275.)				
clipboard	**cb**	String	Global	`""`
Define how the GUI interacts with the system clipboard. (See page 343.)				
cmdheight	**ch**	Number	Global	1
Define the height of the command window. (See page 386.)				
columns	**co**	Number	Global	80 or terminal width
Number of columns in a window. (See page 325.)				
comments	**com**	String	Buffer	`"s1:/*,mb:*,ex:*/,://,b:#,:%, :XCOMM,n:>,fb:-"`
Define what *Vim* considers a comment. (See pages 269-270.)				
compatible	**cp**	Boolean	Global	On (but turned off when a Vimrc file is found)
Enable *Vi* compatibility. (See pages 4 and 401.)				

Option	Abbreviation	Type	Scope	Default
complete	**cpt**	String	Global	**".,w,b,u,t,I"**
Define where *Vim* searches for words to complete. (See pages 127–128.)				
confirm	**cf**	Boolean	Global	Off
Enable a confirmation dialog for some commands. (See page 386.)				
conskey	**consk**	Boolean	Global	Off
Do direct console I/O on Microsoft Windows. (See page 384.)				
cpoptions	**cpo**	String	Global	*Vim* mode: **"aABceFs"**
				Vi mode: All flags
Set compatibility options. (See page 401.)				
cscopeprg	**csprg**	String	Global	**"cscope"**
Define where the CScope program resides. (See page 172.)				
cscopetag	**cst**	Boolean	Global	Off
Use CScope for tag navigation. (See page 172.)				
cscopetagorder	**csto**	Number	Global	0
Define the search order for CScope tag commands. (See page 172.)				
cscopeverbose	**csverb**	Boolean	Global	Off
Output verbose information when using CScope. (See page 172.)				
define	**def**	String	Global	**"^#\s*define"**
Define the string that indicates a macro definition. (See page 284.)				
dictionary	**dict**	String	Global	**""**
Define the files to be searched for dictionary words. (See pages 127–128.)				
digraph	**dg**	Boolean	Global	Off
If set, allow digraphs to be entered with as *ch1***<BS>***ch2*. (See page 200.)				
directory	**dir**	String	Global	Amiga: **".,t:"**
				MS-DOS: **".,c:\tmp,c:\temp"**
				UNIX: **".,~/tmp,/var/tmp,/tmp"**
Define the directory where the swap files go. (See page 151.)				
display	**dy**	String	Global	**""**
If set to **"lastline"**, display partial lines as the last line of a screen. (See page 236.)				
edcompatible	**ed**	Boolean	Global	Off
Change the **g** and **c** flags for the substitute command to be **ed** like. (See page 401.)				
endofline	**eol**	Boolean	Buffer	On
Put an **<EOL>** at the end of an incomplete last line. (See page 121.)				
equalalways	**ea**	Boolean	Global	On
When creating windows, make all window sizes equal. (See page 247.)				
equalprg	**ep**	String	Global	**""**
Define the program to use for the = command. (See page 269.)				

continues

Option	Abbreviation	Type	Scope	Default
`errorbells`	`eb`	Boolean	Global	Off

If set, beep on error. (See page 389.)

Option	Abbreviation	Type	Scope	Default
`errorfile`	`ef`	String	Global	Amiga: `"AztecC.Err"` Others: `"errors.err"`

Define the default error file for the `:clist` and related commands. (See page 89.)

Option	Abbreviation	Type	Scope	Default
`errorformat`	`efm`	String	Global	A long and complex string.

Define how *Vim* parses errors coming out of **make** command. (See page 385.)

Option	Abbreviation	Type	Scope	Default
`esckeys`	`ek`	Boolean	Global	On

Tell *Vim* to accept function keys that send an `<ESC>` string in insert mode. (See page 139.)

Option	Abbreviation	Type	Scope	Default
`eventignore`	`ei`	String	Global	`""`

Define a set of events to ignore. (See pages 85 and 267.)

Option	Abbreviation	Type	Scope	Default
`expandtab`	`et`	Boolean	Buffer	Off

If set, expand tabs to spaces on insert. (See pages 85 and 267.)

Option	Abbreviation	Type	Scope	Default
`exrc`	`ex`	Boolean	Global	Off

Allow reading of initialization files in the current directory. (See page 383.)

Option	Abbreviation	Type	Scope	Default
`fileencoding`	`fe`	String	Buffer	`"ansi"`

Define the encoding of the file. Used for foreign languages. (See pages 137, 176, and 178.)

Option	Abbreviation	Type	Scope	Default
`fileformat`	`ff`	String	Buffer	MS-DOS, OS/2: `"dos"` UNIX: `"unix"` Macintosh: `"mac"`

The format of the current file. (See page 120.)

Option	Abbreviation	Type	Scope	Default
`fileformats`	`ffs`	String	Global	MS-DOS, OS/2: `"dos,unix"` UNIX: `"unix,dos"` Macintosh: `"mac,unix,dos"` Others: `""`

Define the file formats recognized. (See page 120.)

Option	Abbreviation	Type	Scope	Default
`filetype`	`ft`	String	Buffer	`""`

The type of the current file. (See pages 69, 136, and 138.)

Option	Abbreviation	Type	Scope	Default
`fkmap`	`fk`	Boolean	Global	Off

Turn on Farsi keyboard mapping. (See page 176.)

Option	Abbreviation	Type	Scope	Default
`flash`	`fl`	Boolean	Global	Off

Inoperative option put in for *Vi* compatibility. (See page 402.)

Option	Abbreviation	Type	Scope	Default
`formatoptions`	`fo`	String	Buffer	`"tcq"`

Define how text is formatted. (See pages 97, 117-119, and 396.)

Option	Abbreviation	Type	Scope	Default
`formatprg`	`fp`	String	Global	`""`

Define an external command to perform formatting. (See page 119.)

Option	Abbreviation	Type	Scope	Default
`gdefault`	`gd`	Boolean	Global	Off

Make the **g** flag the default for `:substitute` commands. (See page 311.)

Option	Abbreviation	Type	Scope	Default
graphic	**gr**	Boolean	Global	Off

Inoperative option put in for *Vi* compatibility. (See page 402.)

Option	Abbreviation	Type	Scope	Default
grepformat	**gfm**	String	Global	`"%f:%l%m,%f  %l%m"`

Defines how *Vim* interprets the output of **:grep**. (See page 289.)

grepprg	**gp**	String	Global	`"grep -n"`, Win32: `"findstr /n"`

Define the command to run for **:grep**. (See pages 170 and 289.)

guicursor	**gcr**	String	Global	Complex string

Define how the cursor looks in Microsoft Windows *Vim*. (See page 345.)

guifont	**gfn**	String	Global	`" "`

Define the font to use for the GUI. (See page 344.)

guiheadroom	**ghr**	Number	Global	50

Define the amount of space above and below the window used by the window manager. (See page 346.)

guifontset	**gfs**	String	Global	`" "`

Define fonts for English and a foreign language. (See page 175.)

guioptions	**go**	String	Global	GTK: `"agimrtT"`
				UNIX: `"gmrt"`

Sets various GUI options. (See pages 234, 325, 329, and 343.)

guipty		Boolean	Global	On

Use a `"pty"` rather than a pipe to connect to **:shell** commands. (See pag 346.)

hardtabs	**ht**	Boolean	Global	Off

Inoperative option put in for *Vi* compatibility. (See page 402.)

helpfile	**hf**	String	Global	MS-DOS:
				`"$VIMRUNTIME\doc\help.txt"`
				Others:
				`"$VIMRUNTIME/doc/help.txt"`

Define the location of the main help file. (See page 401.)

helpheight	**hh**	Number	Global	Half the current screen.

The height of the help window. (See page 392.)

hidden	**hid**	Boolean	Global	Off

Automatically hide buffers that are no longer visible. (See page 52.)

highlight	**hl**	String	Global	Complex string

Define the highlighting for the *Vim* messages. (See pages 394–395.)

hlsearch	**hls**	Boolean	Global	Off

Highlight search strings. (See pages 29, 97, 203, and 293.)

history	**hi**	Number	Global	20

Define the size of the command (**:**) history. (See page 321.)

continues

Option	Abbreviation	Type	Scope	Default
`hkmap`	`hk`	Boolean	Global	Off
Enable Hebrew keyboard mapping. (See page 177.)				
`hkmapp`	`hkp`	Boolean	Global	Off
Enable Hebrew with a phonetic keyboard. (See page 177.)				
`icon`		Boolean	Global	Off (but on when title can be restored)
If set, display the current filename in the icon. (See page 330.)				
`iconstring`		String	Global	`" "`
The string to be displayed in the icon text. (See page 330.)				
`ignorecase`	`ic`	Boolean	Global	Off
Ignore case differences in a search and name completion. (See pages 126 and 204.)				
`include`	`inc`	String	Global	`"^#\s*include"`
Define the format of an `"include"` directive. (See page 284.)				
`incsearch`	`is`	Boolean	Global	Off
Perform incremental searches. (See pages 30 and 97.)				
`infercase`	`inf`	Boolean	Buffer	Off
Figure out case of insert completion matches from the current text. (See page 127.)				
`insertmode`	`im`	Boolean	Global	Off
Enter the strange world where insert mode is the default. (See page 179.)				
`isfname`	`isf`	String	Global	Complex string
Determine which characters make up a filename. (See pages 186 and 216.)				
`isident`	`isi`	String	Global	Complex string
Determine which characters make up an identifier. (See page 186.)				
`iskeyword`	`isk`	String	Buffer	Complex string
Define what characters make up a word. (See pages 184-185 and 217.)				
`isprint`	`isp`	String	Global	MS-DOS: `"@,~-255"` Others: `"@,161-255"`
Determine which characters are printable. (See pages 186 and 217.)				
`joinspaces`	`js`	Boolean	Global	On
Put spaces between lines joined with the `>` command. (See page 116.)				
`key`		String	Buffer	`" "`
The encryption key. (See page 143.)				
`keymodel`	`km`	String	Global	`" "`
Define how special keys affect selection mode. (See pages 108 and 333.)				
`keywordprg`	`kp`	String	Global	Solaris: `"man -s"` Other UNIX: `"man"` DOS: `" "` OS/2: `"view /"` VMS: `"help"`
Define the command to run for the **K** command. (See page 79.)				

Option	Abbreviation	Type	Scope	Default
`langmap`	`lmap`	String	Global	`" "`

Define a set of mappings for a foreign keyboard. (See page 175.)

`laststatus`	`ls`	Number	Global	1

Determine which windows get a status line. (See pages 246-247.)

`lazyredraw`	`lz`	Boolean	Global	Off

Do not redraw the screen during macro execution. (See page 400.)

`linebreak`	`lbr`	Boolean	Window	Off

Break long lines at nice places. (See page 236.)

`lines`		Number	Global	Screen height

Set the number of lines in the edit window. (See page 325.)

`lisp`		Boolean	Buffer	Off

Set options that make editing Lisp programs easier. (See pages 396 and 401.)

`list`		Boolean	Window	Off

Make invisible characters visible. (See pages 84 and 392.)

`listchars`	`lcs`	String	Global	`"eol:$"`

Define how list mode appears. (See pages 85, 392, and 393.)

`magic`		Boolean	Global	On

Turn on or off the magic properties of some search characters. (See pages 214 and 309.)

`makeef`	`mef`	String	Global	Amiga: `"t:vim##.Err"`
				UNIX: `"/tmp/vim##.err"`
				Others: `"vim##.err"`

Define the name of the file to use for `:make` and `:grep` output. (See page 284.)

`makeprg`	`mp`	String	Global	`"make"`

Define the program to run for the `:make` command. (See pages 87 and 285.)

`matchpairs`	`mps`	String	Buffer	`"(:),{:},[:]"`

Define characters to match for `"%"` and show match. (See page 278.)

`matchtime`	`mat`	Number	Global	5

Define the time (in 1/10 seconds) for `'showmatch'` to work. (See page 278.)

`maxfuncdepth`	`mfd`	Number	Global	100

Define how deeply function calls may be nested. (See page 400.)

`maxmapdepth`	`mmd`	Number	Global	1000

Define the maximum number of nested key mappings. (See page 400.)

`maxmem`	`mm`	Number	Global	512

Define the maximum amount of memory for a single buffer. (See page 399.)

`maxmemtot`	`mmt`	`number`	`global`	2048, or half the amount of memory available

Define the maximum amount of memory total. (See page 400.)

continues

Option	Abbreviation	Type	Scope	Default
`mesg`		Boolean	Global	Off
Inoperative option put in for *Vi* compatibility. (See page 402.)				
`modeline`	`ml`	Boolean	Buffer	`modeline`
If set, look for modelines in the file. (See page 382.)				
`modelines`	`mls`	Number	Global	5
The number of lines at the top and bottom to look for modelines. (See page 152.)				
`modified`	`mod`	Boolean	Buffer	Off
Set to true if the buffer has been modified. (See page 152.)				
`more`		Boolean	Global	On
When displaying more output than a screen of data, page things through **more**. (See page 395.)				
`mouse`		String	Global	GUI, MS-DOS: `"a"` Others: `" "`
Define which modes enables you to use a mouse. (See page 332.)				
`mousefocus`	`mousef`	Boolean	Global	Off
If set, the window focus follows the mouse. (See page 331.)				
`mousehide`	`mh`	Boolean	Global	Off
Hide the mouse while typing in character. (See page 333.)				
`mousemodel`	`mousem`	String	Global	MS-DOS: `popup:` Others: `extend`
Define how the mouse is to be used. (See pages 108 and 331.)				
`mousetime`	`mouset`	Number	Global	500
Time between mouse clicks for a double-click. (See page 332.)				
`novice`		Boolean	Global	Off
Inoperative option put in for *Vi* compatibility. (See page 402.)				
`nrformats`	`nf`	String	Buffer	`"octal,hex"`
Define which formats are recognized for **CTRL-A** and **CTRL-X**. (See pages 198 and 395.)				
`number`	`nu`	Boolean	Window	Off
Display line numbers. (See pages 18 and 100.)				
`open`		Boolean	Global	Off
Inoperative option put in for *Vi* compatibility. (See pages 402.)				
`optimize`		Boolean	Global	Off
Inoperative option put in for *Vi* compatibility. (See pages 402.)				
`osfiletype`	`oft`	String	Buffer	RISC OS: `"Text"` Others: `" "`
The file type as determined by the OS. (See page 179.)				
`paragraphs`	`para`	String	Global	`"IPLPPPQPP LIpplpipbp"`
Define the *troff* macros that begin a paragraph. (See pages 122-123.)				

Option	Abbreviation	Type	Scope	Default
paste		Boolean	Global	Off

Define how *Vim* interacts with the system clipboard. (See page 396.)

pastetoggle	**pt**	String	Global	" "

Define a key to switch between **paste** and **nopaste**. (See page 396.)

patchmode	**pm**	String	Global	" "

Turn on **patchmode**, which saves the original file once. (See page 147.)

path	**pa**	String	Global	UNIX: "./usr/include,,"
				OS/2: ".,/emx/include,,"
				Others: ".,,"

Set the path to be used for locating **#include** and **:find** files. (See pages 127 and 281.)

previewheight	**pvh**	Number	Global	12

Define the height of the preview window. (See page 392.)

prompt		Boolean	Global	Off

Inoperative option put in for *Vi* compatibility. (See page 402.)

readonly	**ro**	Boolean	Buffer	Off

Set to indicate that the buffer is read-only. (See pages 152–153.)

redraw		Boolean	Global	Off

Inoperative option put in for *Vi* compatibility. (See page 402.)

remap		Boolean	Global	On

Allow recursive remapping. (See page 300.)

report		Number	Global	2

Set the number of lines that must be changed before a message is issued. (See page 392.)

restorescreen	**rs**	Boolean	Global	On

Try and restore the screen after editing. (See page 395.)

revins	**ri**	Boolean	Global	Off

Insert character in reverse (for foreign language). (See pages 175 and 396.)

rightleft	**rl**	Boolean	Window	Off

If set, indicates that the file contains right-to-left encoding. (See page 174.)

ruler	**ru**	Boolean	Global	Off

Display the status ruler. (See pages 392 and 396.)

rulerformat	**ruf**	String	Global	Empty

Define the format of a ruler. (See page 392.)

scroll	**scr**	Number	Window	Half the screen height

Define the number of lines to scroll for **CTRL-D** and **CTRL-U**. (See page 190.)

scrollbind	**scb**	Boolean	Window	Off

The window that scrolls with other scroll-bound windows. (See page 275.)

continues

Option	Abbreviation	Type	Scope	Default
scrolljump	sj	Number	Global	1

Define the number of lines to scroll at one time. (See page 193.)

Option	Abbreviation	Type	Scope	Default
scrolloff	so	Number	Global	0

Number of lines to keep above or below the cursor. (See page 193.)

scrollopt	sbo	String	Global	"ver,jump"

Define how synchronized scrolling works. (See page 276.)

sections	sect	String	Global	"SHNHH HUnhsh"

Define the *troff* macros that define a section boundary. (See page 123.)

secure		Boolean	Global	Off

Enable secure mode, which prevents the execution of some risky commands. (See page 383.)

selection	sel	String	Global	"inclusive"

Define how a selection behaves. (See pages 108 and 344.)

selectmode	slm	String	Global	""

Defines the events that can begin select mode. (See pages 108, 258, and 333.)

sessionoptions	ssop	String	Global	"buffers,winsize,options, help,blank"

Defines what is saved by a **:mksession** command. (See page 248.)

shell	sh	String	Global	MS-DOS: **command** OS/2: **cmd** UNIX: **$SHELL** or **"sh"**

The name of the command parser. (See page 319.)

shellcmdflag	shcf	String	Global	MS-DOS: "/c" or "-c" depending on the value of **shell** others: "-c"

The flag that tells the shell that a command follows. (See page 319.)

shellpipe	sp	String	Global	">", "| tee", "|& tee", or "2>&1| tee", depending on the value of "shell"

The string to pipe the output of the command into something else. (See page 319.)

shellquote	shq	String	Global	MS-DOS: "" or "/",depending on the value of 'shell" Others:""

The quote character to put around the command name. (See page 319.)

shellredir	srr	String	Global	">", ">&", or ">%s 2>&1"

String to redirect the shell output. (See page 319.)

shellslash	ssl	Boolean	Global	Off

If set, always use "/" in filenames, even under MS-DOS. (See page 319.)

shelltype	st	Number	Global	0

Define the Amiga shell type. (See page 179.)

Option	Abbreviation	Type	Scope	Default
`shellxquote`	`sxq`	String	Global	MS-DOS: `""` or `"/"`, depending on the value of shell. UNIX: `"\"`

The shell quoting characters for commands and redirection. (See page 319.)

Option	Abbreviation	Type	Scope	Default
`shiftround`	`sr`	Boolean	Global	Off

Adjust all shifts to a **shiftwidth** boundary. (See page 269.)

`shiftwidth`	`sw`	Number	Buffer	8

Define the width of a shift for the `<<` and `>>` commands. (See pages 60, 69, 263, 266, and 269.)

`shortmess`	`shm`	String	Global	**filnxtToO**

Shorten some messages. (See page 387.)

`shortname`	`sn`	Boolean	Buffer	Off

If set, use short filenames for swap filenames. (See page 152.)

`showbreak`	`sbr`	String	Global	`""`

String to display at the beginning of the second part of broken lines. (See page 236.)

`showcmd`	`sc`	Boolean	Global	UNIX: Off Others: On

`showfulltag`	`sft`	Boolean	Global	Off

Show the complete tag when doing a tag search. (See page 130.)

`showmatch`	`sm`	Boolean	Global	Off

Show matching brackets in insert mode. (See pages 345 and 396.)

`showmode`	`smd`	Boolean	Global	On

Display the current mode on the status line. (See pages 386 and 394.)

`sidescroll`	`ss`	Number	Global	0

Define the distance that each horizontal scroll moves. (See page 193.)

`slowopen`	`slow`	Boolean	Global	Off

Inoperative option put in for *Vi* compatibility. (See page 402.)

`smartcase`	`scs`	Boolean	Global	Off

When `'ignorecase'` is set, assume search strings that are all uppercase want the case to be matched. (See page 204.)

`smartindent`	`si`	Boolean	Buffer	Off

Indent like `'autoindent'`, only smarter. (See pages 70-71 and 396.)

`smarttab`	`sta`	Boolean	Global	Off

Insert indents at the beginning of a line, normal tabs elsewhere. (See page 266.)

`softtabstop`	`sts`	Number	Buffer	0

Define what **tabstop** is to be simulated when Tab is pressed. (See pages 265-266 and 396.)

`sourceany`		Boolean	Global	Off

Inoperative option put in for *Vi* compatibility. (See page 402.)

continues

Option	Abbreviation	Type	Scope	Default
splitbelow	**sb**	Boolean	Global	Off

Make **:split** open window at the bottom rather than the top. (See page 247.)

Option	Abbreviation	Type	Scope	Default
startofline	**sol**	Boolean	Global	On

Allow some commands to go past the start or end of a line. (See page 369.)

statusline	**stl**	String	Global	Empty

Define the format of the status line. (See pages 293 and 389.)

suffixes	**su**	String	Global	".bak,~,.o,.h,.info,.swp,.obj"

List of file suffixes to ignore when searching for files that match a wildcard pattern. (See page 397.)

swapfile	**swf**	Boolean	Buffer	On

Turn on or off the use of a swap file. (See page 150.)

swapsync	**sws**	String	Global	"fsync"

Tell the operating system to write the swap file to disk. (See page 151.)

switchbuf	**swb**	String	Global	""

Define how the editor behaves when switching buffers. (See page 288.)

syntax	**syn**	String	Buffer	Empty

The current language used for syntax highlighting. (See pages 136 and 294.)

tabstop	**ts**	Number	Buffer	8

Define how big a tab is. (See pages 263, 267, and 411.)

tagbsearch	**tbs**	Boolean	Global	On

Do a binary search of a sorted tag file. (See page 289.)

taglength	**tl**	Number	Global	0

Define the number of significant characters in a tag. (See page 290.)

tagrelative	**tr**	Boolean	Global	On

Tags are relative to the directory containing the tag files. (See page 290.)

tags	**tag**	String	Global	"./tags,tags"

Define the list of tag files. (See page 290.)

tagstack	**tgst**	Boolean	Global	On

Maintain a tag stack. (See page 290.)

term		String	Global	$TERM, or operating system–dependent value.

Define the name of the terminal. (See pages 137 and 400.)

terse		Boolean	Global	Off

Makes some error messages a little shorter. (See page 388.)

textauto	**ta**	Boolean	Global	On

Obsolete. Use the fileformats option instead. (See page 402.)

textmode	**tx**	Boolean	Buffer	MS-DOS, OS/2: On Others: Off

Obsolete, use fileformats instead. (See page 402.)

Option	Abbreviation	Type	Scope	Default
`textwidth`	`tw`	Number	Buffer	0
Set the width of a line. (See pages 97, 114–115, 118–119, and 396.)				
`tildeop`	`top`	Boolean	Global	Off
Define how the ~ operator works. (See pages 200 and 401.)				
`timeout`	`to`	Boolean	Global	On
Enable time outs for keyboard input for mapping. (See page 385.)				
`timeoutlen`	`tm`	Number	Global	1000
Set the amount of time to wait after a key arrives to see whether it is the start of a function key. (See page 385.)				
`title`		Boolean	Global	Off (but on when title can be restored)
If set, display the current filename in the title bar. (See page 329.)				
`titlelen`		Number	Global	85
Maximum percentage size of the title bar to be used for a title. (See page 330.)				
`titleold`		String	Global	"Thanks for flying Vim"
The fallback old title, which is restored if the real one cannot be restored. (See page 330.)				
`titlestring`		String	Global	""
Define the string to be displayed on the title bar rather than the current filename. (See page 330.)				
`toolbar`	`tb`	String	Global	"icons,tooltips"
Define how the toolbar appears. (See page 329.)				
`ttimeout`		Boolean	Global	Off
Enable time outs for keyboard input. (See page 385.)				
`ttimeoutlen`	`ttm`	Number	Global	–1
Set time out for waiting for mapped keyboard input. (See page 385.)				
`ttybuiltin`	`tbi`	Boolean	Global	On
Search built-in termcap before using the system one. (See page 400.)				
`ttyfast`	`tf`	Boolean	Global	System and terminal dependent
Connection to the terminal is fast. (See page 329.)				
`ttymouse`	`ttym`	String	Global	Depends on the term option
Define how the terminal mouse works. (See page 400.)				
`ttyscroll`	`tsl`	Number	Global	999
Number of lines to scroll. More than this jumps. (See page 401.)				
`ttytype`	`tty`	String	Global	Alias for `"term"`
See the **term** option. (See page 137.)				
`undolevels`	`ul`	Number	Global	UNIX, OS/2: 1000 Others: 100
Define the number of changes remembered for **undo**. (See page 202.)				

continues

Option	Abbreviation	Type	Scope	Default
`updatecount`	`uc`	Number	Global	200
Specify the character typed before data is saved in the swap file. (See page 150.)				
`updatetime`	`ut`	Number	Global	4000
Specify the amount of time (in milliseconds) to wait after typing stops before writing the data to the swap file. (See pages 136 and 150.)				
`verbose`	`vbs`	Number	Global	0
Turn on verbose messages. (See page 402.)				
`viminfo`	`vi`	String	Global	`" "`
Define a file in which to save information between edits. (See pages 231–233.)				
`visualbell`	`vb`	Boolean	Global	Off
Beep by flashing the screen. (See apge 389.)				
`warn`		Boolean	Global	On
Turn on some warning messages. (See page 388.)				
`weirdinvert`	`wiv`	Boolean	Global	Off
Old compatibility option for some weird terminals. (See page 402.)				
`whichwrap`	`ww`	String	Global	`"b,s"`
Define what type of commands can wrap past the beginning or end of a line. (See page 189.)				
`wildchar`	`wc`	Number	Global	`<Tab>`
Define which character starts wildcard completion. (See pages 397–398.)				
`wildcharm`	`wcm`	Number	Global	None (0)
Define the character that starts wildcard completion in mappings. (See page 397.)				
`wildignore`	`wig`	String	Global	`" "`
Pattern of filenames to ignore during wildcard completion. (See page 398.)				
`wildmenu`	`wmnu`	Boolean	Global	Off
When completing wildcards, display a menu of possible files. (See pages 293 and 398.)				
`wildmode`	`wim`	String	Global	`"full"`
Define how *Vim* handles matches. (See pages 398–399.)				
`winaltkeys`	`wak`	String	Global	`"menu"`
Define how Vim uses the <Alt> key in Microsoft Windows. (See page 384.)				
`window`	`wi`	Numeric	Global	Off
Inoperative option put in for *Vi* compatibility. (See page 402.)				
`winheight`	`wh`	Number	Global	1
Define the minimum size of the current window. (See page 247.)				
`winminheight`	`wmh`	Number	Global	1
Define the minimum size of the windows that are not current. (See page 247.)				

Option	Abbreviation	Type	Scope	Default
wrap		Boolean	Window	On

Wrap long lines so that they can be seen on the screen. (See pages 233, 236, and 393.)

Option	Abbreviation	Type	Scope	Default
wrapmargin	**wm**	Number	Buffer	0

Define the margin at which to start text wrapping. (See page 114 and 396.)

Option	Abbreviation	Type	Scope	Default
wrapscan	**ws**	Boolean	Global	On

Define which commands wrap past the beginning or end of a line. (See page 205.)

Option	Abbreviation	Type	Scope	Default
write		Boolean	Global	On

Allows the writing of files. (See page 144 and 399.)

Option	Abbreviation	Type	Scope	Default
writeany	**wa**	Boolean	Global	Off

Automatically write files without the aide of overrides (!). (See page 399.)

Option	Abbreviation	Type	Scope	Default
writebackup	**wb**	Boolean	Global	On

Write backup file over the existing one. (See pages 147–148.)

Option	Abbreviation	Type	Scope	Default
writedelay	**wd**	Number	Global	0

Delay between output characters for debugging. (See page 402.)

Option	Abbreviation	Type	Scope	Default
w300		Numeric	Global	Off

Inoperative option put in for *Vi* compatibility. (

Option	Abbreviation	Type	Scope	Default
w1200		Numeric	Global	Off

Inoperative option put in for *Vi* compatibility.

Option	Abbreviation	Type	Scope	Default
w9600		Numeric	Global	Off

Inoperative option put in for *Vi* compatibility.

Vim License Agreement

By Bram Moolenaar

Summary

The *Vim* editor is Charityware. You can use and copy it as much as you like, but you are seriously encouraged to make a donation to orphans in Uganda. See the section on "Kibaale Children's Centre" later in this appendix.

Details

There are no restrictions on distributing an unmodified copy of *Vim*. Parts of *Vim* may also be distributed, but this text must always be included. You are allowed to include executables that you made from the unmodified *Vim* sources, your own usage examples, and *Vim* scripts.

If you distribute a modified version of *Vim*, you are encouraged to send the maintainer a copy, including the source code. Or make it available to the maintainer through FTP; let him know where he can find it. If the number of changes is small (for example, a modified Makefile) emailing the changes will do. When the maintainer asks for it (in any way), you must make your changes, including source code, available to him.

The maintainer reserves the right to include any changes in the official version of *Vim*. This is negotiable. You are not allowed to distribute a modified version of *Vim* when you are not willing to make the source code available to the maintainer.

The current maintainer is Bram Moolenaar (Bram@vim.org). If this changes, it will be announced in appropriate places (most likely www.vim.org and comp.editors). When it is completely impossible to contact the maintainer, the obligation to send him modified source code ceases.

It is not allowed to remove these restrictions from the distribution of the *Vim* sources or parts of it. These restrictions may also be used for previous *Vim* releases rather than the text that was included with it.

If you are happy with *Vim*, please express that by reading the rest of this appendix. You can also have a look at http://www.vim.org/iccf/.

Kibaale Children's Centre

Kibaale Children's Centre (KCC) is located in Kibaale, a small town in the south of Uganda, near Tanzania, in East Africa. The area is known as the Rakai District. Farmers comprise the bulk of the population. Although people are poor, there is enough food. But this district is suffering from more cases of AIDS per capita than any other part of the world. Some say that it originated in this region. (Estimates are that 10% to 30% of Ugandans are infected with HIV.) Parents are dying, leaving many orphans. In this district, about 60,000 children have lost one or both parents (out of a total population of about 350,000). The deaths are continuing daily.

The children need a lot of help. The KCC works hard to provide the needy with food, medical care, and education—food and medical care to keep them healthy now, and education so that they can take care of themselves in the future. KCC works on a Christian base, but help is given to children of any religion.

The key to solving the problems in this area is education. The regime of President Idi Amin and the following civil wars have negatively impacted on education in the area. Now that the government is stable again, the children and parents have to learn how to take care of themselves and how to avoid infections. There is also help for people who are ill and hungry, but the primary goal is to prevent people from getting ill and to teach them how to grow healthy food.

Most of the orphans live in an extended family. An uncle or older sister takes care of them. Because these families are big and the income (if any) is low, a child is lucky if he or she receives healthy food. Clothes, medical care, and schooling are beyond most children's reach. To help these children in crisis, a sponsorship program was put into place. A child can be financially adopted. For a few dollars per month, KCC sees to it that the financially adopted child gets indispensable items, is healthy, and goes to school; KCC takes care of anything else that needs to be done for the child and the family who supports it.

Besides helping the child directly, the environment where the child grows up needs to be improved. KCC helps schools to improve their teaching methods. There is a demonstration school at the centre, and teacher training is given. Health workers are being trained, hygiene education is carried out, and households are encouraged to build a proper latrine. (I helped setting up a production site for cement slabs. These are used to build a good latrine and are sold below cost.)

There is a small clinic at the project, which provides children and their families with medical help. When needed, transport to a hospital is offered. Immunization programs are carried out, and help is provided when an epidemic threatens (measles and cholera, for example).

From the summer of 1994 to the summer of 1995, I spent a whole year at the centre, working as a volunteer. I helped to expand the centre and worked in the area of water and sanitation. I learned that the help that the KCC provides really makes an impact. Now that I am back in Holland, I want to continue supporting KCC. To do this, I am raising funds and organizing the sponsorship program. Please consider one of these possibilities:

1. Sponsor a child: $15 a month (Holland: fl 27,50)

2. Sponsor a child and the improvement of its environment: $25 a month (Holland: fl 45)

3. Sponsor the health team: Any amount a month or quarter

4. A one-time donation

Compared with other organizations that provide child sponsorship, these amounts are very low. This is because the money goes directly to the centre. Less than 5% is used for administration. This remains possible because this is a small organization that works with volunteers. If you would like to sponsor a child, you should intend to do this for at least one year.

How do you know that the money will be spent right? First of all, you have my personal guarantee as the author of *Vim*. I trust the people working at the centre. I know them personally. The centre is visited at least once a year to check its progress (at our own cost). I have been back to visit the centre myself in 1996, 1998, and 2000.

If you have any further questions, contact the centre directly or send the *Vim* maintainer your queries by email at Bram@vim.org.

The address of the centre is as follows:

Kibaale Children's Centre
P.O. Box 1658
Masaka, Uganda
East Africa

Note

These are Year 2000 prices. Please check the Web page at http://www.vim.org/iccf for the current prices.

Sending Money

United States and Canada

Contact the *Kibaale Children's Fund* (KCF) in Surrey, Canada. You can send them a one-time donation or your sponsorship money directly. Please send me a note so that I know what has been donated because of *Vim*. KCF can also provide more information about sponsorship.

> Kibaale Children's Fund
> c/o Pacific Academy
> 10238-168 Street
> Surrey, B.C. V4N 1Z4
> Canada
> Phone: 604-581-5353

Holland

Transfer to the account of Stichting ICCF Holland in Venlo. You might be eligible for a tax deduction based on your contribution(s) to KCC. For more information about this possibility, check with your tax preparer.

> Postbank, nr. 4548774

Europe

To avoid banking costs, you should send Bram Moolenaar a Eurocheque, written out to Bram Moolenaar in Dutch Guilders (DFL). But any other method should work. Ask for information about sponsorship.

> Stichting ICCF Holland
> Bram Moolenaar
> Clematisstraat 30
> 5925 BE Venlo
> The Netherlands

Others

Transfer to one of these accounts if possible:

> Postbank, nr. 4548774
> Swift code: INGB NL 2A, IBAN: NL47 PSTB 0004 5487 74
>   under the name Stichting ICCF Holland, Venlo
> If that does not work: Rabobank Venlo, nr. 3765.05.117
> Swift code: RABO NL 2U
>   under the name Bram Moolenaar, Venlo

Otherwise, send a cheque in U.S. dollars to the address in the preceding section. The minimal amount is $70. (My bank does not accept smaller amounts for foreign cheques, sorry.)

An alternative is to send a postal money order. That should be possible from any country. Use this name: Abraham Moolenaar (which is how it appears on my passport).

Author's Note

By Steve Oualline

The people behind *Vim* have spent a lot of time and effort to make one of the best editors in the world. Yet they do not ask anything for themselves; instead, they ask that you help some of the poorest and most needy people in Africa. Please send them a donation.

If you work for a medium-size or large company, please take the time to tell your boss how much using *Vim* has helped you and encourage your company to make a substantial donation.

The people behind *Vim* are good people. Please help them out.

I

Quick Reference

The following pages contain the maximum amount of useful information in the minimum space, and thus provide a quick reference. Not all commands are covered, but we have tried to include every command you will encounter in day-to-day editing.

Basic Commands

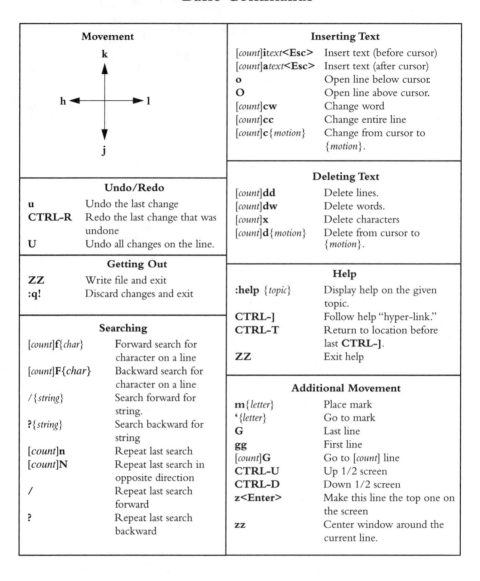

Movement

k

h ◄——► l

j

Undo/Redo

u	Undo the last change
CTRL-R	Redo the last change that was undone
U	Undo all changes on the line.

Getting Out

ZZ	Write file and exit
:q!	Discard changes and exit

Searching

[count]f{char}	Forward search for character on a line
[count]F{char}	Backward search for character on a line
/{string}	Search forward for string.
?{string}	Search backward for string
[count]n	Repeat last search
[count]N	Repeat last search in opposite direction
/	Repeat last search forward
?	Repeat last search backward

Inserting Text

[count]itext<Esc>	Insert text (before cursor)
[count]atext<Esc>	Insert text (after cursor)
o	Open line below cursor.
O	Open line above cursor.
[count]cw	Change word
[count]cc	Change entire line
[count]c{motion}	Change from cursor to {motion}.

Deleting Text

[count]dd	Delete lines.
[count]dw	Delete words.
[count]x	Delete characters
[count]d{motion}	Delete from cursor to {motion}.

Help

:help {topic}	Display help on the given topic.
CTRL-]	Follow help "hyper-link."
CTRL-T	Return to location before last CTRL-].
ZZ	Exit help

Additional Movement

m{letter}	Place mark
'{letter}	Go to mark
G	Last line
gg	First line
[count]G	Go to [count] line
CTRL-U	Up 1/2 screen
CTRL-D	Down 1/2 screen
z<Enter>	Make this line the top one on the screen
zz	Center window around the current line.

Additional Editing Commands

Editing

.	Repeat last change
[*count*]["*register*]**d**{*motion*}	Delete from cursor to {*motion*}
[*count*]["*register*]**dd**	Delete lines
[*count*]["*register*]**c**{*motion*}	Change from cursor to {*motion*}
[*count*]["*register*]**cc**	Change lines.
[*count*]["*register*]**y**{*motion*}	Yank from cursor to {*motion*}
[*count*]["*register*]**yy**	Yank lines
[*count*]["*register*]**p**	Put after cursor
[*count*]["*register*]**P**	Put before cursor
xp	Twiddle characters
[*count*]**r**{*char*}	Replace one character
[*count*]**R**{*string*}**<ESC>**	Replace characters until stopped
[*count*]**J**	Join lines

Windows

:split {*file*}	Split window
:q	Close current window
CTRL-Wj	Go up a window
CTRL-Wk	Go down a window
CTRL-Wo	Make the current window the only one.

Keyboard Macros

q{*register*}	Record commands into a {*register*}.
q	Stop recording
[*count*]**@**{*register*}	Execute the keyboard macro in {*register*}

Text Formatting Commands

[*count*]**gq**{*motion*}	Format selected text
[*count*]**gqq**	Format lines
[*count*]**gq}**	Format paragraphs
:set textwidth={*width*}	Set the width of the text line (turn auto wrapping on)
:[*range*]**center**	Center the text
:[*range*]**left**	Left-align the text
:[*range*]**right**	Right-align the text
:set formatoptions={*characters*}	Set options which control formatting. Options include:
t	Automatically wrap text
2	When formatting text, use the second line of the paragraph to determine what indent to use.
q	Allow formatting of comments with **gq** command.

Commands for Programmers

General	
:syntax on	Turn on syntax highlighting
%	Go to matching brace, comment or **#ifdef**
:set autoindent	Indent each new line the same as the previous one
:set cindent	Use C style indentation
CTRL-D	In insert mode, unindent one level of auto indent.
[*count*]**>>**	Shift lines right
[*count*]**>**{*motion*}	Shift right
[*count*]**<<**	Shift lines left
[*count*]**<**{*motion*}	Shift left
[*count*]**=**{*motion*}	Indent code from cursor to {motion}
CTRL-]	Jump to tag (function definition).
[*count*]**CTRL-T**	Go to location before last tag jump.
[*count*]**CTRL-W CTRL-]**	Split the window and jump to tag under the cursor.
K	Run man on the word under the cursor

Making the program		Grep	
:make	Run *make* and capture the output	**:grep** '{*string*}' {*files*}	Run *grep* and capture the output. Treat matches like **:make** errors.
:cc	Jump to current error		
:cn	Jump to next error		
:cp	Jump to previous error		

Include File Searches	
[*count*] **]CTRL-D**	Find the definition of the macro under the cursor
[*count*] **]CTRL-I**	Search for the word under the cursor
[*count*] **]d**	List first macro definition for the macro the cursor is on.
[*count*] **]D**	List all macro definitions

Commands for directory searches	
:set path={*directory*},....	Tell *Vim* where to search for files
:checkpath	Make sure that *Vim* can find all the files that are referenced in **#include** directives.
:find {*file*}	Edit the {*file*}. If the file is not in the current directory, search through the **'path'** to find it.
gf	Edit the file who's name is under the cursor. Search through the **'path'** if the file is not in the current directory.

Visual Mode Commands

Basic Commands		Editing Commands	
v	Enter character visual~mode	[*"register*]**d**	Delete the selected text.
V	Enter line visual mode	[*"register*]**y**	Yank the text into
CTRL-V	Enter block visual mode		register
$	Move the right side of the block	**>**	Shift text right
	to the end of each line.	**<**	Shift text left
		=	Run the lines through the
Selection Commands			indent program
[*count*]**a(**	Select () block	**J**	Join the highlighted lines
[*count*]**a[**	Select [] block	**gq**{*motion*}	Format text to
[*count*]**a{**	Select { } block		**'textwidth'**
[*count*]**aw**	Select word and space after	**U**	Convert text to all
[*count*]**iw**	Select word only.		UPPER CASE
[*count*]**as**	Select sentence and following	**u**	Convert text to all lower
	space		case.
[*count*]**is**	Select sentence only.	**~**	Invert the case of the
			text.

Insert Mode Commands

Insert Mode Commands	
CTRL-V{*char*}	Insert character literally .
CTRL-D	Unindent one level
0 CTRL-D	Remove all automatic indentation
CTRL-T	Insert one **'shiftwidth'**
CTRL-Y	Copy the character above the cursor
CTRL-E	Copy the character below the cursor
CTRL-N	Find next match for word before the cursor
CTRL-P	Find previous match for word before the cursor
CTRL-R{*register*}	Insert contents of a register
CTRL-K{*char1*}{*char2*}	
	Insert digraphs
CTRL-W	Delete word before cursor

Abbreviations	
:abbreviate {*abbr*} {*expansion*}	
	Define abbreviation.

Ex Mode Commands

Basic Commands

Q	Enter Ex mode
:vi	Enter normal mode
:[*range*]**s/**{*old*}**/**{*new*}**/**{*flags*}	
	Substitute {*new*} for {*old*}. If a flag of "g" is present substitute all occurrences on a line. Otherwise just change the first one.
:[*range*]**write** [*file*]	
	Write text to a file
:[*line*]**read** [*file*]	Read text from another file into the current file.

File Selection Commands

:rewind	Edit the first file
:next	Edit next file
:prev	Edit previous file
:last	Edit the last file in the list
:args	List the files in the edit list.

Editing

:[*range*]**delete**	Delete the specified lines
:[*range*]**copy**[*line*]	
	Copy the specified lines to [*line*] (default = after current line)
:[*range*]**move**[*line*]	
	Like **:copy** but delete the lines as well.

Miscellaneous Commands

:[*range*]**print**	Print the specified lines
:[*range*]**number**	Print the specified lines with line numbers
:[*range*]**list**	Print the specified lines with **'list'** option on.
:dlist {*name*}	List definitions for {*name*}
:[*range*]**retab**[**!**] {*tabstop*}	
	Change the tabbing from the existing setting to the new {*tabstop*}.
:exit[**!**]	Close the current file. If it's the last one, exit the editor
:suspend	Suspend the editor.
:source {*file*}	Read commands from the specified file.
:redir >{*file*}	Record the output of the commands in the specified file.

Options

	Setting
:set {option}= {value}	Set an option
:set {option}?	Display the value of an option
:set	Display the value of options that are set to something other than the default.
:set all	Display the value of all options
:set {option}&	Set an option to the default
:browse set	Set options using a full screen based dialog.
:set {option}+= {value}	Add a value to a list of options (string option). Add a number to a numeric option.
:set {option}-= {value}	Remove a value from a list of options (string option). Subtract a number from a numeric option.
:set {option}	Turn on a boolean option
:set no {option}	Turn off a boolean option
:set inv{option}	Invert a boolean option

	Indent / Tabbing
:set cindent	Turn on C style indentation
:set autoindent	Indent each line the same as the previous one
:set expandtabs	Turn all tabs into space
:set softtabstop	Set the amount of space that the **<Tab>** key uses. (Note: This is not the same as the number of spaces for a Tab.)

	Listing Options
:set list	Turn on list mode where everything is visible
:set number	Display line numbers

	Searching Options
:set hlsearch	Highlight matching search strings
:set incsearch	Do incremental searches
:set wrapscan	If a search reaches the bottom of the file wrap to the top and keep searching. (Also will wrap from the top to the bottom for reverse searches)
:set ignorecase	Make searches case insensitive
:set autowrite	Automatically write files as needed to preserve data.

Regular Expressions

Simple Atoms	
x	The literal character "x"
^	Start of line
$	End of line.
.	A single character .
\<	Start of a word.
\>	End of word.

Range Atoms	
[abc]	Match either "a", "b", or "c".
[^abc]	Match anything except "a", "b", or "c".
[a-z]	Match all characters from "a" through "z".
[a-zA-Z]	Match all characters from "a" through "z" and "A" through "Z".

Sub Patterns	
\(*pattern*\)	Mark the pattern for later use. The first set of \(.\) marks a pattern as \1, the second \2 and so on.
\1	Matches the same string that was matched by the first sub-expression in \(and \). Example: "\([a-z]\).\1" matches "ata", "ehe", "tot", etc.
\2	Like "\1", but uses second sub-expression,
\9	Like "\1", but uses ninth sub-expression.

Modifiers	
*	Match the previous atom 0 or more times. As much as possible.
\+	Match the previous atom 1 or more times. As much as possible.
\=	Match the previous atom 0 or 1 times.
\{}	Match the previous atom 0 or more times. (Same as the "*" modifier.)
\{n}	Match the previous atom n times.
\{n,m}	Match the previous atom n to m times.
\{$n,$}	Match the previous atom n or more times.
\{,m}	Match the previous atom from 0 to m times.
\{-n,m}	Match the previous atom n to m times. Match as little as possible.
\{-$n,$}	Match the previous atom at least n times. Match as little as possible.
\{-,m}	Match the previous atom up to m times. Match as little as possible.
\{-}	Match the previous atom 0 or more times. Match as little as possible.
str1 | *str2*	Match *str1* or *str2*.

Index

See also all the command indices in

<abuf>, 354

<afile>, 353

<amatch>, 354

<bang>, 361

<Break>, 384

<cfile>, 353

<count>, 361

<CR>, regular expression (\r), 217

<cword>, 353

<cWORD>, 353

<Enter> as argument to replace character (r<Enter>), 23

<Line feed> (line ending), 120

<line1>/<line2> (keywords), 361

<register>, 361

<Return> (line ending), 120

<sfile> (file being sourced), 354

! (override), 9
  :bdelete, 246
  :bunload, 246
  :checkpath, 283
  :djump, 314
  :dlist, 314
  :dsearch, 314
  :global, 312
  :ijump, 314
  :ilist, 314
  :next, 42
  :quit, 9
  :recover, 152

:unlet, 353
:vi, 41
:wqall, 242
:write, 41, 168, 202
:wviminfo, 233

!= (operator), 352

!=? (operator), 353

!~ (operator), 352

" (special mark), 221

"* (clipboard register), 163

#
  alternate filename, 353
  instant word search backwards, 206
  special register, 223

#ifdef / #endif matching (%), 77

#include files, 281
  automatic completion search
    (**CTRL-X CTRL-I**), 128
  jump to pattern (**:ijump**), 312
  list pattern (**:ilist**), 312
  search (**:isearch**), 313
  go to end of line, block visual mode, 63
  last line number, 100, 160
  last line, 168
  move to end of line, 16, 234

%
  current filename, 353
  line range, 161
  match braces, 73, 278
  match pairs, 76-77
  operator, 352
  range101, 160
  special register, 223

', line range, 101

'<, line range, 102, 105

'>, line range, 102, 105

E

H

I

M

O

P

Q

S

Advanced Information on Networking Technologies

New Riders Books Offer Advice and Experience

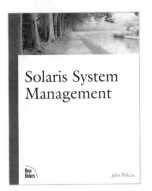

LANDMARK

We know how important it is to have access to detailed, solution-oriented information on core technologies. *Landmark* books contain the essential information you need to solve technical problems. Written by experts and subjected to rigorous peer and technical reviews, our *Landmark* books are hard-core resources for practitioners like you.

ESSENTIAL REFERENCE

The *Essential Reference* series from New Riders provides answers when you know what you want to do but need to know how to do it. Each title skips extraneous material and assumes a strong base of knowledge. These are indispensable books for the practitioner who wants to find specific features of a technology quickly and efficiently. Avoiding fluff and basic material, these books present solutions in an innovative, clean format—and at a great value.

MCSE CERTIFICATION

New Riders offers a complete line of test preparation materials to help you achieve your certification. With books like the *MCSE Training Guide*, and software like the acclaimed *MCSE Complete* and the revolutionary *ExamGear*, New Riders offers comprehensive products built by experienced professionals who have passed the exams and instructed hundreds of candidates.

New Riders \ Books for Networking Professionals

Windows NT/2000 Native API Reference

By Gary Nebbett
1st Edition
528 pages, $50.00
ISBN:1-57870-199-6

This book is the first complete reference to the API functions native to Windows NT and covers the set of services that are offered by the Windows NT to both kernel- and user-mode programs. Coverage consists of documentation of the 210 routines included in the NT Native API, and the functions that will be added in Windows 2000. Routines that are either not directly accessible via the Win32 API or offer substantial additional functionality are described in especially great detail. Services offered by the NT kernel— mainly the support for debugging user mode applications—are also included.

Windows NT Device Driver Development

By Peter Viscarola and W. Anthony Mason
1st Edition
704 pages, $50.00
ISBN: 1-57870-058-2

This title begins with an introduction to the general Windows NT operating system concepts relevant to drivers, then progresses to more detailed information about the operating system, such as interrupt management, synchronization issues, the I/O Subsystem, standard kernel mode drivers, and more.

DCE/RPC over SMB: Samba and Windows NT Domain Internals

By Luke Leighton
1st Edition
312 pages, $45.00
ISBN: 1-57870-150-3

Security people, system and network administrators, and those writing tools for them all need to be familiar with the packets flowing across their networks. Authored by a key member of the Samba team, this book describes how Microsoft has taken DCE/RPC and implemented it over SMB and TCP/IP.

Delphi COM Programming

By Eric Harmon
1st Edition
500 pages, $45.00
ISBN: 1-57870-221-6

Delphi COM Programming is for all Delphi 3, 4, and 5 programmers. After providing readers with an understanding of the COM framework, it offers a practical exploration of COM to enable Delphi developers to program component-based applications. Typical real-world scenarios, such as Windows Shell programming, automating Microsoft Agent, and creating and using ActiveX controls, are explored. Discussions of each topic are illustrated with detailed examples.

Applying COM+

By Gregory Brill
1st Edition
450 pages, $49.99
ISBN: 0-7357-0978-5

By pulling a number of disparate services into one unified technology, COM+ holds the promise of greater efficiency and more diverse capabilities for developers who are creating applications—either enterprise or commercial software—to run on a Windows 2000 system. *Applying COM+* covers the features of the new tool, as well as how to implement them in a real case study. Features are demonstrated in all three of the major languages used in the Windows environment: C++, VB, and VJ++.

Exchange & Outlook: Constructing Collaborative Solutions

By Joel Semeniuk and Duncan MacKenzie
1st Edition
576 pages, $40.00
ISBN 1-57870-252-6

The authors of this book are responsible for building custom messaging applications for some of the biggest Fortune 100 companies in the world. They share their expertise to help administrators and designers use Microsoft technology to establish a base for their messaging system and to lay out the tools that can be used to help build those collaborative solutions. Actual planning and design solutions are included along with typically workflow/collaborative solutions.

Windows NT Applications: Measuring and Optimizing Performance

By Paul Hinsberg
1st Edition
288 pages, $40.00
ISBN: 1-57870-176-7

This book offers developers crucial insight into the underlying structure of Windows NT, as well as the methodology and tools for measuring and ultimately optimizing code performance.

Windows Script Host

By Tim Hill
1st Edition
448 pages, $35.00
ISBN: 1-57870-139-2

Windows Script Host is one of the first books published about this powerful tool. The text focuses on system scripting and the VBScript language, using objects, server scriptlets, and ready-to-use script solutions.

Windows NT Shell Scripting

By Tim Hill
1st Edition
400 pages, $32.00
ISBN: 1-57870-047-7

A complete reference for Windows NT scripting, this book guides you through a high-level introduction to the Shell language itself and the Shell commands that are useful for controlling or managing different components of a network.

Open Source

MySQL
By Paul DuBois
1st Edition
800 pages, $49.99
ISBN: 0-7357-0921-1

MySQL teaches readers how to use the tools provided by the MySQL distribution, covering installation, setup, daily use, security, optimization, maintenance, and troubleshooting. It also discusses important third-party tools, such as the Perl DBI and Apache/PHP interfaces that provide access to MySQL.

PHP Functions Essential Reference
By Landon Bradshaw, Till Gerken, Graeme Merrall, and Tobias Ratschiller
1st Edition
500 pages, $35.00
ISBN: 0-7357-0970-X
February 2001

This carefully crafted title covers the latest developments through PHP 4.0, including coverage of Zend. These authors share their knowledge not only of the development of PHP, but also how they use it daily to create dynamic Web sites. Covered as well is instruction on using PHP alongside MySQL.

Web Application Development with PHP 4.0
By Till Gerken, et al.
1st Edition
416 pages, $39.99
ISBN: 0-7357-0997-1

Web Application Development with PHP 4.0 explains PHP's advanced syntax including classes, recursive functions, and variables. The authors present software development methodologies and coding conventions, which are a must-know for industry quality products and make software development faster and more productive. Included is coverage on Web applications and insight into user and session management, e-commerce systems, XML applications, and WDDX.

Python Essential Reference
By David Beazley
1st Edition
352 pages, $34.95
ISBN: 0-7357-0901-7

Avoiding the dry and academic approach, the goal of *Python Essential Reference* is to concisely describe the Python programming language and its large library of standard modules, collectively known as the Python programming environment. This informal reference covers Python's lexical conventions, datatypes, control flow, functions, statements, classes, and execution model—a truly essential reference for any Python programmer!

GNU Autoconf, Automake, and Libtool
By Gary V. Vaughan, et al.
1st Edition
400 pages, $40.00
ISBN: 1-57870-190-2

This book is the first of its kind, authored by Open Source community luminaries and current maintainers of the tools, teaching developers how to boost their productivity and the portability of their applications using GNU Autoconf, Automake, and Libtool.

Linux/UNIX

Linux System Administration
By M Carling, James T. Dennis, and Stephen Degler
1st Edition
368 pages, $29.99
ISBN: 1-56205-934-3

Today's overworked sysadmins are looking for ways to keep their networks running smoothly and achieve enhanced performance. Users are always looking for more storage, more services, and more Speed. *Linux System Administration* guides the reader in the many intricacies of maintaining a secure, stable system.

Linux Firewalls
By Robert Ziegler
1st Edition
496 pages, $39.99
ISBN: 0-7357-0900-9

This book details security steps that a small, non-enterprise business user might take to protect his system. These steps include packet-level firewall filtering, IP masquerading, proxies, tcp wrappers, system integrity checking, and system security monitoring with an overall emphasis on filtering and protection. The goal of *Linux Firewalls* is to help people get their Internet security measures in place quickly, without the need to become experts in security or firewalls.

Linux Essential Reference
By Ed Petron
1st Edition
368 pages, $24.95
ISBN: 0-7357-0852-5

This title is all about getting things done by providing structured organization to the plethora of available Linux information. Providing clear and concise instructions on how to perform important administration and management tasks, as well as how to use some of the more powerful commands and more advanced topics, the scope of *Linux Essential Reference* includes the best way to implement the most frequently used commands, manage shell scripting, administer your own system, and utilize effective security.

UnixWare 7 System Administration

By Gene Henriksen and Melissa Henriksen
1st Edition
560 pages, $40.00
ISBN: 1-57870-080-9

In great technical detail, this title presents the latest version of SCO UnixWare and is the definitive operating system resource for SCO engineers and administrators. SCO troubleshooting notes and tips are integrated throughout the text, as are tips specifically designed for those who are familiar with other UNIX variants.

Developing Linux Applications with GTK+ and GDK

By Eric Harlow
1st Edition
512 pages, $34.99
ISBN: 0-7357-0021-4

This handbook is for developers who are moving to the Linux platform, and those using the GTK+ library, including Glib and GDK using C. All the applications and code the author developed for this book have been released under the GPL.

GTK+/Gnome Application Development

By Havoc Pennington
1st Edition
528 pages, $39.99
ISBN: 0-7357-0078-8

More than one million Linux users are also application developers. *GTK+/Gnome Application Development* provides the experienced programmer with the knowledge to develop X Windows applications with the popular GTK+ toolkit. It contains reference information for more experienced users who are already familiar with usage, but require function prototypes and detailed descriptions.

KDE Application Development

By Uwe Thiem
1st Edition
190 pages, $39.99
ISBN: 1-57870-201-1

KDE Application Development offers a head start on KDE and Qt. The book covers the essential widgets available in KDE and Qt, and offers a strong start without the "first try" annoyances which sometimes make strong developers and programmers give up.

Grokking the GIMP
By Carey Bunks
1st Edition
342 pages, $45.00
ISBN: 0-7357-0924-6

Grokking the GIMP is a technical reference that covers the intricacies of the GIMP's functionality. The material gives the reader the ability to get up to speed quickly and start creating great graphics using the GIMP. Included as a bonus are step-by-step cookbook features used entirely for advanced effects.

GIMP Essential Reference
By Alex Harford
1st Edition
400 pages, $24.95
ISBN: 0-7357-0911-4

As the use of the Linux OS gains steam, so does the use of the GIMP. Many Photoshop users are starting to use the GIMP, recognized for its power and versatility. Taking this into consideration, GIMP Essential Reference has shortcuts exclusively for Photoshop users and puts the power of this program into the palm of the reader's hand.

Solaris Advanced System Administrator's Guide
By Janice Winsor
2nd Edition
587 pages, $39.99
ISBN: 1-57870-039-6

This officially authorized tutorial provides indispensable tips, advice, and quick-reference tables to help you add system components, improve service access, and automate routine tasks. this book also includes updated information on Solaris 2.6 topics.

Solaris System Administrator's Guide
By Janice Winsor
2nd Edition
324 pages, $34.99
ISBN: 1-57870-040-X

Designed to work as both a practical tutorial and quick reference, this book provides UNIX administrators complete, detailed descriptions of the most frequently performed tasks for Solaris. Learn how to employ the features of Solaris to meet these needs of your users, and get tips on how to make administration easier.

Solaris Essential Reference
By John Mulligan
1st Edition
304 pages, $24.95
ISBN: 0-7357-0023-0

A great companion to the solarisguide.com web site, *Solaris Essential Reference* assumes readers are well-versed in general UNIX skills and simply need some pointers on how to get the most out of Solaris. This book provides clear and concise instructions on how to perform important administration and management tasks.

Networking

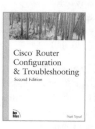

Cisco Router Configuration &Troubleshooting
By Mark Tripod
2nd Edition
330 pages, $39.99
ISBN: 0-7357-0999-8

A reference for the network and system administrator who finds himself having to configure and maintain existing Cisco routers, as well as get new hardware up and running. By providing advice and preferred practices, instead of just rehashing Cisco documentation, this book gives networking professionals information they can start using today.

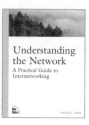

Understanding the Network: A Practical Guide to Internetworking
By Michael Martin
1st Edition
690 pages, $39.99
ISBN: 0-7357-0977-7

Understanding the Network addresses the audience in practical terminology, and describes the most essential information and tools required to build high-availability networks in a step-by-step implementation format. Each chapter could be read as a standalone, but the book builds progressively toward a summary of the essential concepts needed to put together a wide-area network.

Understanding Directory Services
By Beth Sheresh and Doug Sheresh
1st Edition
390 pages, $39.99
ISBN: 0-7357-0910-6

Understanding Directory Services provides the reader with a thorough knowledge of the fundamentals of directory services: what Directory Services are, how they are designed, and what functionality they can provide to an IT infrastructure. This book provides a framework to the exploding market of directory services by placing the technology in context and helping people understand what directories can, and can't, do for their networks.

Understanding Data Communications
By Gilbert Held
6th Edition
620 pages, $39.99
ISBN: 0-7357-0036-2

Gil Held's book is ideal for those who want to get up to speed on technological advances as well as those who want a primer on networking concepts. This book is intended to explain how data communications actually work. It contains updated coverage on hot topics like thin client technology, x2 and 56Kbps modems, voice digitization, and wireless data transmission. Whatever your needs, this title puts perspective and expertise in your hands.

LDAP: Programming Directory Enabled Applications

By Tim Howes and Mark Smith
1st Edition
480 pages, $44.99
ISBN: 1-57870-000-0

This overview of the LDAP standard discusses its creation and history with the Internet Engineering Task Force, as well as the original RFC standard. LDAP also covers compliance trends, implementation, data packet handling in C++, client/server responsibilities and more.

Gigabit Ethernet Networking

By David Cunningham and Bill Lane
1st Edition
560 pages, $50.00
ISBN: 1-57870-062-0

Gigabit Ethernet is the next step for speed on the majority of installed networks. Explore how this technology will allow high-bandwidth applications, such as the integration of telephone and data services, real-time applications, thin client applications, such as Windows NT Terminal Server, and corporate teleconferencing.

Directory Enabled Networks

By John Strassner
1st Edition
752 pages, $50.00
ISBN: 1-57870-140-6

Directory Enabled Networks is a comprehensive resource on the design and use of DEN. This book provides practical examples side-by-side with a detailed introduction to the theory of building a new class of network-enabled applications that will solve networking problems. DEN is a critical tool for network architects, administrators, and application developers.

Supporting Service Level Agreements on IP Networks

By Dinesh Verma
1st Edition
270 pages, $50.00
ISBN: 1-57870-146-5

An essential resource for network engineers and architects, *Supporting Service Level Agreements on IP Networks* will help you build a core network capable of supporting a range of service. Learn how to create SLA solutions using off-the-shelf components in both best-effort and DiffServ/IntServ networks. Learn how to verify the performance of your SLA, as either a customer or network services provider, and use SLAs to support IPv6 networks.

Local Area High Speed Networks

By Dr. Sidnie Feit
1st Edition
655 pages, $50.00
ISBN: 1-57870-113-9

There is a great deal of change happening in the technology being used for local area networks. As Web intranets have driven bandwidth needs through the ceiling, inexpensive Ethernet NICs and switches have come into the market. As a result, many network professionals are interested in evaluating these new technologies for implementation. This book provides real-world implementation expertise for these technologies, including traces, so that users can realistically compare and decide how to use them.

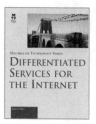

Differentiated Services for the Internet

By Kalevi Kilkki
1st Edition
400 pages, $50.00
ISBN: 1-57870-132-5

This book offers network architects, engineers, and managers of packet networks critical insight into the continuing development of Differentiated Services. It addresses the particular needs of a network environment as well as issues that must be considered in its implementation. Coverage allows networkers to implement DiffServ on a variety of networking technologies, including ATM, and to solve common problems related to TCP, UDP, and other networking protocols.

Wide Area High Speed Networks

By Dr. Sidnie Feit
1st Edition
624 pages, $50.00
ISBN: 1-57870-114-7

Networking is in a transitional phase between long-standing conventional wide area services and new technologies and services. This book presents current and emerging wide area technologies and services, makes them understandable, and puts them into perspective so that their merits and disadvantages are clear.

Quality of Service in IP Networks

By Grenville Armitage
1st Edition
310 pages, $50.00
ISBN: 1-57870-189-9

Quality of Service in IP Networks presents a clear understanding of the architectural issues surrounding delivering QoS in an IP network, and positions the emerging technologies within a framework of solutions. The motivation for QoS is explained with reference to emerging real-time applications, such as Voice/Video over IP, VPN services, and supporting Service Level Agreements.

Designing Addressing Architectures for Routing and Switching

By Howard Berkowitz
1st Edition
500 pages, $45.00
ISBN: 1-57870-059-0

One of the greatest challenges for a network design professional is making the users, servers, files, printers, and other resources visible on their network. This title equips the network engineer or architect with a systematic methodology for planning the wide area and local area network "streets" on which users and servers live.

Understanding and Deploying LDAP Directory Services

By Tim Howes, Mark Smith, and Gordon Good
1st Edition
850 pages, $50.00
ISBN: 1-57870-070-1

This comprehensive tutorial provides the reader with a thorough treatment of LDAP directory services. Minimal knowledge of general networking and administration is assumed, making the material accessible to intermediate and advanced readers alike. The text is full of practical implementation advice and real-world deployment examples to help the reader choose the path that makes the most sense for his specific organization.

Switched, Fast, and Gigabit Ethernet

By Sean Riley and Robert Breyer
3rd Edition
615 pages, $50.00
ISBN: 1-57870-073-6

Switched, Fast, and Gigabit Ethernet, Third Edition is the one and only solution needed to understand and fully implement this entire range of Ethernet innovations. Acting both as an overview of current technologies and hardware requirements as well as a hands-on, comprehensive tutorial for deploying and managing switched, fast, and gigabit ethernet networks, this guide covers the most prominent present and future challenges network administrators face.

Wireless LANs: Implementing Interoperable Networks

By Jim Geier
1st Edition
432 pages, $40.00
ISBN: 1-57870-081-7

Wireless LANs covers how and why to migrate from proprietary solutions to the 802.11 standard, and explains how to realize significant cost savings through wireless LAN implementation for data collection systems.

The DHCP Handbook
By Ralph Droms
and Ted Lemon
1st Edition
535 pages, $55.00
ISBN: 1-57870-137-6

The DHCP Handbook is an authoritative overview and expert guide to the setup and management of a DHCP server. This title discusses how DHCP was developed and its interaction with other protocols. Learn how DHCP operates, its use in different environments, and the interaction between DHCP servers and clients. Network hardware, inter-server communication, security, SNMP, and IP mobility are also discussed. Also, included in the book are several appendices that provide a rich resource for networking professionals working with DHCP.

Network Performance Baselining
By Daniel Nassar
1st Edition
736 pages, $50.00
ISBN: 1-57870-240-2

Network Performance Baselining focuses on the real-world implementation of network baselining principles and shows not only how to measure and rate a network's performance, but also how to improve the network performance. This book includes chapters that give a real "how-to" approach for standard baseline methodologies along with actual steps and processes to perform network baseline measurements. In addition, the proper way to document and build a baseline report will be provided.

Designing Routing and Switching Architectures for Enterprise Networks
By Howard Berkowitz
1st Edition
992 pages, $55.00
ISBN: 1-57870-060-4

This title provides a fundamental understanding of how switches and routers operate, enabling the reader to use them effectively to build networks. The book walks the network designer through all aspects of requirements, analysis, and deployment strategies, strengthens readers' professional abilities, and helps them develop skills necessary to advance in their profession.

The Economics of Electronic Commerce
By Soon-Yong Choi,
Andrew Whinston,
Dale Stahl
1st Edition
656 pages, $49.99
ISBN: 1-57870-014-0

This is the first electronic commerce title to focus on traditional topics of economics applied to the electronic commerce arena. While all other electronic commerce titles take a "how-to" approach, this focuses on what it means from an economic perspective.

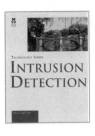

Intrusion Detection

By Rebecca Gurley Bace
1st Edition
340 pages, $50.00
ISBN: 1-57870-185-6

Intrusion detection is a critical new area of technology within network security. This comprehensive guide to the field of intrusion detection covers the foundations of intrusion detection and system audit. *Intrusion Detection* provides a wealth of information, ranging from design considerations to how to evaluate and choose the optimal commercial intrusion detection products for a particular networking environment.

Understanding Public-Key Infrastructure

By Carlisle Adams and Steve Lloyd
1st Edition
300 pages, $50.00
ISBN: 1-57870-166-X

This book is a tutorial on, and a guide to the deployment of, Public-Key Infrastructures. It covers a broad range of material related to PKIs, including certification, operational considerations and standardization efforts, as well as deployment issues and considerations. Emphasis is placed on explaining the interrelated fields within the topic area, to assist those who will be responsible for making deployment decisions and architecting a PKI within an organization.

Network Intrusion Detection: An Analyst's Handbook

By Stephen Northcutt and Judy Novak
2nd Edition
480 pages, $45.00
ISBN: 0-7357-1008-2

Get answers and solutions from someone who has been in the trenches. Author Stephen Northcutt, original developer of the Shadow intrusion detection system and former Director of the United States Navy's Information System Security Office, gives his expertise to intrusion detection specialists, security analysts, and consultants responsible for setting up and maintaining an effective defense against network security attacks.

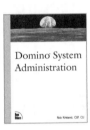

Domino System Administration

By Rob Kirkland
1st Edition
860 pages, $49.99
ISBN: 1-56205-948-3

Need a concise, practical explanation about the new features of Domino, and how to make some of the advanced stuff really work? *Domino System Administration* is the first book on Domino that attacks the technology at the professional level, with practical, hands-on assistance to get Domino 5 running in your organization.

Lotus Notes & Domino Essential Reference

By Dave Hatter, and Tim Bankes
1st Edition
675 pages, $45.00
ISBN: 0-7357-0007-9

If you need something to facilitate your creative and technical abilities—something to perfect your Lotus Notes and Domino programming skills—this is the book for you. This title includes all of the objects, classes, functions, and methods found if you work with Lotus Notes and Domino. It shows the object hierarchy and the overlying relationship between each one, organized the way the language is designed.

Constructing Superior Software

By Paul Clements, et al.
1st Edition
285 pages, $40.00
ISBN: 1-57870-147-3

Published in cooperation with the Software Quality Institute at the University of Texas, Austin, this title presents a set of fundamental engineering strategies for achieving a successful software solution, with practical advice to ensure that the development project is moving in the right direction. Software designers and development managers can improve the development speed and quality of their software, and improve the processes used in development.

Software Architecture and Engineering

Designing Flexible Object-Oriented Systems with UML

By Charles Richter
1st Edition
416 pages, $40.00
ISBN: 1-57870-098-1

Designing Flexible Object-Oriented Systems with UML details the UML, which is a notation system for designing object-oriented programs. The book follows the same sequence that a development project might employ, starting with requirements of the problem using UML case diagrams and activity diagrams. The reader is shown ways to improve the design as the author moves through the transformation of the initial diagrams into class diagrams and interaction diagrams.

A UML Pattern Language

By Paul Evitts
1st Edition
260 pages, $40.00
ISBN: 1-57870-118-X

While other books focus only on the UML notation system, this book integrates key UML modeling concepts and illustrates their use through patterns. It provides an integrated, practical, step-by-step discussion of UML and patterns, with real-world examples to illustrate proven software modeling techniques.

Other Books By New Riders

Switched, Fast and Gigabit Ethernet,
Third Edition
1-57870-073-6 • $50.00 US
Wireless LANs: Implementing Interoperable
Networks
1-57870-081-7 • $40.00 US
Wide Area High Speed Networks
1-57870-114-7 • $50.00 US
The DHCP Handbook
1-57870-137-6 • $55.00 US
Designing Routing and Switching
Architectures for Enterprise Networks
1-57870-060-4 • $55.00 US
Local Area High Speed Networks
1-57870-113-9 • $50.00 US
Network Performance Baselining
1-57870-240-2 • $50.00 US
Economics of Electronic Commerce
1-57870-014-0 • $49.99 US

SECURITY

Intrusion Detection
1-57870-185-6 • $50.00 US
Understanding Public-Key Infrastructure
1-57870-166-X • $50.00 US
Network Intrusion Detection: An Analyst's
Handbook, 2E
0-7357-1008-2 • $45.00 US
Linux Firewalls
0-7357-0900-9 • $39.99 US
Intrusion Signatures and Analysis
0-7357-1063-5 • $39.99 US

LOTUS NOTES/DOMINO

Domino System Administration
1-56205-948-3 • $49.99 US
Lotus Notes & Domino Essential Reference
0-7357-0007-9 • $45.00 US

PROFESSIONAL CERTIFICATION

TRAINING GUIDES

MCSE Training Guide: Networking
Essentials, 2nd Ed.
1-56205-919-X • $49.99 US
MCSE Training Guide: Windows NT
Server 4, 2nd Ed.
1-56205-916-5 • $49.99 US
MCSE Training Guide: Windows NT
Workstation 4, 2nd Ed.
1-56205-918-1 • $49.99 US
MCSE Training Guide: Windows NT Server 4
Enterprise, 2nd Ed.
1-56205-917-3 • $49.99 US
MCSE Training Guide: Core Exams Bundle,
2nd Ed.
1-56205-926-2 • $149.99 US
MCSE Training Guide: TCP/IP, 2nd Ed.
1-56205-920-3 • $49.99 US
MCSE Training Guide: IIS 4, 2nd Ed.
0-7357-0865-7 • $49.99 US
MCSE Training Guide: SQL Server 7
Administration
0-7357-0003-6 • $49.99 US
MCSE Training Guide: SQL Server 7
Database Design
0-7357-0004-4 • $49.99 US
MCSD Training Guide: Visual Basic 6 Exams
0-7357-0002-8 • $69.99 US
MCSD Training Guide: Solution
Architectures
0-7357-0026-5 • $49.99 US
MCSD Training Guide: 4-in-1 Bundle
0-7357-0912-2 • $149.99 US
A+ Certification Training Guide,
Third Edition
0-7357-1088-0 • $49.99 US

Network+ Certification Guide
0-7357-0077-X • $49.99 US
Solaris 2.6 Administrator Certification
Training Guide, Part I
1-57870-085-X • $40.00 US
Solaris 2.6 Administrator Certification
Training Guide, Part II
1-57870-086-8 • $40.00 US
Solaris 7 Administrator Certification Training
Guide, Part I and II
1-57870-249-6 • $49.99 US
MCSE Training Guide: Windows 2000
Professional
0-7357-0965-3 • $49.99 US
MCSE Training Guide: Windows 2000 Server
0-7357-0968-8 • $49.99 US
MCSE Training Guide: Windows 2000
Network Infrastructure
0-7357-0966-1 • $49.99 US
MCSE Training Guide: Windows 2000
Network Security Design
0-73570-984X • $49.99 US
MCSE Training Guide: Windows 2000
Network Infrastructure Design
0-73570-982-3 • $49.99 US
MCSE Training Guide: Windows 2000
Directory Svcs. Infrastructure
0-7357-0976-9 • $49.99 US
MCSE Training Guide: Windows 2000
Directory Services Design
0-7357-0983-1 • $49.99 US
MCSE Training Guide: Windows 2000
Accelerated Exam
0-7357-0979-3 • $69.99 US
MCSE Training Guide: Windows 2000 Core
Exams Bundle
0-7357-0988-2 • $149.99 US

FAST TRACKS

CLP Fast Track: Lotus Notes/Domino 5
Application Development
0-73570-877-0 • $39.99 US
CLP Fast Track: Lotus Notes/Domino 5
System Administration
0-7357-0878-9 • $39.99 US
Network+ Fast Track
0-7357-0904-1 • $29.99 US
A+ Fast Track
0-7357-0028-1 • $34.99 US
MCSD Fast Track: Visual Basic 6,
Exam #70-176
0-7357-0019-2 • $19.99 US
MCSD FastTrack: Visual Basic 6,
Exam #70-175
0-7357-0018-4 • $19.99 US

SOFTWARE ARCHITECTURE & ENGINEERING

Designing for the User with OVID
1-57870-101-5 • $40.00 US
Designing Flexible Object-Oriented Systems
with UML
1-57870-098-1 • $40.00 US
Constructing Superior Software
1-57870-147-3 • $40.00 US
A UML Pattern Language
1-57870-118-X • $45.00 US

 # How to Contact Us

Visit Our Web Site

www.newriders.com

On our Web site you'll find information about our other books, authors, tables of contents, indexes, and book errata. You will also find information about book registration and how to purchase our books.

Email Us

Contact us at this address:

nrfeedback@newriders.com

- If you have comments or questions about this book
- To report errors that you have found in this book
- If you have a book proposal to submit or are interested in writing for New Riders
- If you would like to have an author kit sent to you
- If you are an expert in a computer topic or technology and are interested in being a technical editor who reviews manuscripts for technical accuracy
- To find a distributor in your area, please contact our international department at this address.

nrmedia@newriders.com

- For instructors from educational institutions who want to preview New Riders books for classroom use. Email should include your name, title, school, department, address, phone number, office days/hours, text in use, and enrollment, along with your request for desk/examination copies and/or additional information.
- For members of the media who are interested in reviewing copies of New Riders books. Send your name, mailing address, and email address, along with the name of the publication or Web site you work for.

Bulk Purchases/Corporate Sales

If you are interested in buying 10 or more copies of a title or want to set up an account for your company to purchase directly from the publisher at a substantial discount, contact us at 800-382-3419 or email your contact information to corpsales@pearsontechgroup.com. A sales representative will contact you with more information.

Write to Us

New Riders Publishing
201 W. 103rd St.
Indianapolis, IN 46290-1097

Call Us

Toll-free (800) 571-5840 + 9 + 7477
If outside U.S. (317) 581-3500. Ask for New Riders.

Fax Us

(317) 581-4663

Solutions from experts you know and trust.

www.informit.com

OPERATING SYSTEMS

WEB DEVELOPMENT

PROGRAMMING

NETWORKING

CERTIFICATION

AND MORE...

Expert Access.
Free Content.

New Riders has partnered with **InformIT.com** to bring technical information to your desktop. Drawing on New Riders authors and reviewers to provide additional information on topics you're interested in, **InformIT.com** has free, in-depth information you won't find anywhere else.

- **Master the skills you need, when you need them**

- **Call on resources from some of the best minds in the industry**

- **Get answers when you need them, using InformIT's comprehensive library or live experts online**

- **Go above and beyond what you find in New Riders books, extending your knowledge**

As an **InformIT** partner, **New Riders** has shared the wisdom and knowledge of our authors with you online. Visit **informIT.com** to see what you're missing.

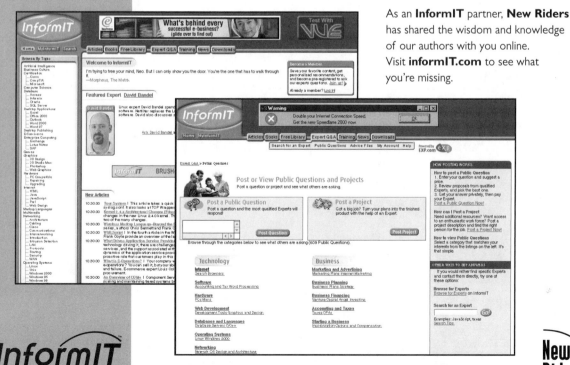